Culinary Service

Fifth Edition

Educational Task Force

JOHNSON & WALES UNIVERSITY College of Culinary Arts *Volume* **II**

Photography: YUM and Others
Photographer: Ronald Manville, YUM
Food Stylist: James E. Griffin

ISBN: 0-7872-7668-5

Printed in the United States of America
10 9 8 7 6 5 4 3 2

Contents

Service Basics   **1**

Mixology **11**

Federal and State Controls for Alcoholic Beverages — 12

Messages

At the end of the year, one takes account and tries to look into the future. Please allow me to say thank you to Johnson & Wales University, who undertook the job of promoting a new generation of foodservice professionals. Every time I visit the United States I am astonished by their expertise and dedication.

Johnson & Wales successfully took their task beyond the borders of the United States. Nevertheless, we shouldn't deceive ourselves that the future will be less difficult for all of us, Europeans and Americans alike. Isn't it a challenge to our profession to look ahead to a joint future with no national borders for our youth in the field of gastronomy?

Therefore, let us master whatever new problems challenge us, whether technical or nutritional, and go hand in hand in human friendship.

Dr. H. C. Siegfried Schaber
President V.K.D. Verbandes der Köche Von Deutschland
Vice President W.A.C.S. World Association Cooks Society

As you prepare for your culinary careers here at Johnson & Wales University, it is very important for you to realize the responsibility and pride you constantly must exercise to uphold the professional ethics, human values, and culinary fundamentals set forth by this great institution.

As the future bearer of the white toque, I encourage you to continuously try to perfect yourself, take great pride in what you do, exercise patience, allow yourself to grow within your limits, share your knowledge and wisdom, respect your peers, and perform every day to the best of your ability.

The culinary profession is an exciting profession where you set the groundwork of your own limits.

Hans J. Schadler, C.E.C., A.A.C.
Executive Chef, Director of Food and Beverage
Williamsburg Inn

When deciding what you want to do as your life's work, think of those things you would do even if you didn't get paid for them. Those things you love doing, that don't get boring, that always have something new to teach you. Become a chef only if you love cooking and are fascinated by the infinite variety of foods and how they work. A cook is basically a chemist, mixing and blending ingredients to find the perfect combination.

When serving others, remember that the customer should always come first. We are there to please them, not the other way around. I always put this note on my menus:

> The "no substitution" rule is not fair and no fun! We reject it since it denies your inalienable right to choose what you want to eat. We believe you should be free to enhance your meal according to your own taste. In other words, be our guest! Make youself at home! And try to enjoy yourself as much as we enjoy serving you!

It works. Try it.

Raymond G. Marshall
Former Owner & CEO
Acapulco y Los Arcos Mexican Restaurants

For the past decade, the world of gastronomy has looked to the United States as a leader for prime quality food products, great advances in the production of fine wines, and top-quality education for young culinarians in schools of culinary arts. The demand for cooks and chefs trained in the United States is greater now than ever. When I started in the kitchen as a young man over 50 years ago, there were no schools teaching culinary arts and opportunities were few.

At Johnson & Wales University, you are attending a world-class culinary school—perhaps the best in the country. You have the finest instructors to teach you not only the basics but also the advanced techniques needed in today's foodservice industry. Learn well, set your goals, and be all that you can be. Don't be discouraged by disappointments or setbacks, but use them as opportunities to do better.

John L. Bandera, C.E.C., A.A.C.
Grand Commander
Honorable Order of the Golden Toque

Johnson & Wales University has continued to be a dynamic force in educating students in culinary arts. Through the creative talents of program founders to the present staff, all have endeavored to be the best they can be. My personal involvement with Johnson & Wales through the Distinguished Visiting Chef program and other activities has been a gratifying experience to me. Working with students has always been enjoyable because I now have the opportunity to give something back in return for all the help given to me as a young culinarian.

I tip my toque to the entire staff of Johnson & Wales for their great contribution to the future of the culinary arts.

Michael L. Minor
U.P. Professional Services
L. J. Minor Corp.

It is the good fortune of a present-day student of the culinary arts to become engaged in a calling that has been recognized by our federal government as a fully acknowledged profession, on a par with law, education, medicine, and the arts. This recognition is a weighty matter. It carries with it the obligation of complete commitment and personal dedication to the entire spectrum of academic preparation for the field of culinary arts. The student must never forget that the obligation is never ending. The health and safety of our nation is technically in your hands and, like all perfect professionals, your complete preparation is the only acceptable foundation for true dedication, technical expertise, and personal success.

Joseph P. Delaney
Retired Educator

Foreword

Though critics of the beverage alcohol business may be blind to our trade's long record of good works—purposely, at times, I'm convinced—there are few industries in this country with a more sensitive social conscience. Medicine, scientific research, higher education, and all sorts of philanthropies that assist the poor and underprivileged have benefited from profits generated by wine, beer, and spirits sales almost since the repeal of the 18th Amendment.

With its growing success, Banfi Vintners has assumed an increasingly broad societal role. Like other firms, year after year, we donate to worthy causes, both national and local. Yet, some time ago, we began experiencing twinges of the corporate conscience because we hadn't made any serious contribution to the trade—and the people of the trade—most responsible for our company's success. We asked ourselves: How can we assist the future development of the hospitality trade; further, how can we assist the people who will lead and administer that trade in decades to come?

The answer was obvious. Through the Banfi Foundation, we now endow schools that specialize in hospitality education; for example, providing them with basic facilities such as the dining room at Johnson & Wales, where food and wine service can be taught under ideal conditions. Equally important, through scholarships and fellowships we help worthy students interested in pursuing a hospitality career. About 15 schools and dozens of students are currently benefiting from Banfi's decision.

The corporate conscience is not at ease, but are our motives entirely altruistic? Admittedly, no. We're convinced that a better and more widely informed hospitality staff will stimulate greater business for hotels and restaurants, including the wines they serve. Experience has proved that, for us anyway, the "trickle down" theory really can work. Well and good. Profits from wine sales fund the Banfi Foundation.

Harry F. Mariani
President and COO
Banfi Vintners

Why did we donate a teaching dining room to Johnson & Wales University?

Because of a family business, I had experience with imports. I decided to go out on my own, moving from the retail side of the business to the institutional market. Therefore, in 1957, my wife, Helena, and I started our own import business.

In the course of our travels in the late 50s and throughout the 60s, we found the "eyes" of the culinary world had shifted to America. Many chefs decided to seek their fortune in the United States, bringing with them culinary knowledge from their individual countries. Many chefs asked us to import certain products that they felt were needed to round out their classical cuisine endeavors, and we continued to import products that were in demand. As we expanded our business, we became aware of the Johnson & Wales University and its commitment to the classical cuisine with an emphasis on creating unique contemporary plates.

We felt a facility such as a dining room with bar and other teaching facilities would be a fitting atmosphere for the training of students on a daily basis. It is very gratifying to know that now hundreds of students use this facility to learn every day. The Tosi dining room is also used by world-renowned chefs, who are invited to demonstrate the culinary achievements that made them famous.

Ernest A. Tosi
President
E. A. Tosi & Sons Company, Inc.

Preface

The Johnson & Wales University, College of Culinary Arts, Volume I—*Culinary: Fundamentals,* Volume II—*Culinary: Service,* and Volume III—*Culinary: Recipes* are the University's commitment to excellence in education. This new edition will enable the college to be on the cutting edge as a trendsetter, introducing new ideas, procedures, and technologies to our students and to the foodservice industry.

Each volume will be used as a reference tool for faculty and students to teach and learn from. These textbooks will emphasize theory and practical applications in nutrition, sanitation, cost control, and marketing.

Volume II: *Culinary: Service,* explains to the student how to serve the guest. The student will be exposed to front-of-the-house operational procedures, customer relations, preparing the dining room for service, and various styles of service. An in-depth study of French, American, German, Italian, and Australian wines is also presented. The mixology component will examine the procedures for opening and closing a bar, how to properly make cocktails and mixed drinks, and the regulations of liquor liability.

Educational Task Force

Acknowledgments

The three volumes of Culinary—I: Fundamentals; II: Service; *and* III: Recipes—*have been written by people who truly love culinary arts. I wish to thank all the faculty, administration, and friends of the University for their support and participation in this tremendous undertaking. Their collective work represents their dedication to educating students who will keep the flame of culinary inspiration alive for future generations.*

Thomas L. Wright

Vice President
Culinary Education

Special thanks to the following individuals for their tireless efforts and dedication in producing these textbooks:

Pauline Allsworth	James Griffin	Paul J. McVety	Christine Stamm
Linda Beaulieu	Karl Guggenmos	Robert Nograd	Michel Vienne
Dr. Barbara Bennett	Edward Korry	Pamela Peters	Bradley Ware
Lynn Dieterich	Victoria A. McCrae	Jacquelyn B. Scott	

Educational Task Force

Carolyn Buster	Jean-Jacques Dietrich	Edward Korry	Christine Stamm
Martha Crawford	Meridith Ford	Robert Nograd	Frank Terranova
Elaine Cwynar	Karl Guggenmos	Pamela Peters	William Travis
Mary Ann DeAngelis	Frederick Haddad	Patrick Reed	Bradley Ware
John Dion	Lars Johannson	Janet Rouslin	

Providence Administration, Faculty and Support Staff

Thomas L. Wright, M.S., Vice President of Culinary Education

Jean-Michel Vienne, C.C.P., C.E.P., C.A.P., Dean, College of Culinary Arts

Dorothy Jeanne Allen, M.S., Associate Professor; A.S., B.S., M.S., Johnson & Wales University

Pauline Allsworth, Office Manager

Frank Andreozzi, B.S., Assistant Professor; B.S., Providence College

Charles Armstrong, A.O.S., Instructor; A.O.S., Culinary Institute of America

Soren Arnoldi, Danish Master Chef, Associate Instructor; Falke Hotel, Tivoli Gardens Wivex, Palace Hotel, Copenhagen, Apprenticeship

John Aukstolis, A.S., Instructor; A.S., Johnson & Wales University

Adrian Barber, A.O.S., Associate Instructor; A.O.S., Culinary Institute of America

Claudia Berube, A.S., Instructor; A.S., Johnson & Wales University

Steven Browchuk, M.A., Certified T.I.P.S. Trainer, Associate Professor; B.A., Roger Williams College; M.A., University of Sorbonne; M.A., Middlebury College

Victor Calise, Associate Instructor

Carl Calvert, B.S., Instructor; A.O.S., B.S., Johnson & Wales University

Gerianne Chapman, M.B.A., Associate Professor; A.O.S., B.S., Johnson & Wales University; B.A., George Washington University; M.B.A., University of Rhode Island

John S. Chiaro, M.S., C.E.C., C.C.E., Associate Professor; B.A., Rhode Island College; M.S., Johnson & Wales University

Cynthia Coston, A.S., Instructor; A.S., Schoolcraft College

Laurie Coughlin, Administrative Assistant

Martha Crawford, B.S., C.W.P.C., Instructor; A.O.S., Culinary Institute of America; B.S., University of Michigan

Elaine R. Cwynar, B.A., Associate Instructor; A.S., Johnson & Wales University; B.A., University of Connecticut

William J. Day, M.S., C.F.E., Associate Professor and Director of Continuing Education; B.S., Bryant College; M.S., Johnson & Wales University

Mary Ann DeAngelis, M.S., Assistant Professor; B.S., M.S., University of Rhode Island

Richard DeMaria, B.S., Instructor; B.S., University of Rhode Island

Jean-Luc Derron, Associate Instructor; Hotel Schwanen Switzerland; steinli Trade School, Switzerland, Apprenticeship; Certification, Department of Labor and Trade, Switzerland; Confiserie Bachmann, Switzerland, Apprenticeship

Lynn Dieterich, Coordinator Faculty Support Services

Jean Jacques Dietrich, M.A., Senior Instructor; A.S., New York City Technological College; B.A., Hunter College; M.A., Johnson & Wales University

John R. Dion, B.S,., C.E.C., C.C.E., Associate Instructor; A.O.S., Culinary Institute of America; B.S., Johnson & Wales University

Rene R. Dionne, Director of Corporate Relations/ Purchasing

Reginald B. Dow, A.O.S., Storeroom Manager; A.O.S., Culinary Institute of America

Kevin Duffy, B.S., Instructor; B.S., Johnson & Wales University

Thomas Dunn, B.S., Instructor; A.O.S., B.S., Johnson & Wales University

Roger Dwyer, B.A., Instructor; B.A., George Washington University

Neil Fernandes, B.S., Storeroom Office Manager; B.S. Johnson & Wales University

Paula Figoni, M.B.A., Instructor; B.S., University of Massachusetts; M.S., University of California; M.B.A., Simmons College Graduate School of Management

Ernest Fleury, M.S., Associate Professor, A.O.S., Johnson & Wales University; A.S., Community College of Rhode Island; B.S., M.S., Johnson & Wales University

Meridith Ford, B.S., Instructor; A.O.S., B.S., Johnson & Wales University

James Fuchs, A.O.S., Instructor; A.O.S., Johnson & Wales University

Nancy Garnett-Thomas, M.S., R.D., L.D.N., Associate Professor; A.O.S., Culinary Institute of America; B.A., Colby College; M.S., University of Rhode Island

William Gormley, B.S., Instructor; A.O.S., B.S., Johnson & Wales University

James Griffin, M.S., C.W.C., C.C.E., Associate Dean & Associate Professor; A.O.S., B.S., M.S., Johnson & Wales University

Frederick Haddad, A.O.S., C.E.C., C.C.E., Associate Instructor; A.O.S., Culinary Institute of America

Rainer Hienerwadel, B.S., Instructor; A.O.S., B.S., Johnson & Wales University

J. Jeffrey Howard, B.A., Instructor; B.A., University of Massachusetts

Lars E. Johansson, C.P.C., C.C.E., Director, International Baking & Pastry Institute

Steven Kalble, A.S., Instructor; A.S., Johnson & Wales University

Linda Kender, B.S., Associate Instructor; A.S., B.S., Johnson & Wales University

Edward Korry, M.A., Assistant Professor; B.A., University of Chicago; M.A., University of Cairo

C. Arthur Lander, B.S.; Instructor; B.S., Johnson & Wales University

Kelly Lawton, Administrative Assistant

Hector Lipa, B.S., C.E.C., C.C.E., Associate Instructor; B.S., University of St. Augustine, the Philippines

Laird Livingston, A.O.S., C.E.C., C.C.E., Associate Instructor; A.O.S., Culinary Institute of America

Michael D. Marra, M.Ed., Associate Professor; B.A., M.Ed., Providence College

Susan Desmond-Marshall, M.S., Associate Professor; B.S., University of Maine; M.S., Johnson & Wales University

Victoria A. McCrae, Assistant to the Vice President

Diane McGarvey, B.S., Instructor; A.O.S., B.S., Johnson & Wales University

Jack McKenna, B.S., C.E.C., C.C.E., C.C.P., Director of Special Projects

Paul J. McVety, M.Ed., Assistant Dean and Associate Professor; A.S., B.S., Johnson & Wales University; M.Ed., Providence College

Michael Moskwa, M.Ed., Assistant Professor; B.A.,

University of Rhode Island; M.Ed., Northeastern University

Sean O'Hara, M.S., Certified T.I.P.S. Trainer, Instructor; A.O.S., B.S., M.S., Johnson & Wales University

George O'Palenick, M.S., C.E.C., C.C.E., Associate Professor; A.O.S., Culinary Institute of America; A.S., Jamestown Community College; B.S., M.S., Johnson & Wales University

Robert Pekar, B.S., Associate Instructor; A.O.S., Culinary Institute of America; A.S., Manchester Community College; B.S., Johnson & Wales University

Pamela Peters, A.O.S.,C.E.C., C.C.E., Director of Culinary Education; A.O.S., Culinary Institute of America

David Petrone, B.S., Associate Instructor; A.O.S., B.S., Johnson & Wales University

Felicia Pritchett, M.S., Associate Professor; A.O.S., B.S., M.S., Johnson & Wales University

Thomas J. Provost, Instructor

Ronda Robotham, B.S., Instructor; B.S., Johnson & Wales University

Robert Ross, B.S., Associate Instructor; A.S., B.S., Johnson & Wales University

Janet Rouslin, B.S., Instructor; B.S., University of Maine

Cynthia Salvato, A.S., C.E.P.C., Instructor; A.S., Johnson & Wales University

Stephen Scaife, B.S., C.E.C., C.C.E., Associate Instructor; A.O.S., Culinary Institute of America, B.S., Johnson & Wales University

Gerhard Schmid, Associate Instructor; European Apprenticeship, Germany

Louis Serra, B.S., C.E.C., Instructor; A.O.S., B.S, Johnson & Wales University

Christine Stamm, M.S., C.W.C., Associate Professor; A.O.S., B.S., M.S., Johnson & Wales University

Laura Schwenk, Administrative Assistant

Adela Tancayo-Sannella, Certified T.I.P.S. Trainer, Associate Instructor

Mary Ellen Tanzi, B.A., Instructor; B.A., Rhode Island College

Frank Terranova, B.S., C.E.C., C.C.E., Associate Instructor; B.S., Johnson & Wales University

Segundo Torres, B.S., Associate Instructor; B.S., Johnson & Wales University

Helene Houde-Trzcinski, M.S., Instructor; B.S., M.S., Johnson & Wales University

Peter Vaillancourt, B.S., Instructor; B.S., Roger Williams College

Paul VanLandingham, Ed.D, C.E.C., IMP, CFBE, C.C.E., Professor; A.O.S, Culinary Institute of America; B.S., Roger Williams College; M.A., Anna Maria College; Ed.D., Nova University

Suzanne Vieira, M.S., R.D., L.D.N., Department Chair, Foodservice Academic Studies; Associate Professor; B.S., Framingham State College; M.S., University of Rhode Island

Bradley Ware, M.Ed., C.C.C., C.C.E., Associate Professor; A.S., Johnson & Wales University; B.S., Michigan State University; M.Ed., Providence College; C.A.G.S., Salve Regina University

Gary Welling, A.O.S., Instructor; A.O.S., Johnson & Wales University

Robin Wheeler, Receptionist

Ed Wilroy, B.A., Continuing Education Coordinator; A.O.S., Johnson Wales University; B.A., Auburn University

Kenneth Wollenberg, B.S., Associate Instructor; A.O.S., B.S., Johnson & Wales University

Robert Zielinski, A.S., Instructor; A.S., Johnson & Wales University

Branch Campuses Administration and Faculty

CHARLESTON

Karl Guggenmos, B.S., C.E.C., G.C.M.C., Director of Culinary Education

Diane Aghapour, B.S., Instructor

Patricia Agnew, M.E., Assistant Professor

Donna Blanchard, B.A., Instructor

Robert Bradham, Instructor

Matthew Broussard, C.W.C., Instructor

Jan Holly Callaway, Instructor

Wanda Crooper, B.S., C.C.E., C.W.P.C., Associate Instructor

James Dom, M.S., Associate Professor

Armin Gronert, G.C.M.P.C., Associate Instructor

Kathy Hawkins, Instructor

David Hendrieksen, B.S., C.C.E., C.C.C., Associate Instructor

Andrew Hoxie, M.A., Assistant Professor

John Kacaia, C.E.C., Instructor

Michael Koons, A.O.S., C.E.C., C.C.E., Associate Instructor

Audrey McKnight, A.O.S., Instructor

Mary McLellan, M.S., Adjunct

Marcel Massenet, C.E.P.C., Associate Instructor

Stephen Nogle, A.A.S., C.E.C., C.C.E., Associate Instructor

Daniel Polasek, Instructor

Frances Ponsford, B.S., Instructor

Lloyd Regier, Ph.D., Adjunct

Victor Smurro, B.S., C.C.C., Associate Instructor

Susan Wigley M.Ed., C.C.E., C.W.C., Associate Professor

NORFOLK

Robert Nograd, Acting Director

Fran Adams, M.S., Instructor; B.S., M.S., Old Dominion University

Guy Allstock, III, M.S., Storeroom Instructor; B.S., M.S., Johnson & Wales University

Christian Barney, B.A., Associate Instructor; B.A., Old Dominion University

Ed Batten, A.O.S., Instructor; A.O.S., Johnson & Wales University

Susan Batten, C.E.C., C.C.E., Culinary Technology Degree, Associate Instructor; Culinary Technology Degree, Asheville Buncombe Technical Institute

Bettina Blank, M.S., Instructor; B.S., Grand Valley State University; M.S., Boston University

Dedra Butts, B.S., Instructor; B.S., Johnson & Wales University

Tim Cameron, M.A., C.E.C., Associate Professor; B.A., Milligan College; M.A., Old Dominion

Donna Curtis, B.A., Instructor; B.A., Northern Michigan University; Reading Specialist Degree, Memphis State University.

Art M. Elvins, A.A.S., C.E.C., Associate Instructor; A.A.S., Johnson & Wales University

Kristen Fletcher, R.D., M.S., Instructor; B.S., M.S., Virginia Polytechnic Institute

Scarlett Holmes-Paul, M.A., Instructor; B.S. Western Michigan University; M.A. Eastern Michigan University

Joan Hysell, M.Ed., Instructor; B.P.S., SUNY Institute of Technology at Utica/Rome; M.Ed., Ohio University

John Keating, M.S., Oenology Instructor; B.S., Georgetown University; M.S., George Washington University

Lisa Kendall, M.A., Instructor; B.A., State University of New York; M.A., Old Dominion University

Greg Kopanski, M.S., Instructor; B.S., New York University; M.S., Old Dominion University.

Jerry Lanuzza, B.S., Instructor; B.S., Johnson & Wales University

Peter Lehmuller, B.A., Instructor; A.O.S., Culinary Institute of America; B.A., State University of New York, Albany

Alex Leuzzi, M.S., Associate Instructor; B.S., Pikesville College; M.S., Fairleigh Dickinson University

Melanie Loney, M.S., Associate Instructor; B.S., M.S., Old Dominion University

Mary Matthews, M.S., Instructor; B.S., M.S., Old Dominion University

Carrie Moranha, A.A.S., Dining Room /Beverage Instructor; A.A.S. Johnson & Wales University

Maureen Nixon, M.A., Instructor; B.A., North Carolina State University; M.A., Norfolk State University.

Shelly Owens, B.A., Baking & Pastry Instructor; B.A., Townson State University

Patrick Reed, A.O.S., C.C.C., C.C.E., Associate Instructor; A.O.S., Culinary Institute of America

Gregory Retz, B.S., Instructor; A.A.S., Johnson & Wales University; B.S., Virginia Polytechnic

Steven Sadowski, C.E.C., A.O.S., Associate Instructor; A.O.S., Johnson & Wales University

Bonita Startt, M.S ., Instructor; B.S., M. S., Old Dominion University

Fred Tiess, A.A.S., Instructor; A.A.S., State University of New York, Poughkeepsie; A.O.S., Culinary Institute of America

NORTH MIAMI

Donato Becce, Instructor; Diploma di Qualifica, Instituto Professionale, Alberghiero di Stato, Italy

Kenneth Beyer, B.B.A., Instructor; A.B.A., Nichols College; B.B.A., University of Miami

Drue Brandenburg, B.S., C.C.E., C.E.C., Instructor; A.O.S., Culinary Institute of America; B.S., Oklahoma State University

Dennis Daugherty, M.Ed., Instructor; B.S., University of Maryland; M.Ed., Pennsylvania State University

Melvin Davis, B.A., Instructor; B.A. University of Maryland

Alberto Diaz, English Master Pastry Chef, Instructor

Claus Esrstling, C.E.C., Instructor

John Goldfarb, B.S., Instructor; A.O.S., Culinary Institute of America; B.S., Florida International University

John Harrison, B.S., Instructor; A.O.S., Culinary Institute of America; B.S., University of New Haven

James Hensley, Instructor

Giles Hezard, Instructor; Certification of Professional Aptitide - College D'Enseignement Technique Masculin, Audincourt, France

Alan Lazar, B.A., Instructor; B.A. Monmouth College

Lucille Ligas, M.Ed., Assistant Professor, Indiana University of Pennsylvania; B.S. Ed. Indiana University of Pennsylvania

Charles Miltenberger, C.E.P.C., Instructor

Betty Murphy, M.S.Ed. Instructor; B.S.Ed. Eastern Illinois University; M.S.Ed., University of Guam

Larry Rice, M.S., Instructor; A.S., Johnson & Wales University; B.S., Florida International University; M.S., Florida International University

Mark Testa, Ph.D., Associate Professor; A.A.S., State University of New York at Farmingdale; B.P.S., New York Institute of Technology; M.A.L.S. State University of New York at Stony Brook; Ph.D., Barry University

Todd Tonova, M. S., Instructor; A.O.S., Culinary Institute of America; B.S., Florida International University; M.S., Florida International University

Karen Woolley, B.S., Instructor; A.O.S., Culinary Institute of America; B.S., Florida State University

VAIL

Todd M. Rymer, M.S., Director; B.A., New College; M.S., Florida International University

Paul Ferzacca, A.O.S., Instructor; A.O.S. Kendall College

David Hite, A.S., Instructor; A.S. Johnson & Wales University

Robert Kuster, Instructor; Diploma, Swiss Hotel School, Lucerne; Diploma, Trade School, Cook's Apprenticeship, Lucerne; Diploma, Institute Stavia, Estavater Le-Lac

Katie Mazzia; B.S. R.D., Instructor; R.D., Saint Joseph's Health Center; B.S., Ohio State

Paul Reeves, B.S., Instructor; B.S., Saint Cloud State University

David B. Sanchez, A.O.S., Instructor; A.O.S., Johnson & Wales University

Culinary Advisory Council

Scott Armendinger, Editor, Journal Publications, Rockland, ME

Michael P. Berry, Vice President of Food Operations and Concept Development, Walt Disney World, Orlando, FL

Edward Bracebridge, Chef Instructor, Blackstone Valley Tech, Upton, MA

Gerry Fernandez, Technical Service Specialist, General Mills, Inc., Minneapolis, MN

John D. Folse, C.E.C., A.A.C., Owner, Executive Chef, Chef John Folse & Company, Donaldsonville, LA

Ira L. Kaplan, President, Servolift/Eastern Corp., Boston, MA

Gustav Mauler, VP, Food & Beverage, Treasure Island Hotel, Las Vegas, NV

Franz Meier, President, MW Associates, Columbia, SC

Roland Mesnier, Executive Pastry Chef, The White House, Washington, DC

Stanley Nicas, Chef/Owner, Castle Restaurant, Leicester, MA

Robert J. Nyman, President, The Nyman Group, Livingston, NJ

Johnny Rivers, Food & Beverage Manager/Executive Chef, Thyme & Associates,

Joseph Schmidt, Owner, Joseph Schmidt Confections, San Francisco, CA

Martin Yan, President, Yan Can Cook, Inc., Foster City, CA

Johnson & Wales University *Distinguished Visiting Chefs 1979–1997*

1 Dr. Jean Joaquin	8 Bernard S. Urban	16 Dr. Pierre Franey 🍴	24 Hans K. Roth
2 Garry Reich 🍴	9 Marcel Paniel 🍴	17 Jean-Jacques Dietrich	25 Gerhard Daniel
3 Dr. Hans J. Bueschkens	10 Lutz Olkiewicz	18 Uri Guttmann	26 Jacques Noe
4 Michael Bourdin	11 Dr. Joel Robuchon	19 William Spry 🍴	27 Andre Rene
5 Christian Inden	12 Ray Marshall 🍴	20 Dr. Stanley Nicas	28 Dr. Anton Mosimann
6 Casey Sinkeldam	13 Francis Hinault	21 Dr. Paul Elbling	29 Dr. Roger Verge
7 John Kempf	14 Wally Uhl	22 Angelo Paracucchi	30 Gerhard Schmid
	15 Gunther Heiland	23 Albert Kellner	31 Karl Ronaszeki

32 Jacques Pepin
33 Klauss Friedenreich
34 Arno Schmidt
35 Lucien Vannier 💀
36 Dr. Wolfgang Bierer
37 Dr. John L. Bandera
38 Albert Marty
39 Dr. Siegfried Schaber
40 Dr. Michael Minor
41 Raimund Hofmeister
42 Henry Haller
43 Dr. Noel Cullen
44 Dr. Carolyn Buster
45 Dr. Madeleine Kamman
46 Udo Nechutnys
47 Andrea Hellrigl 💀
48 George Karousos
49 Warren LeRuth
50 Rene Mettler
51 Dr. Johnny Rivers

52 Milos Cihelka
53 Dr. Louis Szathmary 💀
54 Philippe Laurier
55 Dr. Hans J. Schadler
56 Franz Klampfer
57 Jean-Pierre Dubray
58 Neil Connolly
59 Joachim Caula
60 Dr. Emeril LaGasse†
61 Dr. Roland Mesnier
62 Bernard Dance
63 Hartmut Handke
64 James Hughes†
65 Paul Bocuse
66 Dr. Martin Yan
67 Marcel Desaulniers
68 Heinz H. Veith
69 Benno Eigenmann
70 Johanne Killeen & George Germon
71 Dr. John D. Folse

72 Dr. Christian Rassinoux
73 Dr. Gustav E. Mauler
74 Dr. Keith Keogh
75 Clayton Folkners
76 Kenneth Wade
77 Dr. Roland E. Schaeffer
78 Dr. William Gallagher
79 Van P. Atkins
80 Hiroshi Noguchi
81 Jasper White
82 Albert Kumin
83 Alfonso Contrisciani†
84 Dr. Victor Gielisse
85 Reimund D. Pitz
86 Daniel Bruce†
87 Antoine Schaefers
88 Michael Ty
89 Phil Learned
90 Joseph Schmidt
91 John Halligan

92 Willy O. Rossel
93 John J. Vyhnanek
94 Roberto Gerometta
95 Robert A. Trainor†
96 Ewald & Susan Notter
97 Joseph Amendola
98 David Paul Johnson
99 Thomas Pedersen
100 André Soltner
101 Christian Clayton†
102 Konstantinos Exarchos
103 Christian Chemin
104 Lars Johansson
105 Paul O'Connell†

SPECIAL FRIENDS
John J. Bowen
Joseph P. Delaney
Socrates Inonog
Franz K. Lemoine

† Alumni
💀 Deceased

Partial List of Companies Associated with Johnson & Wales University

Adam's Mark Hotels and Resorts
Allied Domecq Retailing
American General Hospitality, Inc.
AmeriClean Systems, Inc.
Angelica Uniform Group
Antigua Hotel Association
Aramark Services, Inc.
Automatic Sales, Inc.
AVTECH Industries
Bacardi & Company, Ltd.

Bacon Construction Company
Balfour Foundation
Banfi Vintners
Basic American Frozen Foods
Bertoill, USA, Inc.
Boston Chicken, Inc.
Boston Park Plaza Hotel
Braman Motors
Brinker International
Bristol Hotel Company

Bugaboo Creek Steakhouse
Bushiri Hotel Aruba
Campbell Food Service Company
Carlson Companies, Inc.
Carnival Cruise Lines
Cartier, Inc.
Celebrity Cruise Lines
Choice Hotels
Citizens Financial Group
Cleveland Range, Inc.

Club Corporation International
Comstock-Castle Stove Company
Concord Hospitality
Cookshack
Cookson America, Inc.
Coors Brewing Company
Crabtree McGrath Associates
Daka Restaurants, Inc.
Darden Restaurants
Deer Valley Resort

Denny's Restaurants

Dial Corporation

Digital Equipment Corporation

DiLeonardo International

Doral Arrowwood

E.A. Tosi & Sons Company, Inc.

E-H Enterprises

Ecolab, Inc.

Edison Electric Institute

Edwards Super Food Store

EGR International

Electric Cooking Council

Eurest Dining Service

F. Dick

Felchlin, Inc.

Feinstein Foundation

Flik International Corporation

Forbes

Friendly Ice Cream Corporation

Frymaster

G.S. Distributors

Garland Commercial Industries

Gavin Sales Company

General Mills

Godfather's Pizza, Inc.

The Golden Corral Corporation

Grand Western Brands, Inc.

Grisanti, Inc.

Groen, a Dover Industries Co.

Hallsmith-Sysco Food Services

Harman Management Corporation

Harris-Teeter, Inc.

Harvard University

Hasbro, Inc.

Hatch-Jennings, Inc.

HERO

Hiram Walker & Sons, Inc.

Hilton Hotels

Hobart Corporation

Houlihan's Restaurant Group

Houston's Restaurants

Hyatt Hotels Corporation

Ice-O-Matic

Ikon

Intercontinental Hotels

International Metro Industries

Interstate Hotels

Keating of Chicago, Inc.

Kiawah Island Resorts

Kraft Foods, Inc.

Lackman Food Service

Le Meridien Hotel Boston

L.J. Minor Corporation

Legal Sea Foods, Inc.

Loews Hotels

Longhorn Steaks, Inc.

Lyford Cay Foundation, Inc.

Manor Care Health Services

Market Forge Company

Marriott International, Inc.

Max Felchlin, Inc.

Massachusetts Electric Company

McCormick & Company, Inc.

Moet & Chandon

Morris Nathanson Design

Motel 6

MTS Seating

Nabisco Brands, Inc.

Narragansett Electric Company

National Votech Educators

National Banner Company, Inc.

National Prepared Foods Assoc.

National Student Organization

Nestle USA, Inc.

New England Electric System

New World Development Company

Norwegian Seafood Council

Opryland Hotel

Paramount Restaurant Supply

PepsiCo, Inc.

Pillsbury Corp.

The Proctor & Gamble Co.

Providence Beverage

Prudential Insurance Company

Quadlux

The Quaker Oats Company

Radisson Hospitality Worldwide

Ralph Calise Fruit & Produce

Red Lion Hotels

Renaissance Hotels & Resorts

Restaurant Data Concepts

Rhode Island Distributing Company

Rhode Island Foundation

Rich Products Corporation

The Ritz-Carlton Hotel

Robert Mondavi Winery

Robot Coupe

Ruth's Chris Steak House

Saunders Hotel Group

Joseph Schmidt Confections

Schott Corporation

Select Restaurants, Inc.

Servolift/Eastern Corp.

Sharp Electronic Corporation

Somat Corporation

Southern Foods

State of Rhode Island, Department of Education

Stonehard

Sun International

Sunrise Assisted Living

Swiss American Imports, Ltd.

Swiss Chalet Fine Foods

Sysco Corporation

TACO, Inc.

Taco Bell

Tasca Ford Sales, Inc.

Tekmatex, Inc.

The Delfield Company

The Waldorf-Astoria

Thermodyne Foodservice Products

Toastmaster

Tufts University

Tyson Foods, Inc.

U.S.D.A./Bell Associates

United States Army

United States Navy

University of Connecticut

Vail Associates

Vulcan Hart Corporation

Walt Disney World

Wells Manufacturing Company

Wyatt Corporation

Wyndham Hotels & Resorts

1

Service
Basics

1

Service Basics

We define service as "the complete fulfillment of guests' expectations in a friendly, professional, and competent manner." These expectations are based on guests' personal experiences and can vary widely from establishment to establishment, depending on the identity of the restaurant—from casual to fine dining.

Importance of Service

When frequenting a fast-food restaurant, guests' expectations include cleanliness, consistency, and friendly and competent service. If any of these expectations fail to be met, guests would be disappointed and would probably decide that they had not received good service. If guests patronize a fine-dining establishment, their expectations are considerably greater. They expect a much more elegant decor, a more refined style of service, and a more knowledgeable staff. If their expectations are fulfilled, they would assert that they had received good service. *Service* may be elusive to define at times because it is intangible, but any guest receiving it would recognize it. With the complete fulfillment of expectations, guests are satisfied. The establishment will enjoy repeat business and become more profitable. Profit is the bottom line that defines the success of any business.

Service is the most critical ingredient in the recipe for success. It is the "added value" to the purchase of a meal. The server adds value by enhancing the guests' experience. Regardless of the complexity of the service, there are several components that must be included in defining *service*.

What are some of the intangibles of S-E-R-V-I-C-E?

Smiling
Eye contact with the guest
Reaching out with hospitality to every guest
Viewing every guest as being special
Inviting guests to return
Creating a warm environment
Exceeding customers' expectations

Service can only be a team effort and is a reflection of the service philosophy of the establishment. Good service should be consistent among all employees regardless of their position in the service staff: busser, server, host, or maître d'. The expectations of the guests are the same for each employee they encounter in a restaurant. For example, a server could fulfill all the aforementioned elements, but the positive effects could be nullified by rudeness on the part of other service personnel. The service philosophy of an establishment should be understood and executed by every service staff member.

The Server

Quality service does not happen by chance. It is a combination of training and refinement through practice. The professional server is expected to perform the roles of representative, salesperson, and skilled server.

The Representative

Among all restaurant employees, servers have the most direct contact with the guest and must conduct themselves as ambassadors of the restaurant. Servers are directly responsible for setting the mood in the dining room. By demonstrating good interpersonal skills, servers can create a pleasant dining experience for guests. Professional servers are responsible for making guests feel welcome, relaxed, and secure in knowing that they will be well attended.

The Salesperson

Servers are responsible for guiding the guests through their food and beverage decisions. Guiding the guests is the key to ensuring that guests are directed toward the best that the restaurant has to offer. Based on observation and listening to guests, servers can sell items, which will increase the revenue of the restaurant and, thereby, his personal income. Guests can be encouraged by an effective server to try new or different items. This is known as **suggestive selling.** Suggestive selling is a sales technique used by servers which can incorporate several proven sales techniques: **Highlighting, open-ended questions, and upselling.**

Highlighting is emphasizing a particular item to create a lasting impression. It can be used to promote the sale of both menu items and specials of the day. By being enthusiastic and using appropriate adjectives when describing an item, servers help to create a visual image for the guest. Highlighting draws attention to items and is effective when used during the order taking or selling process. Servers can use highlighting to persuade guests to order those items requiring less preparation time by the kitchen staff, or items the chef wishes to sell. This can help facilitate orders through the kitchen during busy periods when tables are needed.

Open-ended questions are ones that can make it difficult for the guest to answer with a "yes" or a "no"—for example, "Would you prefer the soup of the day or the onion soup?" This type of question can create an impression that the guest is expected to order one or the other soup.

Upselling is the technique for suggesting only the products of better quality or greater size than what was originally ordered by the customer. For example, a server taking an order for a scotch and water might suggest Dewars scotch or Chivas Regal. Even though not every guest will accept the suggestion, the consistent attempt to upsell will increase sales over time.

When servers incorporate suggestive selling, guests may be more inclined to try something new or add to their original choices. Increasing sales and enhancing guests' dining experience are the two purposes of sales. Servers cannot fulfill their responsibility to serve unless they are willing to sell. Servers would be doing a disservice to the guests and the establishment by ignoring the sales aspect of service. To sell is to serve.

The Skilled Server

As we shall describe in this book, there are many different positions for a front-of-the-house employee: busser, assistant server, server, captain, wine steward, bartender, host, maître d', and manager. All should have the following attributes:

- Positive attitude
- Good appearance
- Good communication skills
- Thorough job knowledge
- Timeliness

Positive Attitude

When dealing with the public, servers must have a positive attitude at all times. There is no room for allowing guests to be able to read anything into any server's behavior that might detract from their having a positive dining experience. Servers cannot allow a guest to affect their attitude, be it justified or not, because this will affect the other guests' experience. For example, one table of customers should not have to endure a server's poor attitude because of a poor tip from another customer. Servers need to be flexible and adapt to circumstances without allowing their overall attitudes to be affected.

Attitudes need to be differentiated from behaviors. Behavior is the physical expression of a mental process. Behaviors can be learned, adjusted, and manipulated by oneself or by management, but the sincerity of the behavior can come into question when the underlying attitude that drives the behavior is absent. This is why, when we discuss the behavioral skills associated with the front of the house, we must first identify the correct attitude or willingness to please the guest. Without such an attitude or willingness, servers with all the manual skills in the world will not succeed in their responsibilities.

Good Appearance

The appearance of a server is very important. By making a good appearance, guests will form a positive first impression of the server and the establishment. There are three elements to the server's appearance: **personal hygiene, attire,** and **body language.**

Personal Hygiene

- Hair that is longer than collar length must be properly restrained.
- Hands should remain clean. This requires frequent washing, especially after use of the restroom. Washing is required by law and must be observed.
- Fingernails must be trimmed and remain clean.
- Teeth should be clean, and breath should be fresh.
- Servers should pay attention to their body odor and use deodorant as needed.
- Colognes and perfumes should not be worn, because they detract from the aromas of the food and wine.

Attire

- Jewelry should be kept to a minimum (e.g., wedding bands).
- Uniforms should be kept clean and well pressed.
- Uniforms should be properly fitted.
- Shoes should be clean and shined.
- Shirts and blouses should be pressed, free of stains, and not frayed.

Body Language

Servers must be aware of their physical mannerisms, which might reflect poor sanitary standards or a poor attitude. Conversely, mannerisms can be used positively to communicate enthusiasm. The following should be observed:

- Do not smoke, drink, chew gum, or eat during service.
- Do not slouch or lean on walls. If you have time to lean, you have time to clean.
- Be careful about touching your hair, face, mouth, or nose in view of the guests.
- Do not stand around with hands in pockets.
- Do not wipe your brow or nose with your jacket sleeve.
- Do not sneeze into your bare hands.

- Never produce flatware or a napkin from one of your pockets.
- Stand erect and do not lean on the backs of customers' chairs. This suggests familiarity with the customer and is considered unprofessional.
- Maintain your height advantage at the table. It will help you to sell.

Good Communication Skills

The server should be able to communicate. It is imperative that management train the front-of-the-house personnel in good communication skills. The people with whom the server must learn to communicate are the guest, personnel in other work stations (the kitchen and bar), and other dining room personnel (servers, bussers, hosts, maîtres d').

The server must recognize that communication takes place in three ways:

- Writing—transmitting information that will be read by another person or persons. Computer-assisted communication falls into this category.
- Verbal—communicating directly to the person by speaking
- Nonverbal—using body language to communicate *attitudes* and *feelings* knowingly and sometimes unknowingly. As discussed attitudes and feelings affect servers' appearances. Servers should have good eye contact with guests; use facial expressions, such as smiling; and use their hands to communicate in a positive manner.

Servers will be unable to perform their duties unless they are trained in effective communication skills.

Thorough Job Knowledge

Servers should not be permitted to represent the establishment without having a complete knowledge of their profession. This should include knowledge of the menu and wine list, beverages, guest interaction, order taking, check writing, the use of a computer point-of-sale system, the proper serving and clearing protocols, presenting the check, collecting payment, all dining room equipment and its use, preparing for service, and performing necessary **side du-ties.** Servers should be able to answer questions concerning not only the food and beverage selections, but also everything from the history of the restaurant to the previous accomplishments of the chef. Servers may be asked to provide information about local events, directions to the theater or airport, and other significant landmarks. Servers should know how to deal with dining room emergencies, difficult customers, and guest complaints.

Timeliness

Most servers are responsible for the service at more than one table. This group of tables (usually three or four tables) is called a **station** or **section.** The service within the server's station depends on not only the quality of service, but also the speed with which the server can work accurately and safely. To perform effectively, servers must be well organized and, know how to prioritize their workload and execute it with an economy of movement—for example, not making trips to and from the kitchen empty-handed.

The Sequence of Service

Although each restaurant will vary or adjust the service sequence to suit its needs or the needs of its guests, the following sequence is most commonly used in many restaurants. Quality service is achieved when each step is performed correctly from the time the guest arrives until the time the guest departs:

1. Greeting the guest
2. Seating the guest and menu presentation
3. Greeting by the server
4. The beverage order
5. Selling the menu and specials
6. Taking the order
7. Writing the order
8. Transmitting the order to the kitchen
9. Serving (the manner in which the items are placed)
10. Checking back with the customer
11. Presentation of the check
12. Farewell

Greeting the Guest

The initial interaction between a potential guest and any employee of the restaurant is critical. First impressions are lasting. The responsibility of greeting the guest may be designated to the dining room manager or the host. Unfortunately, all too often it seems that only the designated person has been instructed properly or trained in how to greet a guest. All employees should be instructed on how to greet guests properly. Good management should institute a policy that ensures there is always someone at the door to greet the guest.

- Open and hold the door open for guests, if possible.
- Greet guests with a warm smile.
- Make good eye contact and use an appropriate welcoming remark.
- Be warm, friendly, relaxed, and hospitable.
- Advise guests where they can check or hang their coats.
- Help remove their coats whenever possible. (*Note:* Many restaurants dissuade their employees from checking customers' coats because of liability issues. Any well-managed establishment will have the proper controls in place to avoid any potential loss of property, and servers should be of assistance.)
- If a reservation system is being used, inquire if the guests have made a reservation and ask for the name in which the reservation was made.
- Be honest with guests if there is a waiting period or list. Nothing irritates a guest more than to be misled as to how long the wait will be.

Seating the Guest and Menu Presentation

This is usually the responsibility of the host or maître d', but all front-of-the-house personnel should employ the following procedures when greeting guests.

- The host checks that the menus are presentable and contain all additional inserts.
- The host personalizes the way she addresses each party—for example, "Your table is right this way."
- The guests' surnames are used whenever possible.
- The guests are led to the table at a rate that does not make them feel rushed.
- The chairs are pulled out for the guests.
- The menus and wine lists are presented if it is the policy of the restaurant to do so.
- The menus are presented to the women first and the host of the dining party last.
- The host relays to the server any special request concerning the guests.

Note: The host should not rush through these steps, making guests feel that they are unwelcome.

Greeting by the Server

- Give the guests a moment to adjust to the environment before approaching the table.
- Maintain good eye contact with each guest at the table.
- Stand erect at the table. Do not bend down.
- Even if in a hurry, do not appear rushed at the table.
- Welcome the guests to the restaurant.
- Observe the guests' comfort level, body language, and the type of occasion that brings them to the restaurant.

Note: The restaurant host or maître d' determines which guest is the host of the party, (i.e., the person who has brought the other guests to the establishment). She should try to determine who is the guest of honor if there is one and inform the server.

The Beverage Order

Servers must have a knowledge of popular drinks, available brands of liquor, and beers and wines available by the glass. It is essential that beverage service be performed correctly because it is the first point of service. Servers should use appropriate sales techniques to ask guests for their beverage selections.

- Take the order from women first, and from host last.
- Use position numbers to ensure that the beverages are served to the appropriate guest.
- Clarify the guests' preferences regarding the preparation of the drinks (e.g., straight up or on the rocks, olive or twist of lemon).
- Repeat the order for each guest to confirm what has been chosen.
- Serve beverages, whenever possible, from the right side, with the right hand and the right foot forward.
- Avoid reaching across guests.
- Handle glasses as low as possible, with fingers as far as possible from the rim of the glass—by the stem for a stemmed glass and at the base for a base glass.
- Check back for a second round of beverages when the drinks are approximately two-thirds consumed.
- If one customer orders a second round of beverages, be sure that it is the intention of each guest to have another drink at that time.

When serving a fresh drink to a customer, remove the empty glass first. Empty glasses should not accumulate on the table. The procedure for reordering beverages is the same. Refer to the original order to avoid re-asking what each guest is drinking. Unless the glass is empty, ask the guest if you may remove it before doing so.

Selling the Menu and Specials

There are three systems of menu presentation that an establishment can offer. An establishment can have more than a single system, because it can offer a combination of two or three. Each system will affect the organization of the servers' time management and how they try to build the check.

The three systems of menu preparation are

À la carte: Each separate course item is priced individually. For example, the appetizer, soup, salad, entrée, and dessert are priced separately.

Table d'hôte: A menu in which the price of a multiple-course meal changes according to the entrées selected. For example, steak au poivre, at $24.95, might include a soup, salad, and dessert, while grilled chicken with exactly the same courses is $16.95.

Prix Fixe: A meal consisting of multiple courses for one fixed price, regardless of the entrée selected.

Servers must be familiar with the prices and descriptions of all menu items and specials. They should articulate the selections by using the selling methods discussed previously. The food descriptions should include the following:*

- A description of the food item
- How the item is prepared
- The sauce with which the item is served
- The accompaniments
- The server's endorsement of the item (e.g., "It is a best-seller.")

Guests' attention must be focused on the selections that servers feel are particularly outstanding, by using appetizing adjectives that will accurately depict the item, enhance its appeal, and stimulate the appetite of the guest.

- During the verbal presentation, mention those items that have been sold out. (*Note:* The term is *sold out*, not *ran out*.)
- Guide guests by highlighting items they are considering.
- Use your hands to communicate anything from the thickness of a chop to the size of a lobster.
- Assume that guests will probably order a main course. Unlike other retailing establishments, customers do not visit restaurants to browse.
- Focus efforts on selling beverages, appetizers, soups, salads, accompaniments, and desserts to increase the total of the check and enhance the guests' dining experience.
- Politely ask the guests if they would like to order.
- After the food order has been taken, take this opportunity to suggest the appropriate wines to accompany the food.
- Take advantage of suggesting desserts immediately after the meal order has been taken (e.g., "Be sure to save room for one of our fabulous desserts.").

*See Appendix C for update.

- Be prepared to answer specific questions about the food and beverages.

Truth in Menu

It is imperative that servers avoid misrepresenting the products they are trying to sell in an effort to make sales. The following guidelines, established by the National Restaurant Association, should be observed:

- *Representation of quantity*: This must be specific. A "four-egg omelette" must be made with four eggs.
- *Representation of quality:* "Angus Beef" must be certified as Angus.
- Representation of price: If the operation includes a cover charge, service charge, or gratuity, this must be stipulated.
- *Representation of brand names:* Any product brand that is advertised should be the one served. For example, Tabasco sauce must be Tabasco sauce, not a different brand of hot sauce.
- *Representation of product identification:* Bleu cheese must not be substituted for Roquefort cheese.
- *Representation of point of origin:* Atlantic salmon cannot come from any other location.
- *Representation of merchandising terms*: "Fresh" fish must not be previously frozen.
- *Representation of food preparation:* "Charcoal-grilled" steaks must be grilled over charcoal.
- *Representation of verbal and visual presentation:* A server's description of breads that are "baked on the premises" cannot include breads that are delivered to the restaurant already baked.
- *Representation of nutritional and dietary claims*: For example, foods that are represented as fat-free must be totally fat-free.

Taking the Order

Numbering of the guests at the table by seat number must be discussed among servers prior to taking the order. Ail servers in a professionally run restaurant must agree on the numbering of the seats at each table. This system aids the servers in communicating with each other about the needs of individual guests at various tables.

Number the guests at the table by counting clockwise around the table from a **fixed point** or a **focal point** at a booth or banquet table. (See sections on booth and banquette service in Chapter 2.) These points are determined differently at different types of tables by management or by the server. For example, the entrance to the restaurant might be selected as the fixed point, and the seat of each free-standing table closest to the entrance would be numbered position 1.

Generally, the numbering of seats is clockwise from position 1. It would be fairly commonplace for a server to tell another server or busser to serve two coffees to table 213, positions 1 and 3. The server making the request does not need to point to or indicate in any other way the table to which he is referring or which guests should receive the coffee. This also prevents the auctioning of foods ("Who gets the prime rib?"), one of the greatest service sins (see Figure 1–1).

- Stand to the right of each guest while taking the order.
- Stand up straight.
- Look the guest in the eye.

Figure 1–1 Clockwise numbering of seats

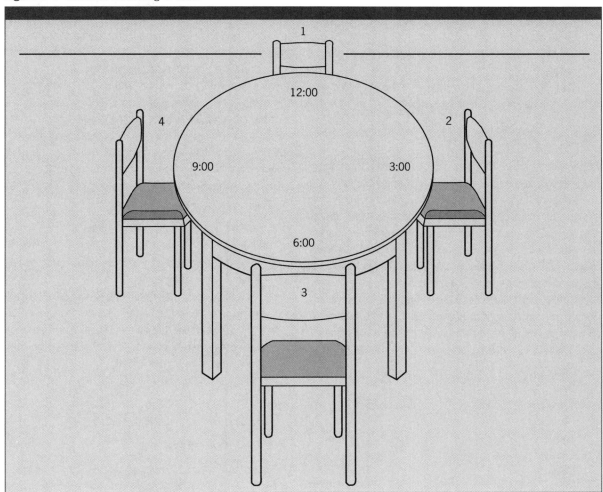

- Maintain a pleasant tone of voice and a smile.
- Reassure uncertain guests about their decision. For example, say "Excellent choice."
- Do not say "next" or point your finger to indicate who is next to give an order.
- Listen attentively to the guest's order.
- Take the entire order from each guest before proceeding to the next.
- Make sure that you have the cooking temperatures on all red-meat items.
- Take the order from the guest of honor first, women next, and the host last.
- Repeat the order for each guest to confirm what has been chosen.
- Remove the menus from each guest when you have taken the order.
- Be sure to check with the kitchen before taking special orders.
- Take into account the work load of the kitchen when timing your orders into the kitchen.

Writing the Order

Servers must know the correct order in which to serve a multiple-course meal. The sequence in which the courses are served will vary according to the courses chosen by the guests. Classically, the rules of service dictate that a cold course precede a hot course and a liquid course precede a solid course. It makes gustatory sense to have a cold course served before a hot course, because it is easier for the palate to appreciate and discern the flavors of the cold food in this order. In most restaurants, however, customers are unlikely to have more than one appetizer or both soup and appetizers. In the United States, therefore, the order in which courses are served is as follows:

- Appetizer
- Soup
- Salad
- Intermezzo
- Entrée
- Cheese
- Dessert
- Coffee

If each guest ordered one of each available course, all of the guests would be served each course simultaneously. Servers will face other scenarios more often. For example, a customer might start with an appetizer and have no salad before her entrée, while her companion may choose a soup and no salad before his entrée. The server will bring the appetizer and the soup simultaneously to his guests (see Figure 1–2A).

In another scenario, there are three customers. The first orders an appetizer, soup, and salad; the second orders a soup and salad; and the third orders only a salad. How should the server coordinate the service? He will serve customer 1 his appetizer first. Then, after clearing, he will serve customers 1 and 2 their soups and, after clearing, will serve customers 1, 2, and 3 their salads. In this scenario, the server might feel uncomfortable that the third guest is without food for two courses and attempt to sell another course by using the phrase, "Join your other guests," or offer a second beverage, but, ultimately, it is the choice of the guest (see Figure 1–2B).

Orders may be taken directly on a guest check, with the beverage order on the back of the check and the food order on the front. In most restaurants, orders are normally taken on a small order pad and then transferred to a guest check or entered directly into a point-of-sale computer terminal.

- Divide the pad into as many sections as there are courses.
- Place the item ordered in the sequentially correct section of the order pad.
- Place the guest's position number next to each item.
- Proceed to the next guest and repeat the procedure.
- If any guest orders the same item as any other previous guest, merely add the guest seat number next to the item (see Figure 1–2C).

Transmitting the Order to the Kitchen

There are three ways to transmit an order into the kitchen: verbally, written, computerized point-of-sales system. Each

Figure 1–2 Examples of how to write an order

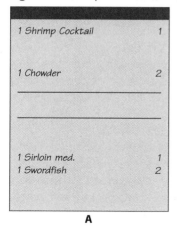

1 Shrimp Cocktail	1
1 Chowder	2
1 Sirloin med.	1
1 Swordfish	2

A

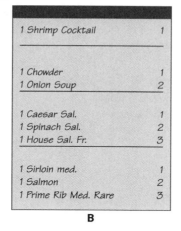

1 Shrimp Cocktail	1
1 Chowder	1
1 Onion Soup	2
1 Caesar Sal.	1
1 Spinach Sal.	2
1 House Sal. Fr.	3
1 Sirloin med.	1
1 Salmon	2
1 Prime Rib Med. Rare	3

B

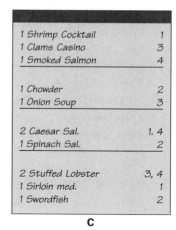

1 Shrimp Cocktail	1
1 Clams Casino	3
1 Smoked Salmon	4
1 Chowder	2
1 Onion Soup	3
2 Caesar Sal.	1. 4
1 Spinach Sal.	2
2 Stuffed Lobster	3, 4
1 Sirloin med.	1
1 Swordfish	2

C

of these methods will depend on the management of the establishment, but the underlying principle for transmitting the information to the kitchen is the same. A verbal ordering system is the least reliable and has limited application. Servers must be competent in hand writing a check to display their understanding of the overall principles. In addition, restaurants that utilize computerized point-of-sale systems should have a hand-written system (a crash kit) ready as a backup for a computer system breakdown or failure.

Check Writing

Before transferring the order from the pad to the guest check, determine if there are more items in a particular course than there are guests—for example, two people ordering three appetizers. Also, check if the same guest number appears twice for one course—for example, one guest ordering two appetizers while the other orders none. If so, that course will have two points of service (intervals) (see Figure 1–2A).

Copy the order pad onto the guest check the way it is written, leaving a space between the separate courses. For example, if a guest is having an appetizer as an entrée, the appetizer would be listed *with* the other guests' entrées (see Figure 1–2B).

Be sure to fill out the information at the top of each check in the boxes provided for date, server number or initials, table number, and number of guests. In the column on the far left, list the quantity of each item ordered. On the upper right of each order, write the number of the guests' positions (see Figure 1–2C).

- Once the check has been properly filled out, servers should proceed immediately to the kitchen.
- The top copy, or dupe, of the check is then given to the chef, coordinator, or kitchen expediter.
- While in the kitchen, servers should be as quiet and unobtrusive as possible.
- Whenever requesting food from the kitchen, the server should request the course by table number rather than by the specific item (e.g., "Chef, may I pick up the soups for table 213?").
- Servers of many establishments may be required to "fire" (instruct the kitchen to begin cooking) the next course they wish to pick up. The process of firing is the server's way of controlling the timing of service.
- The server should never serve a course until all of the items for that course are ready to be served.
- As a representative of the guest in the kitchen, it is the server's responsibility to ensure that the guests receive exactly what they ordered. It is at this point of pick-up that servers should verify correctness of the order.

- If the order is not correct and a problem emerges at this time (e.g., the presentation or temperature is evidently incorrect), it should be solved in the kitchen. The customer's needs should be everyone's first concern.
- Servers should be aware of where each guest's order is located on the tray. This will ensure that the service of the course will be presented in a timely and professional manner.

Communication by Computer

Point-of-sale computer technology is becoming more prevalent in the foodservice industry as a means of communicating. By the turn of the millennium, almost every foodservice establishment will use some form of computer to facilitate communication and service.

Computer-assisted technology makes it easier and faster for the server to transfer the guests' order to the kitchen. Each server is given an identity code or key to prevent any fraudulent use of the computer. To place an order, the server is prompted by the computer to enter information such as whether it is a new check or a continuation of a previously opened check, the table number, and the number of guests. Once this information is entered or displayed, the server enters the order into the computer.

Each computer offers several ways of entering information. Some have codes, while others have a preset key for each item available. Servers using the latter type simply press a key to order an item. This system is less than practical for a very large menu or a large selection of specialty food and beverage items. A third and more popular way of entering information into the computer is by a touch-screen system. The advantage to this system is that it is very easy to master.

Regardless of the type of computer the establishment chooses to use, there are several advantages of using one:

- The computer will transmit various orders to the proper work stations. Each food item ordered will be sent to a printer in the kitchen—hot food to the hot line and cold food to the pantry area.
- Drink orders are transmitted to the bar.

- Sending the order by computer cuts down on steps for the server and speeds up the service. The server could simultaneously enter beverage orders into the computer and have the beverage order print in the bar. Items that do not require a printout for the server to pick them up, such as soups, salads, and coffee, would not be sent to a printer but would appear on the guest's check.
- Orders are legible and organized.
- Printing of the guest's check is expedited by this system and is more accurate.
- The guest receives an itemized and easily understandable guest check with a clearly marked grand total *and* any message that the management might want on the check, such as "Make New Year's Eve Reservations Early."
- The computer can effectively reduce employee theft by requiring a computer printout of every item ordered.
- The computer maintains detailed records of all sales. Each department's sales are recorded accurately, and each server's sales output is available for the manager's perusal. For example, a manager can scrutinize the sales ability of a server.
- The computer manages inventories of each item on the menu and will inform the server of how many portions are available to sell.

The server must input the following data into the computer:

- The server code
- The table number
- The time the order was placed
- The item(s) ordered
- The quantity of each item
- The modifications to each item (temperature of the meat, sauce on the side, etc.)
- The serving sequence of the courses (every computer allows the server to indicate course divisions when placing an order)
- The guest receiving the order (computers allow the server to enter the position numbers or seat numbers for the item ordered)

Figure 1–3 A typical computer printout of a food order

```
Table No: 8                  Server: John
Number of guests: 2          Time: 7:21 PM

     1 Shrimp Cocktail
             no sauce
             lemon only
             position 2
     1 Clams Casino
             no bacon
             position 1
     ************************
     1 Onion Soup
             extra cheese
             position 1
     1 Caesar Salad
             no croutons
             Position 2
     ************************
     2 Sirloin Steaks
             Charred
             MR
             SOS
             Position 1
             MW
             Position 2
     1 Baked Potato
             Position 1
     1 Broccoli
             no butter
             Position 2
```

Figure 1–3 is a typical computer printout of a food order placed in the kitchen. Communication is essential to the success of the restaurant. The computer facilitates this process.

Serving

There are many styles of table service, each offering a varying degree of effectiveness and elegance. Regardless of the style of service, the customer expects courteous and knowledgeable servers who are well groomed. Servers must possess the skills necessary to run an efficient station while making guests feel welcome and comfortable. The following are standard rules of dining room protocol:

- Serve the guest of honor first and the host last.
- Serve children first, then women, and then men.
- Serve and clear beverages from the right side of the guest.
- Clear soiled dishes from the guest's right side, using the right hand with the right foot forward and holding the flatware in place with the thumb.
- Never carry flatware or glasses in hand.
- Never reuse flatware for a subsequent course.
- Never clear a course until everyone at the table has finished that course.
- Never reach across a guest when it is possible to approach the guest from the other side.
- Do not touch (or allow yourself to be touched by) a guest.
- Try not to interrupt the guests who are preoccupied in conversation.
- Serve and clear with the hand farthest from the guest.

Understanding the technical aspects of any given style of service is only the beginning in the overall presentation of good service. The technical aspects of service pertain to how items are physically placed before the guest—for example, whether the guest is served from the left or right side and whether the server's right or left hand is used. The technical aspects of service, however, are of less concern to guests. They are of significance to guests only insofar as servers are intrusive. Of more importance to guests are considerations about the *manner* in which they are served. Guests would more likely evaluate the following:

- Did the server rush to the table with the food, with little regard to the guests' presence?
- Did the server place the food before the guest without forcing the guest to adjust her position?
- Was the position of the plate correct?
- Was the service anticipatory rather than a succession of responses to the guests' requests?
- Did the server take the time to clean or groom the table after serving each course?
- Did the server keep his fingers away from the food when carrying the plates?

- Was each guest's order served without being requested?
- Did the server identify any guest's physical limitations or that a guest is left-handed and make the necessary adjustments?

Adjusting the Flatware

- Flatware needs to be adjusted to suit the food order *before* the arrival of the first course.
- Adjustments may be necessary after clearing each course. For example, the guest may have used a preset utensil intended for another course or may simply need specialty flatware, such as a cocktail fork.
- If the guest used an incorrect piece of flatware, it should be cleared with the course and the appropriate flatware preset for the subsequent course.
- Flatware should not be carried in the the server's bare hands. A service towel or a serviette should be used for this purpose.

Clearing the Table

The purpose of using a tray is for clearing and carrying soiled dishes and service items in an easier, safer, and a more efficient manner. The classical term for clearing is *débarrassage*.

- Before clearing any dish, observe tables regularly to determine if all guests are finished. If unsure, ask if everyone is finished. Guests might indicate that they are finished with a course by pushing the dish away, arranging the flatware in a particular way on the dish, or placing their napkins in a particular way on the table.
- Clear courses from the table once all guests have finished eating.
- Clear from the right side with the right hand. Avoid reaching across the table or in front of the guest while clearing.
- Use beverage trays only for clearing beverages.
- Carry beverage trays at waist level at all times.

- Always carry food trays over the left shoulder.
- Walk around the table clockwise, keeping the cleared plates in the left hand away from the guest and table. (*Note:* This prevents servers from walking backward and causing accidents.)
- Avoid overstacking on the arm or on the tray.
- Never stack plates or dishes on top of food.
- Separate flatware from serviceware and place it to the side of the tray.
- Clear all flatware for a particular course at the same time.
- Always clear salt and pepper from the table with the entrée course.
- Place taller and heavier items on the center of the tray.
- Perform clearing as quietly and unobtrusively as possible.

Crumbing the Table

Crumbing is a procedure used to remove crumbs and food particles from the table. The object is to maintain the clean and elegant appearance of the table and prevent guests from getting crumbs on their sleeves or laps. It should be done as quickly, quietly, and unobtrusively as possible.

- Crumbing should be done between courses as needed.
- Servers should move any glass or utensil as necessary to ensure that the cover or place setting is entirely cleaned.
- Crumbing should be done from either side of the guest so as not to be an inconvenience.
- Crumbers can be in the form of a small dustpan and brush, a pocket-sized bar similar to a tongue depressor, or a self-contained unit resembling a lint brush, or the server may use a service towel folded into a small square.
- Crumbs are swept onto a small plate.
- Servers should crumb from the center of the table, away from the guest, and then diagonally to an open corner. Crumbing directly across the cover may result in crumbs falling into the guest's lap.

Figure 1–4 Method of capping an ashtray

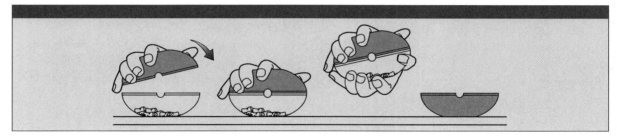

Changing the Ash Trays

Ashtrays should be changed as needed; servers should not allow more than one or two cigarette butts to accumulate (see Figure 1–4).

- The server should invert a clean ashtray and place it quietly over the soiled ashtray before removing it to prevent ashes from flying out of the ashtray into a guest's food or beverage.
- The clean ashtray is then placed on the table.
- The contents of the dirty ashtray are then emptied into a safe container, and the dirty ashtray cleaned.

Note: Do not use napkins to wipe ashtrays.

Checking Back with the Customer

It is imperative that servers check back with their guests to ensure that they are satisfied. It becomes an annoyance to guests, however, if servers check back verbally after each course. The following guidelines should be observed:

- After serving a course, stay within visual range of the guests. Observe their reactions as they taste the food. If they display any displeasure through their facial expressions, return to the table and ask whether the dish is prepared to their liking. Do not use the phrase, "Is everything okay?"
- Do not hover over the table.
- Check back verbally with the guests only after the entrée has been served and they have been given sufficient time to taste the food (1 or 2 minutes), but not while their mouths are full.

The server is principally responsible for ensuring that the guests have proper service and are enjoying their meal. It should not be necessary for the maître d' or the host to inquire, especially as the guests leave the establishment.

Presentation of the Check

- Anticipate the request for the guest check by preparing it as early as possible.
- Verify that all items are accurate.
- Total the check accurately.
- Ensure that the check is unsoiled and legible.
- Clear all items from the table before presenting the check.
- Present the check to the host of the party or in the center of the table.
- Collect payment.
- If payment is by credit card, use the following procedures:
  - Check the card for the guest's signature.
  - Check the expiration date of the card.
  - Use the matching voucher slip for the card.
  - Imprint the credit card onto the voucher so that it is clear.
  - Imprint the credit card onto the guest check.
  - Obtain approval from the credit card company for the amount of the check and estimated gratuity.
  - Fill in the check total on the voucher with the approval code number and date of transaction.
  - Place the check and voucher before the guest along with a presentable pen.

- If the guest has paid with cash, never ask if he needs the change, and always return the change.
- Ensure that correct payment is received.

Farewell

- Whether server, host, or busser, be present when guests depart.
- Assist guests with their chairs.
- Assist guests with their coats.
- Double check that guests have not neglected any personal belongings.
- Thank guests for their patronage and wish them well.
- Hold the door open for guests.

Changing Tablecloths during Service

When changing a tablecloth during service, it is important not to reveal the bare surface underneath. If the establishment is using a second tablecloth as a silencer, however, the following procedures do not have to be followed (see Figure 1–5):

- Remove all dishes and glassware from the table.
- Place standard accessories, such as candles or flowers, on a tray, not on a chair.
- Fold the soiled cloth back approximately one fourth of its length so that it is folded onto the table but does not reveal any of the surface underneath.
- Bring out the new tablecloth and place it over the folded portion of the soiled cloth.
- Drop the end (with the seam down) of the new cloth so that it is opened one fold and hangs over the end of the table.
- Using both hands, grasp the two corners of both the new and old cloths and pull them toward the other end of the table.
- Release the cloth corners when you reach the other end of the table.
- Grasp the hanging corners of the soiled cloth and bring them to the other corners of the folded cloths.
- Hold all corners and drop the top edge of the new cloth over the table, being sure not to release the corners of the soiled cloth.
- Neatly fold the soiled cloth again, ensuring that the trapped crumbs do not fall out onto the floor, and place it on the tray.

Figure 1–5 How to change a tablecloth

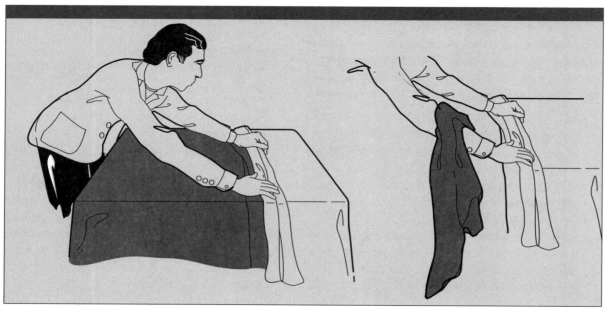

- Empty out the crumbs in the back of the house in a lined trash can before placing the soiled linen in a linen bag.

Resetting Covers

- If the tabletop is the surface of the cover, ensure that it is properly wiped and dried before resetting.
- Have all of your preset (flatware, serviceware, etc.) together before starting.
- Place the cover preset on a tray by the table or at the server station.
- Carry the flatware to the table on a serviette and place it according to the specifications of the establishment.
- Carry the glassware on a beverage tray, ensuring the glasses are right side up, and set them accordingly.
- Place any required china, such as bread-and-butter plates and showplates.
- Place the folded napkin last.

Beverage Service

The service of beverage other than foods is generally grouped into two categories: (1) cold beverages, including spirits, wine, beer, cocktails, soft drinks, milk, and juice; and (2) hot beverages, including coffee and tea. The presentation of beverages varies according to the establishment. The following represent standard procedures that must be observed in the service of all beverages:

- Carry all beverages on a beverage tray (see Figure 1–6).
- Carry beverage trays in the left hand, using the right hand to place the beverage to the right of the guest.
- Keep the tray balanced.
- Place the drinks in such a way that the beverage that is being served first will be closest to the rim of the tray. The tallest and heaviest glasses should be placed in the center of the tray or along the axis of the arm to maintain balance.
- Ensure that all glassware, cups, saucers, and utensils are clean. In some establishments it may be policy to place the glassware over a pot of steaming water

Figure 1–6 Serving from a beverage tray

and wipe the glassware free of any water spots with a clean, unused service towel.

- Present a new glass with each new beverage.
- Determine whether a refill may require a new glass or cup, depending on what is being served.
- Never place the fingers near the rim of the glass or cup. If a stemmed glass is being used in the service, the fingers of the server should be on the stem, not on the bowl of the glass.
- Do not overfill a guest's glass. If a spill should occur due to an accident caused by the server or the guest, the glass should be removed and a new beverage should be served. If spillage occurs onto the saucer during the service of coffee or tea, a new cup and saucer should be provided.
- Use a warmed cup with a hot beverage and a cold glass with a cold beverage.

Cold Beverage Service

Water Service

There are two styles of water service. It may be house policy to serve water automatically to each guest immediately on their being seated. If so, follow these procedures:

- Bring a water pitcher filled with ice water and follow standard protocol.

- Use a neatly folded service towel or serviette to prevent water dripping onto the guest.
- Pour the water with the glass remaining on the table.
- Do not overpour. The water glass should be filled three-fourths full.
- Refill as often as needed throughout the course of service.
- Do not allow the guest's glass to be less than one-fourth full.

Other establishments do not offer automatic water service. In these establishments, the ulterior motive is to have servers sell bottled water or other beverages.

Note: If it is in the interest of the guests' comfort or safety to deviate from these procedures, such as removing the glass from the table to pour, the server needs to adjust to the circumstances, but it should be the exception to the rule.

Other Cold Beverages

- Serve soft drinks and liquors in the appropriate glass.
- Fill the glass to no more than one-half inch from the rim. Overfilling only results in spilling by the server or guest and displays sloppy service.
- Know the appropriate garnishes and ensure that they are fresh.
- Present all beverage items to the right of the guest.
- Place water glasses above and in line with the tip of the entrée knife.
- Place wine glasses to the right of the water glass in a diagonal pattern toward the edge of the table.
- Never refill the glass while it is being held by the guest.
- Never touch the rim of the glass with the service item being used (i.e., water pitcher, wine bottle, coffee pot).
- Never use a glass to scoop ice.
- Place glasses on a beverage or cocktail napkin when the table surface is not covered with a tablecloth.
- When serving bottled beverages, place the appropriate glass before the guest and proceed to fill the glass to no more than two-thirds full. Then place the

bottle to the right of the guest, with the label facing the guest.

Wine Service

Servers must be familiar with the wine list in order to guide customers toward their preference. Servers must know how to pair wine and food and how to guide the guests. Before making a suggestion, ask the guests what kind of wine they enjoy. It is pointless to suggest a wine that the guests do not like.

- Be aware of any wines that may not be available or that have a change in the vintage year.
- Take the wine order from the host either by name or bin number.
- Check the wine label and vintage for accuracy before presenting the bottle.
- Preset the appropriate wine glasses, and bring a wine bucket to the table if serving a white wine. Do not forget to bring an additional tasting glass for the host.
- Determine who will be having the wine.
- Ensure that all guests are of legal drinking age.
- Handle the wine glasses only by their stems.
- Present the wine to the host for verification.
- Determine when the guests want their wine poured.
- Follow correct opening procedures (see next section).
- Pour 1 ounce of wine for the host for tasting purposes.
- If the wine is refused, determine the reason and find the manager.
- Avoid reaching in front of a guest to pour.
- Delicately pour wine for each person from the right side with the right hand, if possible.
- Return the bottle to the wine bucket or onto the table, with the label facing the host.
- Avoid overpouring wine.
- Discreetly allow the host to know when the bottle is empty and determine whether another bottle is desired.
- If the host orders another bottle of wine, bring a clean tasting glass, even if it is the same wine.
- If guests switch to a different wine, bring clean and appropriate wine glasses.

- When guests have finished the bottle and do not require another, remove it from the table before removing the glasses.

Opening Procedures for White and Rosé Wines

- If using a wine bucket, ensure that it is filled three-fourths full with equal amounts of ice and water.
- If using a wine cooler or chiller, place it on the table to the right of the host.
- Present the wine bottle, with the label facing the host, from the right side.
- Place the wine bottle in the wine bucket or chiller.
- Place a service napkin in the form of a collar around the neck of the bottle.
- Remove the top of the seal by cutting it above or below the lip of the wine bottle. If the seal is torn, especially when it is made of plastic, remove it entirely from the bottle. Do not twist or turn the bottle. If the bottle has an exaggerated lip at the top of the bottle with a small seal affixed to the surface of the cork, perforate the seal with the worm of the corkscrew and proceed with cork removal.
- Place the removed portion of the seal in your pocket.
- Insert the worm into the center of the cork by placing the tip of the worm pointing away from the body of the server.
- Twist the corkscrew so that the worm is inserted down four of its turns. Do not turn or twist the bottle.
- Place the lever of the corkscrew onto the lip of the bottle.
- Break the vacuum seal by pulling the cork out. Use your right hand, with two or three fingers wrapped under the handle of the corkscrew and your thumb placed directly over the cork.
- Pull the cork straight out by using the lever as a fulcrum.
- Keep the lever in place over the lip by holding it with your left index finger, which should be wrapped around the neck of the bottle.
- Pull the cork out as far as possible, ensuring that it does not bend. (More expensive wines tend to use longer corks. It might be necessary to turn the corkscrew an additional rotation to maximize the leverage.)

- With a delicate wriggling motion of your right hand, pull the cork completely out of the bottle.
- If the cork does not come out with the lever fully extended, wrap the forefinger and thumb of your right hand around the cork and pull it out slowly and straight up, using a rocking motion.
- Unscrew the cork from the corkscrew.
- Wipe any particles from the top of the bottle rim with a clean napkin.
- Present the cork to the right side of the host by placing it on a *doilied* plate. (The guest will examine the condition of the cork to ensure that it has not dried out, which will suggest the storage condition of the wine.) The cork and doilied plate will be removed from the table after the guests have been served the wine.
- Remove the bottle from the chiller or bucket, holding the bottle over the long folded portion of the service towel collar, leaving the label exposed to the guest's view.
- Pour 1 ounce of the wine into the host's tasting glass.
- Once the wine has been approved, pour wine for the other guests, using standard rules of protocol, before filling the host's glass.
- Serve only 3 or 4 ounces of wine. This will prevent the possibility of the wine's reaching a warmer temperature and becoming less pleasing to the palate.
- Place the bottle back into the ice bucket or the chiller and fold the service towel over the top of the bucket.

Dessert Wines

When serving dessert wines, the server should take special care in not overpouring. These wines are best enjoyed chilled, and guests tend to drink less, savoring them longer.

Opening Procedures for Red Wine

- Bring a wine coaster or doilied bread-and-butter plate to the table along with the bottle of wine.
- Present the wine bottle from the right side, with the label facing the host.
- Place the bottle on the coaster or the doilied bread-and-butter plate and remove the top portion of the seal as previously described.

- Use the same opening procedures described for white and rosé wines.
- Use the doilied plate to present the cork to the host.
- After approval, pour 4 to 6 ounces of wine, depending on the style of glass used. Otherwise, use standard rules of protocol.
- Place the bottle on the coaster or doilied bread-and-butter plate toward the center of the table with the label facing the host.
- Remove and pocket the cork.

Decanting.   The purposes of decanting are threefold:

1. To allow a red wine to "breathe," so that it may display its best bouquet
2. To separate the red wine from the accumulated sediments of several years' aging
3. To bring a red wine to proper serving temperature, called **chambreing**

When serving a young red wine, such as a young claret from Bordeaux, which is high in **tannins,** the server might choose to decant the wine to allow it to oxygenate. This will allow the hard tannins in the wine to seem less astringent and therefore easier to drink. The server will use the same opening procedures as described previously.

When serving an older wine (10 years or more) that has not been standing upright for 24 to 48 hours prior to service, the bottle should be placed and opened in a cradle or wine basket (see Figure 1–7). The server will open the wine, using the same procedures as previously described, but with the utmost caution not to disturb the sediment.

- Decanting should not be done more than a half hour prior to serving the wine.
- To decant, the server should place a glass or crystal decanter (33-ounce minimum) on the table or guéridon.
- A lit candle on a plate or a flashlight should be placed to the right of the decanter.
- Holding the bottle or the handle of the cradle in the right hand, the server should pour the wine into the mouth of the decanter in a slow but continuous

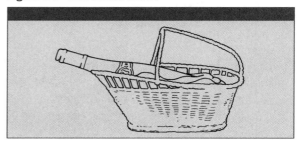

Figure 1–7 Wine service basket

stream. It is very important that this flow not be interrupted, because this will cause the sediment to loosen and spread throughout the wine.
- Depending on the shape of the decanter, one might elect to hold the decanter in the left hand while decanting.
- The key point is to observe the flow of wine going down the neck of the bottle and to stop pouring as soon as the sediment *approaches* the neck of the bottle. The candle or light allows the server to see through the shoulder and neck of the bottle and therefore anticipate the sediment more clearly.
- The server may highlight the sediment of the wine left in the bottle and the clarity of the wine in the decanter to solicit the guests' appreciation and approval.
- For very expensive older bottles of wine, the guest might choose to be served the remaining wine from the bottle. It is imperative that a special funnel with a strainer be used to pour this wine, which will have an abundance of sediment, into a separate glass.

Chambré.   Wine should be stored in a cool cellar (50° F). If a red wine is selected directly from the cellar, it needs to be brought to a warmer temperature (as much as 68° F). Although a bottle can be placed next to a heat source, it can be risky if the wine's temperature becomes too warm, because the taste of alcohol will dominate the wine, and it will seem out of balance. The French word **chambré** means "to bring to room temperature." (The room temperature that was intended at the time the word *chambré* was coined was around 60° F.) The most effective way to warm the wine is to decant it in a warmed decanter.

Opening Procedures for Sparkling Wines

- When serving sparkling wines, it is important to properly chill them (between 40° and 45° F) before opening.
- Ensure that the wine has not been shaken prior to service.
- If possible, use a sparkling-wine bucket, because it is taller and will chill the wine more effectively. It will take the wine 20 minutes to be properly chilled from that of storage temperature.
- Fill the bucket three-fourths full, with equal amounts of ice and water, and bring it to the table as part of the preset.
- Place the appropriate fluted or tulip glasses on the table to the right of the cover.
- Remove the sparkling wine from the ice bucket and wipe it dry with a service towel.
- Hold the bottle at a 45-degree angle at chest height.
- Hold the bottle in the left hand.
- Find the perforation or wire loop and pull it out from under the foil.
- Remove the top part of the foil from the perforation.
- Remove the wire cage with the right hand by twisting the wire loop counterclockwise five times. This will allow the wire cage to be retracted from the lip of the bottle. Place the wire cage in your pocket.
- Holding the bottle at a 45-degree angle and grasping the cork firmly in the left hand, twist the bottle counterclockwise with the right hand. Do not twist the cork, because it will break.
- As you feel the cork being expelled from the bottle, try to counterbalance the pressure by holding it in and simultaneously tilting it toward the body to allow the gasses to escape at an angle from the top of the bottle. This will minimize the loss of gas and preserve the bubbly character of the wine longer. Instead of a loud pop, the guest will hear a soft sigh.
- Maintain the 45-degree angle of the bottle for 10 seconds to equalize the pressure.

- Place a service towel or napkin collar around the neck of the bottle.
- Hold the bottle in the right hand toward the base by resting the bottle on four fingers with the thumb in the punt of the bottle.
- Pour a 1-ounce taste for the host's approval.
- On approval, pour the sparkling wine for all of the guests, using the standard rules of protocol.
- Pour the wine down the center of the glass.
- Wait for the foam to subside and continue pouring until the glass is three-fourths full.
- Place the bottle back into the bucket, draping a service towel over it.

Temperatures

The factor that probably has the most impact on how the wine tastes is its temperature, and the server has control over this most critical element. All of the efforts of the wine grower, wine maker, distributor, and retailer or restaurateur can be in vain if the server does not follow certain guidelines.

Our appreciation of wine is due primarily to our sense of smell. Red wines have heavier molecular weights than do white wines and have less volatile acidity. The higher the temperature of the wine, the more easily the volatile compounds evaporate from its surface. It makes sense, therefore, to serve complex red wines at 61° to 65° F. Additionally, the lower the temperature, the more sensitive the palate to **tannins** and **bitterness,** which may not be elements altogether agreeable to the customer, unless balanced by the wine's other elements.

Conversely, most white wines need to be chilled so that their acidity is more pronounced. To increase the refreshment aspect of a wine, it is best to serve it at a cooler temperature. White wines with greater amounts of complexity need to be served at slightly less chilled temperatures so that it is easier to perceive and appreciate them. Discernable faults in wines can be masked by serving the wines at lower temperatures. The palate discerns sweetness more easily at higher temperatures, and many sweeter wines do not have enough **acidity** to counterbalance their sweetness, so it is best to chill sweet wines so that they taste refreshing and not **flabby**. As a rule, the ranges of temperature for various wines are as follows:

Dessert and sparkling wines (Cava and nonvintage)	40–45° F
White wines, rosés, fino sherries, and best champagnes	45–50° F
Best quality dry whites, light reds (Beaujolais Nouveau)	50–55° F
Light reds, ordinary Bordeaux, Chianti	55–60° F
Full-bodied reds	60–65° F

Hot Beverage Service

Most guests have coffee as their last course for lunch or dinner and may well be paying their check at this time. Therefore, the quality and service of coffee or tea is critical because it is the last impression the guest will experience regarding the meal and service.

Hot beverage service can be more complex than cold beverage service. When a guest orders coffee or tea, the set-up for those items must be presented to the guest before the actual service of the beverage (see Figure 1–8). The following are general rules to be observed when serving a hot beverage:

- Coffee or tea cups and pots should be warmed prior to filling them.
- When using a beverage tray, the lip of the cup and spoons should not come into contact with the surface of the tray.
- Saucers should be stacked in the center of the tray, and cup handles should not be sticking out along the rim of the tray.
- Cream, half-and-half, or milk should always be kept refrigerated.*
- If loose sugar is used, it should be strained prior to placing it in the sugar bowl.
- If sugar cubes are used, claw tongs should be available.
- A serviette may also be used for the service of beverage items.

*See Appendix C for update.

- The handle of the cup should be placed to the right of the guest at the 4 o'clock position.
- The spoon should be placed on the table to the right of the guest, not on the saucer.
- The handle of the creamer also should be positioned at 4 o'clock in front of the guest.
- The sugar bowl should be placed alongside the creamer for the guest of honor or women first.

Coffee Service

Depending on the style of meal being served, coffee cups may be preset on the table as part of the cover or brought to the table when the guest orders coffee. Breakfast service might require the presetting of coffee cups, saucers, spoons, sugars, and sweeteners.

- Use a service towel to catch any drips while pouring.
- Pour the coffee into each cup at the table.
- If individual pots are used, place the pot to the right of the guest.
- Fill the coffee cup only three-fourths full unless the customer specifically orders "black" coffee.
- If the customer orders more coffee after considerable time has elapsed since the first cup, replace the cup with a new one.

There are five fundamentals for brewing the perfect cup of coffee:

1. *Proportion*
   - Accurately measure the amount of coffee to the volume of water.*
   - Always match the portion of coffee to the brewing capacity.
2. *Grind*
   - Coffee beans can be ground from coarse to fine, which will determine, along with the blend and roast, the intensity of flavors. The grind of coffee must be matched to the brew cycle of the coffee machine.
   - Fine grind will require 1 to 4 minutes.
   - Drip/medium grind require 4 to 6 minutes.
   - Regular/coarse grind will require 6 to 8 minutes.

*See Appendix C for update.

Figure 1–8 Coffee and tea service setup

3. *Water*
   - The flavor and quality of the coffee is largely dependent on the quality and temperature of the water. Purification of the water is only essential if the water is too soft or hard. Distilled water is ideal for brewing coffee.
   - The brewer must operate between 195° and 205° F.
4. *Freshness**
   - Coffee beans will lose their essential oils and aromas when oxidized.
   - Ground coffee will lose its freshness faster.
   - Air, light, heat, and moisture contribute to the lack of freshness in coffee.
   - Keep coffee sealed and refrigerated to extend its freshness.

*See Appendix C for update.

5. *Equipment **
   - The coffee brewer must operate at the proper agitation of the water in contact with the coffee grounds.
   - The spray head must be in place and kept clean.
   - The brew basket must be of the proper size and have the appropriate filter.
   - The brew cycle must be completed before removing the coffee pot.
   - Do not combine old and new coffee.
   - Never hold coffee on a warmer for more than 15 minutes.

Espresso

Espresso is Italian for "fast cup." It is a process by which a combination of steam and boiling water are passed quickly

*See Appendix C for update.

through finely ground coffee beans. Brewing espresso extracts the very heart or essence of the bean. Espresso coffee requires a special espresso machine that produces only one or two cups at a time. However, from the time your **portafilter** is placed in the group of the machine, the **shot** should run between 17 and 23 seconds for 1 ounce of espresso. Espresso is traditionally served in a half cup, called a **demi-tasse** and not in the usual coffee cup used for other coffees. When a double espresso is ordered, however, it is served in a regular coffee cup.

The following steps should be used to brew espresso:

- Make sure the demi-tasse is warm.
- Use coffee from the grinder within one hour of grinding.
- Place portafilter under the **doser,** pulling the lever to release the grounds into the portafilter.
- Set the portafilter on the counter and tamp firmly.
- Wipe excess grounds from the rim.
- Insert the portafilter into the group.
- Press the button to pour the shot.
- Use the shot within 30 seconds, or the espresso will not be hot enough for the customer.
- After the espresso is made, remove the portafilter and knock the grounds out into the box.
- Rinse the portafilter under hot water to remove spent grounds.
- Serve espresso with a demi-tasse spoon, sugar, and, in the United States, a twist of lemon zest.

Espresso is made by using a specific blend of Italian roasted beans, brewed in a concentrated manner that yields a beverage consisting of the heart, body, and crema. A shot of espresso is critical to the quality of any drink recipe, such as a latte, mocha, or cappuccino (see Figure 1–9).

Figure 1–9 Espresso machine

- Steam the milk before making a shot of espresso. Always start with cold milk for better foam.
- On some machines, the steam valve should be opened to release any condensation prior to placing the **steam wand** in the milk.
- Place the tip of the steam wand just below the surface of the milk to maximize the volume.
- Open the steam valve, As foam develops, milk will triple in volume.
- When the desired level of foam has been formed, raise the pitcher up to let the steam wand go near the bottom of the pitcher to allow the milk to heat up. Do not allow the milk to overheat, a burned taste will result.*

The finished cup should have a foamy topping of steamed milk on which ground cinnamon or cocoa may be sprinkled.

Cappuccino

Cappuccino is made by combining 1 ounce of espresso and 3 ounces of milk, which will be steamed to triple its volume. The steamed milk will be poured over the shot of espresso in a cappuccino glass or cup.

Coffee Latte

Caffe latte is made with one shot of espresso and mostly steamed milk, topped with a one-fourth inch of foamed milk.

*See Appendix C for update.

Caffee Mocha

Caffe mocha is made with one-half ounce of mocha syrup, one shot of espresso, mostly steamed milk, and is topped with whipped cream.

Tea Service

Tea generally refers to a beverage that is made from an infusion of the leaves of Camellia *Thea sinensis* prepared in boiling hot water. There are five fundamentals to steeping the perfect cup of tea:

1. *Proportion:* The portion of tea to the volume of water will determine the final taste. Depending on the type and quality of tea leaves, 1 rounded teaspoon of tea is required for 6 ounces of water.
2. *Water:* A major contributing factor to the flavor of tea is the type of water used. Bottled spring water or distilled water is preferable. Restaurants may also install a filtering system. The objective is to remove trace chemical and mineral flavors that are present in tap water.
3. *Freshness:* The tea should be kept in a sealed container because light, temperature, humidity, and oxygen will have a significant effect on the tea leaves.
4. *Infusion:* Two factors are important to consider when infusing tea in fresh water:
   - The temperature of the water. Tea must be infused in water at or near the boiling point in order to release all of its desired aromas and flavors. Generally, the greater the fermentation of the tea, the higher the temperature of the water.
   - The length of time the leaves are in contact with the water. The time needed to steep tea leaves is also based on the level of fermentation or oxidation. Generally, the greater the level of oxidation, the less time needed for brewing.

Green tea	Steeped at 160° to 180° F for 2 minutes
Oolong tea	Steeped at 195° to 212° F for 30 to 90 seconds
Black tea	Steeped at 200° to 212° F for 20 to 60 seconds

Teas can be steeped more than once, but later infusion will require more time. Avoid using color as a determining factor for the length of time to infuse tea because color does not necessarily result in a better tasting cup of tea; the determining factors are the aromas and flavor.

5. *Equipment:* Tea can be steeped in a wide variety of equipment. Teapots, teacups, kettles, infusers and strainers can be made from silver, stainless steel, pottery, stoneware, fine china, porcelain, bone china, and glassware. These may be very decorative and ornate or simple in design. Teaware design is as varied as the people and cultures producing them. From the unglazed clay pots of the Chinese Ming Dynasty (A.D. 1368–1644) to the formal delicacy of Victorian era teaware, to the contemporary use of colors, shapes, and angles, the basic usage of teapots and teacups has changed little throughout history.

   Regardless of the equipment used, it must be spotless. Constant use can lead to a build-up of mineral deposits left by the water and tea, which will impart off-flavors into the tea.

Most establishments use a commercial grade of bagged tea. Packaged as individual servings, it provides convenience. Higher-quality loose-leaf teas, however, are available and should be used in fine-dining establishments. Steeping teas is a rather simple procedure, but certain points should be observed in order to provide a quality product.

- When a guest orders tea, bring a selection of the available teas for the guest's perusal.
- Once the guest has made a selection, place the tea packet on a doilied bread-and-butter plate, or place the loose-leaf tea in a tea strainer (preferably nonmetallic).
- Preset a warm cup on a saucer, a spoon on the table to the right of the guest, sugar and sweeteners, and lemon wedges if the guest has ordered tea with lemon, or a creamer with milk.
- If using a teabag, the guest should be allowed to have the option of how strong or weak the tea should be. The teapot is placed on a doilied bread-and-butter plate, with the teabag propped against it to the right of the cup.

- If using loose-leaf tea, the tea is placed in a warmed teapot, which is then filled with boiling water. The server should allow the requisite time for the tea to steep and then proceed to pour the tea through a tea strainer, which is placed over the tea cup.

High Tea Service

The nineteenth century practice of Victorian society eating early breakfasts and late dinners created a void that was filled by the development of a full afternoon tea. Sipping tea was accompanied by a variety of breads, scones, cakes, fruit, jams and preserves, small finger sandwiches, and tartlets. The afternoon tea sometimes developed into an elaborate social event and was referred to as **high tea.**

In hotels throughout Europe and the United States, afternoon tea is a welcome service to guests and an opportunity to serve food and beverage at a time when full-service meals are not available. In such a setting, there may be greater formality to the tea service, and loose-leaf tea will definitely be used.

- Ensure that the table is preset with small plates, bread-and-butter knives, a salad fork, teaspoons, and napkins, as appropriate.
- Once guests have made their selection, steep the tea in a preheated teapot by placing the tea leaves in a tea ball or strainer or placing the leaves in the bottom of the pot before pouring the freshly boiling water into the pot.
- Present a cart or tray that carries the teapot, warmed cups and saucers, lemon wedges on a doilied plate, a sugar bowl and sweeteners, and a small creamer filled with milk.
- Bring a second pot of boiling water to the table to allow the guest to dilute the tea in the cup or to add to the original pot to make more tea.
- Know how long the tea should be steeped and begin pouring it into the cups when it is ready, unless the host of the party chooses to do so.
- If the guests are not sitting in very close proximity to each other, serve each guest's cup.
- Present and serve, butler style, the available choices of sandwiches, tartlets, and so on.
- Use a **tea cozy,** if available to help insulate the teapot.

Iced Tea

More than 80% of the tea consumed in the United States is consumed as an iced beverage. Iced tea is made in four ways:

1. From a liquid tea concentrate, a commercial source
2. From liquid tea concentrate prepared on the premises from loose tea or tea bags
3. From powdered tea concentrate
4. From a dispenser using powdered tea.

- To make a liquid tea concentrate, use less than one-fourth of the water necessary to make regular tea.
- Steep the tea for 10 minutes. Remove the tea bags or strain if using loose-leaf tea.
- If the liquid concentrate is to be sweetened, add the sugar when the concentrate is still hot, so that all of it dissolves.
- To prepare an individual portion, fill the iced glass one-third full with the concentrate, and fill the remainder with water.
- Serve the iced tea in a highball glass or tall goblet, with an underliner, a tall spoon, sugar and sweeteners, and a wedge of lemon to the side.

Bread-and-Butter Service

The sequence of the bread-and-butter service is determined by the restaurant's policy. However, many restaurants require that it be served once the beverage order has been taken and served. If there is more than a 2-minute delay at the service bar, the server might first serve the bread and butter. Regardless of the sequence, the following procedures should be observed:

- Ensure that the bread basket or plate is lined with a clean napkin fold dictated by restaurant policy.
- Provide each guest with one and a half rolls per initial serving.
- Store the bread or rolls in a bread warmer.

- Place the bread in the center of the napkin fold by using bread tongs or service sets. Never handle the bread or rolls with hands!
- Bring out butter with the bread or rolls. Butter may be in the form of chips, curls, balls, or florets or in a ramekin. Attention should be placed on the presentation of the butter. Its preparation is normally the responsibility of the server. If it is in a ramekin or a bowl, it should be placed on a doilied underliner. Some restaurants prefer that the butter is served on ice, while others prefer it served at room temperature.
- Place the butter dish(es) in the most accessible position for the women at the table.
- Place the bread basket in the center of the table. Some restaurants require the servers to "Russian service" the bread and/or butter. (See the section on Russian service in Chapter 2.)
- When replenishing bread, always ensure there is sufficient butter.
- If flavored butters are being served, always inform the guests of the ingredients used.

Note: The method for heating and storing bread or rolls in a bread warmer is described in Chapter 3.

Appetizer Service

An appetizer is sometimes offered on a menu to provide the guest with an alternative to the soup or salad course. Generally, the portion size of an appetizer is small and gives insight into the creativity of the chef. The time needed to prepare an appetizer should not be lengthy. Appetizers may be served hot or cold. The following procedures should be observed:

- When a guest orders a cold and a hot appetizer, the cold appetizer should be served first, unless the guest requests otherwise.
- The side of the guest from which the appetizer will be served will depend on the style of service being given.
- An appetizer should be skillfully and neatly divided if

two or more guests are sharing it. This cannot always be done in the kitchen, because the presentation would be ruined. It then becomes necessary to divide and plate the appetizer into equal portions in as attractive a manner as is possible.
- The flatware used will vary, but most establishments will have an appetizer or salad fork and knife for use with this course, as well as a specialty flatware, such as a cocktail fork.
- Certain appetizers may require finger bowls. These should be set up in accordance with the restaurant's policy.
- Finger bowls can be brought out either before or immediately after clearing the appetizer.
- All flatware for the appetizer course should be removed when clearing the appetizer course.
- Any flatware should be adjusted prior to serving the next course.

Soup Service

There are two distinct categories of soups: clear soups, such as consommé, and thick or cream soups, which include chowder. The **preset** used in the service of soup will vary with the style of soup served.

- Serve cream soups and chowders in a bowl or soup plate, unless the guest requests a cup.
- Provide a potage spoon or soup spoon when a soup bowl is used.
- Use an underliner in the service of either the soup cup or bowl.
- If the underliner does not have an insert for the cup or bowl, use a doily to prevent slippage.
- Preset a consommé or bouillon spoon when serving a soup cup.
- If soups are carried on a food tray into the dining room, assemble the cups and bowls onto liners in the dining room, not in the kitchen, to avoid the ramifications of spilling onto the underliners.
- Wipe the rim of the soup plate clean, if necessary, before serving.

- To prevent accidents and spills, ensure that the spoon is placed on the underliner before clearing the soup.

Note: Many establishments require servers to fill the guests' soup cups or bowls in the kitchen. It is the servers' responsibility to ensure that the soup has been stirred and that it is the appropriate temperature before ladling it. Hot soup are placed in warmed cups or bowls, and cold soups are ladled into chilled cups.

Salad Service

The service of salad as part of a meal can be presented either before or after the service of the entrée. In the European style of dining, the salad is served after the entrée because the greens contained in the salad are considered an aid in the digestion of the meal. In addition, only a vinegar-based dressing would be considered appropriate, and vinegar would ruin any accompanying wine. In most instances in the United States, however, the salad is served before the entrée, unless the guest requests otherwise.

- Cold salads should be served on chilled plates.
- A salad fork and knife should be preset.
- If freshly ground pepper is available, it should be offered to the guest when serving the salad.
- If requested, oil and vinegar should be brought out in filled, clean cruets.
- The salad plates should be cleared according to standard rules of protocol.
- Time should be allotted to bring more bread and butter, if appropriate, and pour or refill wine.

Intermezzo Service

Intermezzo service is a pause or intermission between two courses. Usually, a sorbet, sherbet, or granité is served to cleanse the palate between two courses of very different flavors.

- Preset a teaspoon to the right of the guest.
- Serve the intermezzo as quickly as possible. The dish in which it is served will generally require an underliner.
- Because this is a very quick course, expect it to last no more than 5 minutes.
- Clear the intermezzo by first placing the spoon to the side of the dish on the underliner.

Entrée Service

The technical aspect of serving the entrée will depend on the style of service being performed. However, there are general rules of service protocol that should be followed:

- If the accompaniments are presented on the same plate as the entrée, be aware of how the chef intended the plate to be positioned in front of the guest.
- When either hand-carrying or using food trays, take care to ensure that the plates stay as level as possible. This will prevent the presentation of the entrée from being ruined. For example, it will prevent sauces from being intermingled.
- If the entrée is hot, present it on a hot plate.
- Use a clean, folded service towel in the handling of hot plates to expedite safety and sanitation procedures.
- Inform the guest when plates are hot.
- Allow approximately 1 inch of distance between the edge of the plate and the table. This will lessen the likelihood of the guests' clothes being soiled.
- While serving an entrée, if a guest chooses to leave the table, either take his plate back to the kitchen or cover it with a plate cover until he returns.
- When clearing, use standard rules of protocol.
- Clear the wine glasses if all guests have finished the wine.
- Remove all of the flatware set for the entrée course, the salt and pepper shakers, and the bread-and-butter plates and knives, unless the guests are having a cheese course.

Cheese Service

Cheeses taste best and show their finest flavor when served at room temperature. Semi-firm and firm cheeses need at least an hour to warm to room temperature. Soft and semi-soft cheeses usually need a half hour or more before full enjoyment can be obtained. Very large pieces of cheese require more time than smaller ones (see Figure 1–10 on page 30).

- Cut cheese according to its shape, so that the rind is evenly distributed.
- Present cheeses on wooden cheese boards, trays, or a cheese cart.
- Arrange the cheeses with enough room between them to make cutting easy.
- Provide a cheese cutter or knife for each cheese offered.
- Provide bread or crackers with the cheese. (If presented as a course during the meal service, the bread plate and bread knife should be left on the guest's table when the entrée is cleared.)
- If fruit is served with the cheese, ensure that it is washed, wiped dry, and cut into bite-sized portions, and if grapes are used in the presentation, section them into small bundles.

Dessert Service

The dessert course is perhaps the most anticipated by the guest. For the establishment, it is the last opportunity to impress the guest. Many establishments use rolling pastry carts or may even display their desserts at the entrance of the restaurant to help sell them. The procedure for serving the dessert will vary with the style of service performed as well as the type of dessert served.

- Present flatware for the dessert course.
- Place the fork to the left and the spoon to the right of the cover.
- If the dessert fork and spoon are part of the place setting, place them (usually) above the cover.
- When placing flatware above a guest's cover, point the handle of the flatware toward the same side of the cover that would receive it if it were placed *beside* the cover.
- Place the spoon above the fork.

Figure 1–10 Methods of cutting cheeses according to their shapes

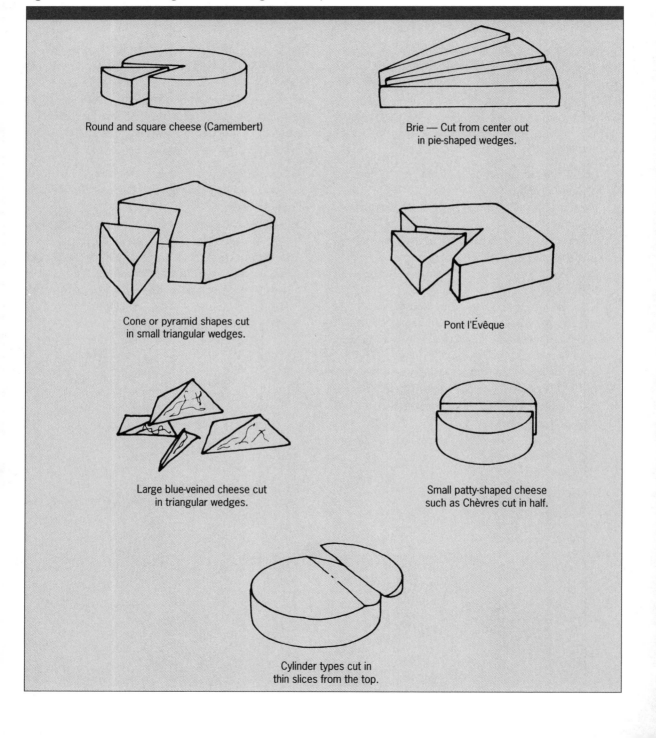

Round and square cheese (Camembert)

Brie — Cut from center out
in pie-shaped wedges.

Cone or pyramid shapes cut
in small triangular wedges.

Pont l'Évêque

Large blue-veined cheese cut
in triangular wedges.

Small patty-shaped cheese
such as Chèvres cut in half.

Cylinder types cut in
thin slices from the top.

2

Styles of
Service

2

Styles of Service

A number of different styles of service have developed over the centuries to suit the types of menus and needs of the dining public.

In examining different styles of service, it is important to understand that different elements of each style can be intermingled. Certain establishments utilize all elements of a particular service, but for the most part, in United States, if modern American plated service is not utilized, we find an amalgamation of these different styles.

The major styles of service are

Modern American plated service
Booth service
Banquette service
French service
Wagon service
Russian service
Family-style service
Butler service
English service
Buffet service

Modern American Plated Service

Modern American plated service originated in the United States but is now used internationally. This service is popular because it requires fewer and less extensively trained dining room personnel than do other services, such as classical French service. It is theorized that American service developed because Americans consumed more beverages than Europeans during a meal, and by serving food from the left there would be less likelihood for interrupting the guest. It is defined as service in which the food.is completely prepared, portioned, plated, garnished and or sauced in the kitchen. The servers do no table-side cook-

ing or plating. The server merely places the dishes in front of the guest. Service is, therefore, more streamlined to allow for more speed and efficiency. The net effect is an overall savings in labor cost that is desirable to both management and the guest, as cost savings can be passed on to the guest in the form of reasonable menu prices.

General rules of modern American plated service are the following:

- Beverages and soup are served to the right side of the guest, with the server's right hand and right foot forward.
- When serving to the right of a guest, the server proceeds to the next guest in a clockwise direction.
- Solid foods are served to the guest's left side, with the server's left hand and left foot forward.
- When serving to the left of a guest, the server proceeds to the next guest in a counterclockwise direction.
- Clearing is performed from the right, with the right hand and the right foot forward, except when clearing items placed to the guest's left, such as a bread-and-butter plate.

Modern American Plated Service in a Banquet Setting

A banquet is a predetermined meal for a group of guests. It may be for a few guests or as many as 3000. Most banquets in the United States use modern American plated service. The servers are required to act in unison so that the guests are served each course at the same time. Servers are assigned 20 to 30 guests, depending on the number of courses. For example, a breakfast would usually require only one food course, juice, and coffee service. A typical dinner, however, would consist of an appetizer, soup, salad, entrée, and dessert.

- Follow standard rules of protocol.
- Pay attention to the maitre d' or captain at all times as he sets the pace of service.
- Always serve the guest of honor's table first.
- If there is a **split menu,** from which there is a choice of entrées, ensure that the proper order is communicated to the kitchen. (*Note:* There are a number of systems that an establishment can employ to prevent customers from changing their orders at the last minute—for example, coded cards, which are placed in front of each guest.)
- Serve the entire table at the same time for each course.
- Do not carry more than twelve entrées on a service tray.

The advantages and disadvantages of American plated service are as follows:

Advantages
1. It is the fastest form of table service.
2. It is easy to master.
3. Service staff need less training.
4. There is no added equipment cost.
5. Less space is required between tables.
6. More guests can be seated.
7. Menu prices can be more reasonable.
8. Professional chefs can better maintain the quality control of the food.

Disadvantages
1. It is not as elaborate as French or Russian service.
2. The visual presentation of food is not as impressive to the guest.

Booth Service

A booth is generally a table that rests against or is attached to a wall. It has high-backed, bench-like seats. A booth has only one focal point: the end of the table. Guests are served from that focal point, and the server addresses all guests from that position.

The following procedures must be observed at a booth:

- Number the seat to the immediate left of the focal point as seat 1, and number the rest in a clockwise fashion (see Figure 2–1).
- Serve guests farthest away first, using the right hand to serve guests seated on the left and the left hand to serve guests seated on the right.
- Clear soiled tableware from the guests seated closest to the end first, using the same hand procedure described previously.
- For beverage service, do not switch hands. The tray should remain in the left hand and beverages served with the right.
- Always keep the hands as low to table level as possible, to maintain proper etiquette.
- Avoid handing an item to a guest; place it on the table.

Banquette Service

A banquette is a type of seating arrangement in which guests are seated facing the server with their backs against or to the wall. This arrangement generally is used to minimize space in a small restaurant. The following procedures should be observed:

- Treat both ends of the banquette as focal points (see Figure 2–2).
- When facing the table, number the guest on the far left as seat 1 and number in a clockwise direction.
- When standing at the focal point to the left of the banquette, serve the guest in seat 1 using the right hand, then the guest in seat 4 using the left hand. Proceed to the other focal point and serve the guest in seat 2 with the left hand and the guest in seat 3 with the right hand.

Figure 2–1 Booth table with seat numbers

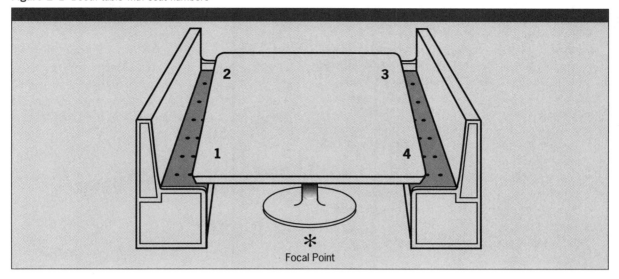

Figure 2–2 Banquette table with seat numbers

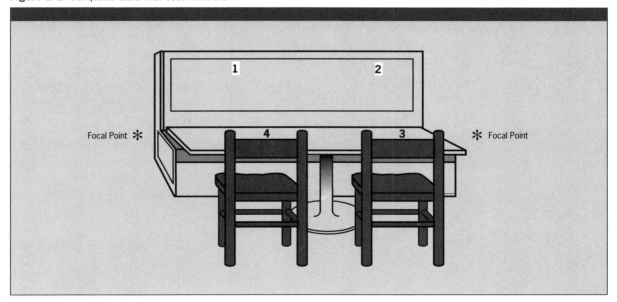

- When clearing dishes, use the same hand procedures.

- Hold the beverage tray in the left hand, and serve with the right hand. Stand with the right hip close to the table and the left arm farthest away.

The Serving of Children

In today's fast-paced society, families dine out with increasing frequency. According to the National Restaurant Association (NRA), families eat out 3.5 times per week. Servers need to be more mindful of children's service needs.

The rules for serving children up to the age of 8 years are as follows:

- Ask the parents whether a **booster seat** or **high chair** is needed.
- Ensure that the seats are clean.
- Remove all sharp objects from the cover.
- Remove glassware from the covers of small children.
- Bring to the table any activities for children (e.g., paper placemats and crayons) that the establishment may have.
- Help children select an appropriate food item on the menu once it has been approved by the parents. Many parents prefer to have all orders for their children discussed only with them.
- Serve children as quickly as possible. It is proper etiquette to serve children before the adults, as long as it has been previously discussed.
- Serve beverages in suitable cups or glasses. For example, serving milk in a stemmed glass is courting a disaster.
- During the service, engage the children in conversation.
- After the guests have departed, verify that the area under the table is swept clean.

The Serving of Guests with Disabilities

In keeping with taking care of guests' needs, the establishment should provide for guests with disabilities. With the passage of the Americans with Disabilities Act (ADA), owners of establishments now have legal requirements to provide accommodations for these customers. There are space requirements for accommodating guests in wheel-chairs. The tabletop should have a 27-inch clearance and unobstructed width of 30 inches. There should also be a minimum of 6 feet between free-standing tables in the dining area.

Servers should take care not to appear condescending, nor should they ask other guests what the person with disabilities needs or would like. Servers should address these guests directly and not assume that a disabled guest wants or needs help.

Classical French Service

Classical French service is the most elegant and elaborate style of service. It is used internationally when a fairly high degree of formality is desired. More complex and involved than American service, it is more labor intensive and time consuming. The servers involved must be highly skilled and possess in-depth knowledge of all facets of food preparation and fine-dining service. Successful French service is in the hands of not one, but a number of servers, using a **brigade** system, each one responsible for specific duties, and all of whom must strive to create a dining experience of the highest quality.

- Tableside preparation and plating is an integral part of this service; therefore, special equipment is required.
- The act of preparing special dishes in full view of the guest calls for the server to possess a high degree of skill that is absolutely flawless, allowing no room for the slightest error.
- The entire staff must work in concert, with the same commitment to excellence, to achieve the desired effect.

General Rules of French Service

In contrast to other services, classical French service differs in a variety of ways:

- All food and beverages are served from the right with the right hand.
- All food and beverages are cleared from the right with the right hand, with the exceptions of bread-and-butter plates and knives.
- Servers walk around the table in a clockwise direction.
- Not all food is prepared or plated in the kitchen.
- Food may be prepared tableside or plated on a **guéridon** or a side stand.
- Accompaniments may be plated directly from a service platter onto the guest's plate.
- Some entrées may be prepared tableside, while others for the same table are prepared in the kitchen. If this is the case, the items requiring tableside preparation are brought out first.
- The plates prepared in the kitchen are brought out only when the plates prepared tableside are ready to be served. The object is to have all the items served simultaneously. This example demonstrates the need for the constant communication between the brigade to orchestrate service properly. Timing is critical.
- Plates also may be presented to the guests *sous cloche* (under an elegant domed cover).
- Because this service is specialized and has developed over the centuries, there are many flatware pieces that have been designed specifically for certain foods—fish forks and knives, snail tongs and forks, lobster crackers and picks, pastry forks, parfait spoons, and espresso or demi-tasse spoons with demi-tasses (cups) for coffee. Therefore, flatware is not part of the preset cover but is set immediately prior to the course served.
- Elegant service also includes the use of **show plates** and **service plates.**
- Show plates are used as part of a cover for the purpose of decoration only. They are usually expensive china that add to the table presentation and help create a rich and elegant ambience.
- Showplates are removed once the guest has ordered. These are replaced by service plates, which serve as underliners for all courses except the entrée. If removed and reset, service plates must be clean.

- When napkins are preset, they should not cover the logo on the plates.

The advantages and disadvantages of French service are as follows:

Advantages

1. Service is very personalized.
2. Service is very elegant and stylized.
3. Food is prepared with a great deal of finesse and flair.

Disadvantages

1. More servers are required, resulting in high labor costs.
2. Highly skilled wait staff is required.
3. Costly equipment, such as guéridons, réchauds and chauffe plats are needed.
4. Fewer seats are available in the restaurant, due to the space needed for guéridons and specialty carts.
5. It takes longer to serve guests, so turns are less frequent.
6. Menu prices are high to cover the costs.

The Brigade

The brigade, or service staff, within a dining room offering French service may consist of as many as six members. When using the entire brigade in the service of food items, the duties of each of the members are as follows:

Chef de Service

The chef de service, or chef de salle, is the dining room manager who must be in close contact with every department and know all aspects of the business: dining room, banquet facilities, service bar, front bar, kitchen, dishwashing area, and front office. The position's responsibilities include the following:

- Hires and trains the dining room staff
- Ensures the proper set-up of the dining room

- Inventories all dining room equipment
- Requisitions the necessary supplies
- Supervises the reservation system
- Schedules the dining room staff
- Opens and closes the dining room each day
- Seats guests
- Solves all customer issues or complaints
- Is responsible for check reconciliations and cash reconciliation at the end of each shift

Chef de Rang (Captain)

The chef de rang, or station captain, has the responsibility of supervising and organizing all aspects of the classical French service in his station. Responsibilities include the following:

- Ensures that the tables are positioned and set correctly in his station
- Ensures that the guéridon, réchaud, and all other equipment needed is ready
- Greets guests with a smile
- Observes all guests within his station at all times. (He should never leave the station.)
- Is attentive to all verbal and nonverbal communication of the guests
- Develops a good rapport with guests
- Sells food and beverages via suggestion
- Accurately takes all orders
- Answers all questions regarding ingredients and the preparation of all food and beverages
- Prepares and portions foods tableside
- Synchronizes service within the brigade system
- Oversees all tables to ensure guest satisfaction
- Accurately totals each check and collects payment
- Is held accountable for all check reconciliations for his station

Commis de Rang

The commis de rang, or front waiter, assists the Chef de Rang when serving food and should be able to perform all duties of the Chef de Rang in his absence. The commis de rang is responsible for

- Actual service of food and beverage items to guests
- Beverage items served immediately upon receiving the order from the chef de rang
- Serving food once the course is plated by the chef de rang
- Opening and serving all bottled wine ordered by the chef de rang unless the sommelier is performing this service
- Giving assistance to the commis débarrasseur in clearing guests' tables
- Ensuring that the flatware is adjusted properly

(*Note:* All food items should be taken from the guéridon from the right side with the waiter's right hand and presented to the guest.)

Commis De Suite

The commis de suite, or back waiter, brings all food orders from the kitchen to the service area. This person is the link between the brigade and the kitchen staff. His/her responsibilities include

- Placing and picking up all orders, service equipment, and utensils from the kitchen to be taken into the dining room
- Presenting platters prepared by the kitchen to guests prior to plating
- Assisting in the clearing of both the guéridon and the guests' tables
- Delivering the necessary ingredients for the preparation of tableside dishes
- Providing all equipment and utensils for the plating of items (plates, service sets)
- Knowing the ingredients, methods of preparation, and garnishes
- Being aware of the stage of service for each table in the station
- Coordinating efforts with the chef de rang, the chef in the kitchen, and other members of the brigade

Commis Débarrasseur

The commis débarrasseur is the busser and is usually the entry position in the apprentice system. His/her responsibilities include

- Serving bread, butter, and water, and replenishing these when necessary
- Clearing the table after each course
- Changing the ashtrays, when necessary
- Cleaning the table after the guests have departed
- Resetting each table
- Ensuring that a supply of clean linens and flatware is on hand
- Performing any other duties necessary to keep the dining room in smooth running order.

Note: In most European countries, bread and water are served only if ordered.

Sommelier

The sommelier is the wine steward who must have extensive knowledge of wines and is in charge of the purchasing and service of wine. In formal restaurants, the sommelier may be wearing the tastevin cup, a silver cup hanging on a chain around his neck, which was used in Burgundy to taste wine. Today it is more a symbol of the position of sommelier and is rarely used as it was originally intended. His/her responsibilities include

- Selling and serving bottled wines
- Assisting guests in making wine selections based on their selection of food items
- Maintaining the wine inventory
- Maintaining the correct storage and cellaring of all wines
- Helping the chef de service develop wine lists
- Establishing the pricing for the wines
- Developing wine programs to augment sales in the restaurant (e.g., wine dinners or wines by the glass).

Tableside Service

Tableside service, while an integral part of French service, can be incorporated into other services to enhance the guest's dining experience. Tableside preparation includes assembling, carving, cooking, and flambéing. Many dishes that have evolved over the centuries lend themselves to tableside preparation. The underlying principles that have led to the success and suitability of many dishes include the following:

- The time needed to prepare the dish is not excessive.
- Only one pan, bowl, or carving board is needed for the preparation.
- The dish is conducive to preparation without handling any ingredients by hand.
- The number of ingredients is limited.
- The dish will enable the server to prepare it with flair.
- The dish is enhanced because it is served at the optimum temperature.

Tableside preparation or service can be classified into four types:

1. **Assembling:** Salads or dishes that involve simple assembly of ingredients (e.g., Caesar salad or steak tartare).
2. **Saucing** and **Garnishing:** Dishes that have been precooked in the kitchen that require finishing touches or saucing and garnishing
3. **Sautéing/Flambéing:** Items that are cooked quickly in the dining room, such as shrimp with garlic or hot beverages or desserts that are flamed tableside as part of the preparation.
4. **Carving** and **Deboning:** Fish, poultry, game, and meat dishes that require carving or deboning for the guest's enhanced enjoyment. This category also includes peeling and slicing of fruit and cheese. Peeling, coring, pitting, and slicing fruit enables guests to eat fruit easily without using their fingers.

Assembling

The tableside preparation of salads, dressings, and other foods allows the server to demonstrate individual style and flair. However, a salad is enhanced by being prepared *à la minute*, because acids in a dressing will quickly break down the texture of the greens.

Traditionally, wooden salad bowls, spoons, and forks are used for tossing. When using a glass salad bowl, place it in a larger bowl filled with crushed ice and rotate the bowl as the salad is tossed with the dressing to provide added flair.

The most commonly used greens in a tableside tossed salad include

Bibb lettuce	Soft texture; tender and nutty flavor
Chicory	Curly leafed and slightly bitter
Dandelion greens	Bitter
Endive	Crunchy texture and tangy
Escarole	Similar to chicory but with broader leaves and stronger flavor; bitter
Romaine	Good texture and taste
Watercress	A spicy green used for accent
Mâche or Lamb's Head	A mild spiciness and buttery quality

Basic Ingredients for Dressings

Oils. The best oil in salad dressings is virgin olive oil, which is from the first pressing. Other oils include corn oil, which is light and fresh tasting, and ground nut oil, such as peanut oil. The oil should be clean, clear, and free of any strong odors.

Acids. Vinegars and lemon and lime juices are the most commonly used acids. Vinegars may be wine vinegars, balsamic vinegars, or other fruit-based vinegars. Lemon or lime juice will also provide excellent flavor components to dressings.

Mustards. Mustard is often used in a wide range of dressings. French mustard should be the choice for vinaigrette-style dressings. The best known and used style of mustard is the *moutarde forte de Dijon*. Although this is a pungent mustard, it will provide an underlying zest and spiciness to the dressing that will not be overpowering if used discretely.

Herbs and Seasonings. There are many herbs and seasonings that will alter not only the flavor, but also the appearance of a dressing. Herbs that may be used in a dressing include chopped chives, fennel, tarragon, mint,

and dill. To lend different seasonings to a dressing, the following will most commonly be found in a guéridon set-up: shallots, horseradish, chopped olives, grated cheese, Tabasco, chili sauce, soy sauce, and Worcestershire sauce.

A selection of peppers (both white and black peppercorns in separate mills), cayenne, or paprika may be used to enhance a dressing. Garlic is another worthy addition to the seasonings the server might use. Rubbing the wooden mixing or salad bowl with a clove of garlic and then removing the remainder is the best technique for imparting the flavor without it becoming overwhelming.

In blending dressings in the dining room, there is room for some individuality, and recipes can be adjusted to the tastes of the guests who are being served. It is an opportunity for the server to demonstrate flair and finesse, which will enhance the guests' experience, if done professionally.

Recipes

Hazard Analysis Critical Control Point. In the dining room setting, it is imperative that food safety guidelines are followed. These guidelines are known as **hazard analysis critical control point (HACCP).** The HACCP system was established by the Pillsbury Company in 1971 for the National Aeronautics and Space Administration (NASA). The primary purpose of HACCP is to ensure that food served to the customer is safe. (See Volume I, Chapter 2 for further details and specific guidelines.)

In the recipes that follow, the HACCP foods have been identified.

Anaphylaxis. A customer's health and safety is a very important priority. Anaphylactic (allergic) reactions can be life-threatening. The Food Allergy Network (4744 Holly Avenue, Fairfax VA 22030-5647) has indicated the most common food-borne allergies. The ingredients that most often cause allergic reactions are dairy products, nut products, seafood, and flour (breads, pastas, etc.). If a reaction to a particular food item occurs, 911 should be called *immediately*.

HACCP:
Egg yolk

Caesar Salad

YIELD: 2 FOUR-OUNCE SERVINGS

INGREDIENTS:

Mise en Place by Chefs in the Kitchen:

1 large clove	Garlic, peeled and cut in half
1 teaspoon	Salt
1 large	Anchovy fillet
1 teaspoon	Dijon mustard
2 ounces	Olive oil
½ teaspoon	White wine vinegar
1 ounce	Freshly squeezed lemon juice
1 each	Egg, boiled 3 minutes and white discarded
1 teaspoon	Freshly ground black pepper
4 ounces	Romaine, washed, dried, and torn into bite-sized pieces Croûtons, see Culinary Recipes
1 tablespoon	Grated Parmesan cheese

TABLESIDE METHOD OF PREPARATION BY CHEF DE RANG:

1. Season the bowl with garlic, using salt as an abrasive; then discard garlic pieces.
2. Add anchovy and mash with a fork. Move the anchovy to one side of the bowl and add mustard.
3. Blend oil into mustard, slowly and steadily.
4. Add wine vinegar, lemon juice, egg yolk, and pepper. Mix well.
5. Add romaine and toss lettuce. Toss all the above by rotating service spoon and fork from back to front of bowl until lettuce is fully coated.
6. Add croûtons and toss as in step 5.
7. Add cheese and toss. Serve immediately.

Variations:

1. Supplement with 2 dashes of Worcestershire sauce and 1 dash of Tabasco sauce when adding lemon juice.
2. Supplement with 2 dashes of soy sauce when adding lemon juice.
3. Blend oil and lemon juice and emulsify; then add dry mustard instead of Dijon.
4. Egg yolk may be omitted due to the concern over salmonella poisoning.

CHEF NOTES:
1. When increasing Caesar salad to a larger amount, do not increase the amount of garlic, anchovies, and mustard proportionately; that is, if you double the recipe, use less than twice the amount of garlic, anchovies, and mustard.
2. All ingredients must be chilled to 40° F or less.

HACCP:

Eggs

Cold Spinach Salad

YIELD: 2 FOUR-OUNCE SERVINGS

INGREDIENTS:

Mise en Place by Chefs in the Kitchen:

1 large clove	Garlic, peeled and cut in half
1 teaspoon	Salt
1 tablespoon	Olive oil
1 teaspoon	Red wine vinegar
½ teaspoon	Freshly ground black pepper
8 ounces	Fresh spinach leaves, cleaned, dried, stemmed, and torn into bite-sized pieces
1 each	Hard-boiled egg, finely chopped
2 each	Large mushrooms, cut in quarter-inch slices
2 ounces	Bacon, cut in half-inch pieces and crisply fried

TABLESIDE METHOD OF PREPARATION BY CHEF DE RANG:

1. Season the bowl with garlic, using the salt as an abrasive; then discard garlic pieces.
2. Add the oil, vinegar, and pepper.
3. Add spinach and toss greens from front to back and top to bottom, within the bowl.
4. Add egg, mushrooms, and bacon; toss.
5. Serve immediately.

Variations:

1. Supplement with lemon juice or Worcestershire sauce.
2. Supplement with white or brown sugar.
3. Supplement with honey.

CHEF NOTES:

All ingredients must be chilled to 40° F or less.

Hot Spinach Salad

YIELD: 2 FOUR-OUNCE SERVINGS

INGREDIENTS:

Mise en Place by Chefs in the Kitchen:

2 ounces	Bacon, cut in 1-inch pieces
2 teaspoons	Granulated sugar
1 teaspoon	Olive oil
1 teaspoon	Red wine vinegar
1 ounce	Freshly squeezed lemon juice
	Salt, to taste
½ teaspoon	Freshly ground black pepper or to taste
8 ounces	Fresh spinach leaves, cleaned, dried, stemmed, and torn into bite-sized pieces

TABLESIDE METHOD OF PREPARATION BY CHEF DE RANG:

1. In a heated Suzette pan, place bacon.
2. When bacon is half-cooked, add sugar and melt.
3. When bacon is fully cooked, add oil, vinegar, lemon juice, salt, and pepper.
4. Mix well and pour over spinach leaves.
5. Toss and serve immediately.

Variations:

1. Supplement spinach with ripe olives, onions, cooked eggs, or sliced mushrooms, finely chopped or cut julienne.
2. Supplement with Worcestershire sauce or garlic.
3. Supplement with flambéed brandy, and pour, flaming, over spinach.
4. Substitute brown sugar for white.

Glossary:
Brunoise—fine dice

HACCP:
Egg
Tenderloin

Steak Tartare

YIELD: 2 SERVINGS

INGREDIENTS:

Mise en Place by Chefs in the Kitchen:

4 each	Anchovy fillets
1 teaspoon	Dijon mustard
1½ teaspoons	Olive oil
½ teaspoon	White wine vinegar
1 tablespoon	Lemon juice, freshly squeezed and strained
1 ounce	Cognac
2 teaspoons	Onion, peeled and cut **brunoise**
1 teaspoon	Capers
1 teaspoon	Chopped fresh parsley
2 each	Raw pasteurized egg yolks
10 ounces	Tenderloin, minced
6 slices	Rye bread, sliced, toasted, and cut into points

TABLESIDE METHOD OF PREPARATION BY CHEF DE RANG:

1. In a chilled salad bowl, mash anchovies with a fork.
2. Add mustard and blend in oil.
3. Add vinegar, lemon juice, Cognac, onions, capers, parsley, and egg yolks. Mix all ingredients together.
4. Add meat and mix thoroughly.
5. To serve, mold mixture into original shape on two cold dinner plates.
6. Arrange toast points around steak tartare.

Variations:

1. Substitute shallots for onion.
2. Supplement with Worcestershire sauce, soy sauce, Tabasco, or a combination.
3. Supplement with Hungarian paprika.
4. Supplement with horseradish.
5. Substitute pumpernickel or toasted French bread for rye bread.
6. May omit egg yolk and parsley from dressing and use as a garnish.

CHEF NOTES:
1. Chopped tenderloin is the leanest beef available. Even the leanest sirloin would have at least a 12% fat content. The leanest possible meat should be used to make it easily digestible.
2. State and local health departments caution against the use of raw eggs due to the risk of salmonella poisoning.

Glossary:
Al dente—to the bite

HACCP:
Cream
Egg yolk

Fettuccine Alfredo

YIELD: 2 SERVINGS

INGREDIENTS:

Mise en Place by Chefs in the Kitchen:

1 ounce	Unsalted butter
4 ounces	Heavy cream
1 ounce	Pasteurized egg yolk
8 ounces	Fettuccine, cooked **al dente**
2 tablespoons	Grated Parmesan cheese
	Salt and freshly ground black pepper, to taste

TABLESIDE METHOD OF PREPARATION BY CHEF DE RANG:

1. In a sauté pan, add butter and melt; add cream and whisk together.
2. While whisking, add egg yolks slowly, being careful not to touch sides of pan with egg so yolks will not cook separately from the sauce.
3. Add fettuccine and keep mixture moving, shaking pan until pasta is heated throughout.
4. Add cheese, salt, and pepper, and mix well.
5. Portion on preheated dinner plates.

Variation:

Substitute hollandaise sauce for egg yolk for easier blending and richer taste.

Saucing and Garnishing:

This type of tableside cooking is quick and allows the server the advantage of performing with flair while improving the dish, because it will be served at its optimum temperature without adversely affecting the main ingredient, such as pasta. The sauce is made in a blazer pan (see section on blazer pans, this chapter), and the pre-cooked ingredient is added to the pan and tossed to coat the ingredient, heating throughout. It is then portioned, plated, and served.

Sautéing and Flambéing

These procedures should be used only if the main ingredient requires a short cooking time (e.g., shrimp or a scaloppine). The advantage to the guest is that the dish will remain hot. Generally, the main ingredient will be accompanied by a sauce that is also prepared tableside and includes a wine, which may be fortified. Fortified wines are appropriate in tableside cooking because they require less reduction to transmit their flavors and bouquets. The following are the tableside fortified wines most often used for cooking:

Wine	Place of Origin
Marsala	Italy
Port	Portugal
Sherry	Spain
Madeira	Portugal
Vermouth	France and Italy

If the sauce requires stronger flavors, the main ingredient, such as a tournedo of beef, may be flambéed with a higher-proof spirit. This not only allows the sauce be imparted with these flavors, but also enables the server to provide the most dramatic tableside preparation. The most desirable spirits to use in flambéing are brandies (e.g., Cognac, Armagnac, or Calvados) and rum or whiskey.

- To flambé, the server removes the hot pan containing the main ingredient from the réchaud to prevent premature ignition and expose guests to harm.
- The liquor is added to the pan.
- The pan is returned to the flame at a 35-degree angle to ignite.
- If the liquor does not ignite immediately, the server should swirl the pan gently and tilt the pan again at a 35-degree angle, which will cause the alcoholic fumes to come into contact with the flame and ignite.
- When using wines, fortified wines, or spirits, it is important that most of the alcohol evaporate, because the intention in adding the wine or spirit is to impart flavor, not alcohol.

Recipes

Flambéing desserts employs some of the same techniques described previously. Desserts are often accompanied by ice cream, which is brought out by the commis de suite or another server while the tableside preparation is being performed.

Many recipes for desserts and international coffees call for both a spirit and a liqueur. The spirit is added first to enable the flaming to occur.

Spirits most often used in flambéing are:

Spirits	Brandy from	Place of Origin
Armagnac/cognac	Grapes	France
Calvados	Apples	Normandy, France
Kirsch	Cherries	Alsace, France, and Switzerland
Mirabelle	Plums	France
Rum	Sugar cane	Jamaica
Whiskey	Barley	Scotland, Ireland, the United States

The liqueur is added at a later point and the alcohol is evaporated during the cooking. Liqueurs that are used most often include

Liqueur	Predominant Flavor
Crème de Banana	Banana
Benedictine	Aromatic compound
Crème de Cacao	Chocolate or cocoas and vanilla
Crème de Cassis	Black currant
Cherry brandy	Cherries
Cointreau	Orange
Curaçao	Orange
Crème de Fraises	Strawberry
Crème de Framboise	Raspberry
Grand Marnier	Orange
Maraschino	Cherry
Crème de Peche	Peach

HACCP:
Shrimp

Shrimp Sauté with Garlic

YIELD: 2 SERVINGS

INGREDIENTS:

Mise en Place by Chefs in the Kitchen:

2 ounces	Clarified butter
8 each (16–20)	Shrimp, peeled, deveined, and butterflied
1 ounce	Sherry
1 teaspoon	Crushed garlic
2 ounces	Lemon juice, freshly squeezed
	Salt and cayenne pepper, to taste
1 tablespoon	Freshly chopped parsley

TABLESIDE METHOD OF PREPARATION BY CHEF DE RANG:

1. Heat pan, add butter, and melt.
2. Add shrimp and sauté on both sides.
3. Remove pan from heat, pour in sherry; then return to heat.
4. Add garlic, lemon juice, and season to taste. Mix well and simmer 2 minutes.
5. Place four shrimp per portion on preheated dinner plate, spoon sauce over, and garnish with parsley. Serve immediately.

CHEF NOTE:

When using a réchaud, apply the safe and proper techniques. (See the section, "The Rechaud," in this chapter.)

Glossary:
Nappé—coat

HACCP:
Veal

Veal Scallops in Wine Sauce

YIELD: 2 SERVINGS

INGREDIENTS:

Mise en Place by Chefs in the Kitchen:

1 ounce	Butter
1 ounce	Olive oil
6 1½-ounce	Veal scallops
1 ounce	Seasoned flour
2 ounces	Mushrooms, washed and sliced
1½ ounces	Marsala wine
2 ounces	Veal demi-glace
	Salt and ground white pepper, to taste
2 each	Croûtons
1 tablespoon	Freshly chopped parsley

TABLESIDE METHOD OF PREPARATION BY CHEF DE RANG:

1. Warm pan, add butter and oil, and heat.
2. Coat veal slices in seasoned flour, shaking off excess.
3. Place veal slices in pan and brown over high flame on both sides.
4. Add mushrooms and sauté.
5. Add Marsala wine and simmer 2 minutes.
6. Add demi-glace, heat to boil, and season. Cook veal to an internal temperature of 145° F.
7. Place croûton on preheated dinner plate, arrange veal slices on croûton, and **nappé** with sauce.
8. Garnish with chopped parsley.

Glossary:
Nappé—coat

HACCP:
Veal

Veal Piccata

YIELD: 2 SERVINGS

INGREDIENTS:

Mise en Place by Chefs in the Kitchen:

1 ounce	Olive oil
1 ounce	Butter
6 two-ounce	Veal scaloppine
	Seasoned flour, as needed
	Salt and freshly ground black pepper, to taste
2 tablespoons	Lemon juice, freshly squeezed
3 ounces	Dry white wine
4 slices	Lemon pinwheels (without rind)

TABLESIDE METHOD OF PREPARATION BY CHEF DE RANG:

1. In a heated sauté pan, add olive oil and butter.
2. Lightly coat the scaloppine with flour, shaking off excess.
3. Sauté the scaloppine on both sides and season to taste.
4. After turning scaloppine, add lemon juice.
5. Add wine and simmer. Cook veal to an internal temperature of 145° F.
6. Remove the scaloppine to a preheated dinner plate, overlapping slices, and **nappé** with sauce.
7. Garnish with two lemon pinwheels on side of plate.

Variations:

1. Supplement with capers to create grenobloise.
2. For à la Française, use flour and egg wash on scaloppine.

HACCP:
Beef

Flaming Steak with Peppercorns

YIELD: 2 SERVINGS

INGREDIENTS:

Mise en Place by Chefs in the Kitchen:

1 ounce	Butter
1 teaspoon	Olive oil
2 five-ounce	Sirloin steaks, coated with crushed black peppercorns, as needed
2 ounces	Cognac
4 ounces	Demi-glace
	Salt, to taste

TABLESIDE METHOD OF PREPARATION BY CHEF DE RANG:

1. Heat a Suzette pan until very hot; then add butter and oil.
2. When butter is melted, add steaks.
3. Cook to desired doneness.
4. Remove pan from heat, add Cognac; then return to heat, and flame.
5. When flame subsides, remove steaks and place on preheated dinner plates.
6. Add demi-glace to pan and mix with Cognac. Season with salt.
7. Spoon sauce alongside steak.

Variations:

1. Dijon mustard may be lightly brushed on steak before coating with peppercorns, or add mustard to sauce in pan.
2. Medallions of tenderloin may be substituted for sirloin.
3. Green peppercorns also may be used.
4. Supplement with light cream.

CHEF NOTE:

The FDA recommends that beef be cooked to an internal temperature of 145° F.

HACCP:
Chicken

Émincé of Chicken with Fines Herbes

YIELD: 2 SERVINGS

INGREDIENTS:

Mise en Place by Chefs in the Kitchen:

2 ounces	Butter
12 ounces	Chicken fingers, precooked to 165° F.
2 ounces	Seasoned flour
1 ounces	Dry sherry
1 teaspoon	Minced shallots
1 teaspoon	Chopped fresh tarragon
2 teaspoons	Freshly chopped parsley
2 tablespoons	Lemon juice, freshly squeezed
	Salt and ground white pepper, to taste

TABLESIDE METHOD OF PREPARATION BY CHEF DE RANG:

1. Place 1 ounce of the butter in a sauté pan and heat.
2. Coat chicken fingers in flour, shaking off excess.
3. Place chicken fingers in hot butter and brown.
4. Remove pan from heat, add sherry, and return to heat.
5. Remove chicken fingers to a preheated plate to hold.
6. Place second ounce of butter in pan.
7. Add shallots, herbs, and lemon juice and allow to simmer.
8. Return chicken fingers to pan and allow to heat throughout. Season to taste.
9. Portion into servings on preheated dinner plates.

Pommes Normande

YIELD: 2 SERVINGS

INGREDIENTS:

Mise en Place by Chefs in the Kitchen:

1 tablespoon	Granulated sugar
1 ounce	Butter
2 each	Sweet apples, peeled, cored, and cut into quarter-inch slices
2 ounces	Calvados or Applejack
½ teaspoon	Cinnamon sugar mixture
2 ounces	Heavy cream

TABLESIDE METHOD OF PREPARATION BY CHEF DE RANG:

1. Heat a crêpe pan, add sugar and butter and allow to lightly caramelize.
2. Add apples and sauté.
3. Remove pan from heat, add Calvados; then return to heat and flame.
4. Sprinkle cinnamon sugar over flame.
5. When flame subsides, remove apples to preheated dessert dishes. Add cream to pan, bring to a boil, and blend well.
6. Spoon sauce over apples.

Variations:

1. Substitute brown sugar for granulated sugar.
2. Substitute nutmeg for cinnamon.

Glossary:
Coupe—stemmed dish with wide, deep bowl
Nappé—coat

Banana Flambé

YIELD: 2 SERVINGS

INGREDIENTS:

Mise en Place by Chefs in the Kitchen:

2 tablespoons	Granulated sugar
1 ounce	Butter
2 each	Bananas, split in half crosswise and lengthwise
1½ ounces	Dark rum (preferably Myers)
½ teaspoon	Cinnamon sugar mixture
1½ ounces	Banana liqueur
2 scoops	Vanilla ice cream (4 ounces each), in **coupe**

TABLESIDE METHOD OF PREPARATION BY CHEF DE RANG:

1. Heat Suzette pan and add sugar and butter.
2. Lightly caramelize; then add bananas and coat with caramel.
3. Remove pan from réchaud, add rum; then return pan to réchaud and flame.
4. While still flaming, sprinkle cinnamon sugar over pan.
5. Lower flame and remove pan from heat. Add banana liqueur and return pan to réchaud and allow sauce to reduce.
6. Arrange four quarters of banana around ice cream and **nappé** with sauce, covering ice cream.

Variations:

1. Replace granulated sugar with brown sugar or honey.
2. Supplement with lime or lemon juice.
3. Serve with lemon wedge.

Glossary:
Coupe—stemmed dish with wide, deep bowl
Nappé—coat

Cherries Jubilee

YIELD: 2 SERVINGS

INGREDIENTS:

Mise en Place by Chefs in the Kitchen:

2 tablespoons	Granulated sugar
10 each	Dark, sweet, pitted cherries
2 tablespoons	Lemon juice, freshly squeezed
1½ ounces	Kirschwasser
1½ ounces	Peter Heering
3 ounces	Cherry juice
2 scoops	Vanilla ice cream (4 ounces each), in **coupe**

TABLESIDE METHOD OF PREPARATION BY CHEF DE RANG:

1. Heat Suzette pan; then sprinkle in sugar. When sugar is totally caramelized, add cherries.
2. Add lemon juice and shake to remelt sugar.
3. When sugar is melted, remove pan from heat, add both liqueurs; then return to heat and flame.
4. Add cherry juice. Move cherries to the side of the pan to prevent their being overcooked.
5. Heat sauce to a froth.
6. Spoon cherries over ice cream and **nappé** with sauce.

Variations:

1. Sprinkle a mixture of cinnamon and sugar over cherries while the liquor is still ignited.
2. Replace Peter Heering with Crème de Cocoa or Vandermint.
3. Replace Kirschwasser with brandy.

CHEF NOTE:

To reduce preparation time, cornstarch may be premixed with cherry juice.

Glossary:

Nappé—coat

Crêpes Suzette

YIELD: 2 SERVINGS

INGREDIENTS:

Mise en Place by Chefs in the Kitchen:

2 tablespoons	Granulated sugar
1 ounce	Butter
Zest of 2	Oranges
Zest of 1	Lemon
4 ounces	Orange juice
2 ounces	Grand Marnier
4 each	Crêpes
1 ounce	Cognac

TABLESIDE METHOD OF PREPARATION BY CHEF DE RANG:

1. Heat Suzette pan and add sugar. Add butter and mix until all sugar is dissolved.
2. While sugar is dissolving, add the zest of one orange and the lemon.
3. Add orange juice. (If sugar caramelizes too quickly, add juice to pan while zesting.)
4. Remove pan from heat and add Grand Marnier.
5. Return pan to heat, but do *not* flambé. Dip crêpes in sauce, one at a time; then fold into quarters. Move crêpes to the side of the pan.
6. When all crêpes are folded, remove pan from heat, add Cognac; then return to heat and flame.
7. Heat sauce to a boil. Serve two crêpes on a preheated plate and **nappé** with sauce.
8. Garnish with additional orange zest.

Variation:

For a more syrupy sauce, caramelize sugar first, then add butter.

CHEF NOTE:

Zest can be removed from orange and lemon at the time of preparation (step 2).

HACCP:

Egg yolks

Zabaglione

YIELD: 2 SERVINGS

INGREDIENTS:

Mise en Place by Chefs in the Kitchen:

2 ounces	Pasteurized egg yolks
2 teaspoons	Granulated sugar
3 ounces	Marsala

TABLESIDE METHOD OF PREPARATION BY CHEF DE RANG:

1. Beat egg yolks and sugar in a cold zabaglione pan.
2. When some volume is reached, add Marsala and beat a little more.
3. Apply to low heat, whisk, keeping sides of pan clean so as not to cook yolk on sides, which could become mixed with final product.
4. When mixture has reached a ribbon-like texture (determined by testing on the back of a spoon), pour into champagne glasses.

Variations:

1. Lady fingers may accompany this dish.
2. Zabaglione may be poured over fruit.
3. Grand Marnier or Kirschwasser may be poured in champagne glasses ahead of time.
4. Marsala may be replaced with a sweet white wine.

Café Diable

YIELD: 2 SERVINGS

INGREDIENTS:

Mise en Place by Chefs in the Kitchen:

1 teaspoon	Sugar
1 each	Cinnamon stick
1 each	Horse's neck (see chef note 2)
1 ounce	Cognac
1 ounce	Grand Marnier
5 ounces	Espresso

TABLESIDE METHOD OF PREPARATION BY CHEF DE RANG:

1. In a diable réchaud, add sugar, cinnamon stick, horse's neck, Cognac, and Grand Marnier.
2. When liqueurs start to steam, pierce one end of horse's neck with a long-handled fork. With the other hand, use a ladle and remove a small amount of liquor from bottom of réchaud and expose it to the flame until it ignites.
3. Raise horse's neck about 12 inches above pan and pour liqueur down rind. Continue until cloves glow bright red. Extinguish flame in réchaud by pouring in espresso.

CHEF NOTES:
1. *Diavolo* in Italian; *Diablo* in Spanish.
2. Horse's neck: The skin of an orange that has been removed by carefully peeling from top to bottom while rotating orange in hand. Stud with cloves approximately 1 inch apart.

HACCP:
Cream

Irish Coffee

YIELD: 2 SERVINGS

INGREDIENTS:

Mise en Place by Chefs in the Kitchen:

2 each	Lemon wedges
2 tablespoons	Granulated sugar
2 ounces	Irish whiskey
10 ounces	Coffee
2 ounces	Heavy cream, whipped

TABLESIDE METHOD OF PREPARATION BY CHEF DE RANG:

1. Rim footed glass with lemon and dip it in sugar.
2. Heat over flame slightly, rotating glass.
3. Remove from heat, add whiskey, return to heat, and flame. Swirl glass so flame rises. Flame for approximately 1 minute.
4. Add coffee and fill to about a half-inch below rim.
5. Add whipped cream.

Variations:

Use liqueurs from any country to create different international coffees:

1. Jamaica: Jamaica Rum and Tia Maria
2. Mexico: Kahlua
3. Amaretto: Lover's Coffee

CHEF NOTE:
Coffee with two liqueurs is prepared by the same method, except that the second liqueur, usually a cordial, is floated on the whipped cream or heated in a ladle and then poured over the whipped cream. The first liquor is usually of high alcohol content (e.g., brandy or whiskey).

Carving and Deboning

There are a number of ways to carve, but the underlying principles are the same. Carving in the dining room differs from carving in the kitchen.

- Handling of the food should be restricted to utensils.
- Carving or deboning must be accomplished quickly because the item will be cooling.
- The appearance of all implements and equipment must be scrupulously clean.
- Portioning should be as equal as possible, while recognizing that it is more difficult to gauge portions of jointed items such as roast ribs of beef than those of a chateaubriand.
- The presentation should be accomplished not only with dexterity, but also with flair.

Carving Tools

There are a number of carving and boning tools, which are illustrated in Figure 2–3, to accomplish the tasks of carving, boning, peeling, coring, pitting, and slicing.

A *serrated slicing knife* is ideal for slicing items presented in puff pastry or brioche dough.

A flexible, *narrow-bladed slicing knife* is ideal for slicing salmon and roast ribs of beef.

A *slicing knife with pointed tip* is used primarily for slicing and carving red meat items and fowl.

A light 8-inch or 10-inch *French knife* and 4-inch to 6-inch *boning knife* can be used for boning chicken, duck, or squab. The French knife is usually used for the larger items, and the boning knife for the smaller items.

A *paring knife* is used for peeling fruits and vegetables. Additional tools include various styles of meat forks, an apple corer, a pineapple corer, and a zester.

Figures 2–4 through 2–11 (starting on page 60) detail carving and/or boning of various foods.

(Text continues on page 65)

Figure 2–3 Carving and boning tools

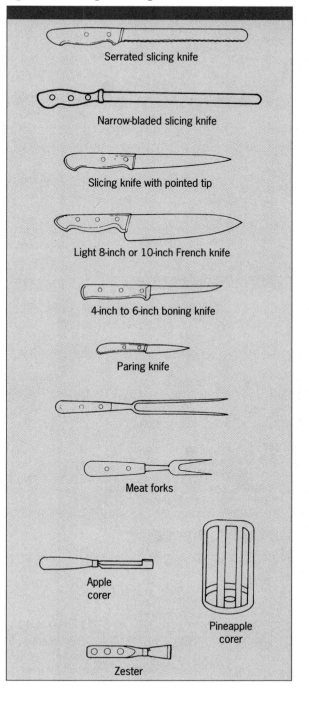

Serrated slicing knife

Narrow-bladed slicing knife

Slicing knife with pointed tip

Light 8-inch or 10-inch French knife

4-inch to 6-inch boning knife

Paring knife

Meat forks

Apple corer

Pineapple corer

Zester

Figure 2–4 Carving fowl (chicken, duck, pheasant, and goose).

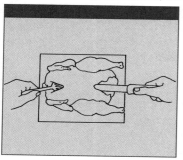

1   Present the fowl with the breast of the bird facing the guest. To transfer the bird from the platter to the carving board, insert the fork into the neck cavity while inserting the carving knife into the large stomach cavity.

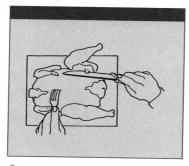

2   **Transferring the whole bird**

Insert the fork under the neck cavity and through the spine or on the top of the bird. Slice through the skin around the leg joint with the carving knife, cutting away any fat and connective tissue near the thigh joint.

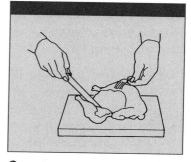

3   **Cutting away fat and connective tissue**

With the tip of the knife, find the joint and separate it. This will disconnect the leg from the body.

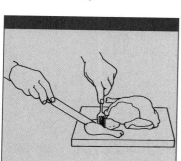

4   Hold down the leg with the fork and slice through the knee joint to separate the thigh from the drumstick. Repeat the procedure to remove the other leg and return the legs to the platter.

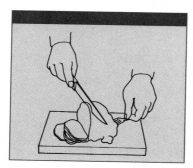

5   To carve the breast while it is still attached, insert the fork under the wing and through the spine. With the tip of the carving knife, make a cut along the wishbone and along the breastbone. Slice down between the breast meat and breastbone using the entire blade of the knife.

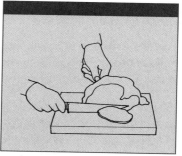

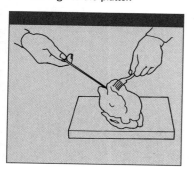

6   **Removing the breast with the wing attached.**

Follow the contour of the rib bones down to the carving board and slice through the wing joint. This will remove one half the breast with the wing attached. Repeat the procedure to remove the opposite side of the breast. The wing may be removed from the breast meat at this time if so desired and returned to the platter.

Figure 2–5 Chateaubriand

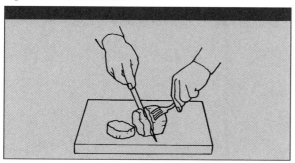

Present the platter to guest. Transfer the Chateaubriand to the carving board using a large serving spoon and fork. Hold the meat steady with the serving fork and slice half-inch portions using the entire length of the carving knife. Slice from one end to the other end, making sure not to pierce the meat with the tines of the fork. Carve all slices *across the grain* of the meat to ensure a more tender product. Transfer slices back to the platter, have the assistant waiter remove the carving board, arrange plates, and portion slices equally.

Figure 2–6 Carving rack of lamb

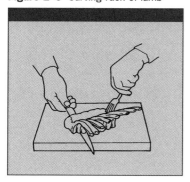
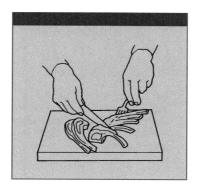

1   Present platter to guest. Transfer rack to the carving board using a large carving fork and slicing knife. This is done by lightly piercing the fork between the rib bones and the meat.

2   Slice down between each rib bone separating the chops. Continue until all the ribs have been separated.

3   Transfer the chops to a platter and remove the carving board. Place 4 chops on each plate.

Figure 2–7 Boning sole

1   Hold the sole steady using a fish fork or serving fork. Press and scrape away the outer edges of the fins using a fish knife, palette knife or serving spoon.

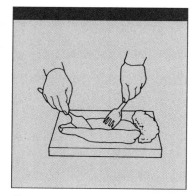

2   Draw the knife or spoon down the center line of the fish from head to tail.

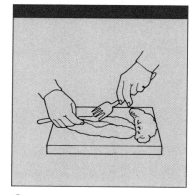

3   Place the fork into the slit just made to hold the fish steady.

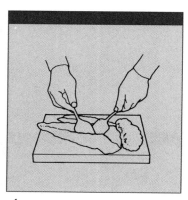

4   Gently push the top fillets away from the skeleton using the knife or spoon.

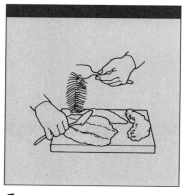

5   Wedge the backbone between the first two tines of the fork and lift it away from the bottom fillets while holding down the fillets with the spoon or knife.

6   The sole is now ready to plated.

Figure 2–8 Bonding trout

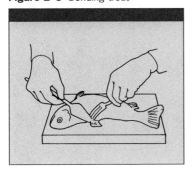

1 Present platter to guest. Remove all the fins by pulling them away from the fish using a fish fork and fish knife or palette knife. Place fins to the outer edge of the platter.

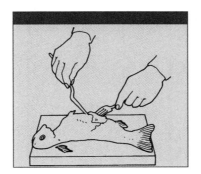

2 Slide the knife under the skin and peel the skin away from the flesh with the help of the fork.

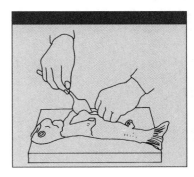

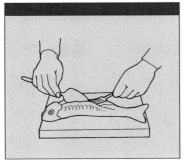

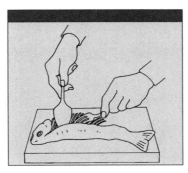

3 Draw the knife along the center line from the head to the tail. Place the fork into the slit just made to hold the fish steady. Gently push the top fillets away from the skeleton using the knife.

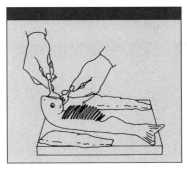

4 Insert the first two tines of the fork into the backbone just behind the head.

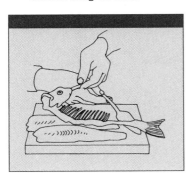

5 Lift the head with the fork while pushing the bottom fillets away from the skeleton with the knife. Usually the head and tail will remain attached, but it is not uncommon for the head to fall off during boning. Do not be concerned if it does—just remove it.

6 Plate the trout fillets in an attractive manner.

Figure 2–9 Carving an apple or a pear

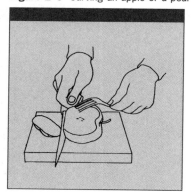

1   When carving fresh fruit, it is customary to first peel the fruit. Place the fruit on its side and steady it using the curved side of a fork. Slice off the end with a small, sharp knife.

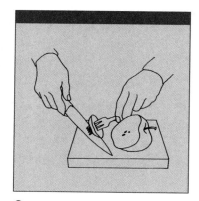

2   Now place the cut end on the fork while bracing the end with the knife.

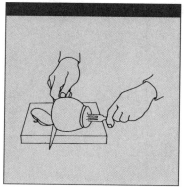

3   Insert the fork into the cut end of the apple and slice away the other end.

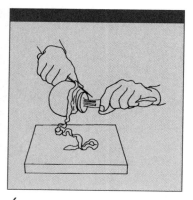

4   Now hold the fork up on one hand and peel the skin away while turning the apple. Be sure the fork is firmly inserted into the apple to avoid having it fall off the fork.

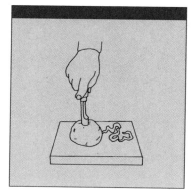

5   Once peeled, remove the fork and lay the apple on one of the flat cut ends. Remove the core using a fruit corer.

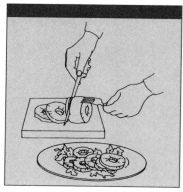

6   The fruit may now be sliced into rings or wedges as desired and served or used for a hot dessert such as Apples Normandy.

Figure 2-10 Carving a banana

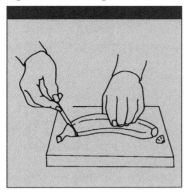

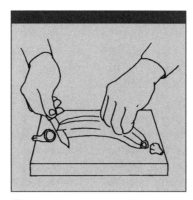

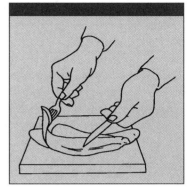

1 Bananas may be carved on a china plate, sliver platter or carving board. Slice away the two ends far enough back to expose the flesh.

2 Now slice the banana in half lengthwise.

3 With the two halves laying flat side down, remove the skin. This is done by piercing the skin with the first tine of a fork and peeling it away from the flesh. Use the knife to steady the banana as it is peeled.

Figure 2-11 Carving a peach

Peeling a peach depends on the desire of the guest. Peach skin, although fuzzy, contains desirable flavors and many people like to eat it. If peeling is desired, the same procedure as for peeling an apple can be used. To carve, lay the peach on a plate or carving board and steady it with a fork. Slice wedges lengthwise and roll the peach as carving proceeds until all the flesh is removed from the stone. Be sure to slice down to the stone to ensure a clean separation of flesh from stone.

Tableside Equipment

To be able to properly perform tableside service, there are a number of indispensable pieces of equipment and small wares the server needs.

Figure 2-12 Correct position for grasping the service fork and spoon

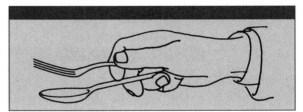

The Service Set

Service set refers to a large spoon and fork. The spoon is shaped like a soup spoon, and the fork is similar to a meat fork, but both are larger. The service set is used so that service personnel never touch food items with their hands. Professional servers must be able to use the service set with the same dexterity with which they command their hands. The correct position for grasping the service fork and spoon is shown in Figure 2-12. Place the spoon in your hand as the lower of the two utensils, with the bowl of the spoon facing up and the fork placed directly above it, tines pointing up.

When performing tableside plating, it is essential that the server understand the aesthetics of both performance and the finished plate. This makes French service elegant. Plating should be performed by using a service set, the service fork in the left hand and the service spoon in the right. The main food item ordered should be placed at the 6 o'clock position on the guest's plate, with the accompaniments strategically placed around it.

Service sets are used in **French casserole service.** In this type of service, plating of the casserole is completed on the guéridon. If the accompaniments are preplated in the kitchen, the server merely transfers the entire contents of the casserole dish to the guest's plate by using the service set with both hands.

The Guéridon

The guéridon is a service cart or trolley. It is a portable work station that is used for all tableside preparations, including portioning, cooking, finishing, and plating.

Guests are usually impressed by the skills demonstrated by the chef de rang. Tableside preparations often pique the interest of other guests, thereby boosting sales. The flickering flame of a réchaud or the flaming of liquors in a pan substantially contributes to the restaurant's ambience (see Figure 2–13).

- The guéridon is generally 18 inches wide by 30 inches long.
- The guéridon generally has three shelves.
- The top shelf is used for the preparation and plating of the dishes.
- The middle shelf is used to store underliners, napkins, condiments, and service sets.
- The lower shelf is used to store the carving board and sets.
- All of the shelves on the guéridon should be covered with linen.
- The linen on each shelf of the guéridon should be neatly folded so that it does not drape or hang over the sides of the shelf.

Figure 2–13 Guéridon with a built-in réchaud.

Figure 2–14 Types of réchauds. (Left) Réchaud using wick and fuel. (Middle) Réchaud using alcohol/gel. (Right) Fuel reservoir with flame control lever and extinguisher cap.

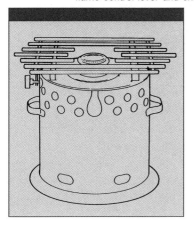 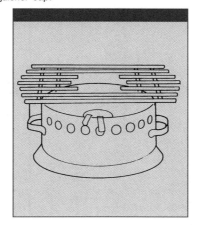 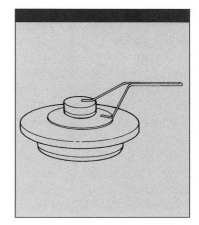

- Position the cart close enough to the table so that the performance of the chef de rang can be enjoyed by the guests, while maintaining a safe distance.
- Preparing or plating should be performed from the left end of the guéridon.
- If using a **réchaud** for flaming or **flambéing,** it should be placed on the left end of the guéridon, with all liquor bottles placed on the opposite end.
- When the service has been completed, the cart should be removed from the table.
- When not in use, the guéridon should be kept off to the side of the station.

The Réchaud

The réchaud is a portable stove designed to cook, flambé (flame), or keep food warm. It is made of stainless steel, copper, brass, or silver plate. The base is cylindrical and of varying heights with a detachable grate. The pan rests on the grate. The heat sources used are propane gas, alcohol, or solid fuel. It is used in the dining room for tableside preparation of food items. Some réchauds may be built into the guéridon, while others may be placed on the top of the guéridon. Utmost care must be taken when using this equipment because of the dangers involved in using flammable products in a dining room environment.

It is the responsibility of management to ensure that those using this equipment are trained properly (see Figure 2–14).

- All réchauds should be clean.
- The server should inspect the réchaud to ensure proper functioning.
- Refueling of the réchaud should never be performed in the dining room. It is done in an open, well-ventilated area.
- After refueling, the réchaud should be wiped clean of any spilled fuel before lighting.
- Light the réchaud with a match unless using propane gas.
- A spirit or liquor should never be added to an already flaming pan.
- The liquor bottle used should have a pour spout, or the liquor should be poured from a small silver pitcher.
- Never leave a lit réchaud unattended.
- Always extinguish the réchaud before moving the guéridon.
- When flambéing, remove the pan from the flame and bring it to the right of the guéridon. Add the liquor and return the pan to the flame.
- Tilt the pan at a 45-degree angle to allow the vapors of the liquor to ignite.

- When not in use, the réchaud should be stored on the lower shelf to the guéridon away from the traffic flow.

Blazer Pans

Blazer pans may be oval, rectangular, or round. The oval blazer-type pan should be made of copper or stainless steel. Copper, a more efficient conductor of heat, provides an even spread of heat throughout the pan relatively quickly. Copper has more aesthetic value and is thus preferred. The shape of the pan is generally designed to suit particular items; however, its use is not restricted to those items. For example, Crêpes Suzettes pans are copper-plated shallow pans, normally ranging in diameter from 9 to 16 inches. They are used primarily for tableside dessert items, particularly crêpes Suzette (see Figure 2–15).

Chauffe Plats

Chauffe plats are heat-retaining panels that may be stacked in a small battery at a convenient service point inside the dining room and brought to the guéridon for use as required. These are used for keeping foods warm when tableside plating is performed or when direct flame is not needed.

Flaming Swords

Flaming swords are swords designed specifically for flambé service. They resemble regular military swords, although the bowl-shaped guard is inverted to catch any drips. The food items, whether meat or vegetables, are flambéed on the sword in the kitchen and presented flaming to the guest, before being removed from the sword onto a plate (see Figure 2–16).

Wagon Service

Wagon service differs from French service in that the skill level and formality required is considerably less. It is usually employed as a carving cart. For example, the server carves prime rib tableside according to the specifications of the guest and places it on the guest's plate with the accompaniments. This type of service gives the illusion of being more elaborate and helps to sell featured items. The server should maintain the cleanliness of the cart and carving set at all times.

Russian or Silver Service

Russian service is used internationally for very formal banquets and at elegant restaurants. The food items are completely prepared and portioned in the kitchen and then placed on platters, in tureens, or on a service plate.

Figure 2–15 Blazer pans. (Left) Oval blazer pan, commonly used for trout and sole. (Middle) Rectangular blazer pan, commonly used for duckling. (Right) Round blazer pan, commonly used for crêpes Suzette and cherries jubilee.

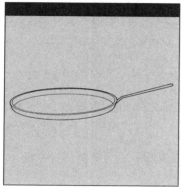

Figure 2–16 Flaming sword used in flambé service

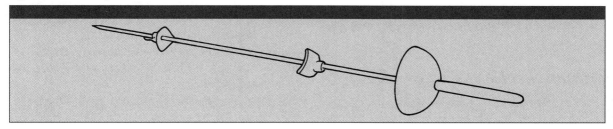

This service was developed in Russia during the reign of Catherine the Great. She was an avid admirer of French culture and imported a number of French chefs to her palace. To impress her court, the foods were beautifully prepared and displayed on silver platters. This service was copied by the French, who named it Silver service.

The procedure to be followed using Russian service is the same whether serving one guest in a restaurant or a number of guests in a banquet setting.

General Rules of Russian Service

- All food is completely prepared, portioned, and garnished prior to being placed on platters, in tureens, or on a service plate.
- All servers should have clean service towels draped over their left forearms.
- Beverages and empty plates, soup bowls, or salad plates are placed before the guest on the right side.
- One server or a team of servers can be involved.
- Items are served using the right hand from the left of each guest, the server standing with the left foot forward.
- When pureed foods are served as a starch, a separate serving spoon should be used.
- Service proceeds in a counterclockwise direction.
- Serving sets are used to transfer food from the platter to the guest's plate.
- A server must never use two of the same service utensil.
- All items are removed with the server's right hand from the right of the guest.

Tureen Service

- Preset the warmed soup plates or bowls on underliners.*
- Place the tureen of soup on a serviette underliner before leaving the kitchen, and place a ladle in or beside it.
- Remove the cover before approaching the table.
- Approach the guest from the left, with the tureen held in the server's left hand with the left foot forward.
- While holding the tureen in the left hand just above table level and as close to the soup plate or bowl as possible, ladle the soup.
- When ladling soup, draw the handle of the soup ladle toward yourself to avoid spillage. Replace the ladle in the tureen before moving to the next guest.
- Proceed in a counterclockwise direction.

Platter Service

- All foods are prepared, portioned, garnished, and placed on the platter in the kitchen.
- Warmed plates are placed from the right side of the guest prior to the food being presented.
- Platters are held in the left forearm and hand.
- Platters are held parallel to the table at all times.
- The platter is held to the left of the guest 1 to 2 inches above the table.
- The platter must never touch the table or cover.
- If there is a sauce boat on the service platter, it should be placed furthest away from the server and closest to the guest.

*See Appendix C for update.

- A clean service set is used for each new platter.
- A separate serving spoon is used for sauce.
- The service sets are used as described previously.

Russian Service of a Casserole

- Using the right hand, place the dinner plate containing the accompaniments before the guest from the guest's right side.
- Holding the casserole dish in the left hand by the underliner, and using a service set in the right hand, serve the entire contents of the casserole dish from the guest's left side as low and as close as possible to the guest's plate.
- Using the right hand, clear from the right of the guest.

Russian Banquet Service

- It is a very formal service seen at elaborate functions. Russian banquet service usually involves a team-type service, with each server assigned to a specific task.
- White gloves are generally worn at these events.
- It can be executed as controlled service in a precise parade-like manner. Each server stands at the same designated place, or the servers line the perimeter of the dining room.
- On a given signal from the headwaiter, such as the nod of his head, the waitstaff enters and leaves the dining room in unison and in a single file.
- All actions of the waitstaff are orchestrated so that their actions are synchronized. In the team service, for example, one server places the warmed soup bowls, while the other follows to ladle the soup. While one server places the main food item onto the guests' plates, another serves the accompaniments and a third ladles sauce.
- Servers or teams of servers begin and end the serving of each course for their designated guests at the same time.

The advantages and disadvantages of Russian Service are as follows:

Advantages

It is ideal for serving a function in an elaborate way. The food can be displayed impressively.

It is quicker service than French service.

The waitstaff does not have to have the same skill level as for French service.

The guests are generally given more space at the table.

Food quality can be controlled by the kitchen staff more easily than in French service.

Guests can determine the amount of food placed on their plates.

Disadvantages

There is less flexibility in positioning tables.

Servers have to be skilled in handling service sets.

There are high equipment costs in the initial purchase.

There is a high risk of theft of silver tableware.

There are numerous restrictions placed on menu selections.

The last guests served face an unappetizing platter.

There is excessive temperature loss in the food items served on a platter.

Family-Style Service

Family-style service is used in a casual dining atmosphere. It is particularly prevalent in the South. Guests serve themselves and pass the food around the table for each guest. This service creates an atmosphere of eating dinner at home with the family.

- The dishes are prepared completely in the kitchen but are placed on platters, tureens, or casseroles and then placed in the center of the guests' table.
- An appropriate serving utensil is placed beside the food.
- Guests pass each food item to the next person after serving themselves.
- Modern American plate service protocol is used for clearing.
- This style of service is usually combined with other

styles when serving a number of courses, especially for banquets, at which the entrée is individually plated and served using modern American plated service. The accompaniments may be served family style.

Server responsibilities include

- Ensuring that serviceware temperature is appropriate to the dish served
- Presenting tureens on underliners
- Placing appropriate serving utensils with each tureen or platter
- Removing all serviceware when emptied by the guests and replenishing if necessary

Note: If children are present at the table, servers should offer to help plate.

The advantages and disadvantages of family-style service are as follows:

Advantages

It is cost effective for dining room labor.
If used propitiously, it can give the guests the sense of good value.
It helps provide a warm and informal atmosphere.
Guests can determine their own portion sizes.

Disadvantages

It lacks personalized service.
There is no expertise in plate presentation.
Portion control is minimized.
It can create a great deal of food waste.

Butler Service

Butler service is most often employed at a banquet reception. The server carries the prepared food on a silver tray and allows the guest to select whatever she would like. For bite-sized hors d'oeuvre, this is a very cost-effective and efficient method of serving a large number of guests.

- The server not only carries the hors d'oeuvre tray or platter but offers a cocktail napkin with each serving.

- The cocktail napkins should be fanned in a spiral and held in the right hand, if no space is available on the tray.
- If a large rectangular tray with handles is used, cocktail napkins must be placed on the tray, because the server carries it by the handles.
- There must be appropriate frill picks for small bite-sized items.
- Tray stands or jacks must be draped with linen and lined with a service tray. There should be one tray stand per 25 guests.
- One server per 50 guests should circulate the room to collect empty beverage glasses and used cocktail napkins onto a beverage tray.

Sit-Down Butler Service

For a full-service meal, one would most likely find this type of service at a banquet or a private club. The advantage for guests is that they can select as little or as much as they would like of any food offered.

The rules of service are as follows:

- Food items are prepared completely and placed on platters or in tureens.
- The guests' bowls, cups, or plates are preset before each course.
- Appropriate service utensils are placed in or on the serviceware.
- Food is presented to the guest's left side, as in Russian service, but with the handles of the service utensils pointed closest to the guest.
- Guests serve themselves.
- Serviceware is not placed on the table.
- If the food is presented a second time, all food is presented on clean serviceware with clean service utensils.
- Standard rules of protocol are used.

The advantages and the disadvantages of butler service are as follows:

Advantages

It is cost effective and efficient for serving guests at a stand-up reception.

It allows the guest to select how much of a food item she desires.

It allows for a creative display of the food on a tray.

Disadvantages

There is no portion control.

If guests choose not to serve themselves, the host might be embarrassed.

If guests are not dextrous, the presentation of food on their plates might not be as appetizing.

In a stand-up reception, many cocktail napkins are wasted needlessly.

English Service

English service is most often combined with other styles of service, such as modern American plated service and family-style service. In English service, the main course is carved by the host. English service is conducted primarily in private homes. On occasions such as Thanksgiving and Christmas, it also can be utilized in a restaurant setting. When using this style, it is best to use a prix-fixe style of menu.

Buffet Service

Buffets are used in both à la carte and banquet settings, although they are much more commonplace in the latter. One would typically find the buffet used for a Sunday brunch as well as in a family-style restaurant.

A buffet is a table where all the food prepared in the kitchen is attractively displayed in the dining room (see Figure 2–17). There are many types of tables that can be used to augment the presentation. The buffet can encompass both cold and hot foods. Cold food platters should be kept chilled, while hot food can be kept at a safe temperature zone by placing it in chafing pans. There are sanitary regulations that should be observed by utilizing a sneeze guard and maintaining proper temperatures to ensure the safety of the customer. Today, these regulations are becoming more commonplace in the foodservice industry.

There are three types of buffet service:

1. Simple Buffet
2. Modified Deluxe
3. Deluxe

The *simple buffet* hardly rates as a service, because it is basically nonstaffed. The customers serve themselves to all food, utensils, and beverages. The server is responsible only for setting up, replenishing and breaking down the buffet table, clearing the customers' tables, and presenting the check. This buffet might be utilized in a conference center or hotel, where a buffet might be wheeled into a meeting room to allow the customers to serve themselves during their meeting.

The *modified deluxe buffet* requires the servers to serve beverages and perhaps the dessert course. The customer serves himself to the appetizer or salad and entrées. In some cases, a chef is positioned at the carving station. This type of buffet is most often used in the foodservice industry.

The *deluxe buffet* provides the guest with the most service. All of the courses are plated and served to the customer, with the exception of the entrée. In this service, **buffetiers** may assist the guests with the entrée choices.

Modern American plated service is generally used in buffets. The responsibilities of the servers are lessened by the self-service aspects of buffets, so the ratio of guests to server is greater. With the modified deluxe buffet, there are up to 40 customers per server in a banquet, but only 30 customers per server with the deluxe buffet.

The server's responsibilities include

Figure 2–17 Buffet table layout

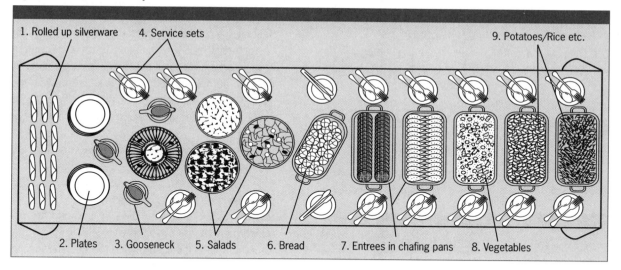

1. Rolled up silverware   4. Service sets   9. Potatoes/Rice etc.

2. Plates   3. Gooseneck   5. Salads   6. Bread   7. Entrees in chafing pans   8. Vegetables

- Following standard rules of protocol
- In a banquet, inviting the guests up to the table
- In an à la carte setting, informing the guests of the available choices and making recommendations
- Serving and clearing all beverages
- Serving any plated or portioned course using modern American plated service
- Keeping a close eye on the assigned tables and clearing any soiled plates and flatware
- Replacing flatware as needed
- Folding guests' napkins neatly to the side of the cover each time the guests go to the buffet
- Helping women with their seats
- Presenting the check

In addition to the server, buffets require the position of the **buffetier.** The buffetier's responsibilities include

- Knowing all of the ingredients and method of preparation of each food item.
- Being able to articulate this knowledge effectively to the guest.
- Ensuring the proper positioning of the buffet table(s). The service staff must be aware of the traffic flow that the customers will create in coming to the buffet

table. For example, if the buffet tables are placed too close to guests' tables, seated guests could be bumped by the customers at the buffet line. The traffic flow of the buffet line should run from left to right (when facing the table). This enables the guest to hold her plate in her left hand and use the service utensils with her right hand. Additionally, if there are separate courses offered in the buffet, it is advantageous to separate the buffet tables.

- Considering the number of customers that a buffet table can accommodate. One side of a buffet is referred to as a **line.** A buffet line can accommodate between 75 and 125 customers, depending on the type of buffet. Management would determine whether to run another line if this number is exceeded.
- Ensuring the proper organization of the buffet table. Cold items are displayed first and hot items last.
- Generally, determining the order in which the food items are placed via the joint efforts of the chef and dining room staff. Entrées may be placed before the vegetables and accompaniments. If there is a carving station, it would be placed at the end of the buffet line.
- Placing hot foods in a chafing pan. The insert pan is

filled at least a third full with *hot* water. At least two sources for heat are used, unless an electric heating element is chosen (see Figure 2–18).

- Keeping the buffet surface clean at all times
- Checking the cleanliness of both sides of all plates before arranging them on the tables
- Chilling the appetizer and salad plates for the appetizer and salad courses
- Heating the dinner plates so that they are warm to the touch. (Do not overheat the plates.)

Figure 2–18 Chafing dish shown with foldback lid in closed and open positions

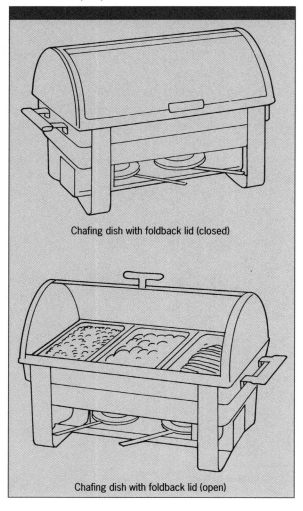

Chafing dish with foldback lid (closed)

Chafing dish with foldback lid (open)

- Replenishing any service utensils whose handles have become soiled
- Keeping the food pans covered at all times when the customers are not serving themselves. (*Note:* Chafers have attached lids, lids that hinge from the side or that can be held in place by harps, which allow the lids to hang 18 inches above the pan. If using a hinged chafer, ensure that the side of the hinge is away from the guest.)
- Placing any pan with shingled food items so that the first piece is on top, not under the piece behind it. If it is a two-sided buffet, the food should be shingled in two lines opposite to each other.
- Reordering hot food when the pan is a third full and replenishing before it is empty
- Reordering food if it has remained in the pan too long and the appearance or texture has diminished (e.g., the discoloration of scrambled eggs)
- Never transferring food from one bowl, pan, or platter to another in the dining room
- Placing all accompaniments and condiments by the appropriate item—for example, different choices of salad dressings would be placed right after the salad(s).
- Using appropriate serviceware for all condiments on appropriate underliners
- Never stacking plates too high (no more than 30 plates to a stack)
- Replenishing plates or bowls before they are all used
- Informing the chef of the status of the buffet on a regular basis
- For large numbers of guests, possibly utilizing a **runner** to carry the food from the kitchen to the dining room and empty pans back to the kitchen
- Changing a hot chafing pan safely, by requiring two people. One buffetier removes the used pan, while the other server replaces it with a new pan in the chafer.
- Only removing a used pan when the replacement pan is ready to take its place
- Cautioning any guests when approaching the buffet with a hot pan or when replacing the pan
- Always using a service towel to change chafing pans

- When breaking down the buffet, ensuring that all left-over food is discarded. The chef may want to be informed of any significant amounts of left-over food.
- Wiping the table clean.
- Covering chafing pans. Extinguish all sterno fuel containers before moving the chafing unit.
- Discarding the hot water in a safe manner
- Saving for future use any sternos that are not empty
- Cleaning the chafing unit thoroughly before storing
- Breaking down the buffet table once the guests have left the room

The advantages and the disadvantages of buffet service are as follows:

Advantages

Customers have a wider selection of foods from which to choose.

Customers can choose as much food as they would like.

Buffets can present the customers with an impressive food display.

There are lower dining room labor costs.

It provides an outlet for excess foods and for the creativity of the chef.

If managed properly, it can expedite service time.

Disadvantages

Customers serve themselves.

There is no food-portion cost control.

There is left-over food.

There is a considerable lag between the first and last table of customers serving themselves.

The appearance of the buffet can suffer if it is not properly maintained.

Customers with physical disabilities may be placed at a greater disadvantage.

3

Dining Room Environment and Equipment

3

Dining Room Environment and Equipment

By environment, *we are referring to the colors, textures, sounds, and smells that create an image and experience.*

The Environment

The environment of the establishment dictates the type of menu and the style of service that is employed. This symbiotic relationship will create a "concept" to which the guest can easily relate.

Each element that helps to create the environment is critical. For example, harsh lighting would be inimical to creating a soft and romantic mood. The playing of heavy metal music in a fine dining restaurant would be equally discordant. Unpadded hardwood chairs would be inappropriate to relaxing in a leisurely fine-dining restaurant. The exotic spicy aromas of Indian cuisine would be anomalous in an Italian restaurant.

Just as significant is the tableware and serviceware, which need to fit into the concept that the establishment is trying to create. Servers need a complete understanding of all dining room equipment and its proper usage to be able to provide quality service.

Quality service begins with properly preparing and placing all equipment needed so as to ensure smooth and efficient service. Each establishment will have clearly defined duties for each service member to perform prior to the opening of the dining room to the public. These duties are referred to as **side work.** Although side work may vary by establishment, it typically includes

1. Setting tables for service
2. Cleaning and refilling salt and pepper shakers
3. Refilling sugar bowls
4. Cleaning and refilling vinegar and oil cruets
5. Folding napkins for service
6. Polishing flatware and glassware
7. Stocking side stations for service

Dining Room Equipment and Serviceware

The Table

A primary concern in selecting the table size is not only the layout of the dining room, but also the amount of space available for each guest. The style of menu and service will dictate the type of cover that will be used. This will influence the amount of space needed for the cover. It may be as simple as a napkin and a bread-and-butter plate or as elaborate as a show plate, appetizer fork and knife, soup spoon, salad fork and knife, dinner fork and knife, dessert fork and teaspoon, water glass, and three wine glasses.

- Most establishments place additional items on the cover to enhance the aesthetics of the table.
- Linen may or may not be used as a tabletop. It adds to the ambience of the dining room and acts as a silencer, reducing the noise level. The types and styles of linen will be discussed further.
- The arrangement of the tables in the dining room is significant for two reasons. First, it helps to create a sense of order, which is important in creating a positive impression on the guest, and second, it affects the flow of traffic in the room, which impacts on the guest's comfort.
- The type of seat used is of great significance and must fit the concept of the establishment. A comfortable chair lends itself to a more leisurely paced dining experience. This can work against the establishment's turnover rate, so such seats would be found in a fine-dining restaurant.

- There should be sufficient space between each chair for the guests' comfort, so they can be seated and leave the table with ease.
- The chair should be centered to each cover at the table.
- The seat of the chair should barely touch the overhanging tablecloth.
- The chairs should be placed at a table with their legs away from the table legs so that they don't discomfit the guest.

The establishment determines the table setting, but the three most important factors for setting the table are cleanliness, guest comfort, and uniformity. All preset items should be spotless; anything less will cause the guest to question the sanitary practices of the establishment.

- If the settings are placed too closely together, it will be to the discomfort of the guest.
- If the place settings are not uniform, it will draw attention to the jarring incongruence. Guests may question the degree of attention to detail by the server and lose confidence in their selection of the establishment.
- To achieve uniformity of appearance, it is best to place tables with the legs positioned to the corners of the room.
- If a round table is set with an even number of settings, each setting should align with the setting directly across the table. The table is divided into an even number of wedge-shaped sections. When setting a table for two, called a deuce, the settings should be directly across from each other.

Setting a round table with an odd number of settings requires that each place setting align directly between two place settings across the table. Figure 3–1 illustrates this setting. It is important that care be taken to ensure equal distance between settings to maintain uniformity.

Table Settings

Whether setting with paper placemats or fine linen, the server must ensure that not only the tabletop is clean, but

Figure 3–1 A round table with an odd number of settings

also chairs, benches, and the area around each table. Constant inspection of the table should take place during service, particularly when tables are being reset.

When using a placemat , whether paper, vinyl, or linen, it should be centered on the cover, or guest's position, about 1 inch from the edge of the table. A napkin (paper or cloth) may be placed to the left side of the mat or in the center. Placement of flatware, vases, condiment trays, salt and pepper shakers, and any other item should be consistent and uniform on each table.

- When placing a cloth on the table, ensure that the sewn seam is on the underside and not visible to the guest. The cloth should be placed so that it falls evenly on all sides.
- Ideally, cloths should not fall below the surface or cushion of each seat.
- When setting a round table with four legs, as opposed to a round table with a pedestal, the tablecloth should be laid to allow the corners of the cloth to hide the legs of the table.
- Cloths that are stained, torn, frayed, or contain burn

marks or holes should be sent for repairs or converted into rags. Never attempt to hide stains or holes by placing vases or ashtrays over them. These cloths should be folded neatly and tagged so that they are separated from the inventory in use.

- Cloth napkins should be placed in the center of the setting unless a show plate is utilized. Covering the show plate defeats the purpose of using a decorative plate. The napkin can then be placed to the side or above the place setting.

Note: The undersides of tabletops should be checked for any chewing gum that may have been placed by a guest.

Whether setting flatware for breakfast, lunch, dinner, or banquet service, it is essential to follow certain rules:

- The show plate or napkin should be placed first, to center each place setting.
- The place setting should allow the placement of the largest service or show plate in the center without requiring moving the utensils when serving.
- Forks are set on the left side of the cover.
- Knives and spoons are set on the right side of the cover.
- Knives are always set with the cutting edge toward the center of the place setting.
- Flatware should be placed so that it does not hang over the edge of the table. One inch from the edge of the table is standard.
- Any other flatware will be placed parallel to the entrée knife and fork. The flatware can be staggered or placed with the handles at the same distance from the edge of the table.
- All flatware is set from the outside in, following the sequence of use.
- Flatware must not be placed to the inside of the entrée knife and fork.
- The dessert fork and spoon is placed on the top of the cover perpendicular to the other flatware.
- Bread-and-butter plates are set on the left, next to or above the forks.
- The water glass is set above the tip of the dinner knife. Wine glasses are set from the outside, following the sequence of use.

- If several wine glasses are preset in a **flight,** or row, the water glass may be set directly above the place setting or off to the right.
- Coffee and tea cups are preset to the right of the knives and spoons, with handles at the 4 o'clock position.
- China, flatware, and glassware should not touch.
- On rectangular, square, or round tables with an even number of settings, all flatware items on one place setting should be aligned with those on the opposite side in a straight line.
- In some European countries, forks are set with the prongs facing down and knives are set on **knife rests** to prevent damaging the table cloth.
- If each cover includes an entrée knife and fork and is set directly across from another cover, each knife is placed directly across from the fork.
- Each establishment will require different settings to suit the needs of the menu.

The following is a typical lunch or dinner table setting (see Figure 3–2):

1. Salad fork or dinner fork
2. Dinner fork
3. Napkin
4. Dinner knife
5. Teaspoon
6. Spoon
7. Bread-and-butter plate
8. Butter knife
9. Water glass

Figure 3–2 Lunch and dinner table setting

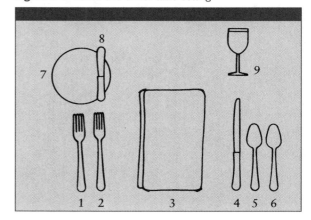

À la Carte Place Setting

When guests are served an à la carte menu, a basic table setting is placed on the table in advance. The guest chooses each desired food item from the menu, and the appropriate flatware is brought to the table using a serviette (see Figure 3–3).

1. Show plate
2. Napkin
3. Dinner knife
4. Dinner fork
5. Bread-and-butter plate
6. Butter knife
7. Wine glass

Preset Menu

A preset menu is a meal served to a group of guests who have determined the menu and the time of service in advance, such as in a banquet. The table setting will be set according to the particular menu as illustrated in the following settings. One example illustrates a banquet preset menu (see Figure 3–4); the other shows a continental breakfast.

Figure 3–3 French table setting, à la carte.

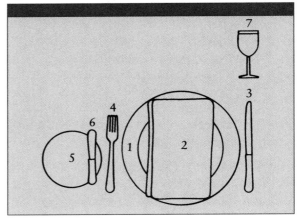

1. Bread-and-butter plate
2. Butter knife
3. Salad fork
4. Dinner fork
5. Dinner knife
6. Spoon
7. Coffee cup
8. Wine glass
9. Water glass
10. Dessert spoon
11. Dessert fork
12. Napkin
13. Show plate

Figure 3–4 Banquet preset menu table setting

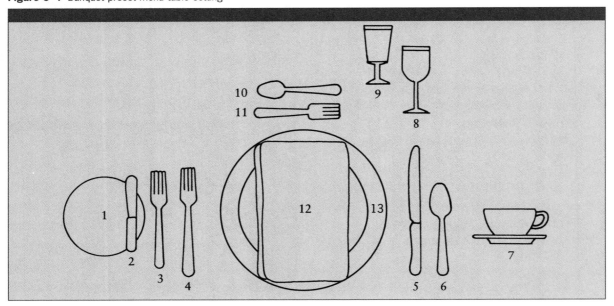

Continental Breakfast (see Figure 3–5)

1. Napkin
2. Bread-and-butter plate
3. Butter knife
4. Coffee cup and saucer
5. Coffee spoon
6. Creamer and sugar bowl
7. Juice glass
8. Water glass

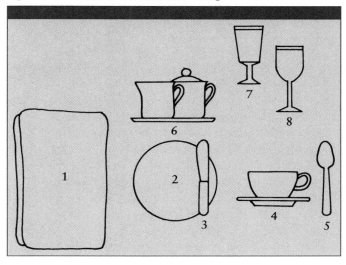

Figure 3–5 Continental breakfast table setting

The Food Tray (Oval)

A large oval food tray is used to allow servers to carry several dishes to the table at once. Food trays are usually lined with cork or rubber to prevent plate slippage and accidents. If food trays are not lined in this manner, a service napkin should be used to line the tray.

Basic handling of the tray is as follows:

- Carry a service tray in the left hand, above the shoulder. This is done to enable the server to proceed through a doorway without the door swinging back and hitting the tray.
- The tray should always be placed on a tray stand, with the length of the tray crossing the bars of the tray stand.
- Distribute items on the tray so that the tray is as evenly balanced as possible.
- Place tall or heavier items in the center of the tray.
- Never stack plates on top of food when clearing a guest's table.
- Remove all flatware from plates and place off to the side on the tray.
- When setting up the tray, do not place it close to the guest's table. (It is not part of the guest's dining experience.)
- Always carry the food tray over the shoulder, never at the side of the body, even if the tray is empty.
- Signal a server in front of you by saying, "Behind you," to prevent collisions.
- Be particularly alert when walking behind guests in case they stop suddenly.
- Never carry glassware on a food tray. Glassware is carried only on a beverage tray.
- After clearing a guest's table, cover the tray with a service towel before carrying it from the dining room.
- Never leave unsightly trays in the dining room. As soon as the table is cleared, remove the tray from the dining room.

The Beverage Tray

A beverage tray is a small hand-held tray used in the service of any beverage. General rules for the use of this tray are as follows:

- Ensure that the tray is clean and dry before being used at a table.
- Place all glasses or cups as close to the center of gravity as possible and continue to adjust the position of these items as the service from the tray proceeds.
- Carry the tray at waist level and in the left hand.
- Never hold the tray between the server and the guest or the server and the table.
- Be particularly careful not to tilt the beverage tray at an angle when placing the beverage onto the table. (*Note:* If you tuck your left elbow into your side, you are less likely to spill the remaining beverages on the tray.)
- Hold the tray with the left hand under the center of the tray, not by the edge.
- When removing glassware from a beverage tray, always hold the glasses from the base, with fingers away from the rim of the glassware.
- Never allow a guest to remove items from a beverage tray held by the server.

Tray Stands (Jacks)

Tray stands, or jacks, have collapsible leg frames, usually connected by two cloth or fiber support straps to hold the legs rigid when set up. Frames can be heavy plastic, wood, or metal. Some include a low-level shelf that can be used as a small side stand.

When not in use, stands should be collapsed and placed out of busy traffic lanes to prevent accidents. Some establishments designate permanent locations in the dining room for tray stands. Other establishments require the service staff to carry the stands with them as they carry food trays in and out of the dining room. The following procedures should be observed:

- Carry the tray on the palm or fingertips, depending on its weight.
- Use the left shoulder to help balance the tray, if necessary.
- Carry the tray stand in the collapsed position on your right, while walking in the dining room.

- Extend the right arm, which holds the tray stand and flick the wrist so that the support legs separate, bringing the tray stand to an upright position. The legs should be parallel to the body.
- Turn to the right, bend the knee, and lower the tray in a horizontal position until it sits on the support frame. Slide the tray across the top of the frame so that its weight is distributed evenly.
- When picking up or placing down a loaded tray, keep the back straight and bend and lift with the knees and legs.

When removing the tray, reverse the process. Collapse the tray stand against the right hip, while holding the tray level.

Glassware

There are many styles of glassware in the foodservice industry. Restaurateurs are faced with numerous patterns and varying degrees of cost and quality. Each operator will select the glassware that best suits the particular needs of the operation, but caution should be taken because patterns are frequently discontinued, all of the glassware will need to be replaced if supplies become unavailable. The glassware available to the foodservice operator falls into two general categories: heat-treated and lead crystal (see Figure 3–6).

Heat-Treated Glassware

Most glassware used in the food service industry is heat-treated. This process involves heating the glass and cooling it rapidly. This is a mild form of tempering that gives strength to the glass, adding resistance to chipping and breakage. Heat-treated glassware by manufacturers such as Cardinal Glassware is recommended for high-volume establishments.

Figure 3–6 Types of glassware.

Bordeaux Bordeaux white Burgandy red Burgandy white Rheingau Hock wine Prestige cuvee

Muscato Champagne flute Port Brandy snifter Sherry Footed pilsner Mug

Pilsner Rocks Footed rocks Highball Footed highball Zombie sling Old-fashioned Whiskey sour

(continued)

Figure 3–6 Types of glassware (continued)

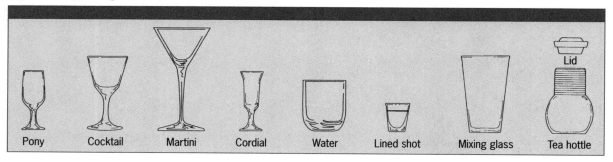

Pony Cocktail Martini Cordial Water Lined shot Mixing glass Lid Tea hottle

Lead Crystal

Often called 24% lead crystal, it is glassware that has lead oxide added during the formation of the glass. This creates a very hard glass and adds brilliance and clarity. Crystal glassware is expensive, chips easily, and is not conducive to high-volume establishments. Most crystal glassware is found in fine-dining establishments where the emphasis is on a formal, relaxed atmosphere.

Crystalware can be machine made or hand blown. Hand-blown crystal is the most expensive type of crystal and is found in only the most exclusive establishments. Some manufacturers, such as Schott Zweisel, make a crystal glass bowl that is attached to a heat-treated glass stem; this is considerably less expensive and is popular with upscale fine-dining establishments. Glassware should be handled with care at all times.

The style of glass and its shape are significant when tasting wine. The many different sizes and shapes of wine glasses affect the way in which the aromas and flavors are perceived. The basic styles are Bordeaux white and red wine glasses, Burgundian white and red, Treviris Mosel and a Hock glass, a champagne flute or tulip, a sherry copita, and a port glass.

The following guidelines for the use and care of glassware should be observed:

- Glassware should be stored in an appropriate glass rack.

- A glass rack's height should exceed the length of a stemmed glass.
- Stems should not be in contact with each other.
- Glassware should be placed upside down in a rack.
- Glassware should always be held by the stem or base.
- If steaming a clean glass, use a lint-free cloth.
- Glassware should be free of cracks or chips.
- All glassware should be cleaned to an immaculate state.
- When carrying glasses in the dining room, a beverage tray should be used.
- When storing glasses on a shelf, they must be placed upside down on air mats.

Corkscrews

There are many different models of corkscrews, ranging from the first patented design of the Henshall to the Leverpull of the 1980s . The Romans used cork as a stopper, but this use had long been forgotten until the middle of the sixteenth century. The first known written reference to a corkscrew was in 1681 by an Englishman. The key to any good corkscrew is that its worm not to be too thick and that its edges be sharp enough to cut into the cork, rather than tear it. The most commonplace corkscrew in the food service industry is "the waiter's friend." This corkscrew most often has a knife blade to cut the capsule

Figure 3–7 Corkscrews. The waiter's friend is best adapted for restaurant service.

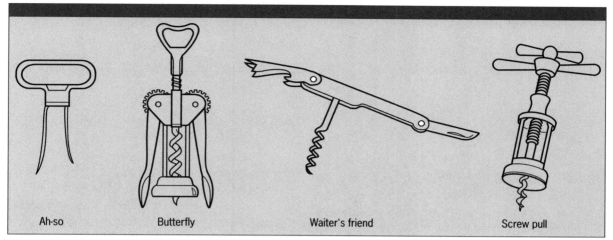

Ah-so   Butterfly   Waiter's friend   Screw pull

of the wine bottle. Its edge should be kept sharpened. This corkscrew should have five turns to the screw, and the server should ensure that the worm is not bent, but straight, in order to maximize its effectiveness (see Figure 3–7).

Tableware: Plateware

Pottery

The term *pottery* applies to clay products made of unrefined clays. As a generic name, *pottery* includes all fired clayware. As a specific name, it describes low-fired porous clayware, which is generally colored.

Ceramic products acquire strength through the application of heat. Along with the heat, the chemical composition of the materials used determines the strength, porosity, and vitrification of the fired product. There are many types of tableware available to the restaurateur. The final choice is determined by how it fits into the concept of the establishment and its cost.

Earthenware

Earthenware is a porous type of ceramic product that, fired at comparatively low temperatures, produces an opaque body not as strong as stoneware or china. The product may be glazed or unglazed.

Stoneware

Stoneware is a nonporous ceramic product made of unprocessed clays, or clay and flux additives, fired at elevated temperatures. It is quite durable but lacks the translucence and whiteness of china. It is resistant to chipping. It differs from porcelain in that it produces colors other than white. These result from the iron or other impurities in the clay.

Ironstoneware

Ironstoneware is the historic term for the durable English stoneware. The composition and properties of this product are similar to porcelain, except that the body is not translucent and is off-white.

Cookingware

Cookingware is a broad term applied to earthenware, stoneware, porcelain, and china designed for cooking or baking as well as serving. It has a smooth, glazed surface and is strong and resistant to thermal shock.

Fine China

Fine china is a term applied to a thin, translucent, vitrified product generally fired twice at relatively high temperatures: first, to mature the purest of flint, clay, and flux materials; and second, to develop the high gloss of the beautiful glaze. Fine china is the highest quality tableware made for the domestic or retail trade.

Porcelain

Porcelain is a term used frequently in Europe to mean china. European porcelain, like china, is fired twice. In the United States, porcelain may be fired in a one- or two-fire process. Porcelain has a hard, nonabsorbent, strong body that is white and translucent. European porcelain is made primarily for the retail market, but manufacturers such as Lennox and Rosenthal make commercial-grade porcelain, which is purchased by upscale hotel and fine-dining establishments.

Bone China

Bone china is a specific type of china manufactured primarily in England. The body contains a high proportion of bone ash to produce greater translucency, whiteness, and strength. Like fine china, it is made primarily for the retail trade.

Restaurant China

Restaurant china is a uniquely American blend of china and porcelain, designed and engineered specifically for use in commercial operations. The body was developed in the United States to give it greater impact strength and durability, as well as extremely low absorption, which is required of china used in public establishments. Decorations are applied between the body and the glaze, thereby protecting the decoration during commercial use. Most of this tableware is subject to a high temperature during its first firing and a lower temperature during its second. Some restaurant china, however, is fired in a one-fire operation, during which the body and glaze mature at the same time. Like fine china, America restaurant china is vitrified.

The following guidelines for handling china should be observed:

- Check all china for cleanliness prior to service.
- Store all china by category.
- Store china soup and coffee cups in appropriate racks.
- Handle china plates by the rim.
- Avoid overstacking china cups.
- Do not stack cups with handles.
- Use underliners for china cups and bowls.
- Bleach all coffee cups every 2 weeks or according to the establishment's policies.
- Do not use china that has chips or clearly visible cracks. (The manager should make the decision on how to dispose of damaged china.)

Flatware and Cutlery

The term *flatware* refers to all dining utensils, such as forks, spoons, and knives. *Cutlery* refers to all knives. The selection of flatware is determined by the concept of the establishment. The composition can vary from different quality grades of stainless steel to silver, and there are many styles available (see Figure 3–8). In handling flatware and cutlery within the dining room, the following guidelines should be observed:

- Use a clean side towel to wipe all flatware before placing it on the table.
- Carry flatware through a dining room on a serviette.
- Place flatware on the appropriate side of the guest's cover.
- Handle flatware by the "waist," or midsection, so that fingers do not come in contact with the end of the utensil that will go into the customer's mouth or leave fingerprints on the handles.
- Place most flatware parallel to each other and perpendicular to the table. On round tables, the flatware should not follow the contour of the edge of the table.

Figure 3–8 A selection of flatware and cutlery

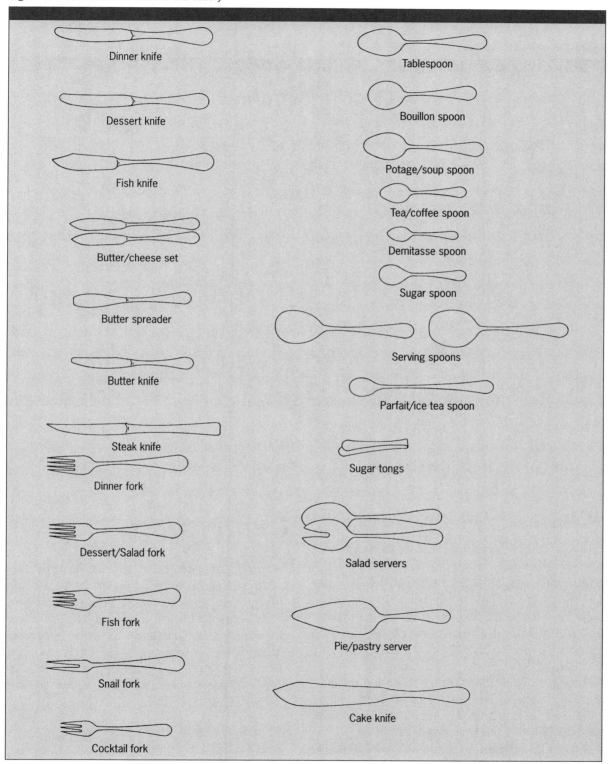

Dinner knife

Tablespoon

Dessert knife

Bouillon spoon

Fish knife

Potage/soup spoon

Butter/cheese set

Tea/coffee spoon

Butter spreader

Demitasse spoon

Butter knife

Sugar spoon

Steak knife

Serving spoons

Dinner fork

Parfait/ice tea spoon

Dessert/Salad fork

Sugar tongs

Fish fork

Salad servers

Snail fork

Pie/pastry server

Cocktail fork

Cake knife

Figure 3–8 A selection of flatware and cutlery (continued)

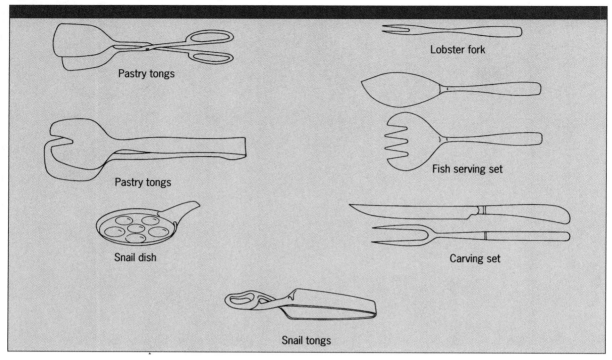

Pastry tongs

Lobster fork

Pastry tongs

Fish serving set

Snail dish

Carving set

Snail tongs

- Preset dessert forks and spoons horizontally on the top of the cover, with the spoon above the fork.

only if the correctly sized holloware piece is used and if it is properly maintained and cleaned (see Figure 3–9).

Holloware

Holloware is a term that originally described service pieces that were hollow but now includes the following: chafing dishes, coffee urns, samovars, coffee pitchers, tea pots, creamers, water pitchers, sauce boats, goose necks, sugar bowls or basins, tureens, silver salt and pepper shakers, butter dishes, compotes, silver bowls, oval platters, round platters, rectangular serving trays, plate covers, cloches, torte stands, tiered pastry stands, cake server holders, wine stands, wine buckets and coolers, champagne buckets, and candlesticks and candelabra.

Holloware can be of different quality levels, from different grades of stainless steel to sterling silver. The purpose is to enhance the presentation of a meal, which can occur

Centerpieces

Centerpieces are decorative objects that are placed on a table to enhance its aesthetics and attract the attention of the guests. Depending on the table setting and the concept of an establishment, a table without a centerpiece can look barren. Centerpieces can be used for the guests' or buffet tables. Centerpieces for buffet tables allow the establishment more dramatic license, but the rules discussed here are as applicable. There are five types of centerpieces:

1. Floral and foliage
2. Edible

Figure 3–9 Types of holloware

Water pitcher

Soup tureen with lid

Champagne bucket

Teapot, 8 oz. / coffeepot, 32 oz.

Soup ladle

Cake server holder

Water pitcher with ice guard

Cloche (plate cover)

Plate cover (stackable)

Pastry display stand
(three tier)

Sugar basin with lid

Sugar basin

Sauce boat

Wine bucket

Table crumber/scraper

Sauce ladle

Wine stand

3. Sculpted
4. Ceramic
5. Lighting pieces

Floral Centerpieces

Floral centerpieces can be made from fresh flowers, foliage, dried flowers, and silk or synthetic flowers and foliage. When selecting floral centerpieces, one should take a number of factors into account. The floral selection should be sized properly to the table. The centerpiece should not be an obstruction or impediment to the guest. When selecting a centerpiece, the following considerations should be examined: the theme of the event, the seasonality, the color coordination with the colors of the tabletop and the establishment, the condition of the flowers and foliage, the scent of the flowers, and the cost. The scent of the flowers should in no way interfere with the food or wine being served.

The disadvantage to using fresh flowers and foliage is not only the cost and availability, but also the care needed on the part of the servers if the centerpieces are to be reused. Flowers need to be removed from their containers (bud or flower vase) at the end of the day, placed in a suitable storage vessel under refrigeration, and the stems recut to maintain their fresh appearance. The flower container, bud or flower vase, needs to be cleaned daily.

The advantage of using synthetic arrangements is that they can be reused for extended periods if properly tended. The establishment will have to provide the necessary storage space. Dried and synthetic flowers are initially expensive if they appear to be a reasonable facsimile to fresh flowers. Caution should be used in selecting dried, silk, or synthetic arrangements if candles or heavy smoking is expected. Local fire ordinances may prohibit their use.

Almost as significant as the selection of flowers is the container in which they are placed. The containers can range from a simple bud vase to an elaborate flower vase. Vases should be sized according to the arrangement, appear free of chips or cracks, and always be kept clean. Glass vases are generally the least expensive, but they have the disadvantage of revealing the stems of the flowers.

Edible Centerpieces

Edible centerpieces are of three types: natural, carved, or sugar-based. Natural foods would primarily include a carefully displayed bowl or epergne of a variety of fresh fruit. The arrangement may include nuts and be used in combination with flowers, which is traditionally French. A vegetable crudité display also might provide a colorful and appropriate enhancement.

Carved centerpieces include vegetable carvings, which can showcase the artistic skills of the chef. Although technically edible, one would not expect a guest to indulge. One should use the same considerations for a vegetable carving as for a fresh floral arrangement—that it is fresh in appearance and its aromas are not overpowering.

Sugar-based centerpieces may include very ornate or delicate show pieces, which should be both color and theme coordinated. Centerpieces also may include marzipan figures, which might replicate a bowl of fruit. Sugar centerpieces can be dramatic and showcase the artistry of the chef. The disadvantages include the temperature, humidity, and the delicate or brittle nature of the pieces. These centerpieces need to be displayed on an appropriate mirror or tray.

Sculpted Centerpieces

Sculpted centerpieces fall into five categories: tallow, beeswax, butter, chocolate, and ice carvings. The first four are seldomly seen today, but ice carvings are particularly appropriate for buffets. An appropriately sized and lit glow pan and base are necessary to hold the sculpture and ensure that the melted ice can drain unobstructed into a sufficiently large receptacle.

Ceramic Centerpieces

Ceramic centerpieces were particularly prevalent in the eighteenth and nineteenth centuries. The ceramic sculptures were often made by manufacturers to coincide with the patterns, colors, and themes of the plateware that was produced. Porcelain centerpieces are beautifully hand-crafted but are expensive and delicate.

Lighting Centerpieces

Lighting centerpieces are the most common type in the foodservice industry. They may range from antique and elaborate candelabra to a simple votive candle holder. The use of artificial light is generally limited to the evening hours and can be used to create a more soothing environment. Candlesticks and candelabra should be kept polished and should not obstruct the guests' view. Most municipalities have strict ordinances prohibiting the use of an open flame in a dining room. Most frequent is the use of votive or glass-enclosed candles, which can range from the plain and inexpensive to the elaborate and costly. Additionally, there are artificial lights on tables that can be electrically powered, battery operated, or lit by fuels. The server's primary concern should be the safety of the guest; this is achieved by maintaining the equipment properly and keeping it clean and serviceable.

Table Accessories

In addition to centerpieces, the server needs to be concerned with table accessories, which include dry sundries and condiments. Fine-dining establishments have minimal accessories, but high-volume establishments, where the wait staff is under severe time constraints, often have a number of accessories on the table at one time. Accessories include

Ashtrays
Matches
Straws
Napkin dispenser
Menu stands and table tents
Sugar
Sweeteners

Salt
Pepper
Cream
Relish or relish trays
Ketchup
Mustard
A-1 sauce
Tabasco sauce
Worcestershire sauce
Oil and vinegar cruets
Crackers

Linen

Linen is referred to as one of the "big four" in the foodservice industry: linen, china, flatware, and glassware. Linen is an expense that must be carefully controlled or there will be a negative impact on the profit-and-loss statement of the establishment. Due to the high capital expense for a laundering facility, only those establishments that have a large volume of business and are usually associated with a hotel can afford it. Because of the expense involved, many foodservice establishments are opting to forego the use of tablecloths and are using placemats, paper, vinyl, and glass tabletops.

The vast majority of establishments rent their linen from rental companies that specialize in linen. The operator, however, is still accountable for the linen that is rented. For example, the establishment will be charged at full value for missing linen. Many rental companies have an automatic replacement charge of 5%. It is critical that the establishment have an inventory control system and that it ensure that the linen is being used properly. A growing number of establishments are purchasing linen and contracting their laundering.

There are many different types, styles, and colors of linen, and the choices should reflect the environment and concept that is being created. Linen can enhance dramatically the appearance of a room. While many restaurants use accent pieces of linen, such as chintz or lace for a tea room, we will concern ourselves with napkins, tablecloths, and drapery linen, such as skirting.

There are three types of linen: **100% natural fibers,** such as cotton, flax, or linen; a **blend of cotton and polyester,** usually a 50-50 blend; and **100% polyester.** Polyesters have improved dramatically over the past few years and are becoming more prevalent in the foodservice industry. While these materials have the advantage of having better longevity and being color-fast, they have the disadvantage of lacking absorbency and holding many napkin folds. This is significant to servers if they are using the napkins as service towels or are instructed to fold the napkins in an elaborate fold.

The second factor that is of concern to the establishment is the type of weave, which gives the linen a particular appearance. **Momie** weave is prevalent in restaurants and is generally made from the cotton polyester blend. It gives the linen the appearance of richer texture. **Damask** is a heavier weave, which is always associated with elegantly patterned linens found in fine-dining establishments. Damask-woven linen was once made only of cotton, but today it can be made of all three types of linen. Cotton linens have the disadvantage of losing their shapes and colors, although operators can buy dye kits to resolve color fading.

There are standard guidelines for purchasing linen, but the difficulty is that there are many size variances according to the brand and fabric type. Linen is sold by three size types: **cut, finished,** and **laundered.** *Cut linen* refers to the size before it is hemmed or seamed. Finished cotton or blended linens are hemmed, while polyester linen is seamed by **merrowing** or **serging,** a process that gives the edge of the linen a rolled stitch. This has the disadvantage of the linen's being ruined if this stitch is cut. *Laundered size* is the size of linen after it is washed.

All linens will shrink at least 3%. If cotton linen is unmercerized, it will shrink up to 7%. **Mercerization** is the process of bathing the cotton in chemical additives, which gives it strength and durability. Many imported cottons are unmercerized and, although frequently less expensive, will wear out quickly. Many operators purchase linen without understanding these differences, which can result in the incorrect sizing of the tablecloth.

There is a standard guideline for purchasing tablecloths. The overhang on a square or rectangular table should be a minimum of 7 inches and a maximum of 12 inches. For round tables, the hang of the cloth should be 10 inches minimum.

It is important to note that when purchasing linens, there are standard sizes. If purchasing sizes are not among those in the following list, they are custom made and will cost considerably more. The server needs to recognize the appropriate sizes of all linens and their proper use so that costs are minimized. Standard sizes of tablecloths are as follows:

Square and rectangular	Round
36″ × 36″	51″ round
45″ × 45″	60″ round
54″ × 54″	69/72″ round
63″ × 63″	81″ round
72″ × 72″	87″ round
83″ × 83″	90″ round
54″ × 72″	120″ round
54″ × 96″	132″ round
54″ × 108/110″	
54″ × 120″	

Standard finished napkin sizes include the following:

17″ × 17″
20″ × 20″
22″ × 22″

Skirting

Skirting is specialized linen that is used for draping tables. Tables may be draped using tablecloths, but skirting is used more frequently because it has the advantage of saving on the cost of tablecloths and labor. It also gives a uniform appearance at all times. There are three styles of pleats that are currently available in skirting: **sheer, accordion,** and **box.** Sheer skirting is used as an overlay, such as lace. The accordion is sometimes referred to as a *closed pleat,* while a box pleat is referred to as an *open pleat.*

The standard height of skirting is 29 inches; all other lengths are customized. Skirting is attached to the table with clips, pins, or tape. If using clips, it is important to have a system that will control the use and inventory of the clips. Servers should have the technical skill to pleat a table using tablecloths, in the event that skirting is unavailable.

Linen Handling

When handling linen, the following guidelines should be observed:

- Obtain only the linen you will need for the shift, including 5% overage for emergencies.
- Treat the linen with care.
- Check that the order has been filled properly.
- Never place clean linen on a floor.
- Place the package of linen on a clean surface.
- Ensure that your hands are clean prior to handling linen.
- When storing tablecloths, place them on shelves with the folds facing out.
- Open the package of napkins and fold each napkin in half; restack them when storing.
- Organize the linen storage closet by type, size, and color.
- When in doubt, check the label of a cloth before unfolding it.
- Most linen companies have a specific fold for a specific size of tablecloth.
- Place tablecloths on the table with their seams facing down.
- Handle guest napkins as little as possible.
- When removing a tablecloth from the table during service, use the steps described in the section on resetting a table.
- Remove any debris from the tablecloth before folding and bagging it for laundering.

Napkin Folding

The napkin folds illustrated starting on page 98 are a few decorative presentations. The choice of which fold to use

in a dining room is determined by the personal taste of the owner or chef de service.

Table Draping for Buffets

Straight drape (see Figure 3–10)

- After the tables have been positioned, cover each with a silencer.

Figure 3–10 Pleated drapes

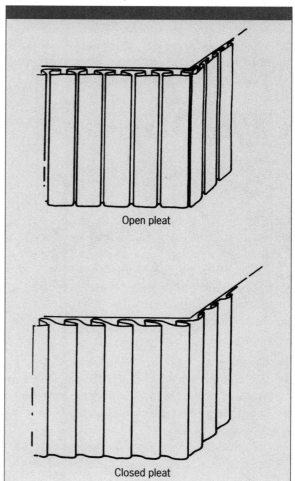

Open pleat

Closed pleat

- Lay draping cloth over the front of the table, allowing it to hang down 1½ to 2 inches from the floor.
- Do not allow the drape to touch the floor.
- Leave sufficient cloth to cover the side of the table.
- Pin the drape to the silencer.
- Cover the table with a cloth folded to the exact dimensions of the tabletop(s).

Pleated Drapes (see Figure 3–10)

- If using pleats, order three times the amount of cloths used for a straight pleat.
- Prepare the tables with silence cloths.
- Measure the desired pleat size by folding the cloth under, and hold it by pinning it to the silencer.
- Repeat the procedure until the table is fully draped.
- If using an accordion (closed) pleat, have the pleats folded away from the guests' approach to the table.
- When the table is fully draped, cover the top as in the directions for straight draping.

Coffee Makers

There are many different types as well as brands of coffee makers. There are machines that make only regular grind coffee and others that make only espresso and cappuccino. The mechanical features of these makers vary, as do the procedures for usage and maintenance. Most establishments lease the coffee makers from the company that is supplying the coffee. The advantages are that there is less capital expenditure and maintenance is provided by the company in a timely manner. The following guidelines should be observed when using most **drip** coffee makers (see Figure 3–11).

- Turn the maker on before each shift.
- Turn on the hot plates. Set adjustable plates to the high position, enabling water to boil for tea service.
- Do not place empty glass or near-empty coffee pots on warming plates.
- Use the coffee within 15 minutes of its being made.
- Keep coffee in a glass pot, not a reactive stainless steel pot.

Figure 3–11 Coffee makers

- Remove the used filter and grounds by hand, not by inverting the basket over a trash barrel.
- Shut off and/or unplug the machine.
- Remove the water spray fixture and clean it.
- Ensure that the filter basket is cleaned and replaced.

Glass and stainless steel coffee pots should be cleaned at the end of each shift. Use a commercial cleaner and brush or a mixture of vinegar or lemon juice, salt, and ice cubes, which will act as an abrasive.

Ice Makers and Bins

- Always treat ice as food!
- Always use metal or plastic scoops when obtaining ice. Never use a glass to scoop ice.
- Use a plastic scoop when serving ice into a glass.
- Do not leave an ice scoop in an ice maker after use. It is unsanitary and will be buried by new ice.
- Do not use the ice machine to chill any other objects or food.
- Ensure that the door or cover to the ice bin is closed when not in use.
- If glass breakage occurs within close proximity to the

ice bin or ice maker while the door is open, all ice should be emptied and the bin cleaned thoroughly.

- Keep the floor around the ice machine dry to prevent accidents.

Soda Machines

Soda can be dispensed by using a dispensing system with a gun. Two types of containers are currently on the market: the soda tank and the "bag in the box." If a tank system is used, each tank is connected to two plastic lines. One leads to the carbon dioxide (CO_2) tank and allows it to pressurize the soda syrup; the other line allows the soda to pass to the dispensing mechanism.

- A soda tank is completely empty when there is no visible color in the plastic line. The tank will also weigh considerably less. Each tank will have a tag attached to it indicating if it is full or empty. The server should detach the portion of the tag indicating it is empty when changing the tank.
- When soda is dispensed and there is no carbonation, it is a clear indication that the CO_2 tank is empty. Reading the gauge on the CO_2 tank should verify this.
- To change the tank, each line is removed by pressing down on each housing unit of each terminal; pull up on metal collars and remove them.
- To replace the tank, each housing unit is positioned over the proper post. The post for the CO_2 line will be marked IN on the soda tank. Press the housing over the position. Pull up on the collar and push the unit into place. Release the collar, which should now be secure on the post. Repeat the procedure for the syrup line.
- Each CO_2 tank comes with a built-in wrench that allows for easy removal of the connector housing. First, turn the gas valve to "off." Then, unscrew the housing nut with the wrench.
- Position the new tank and screw in the housing nut, making sure that the nut is very tightly secured. Turn

the gas valve to "on." The indicator needle should then jump to the full position. In some units, a rubber gasket is needed to prevent CO_2 leakage. Make sure that the gasket is placed inside the housing unit before securing to the CO_2 tank.

Bread Warmer

The bread warmer should be turned on ahead of time (approximately 1 hour) so that it is heated properly before it is filled. For soft rolls or breads, place a small cup containing a water-soaked sponge or napkin in each drawer, as this will keep the rolls moist and prevent them from becoming dry and hard. This procedure is unnecessary for hard rolls and crusty breads. At the end of each shift:

- Turn off the warmer.
- Remove the water cups.
- Remove the drawer, empty it of its contents, and wipe it clean. Return bread and rolls to the kitchen for use as crumbs.
- Replace the drawer.

Note: Refrigerated or frozen rolls need to be rebaked in an oven prior to storing in the bread warmer.

Toaster

The conveyor toaster is the most prevalent type used in the foodservice industry. Some toasters use a timer-setting method to ensure proper toasting. Others use a rotisserie cycle span.

To clean the toaster:

- Shut the toaster off.
- Remove grills and crumb catch pans from the unit.
- Clean crumbs and burned product from each.
- Replace the parts in the toaster.

Figure 3–12 Bird

1. Fold the napkin into four equal parts.
2. Fold A into center line as shown.
3. Now fold B to match A.
4. Fold the front corners of A and B diagonally.
5. Lift folds A and B and support on the turned back corners to create the wings. Place on table with points facing the diner.

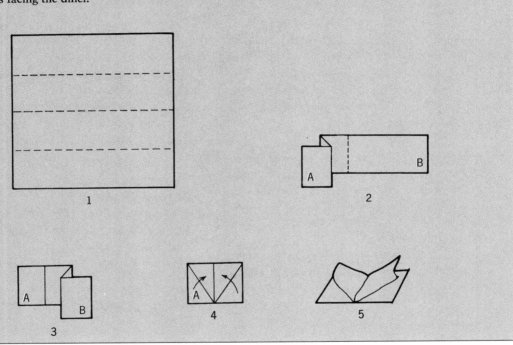

Figure 3–13 Bishop's hat

1. Fold the napkin in half.
2. Fold corners A to B and C to D.
3. Fold top back at the dotted line.
4. Turning the points to the top, bring the left-hand corner around and tuck behind the front flap.
5. Napkin after step 4.
6. Turn the napkin around and repeat step 4.
7. Finished fold.

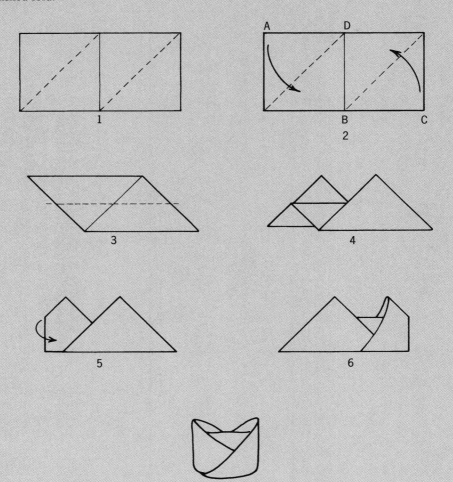

Figure 3–14 Chinese fan

1. Lay the napkin flat and fold along dotted lines bringing points A to point B.
2. Fold A to B. This will give a W effect if viewed from the end of the napkin.
3. Pleat the napkin, making 2-inch pleats.
4. Hold the napkin at the bottom bringing points A and B together.
5. Open the pleats and pull down one side.
6. Turn the napkin around and repeat step 5.
7. Open the napkin into a fan shape and stand on the place setting.

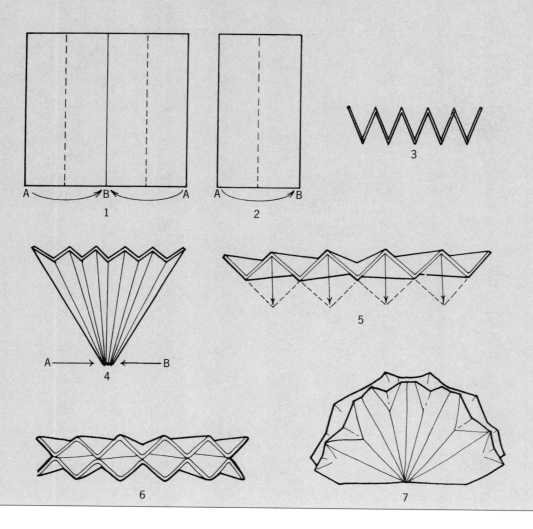

Figure 3–15 Cock's comb

1. Fold in fourths as indicated by dotted lines.
2. Fold diagonally.
3. Turn napkin so that points are away from you. Fold sides B along dotted line to meet at center A.
4. Turn the points of B under.
5. Fold along the center line A and stand the napkin with fold uppermost.
6. Pull up the four pleats and arrange to produce the finished fold.

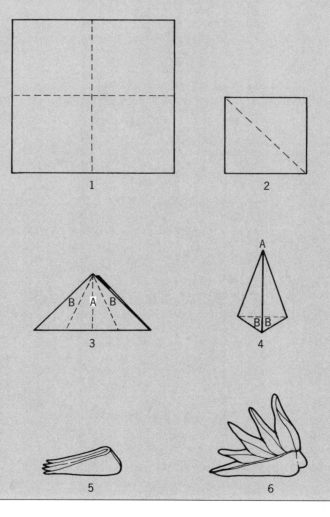

Figure 3–16 Cone

1. Fold the napkin into thirds.
2. Fold corners A and B upward to center line.
3. Fold corner C to D and E to F.
4. Place fingers of left hand inside fold and turn down point GH at the dotted line to form a cuff.
5. Mold the napkin into a cone and set on the table with the points of the cuff facing the diner.

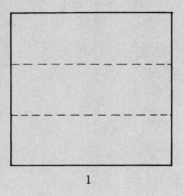

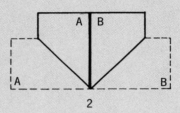

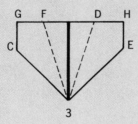

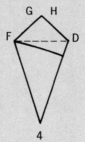

Figure 3–17 Fan

1. Fold the napkin into thirds as shown.
2. Fold at line B leaving about 6 inches at end A.
3. Pleat from C to B.
4. Fold in half as shown.
5. Fold triangle A over along the dotted line; this will form a support for the finished fold.
6. Open out the pleats and arrange as shown.

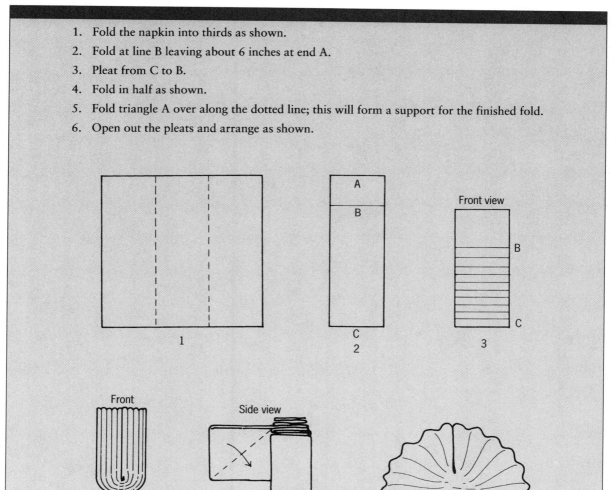

Figure 3–18 French pleat

1. Fold the napkin in thirds along the dotted lines to form a rectangle. Turn the napkin so that the narrow side is toward you.
2. Fold ends A and B over 1/4 of napkin along the dotted lines.
3. Fold B over once more to center.
4. Turn edge A over so that it meets the edge of the top fold B.
5. Turn edge C under so that A is now the top. Position on plate.

Note: The name card or menu may be placed in between the steps of this fold.

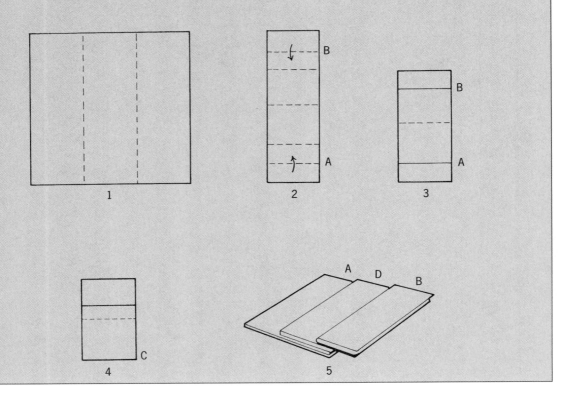

Figure 3–19 Lazy butler

1. Fold the napkin into thirds as shown.
2. Fold edges A to center line B.
3. Fold corners C to center line.
4. Napkin after step 3.
5. Take the napkin in both hands and turn it over with the points toward you and the plain side uppermost; roll to form a cone.
6. Tuck corner A into corner B.
7. Place on the table with the opening down and the points toward the diner.

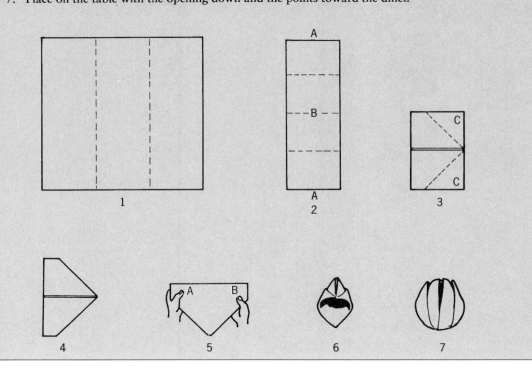

Figure 3–20 Lily

1. Fold the napkin at the dotted line.
2. Fold corners A up at the dotted lines.
3. Fold B up at the dotted line.
4. Fold B down at the dotted line.
5. Napkin after step 4.
6. Turn the napkin so that side C to D is away from you. Fold corner C as shown. Fold corner D up at the dotted line and tuck into the pleat at C.
7. Stand the napkin on the table with point E up.
8. Pull down the pleats to produce the finished fold.

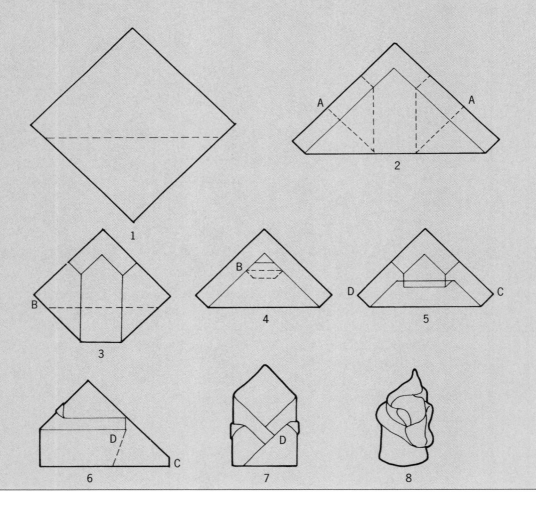

Figure 3–21 Lotus

1. Lay napkin flat and fold along the dotted lines.
2. Turn through 45° and fold along the dotted lines.
3. Turn again and fold along the dotted lines.
4. Turn napkin over and fold along the dotted lines.
5. Napkin after step 4.
6. Place a tumbler over the points in the center.
7. Pull each of the 12 points gently away from underneath, taking opposing corners in turn.
8. Finished fold.

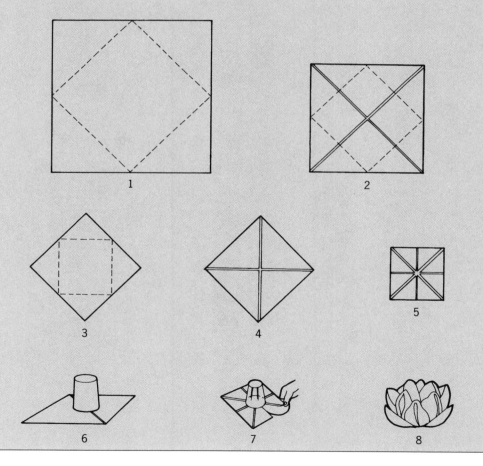

Figure 3–22 Pixie

1. Fold the napkin into thirds.
2. Fold at lines A to bring sides B to the center.
3. Napkin after step 2.
4. Turn the point to the right, folding along the center line.
5. Turn the napkin over and fold the portion BB up and away from you at the dotted line shown in previous diagram.
6. Fold CC in half toward you; this will make the heel.
7. Fold CC around and tuck into pleat D.
8. To finish this fold, insert the fingers between the folds and curl this part around the slipper..

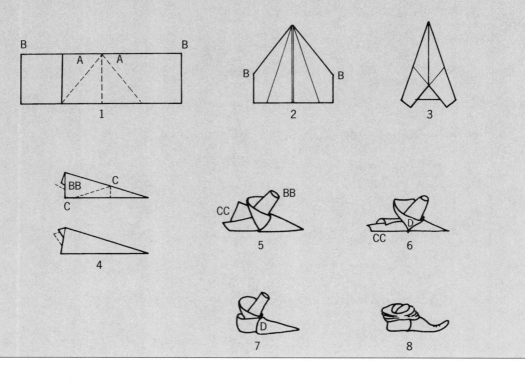

Figure 3–23 Pocket

1. Fold the napkin into four, ensuring that four loose edges are at A.
2. Fold down top flap as indicated.
3. Fold along dotted line.
4. Fold down second flap.
5. Fold second flap along dotted line.
6. Tuck second fold under first fold.
7. Fold napkin along dotted line, putting the fold underneath.
8. Fold napkin along dotted line.
9. Finished fold.

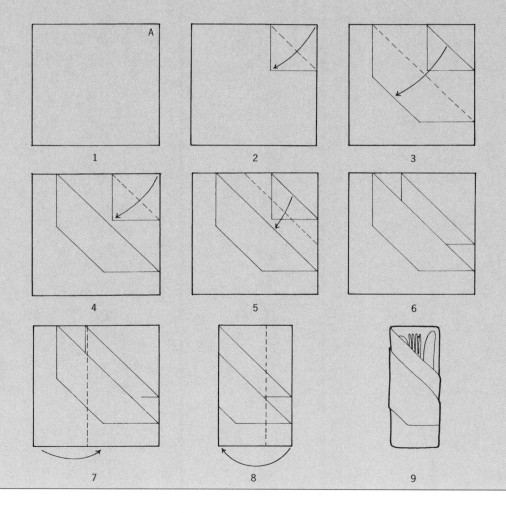

Figure 3–24 Rocket

1. Fold the napkin into fourths as shown.
2. Fold corners A and B along the dotted lines to center line C.
3. Turn the napkin over.
4. Roll corners A and B outward as shown.
5. Fold corners A and B to the top along the dotted lines.
6. Napkin after step 5.
7. Turn napkin over. Arrange on the table with the point toward the diner.

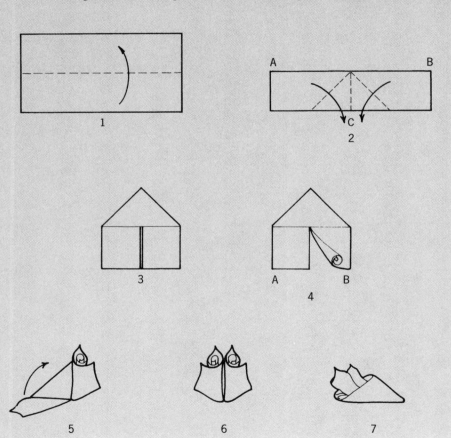

Figure 3–25 Spear

1. Fold the napkin into thirds as shown.
2. Fold corners A diagonally to center line.
3. Fold back corners A.
4. Keeping the two sides flat on the table, press them toward the middle; this will make the center line stand up. Fold sections B under at the dotted line.
5. Open out the center fold and arrange on the table with the point away from the diner.

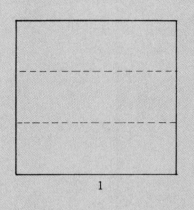

1

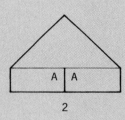

2

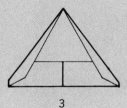

3

4

5

Figure 3–26 Twirl

1. Fold the napkin into thirds along the dotted lines.
2. Lay both hands, palms up, on the napkin, taking corner A between the thumb and forefinger of the left hand and corner B with the right hand.
3. Turn the hands palm down, retaining hold of the corners.
4. Turn hands in toward body in a circular motion.
5. Complete the motion; this will trap hands.
6. Release hands and place the napkin into a glass or arrange it flat on showplate.

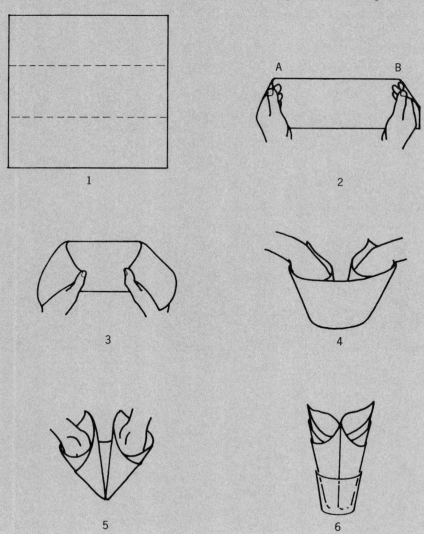

Figure 3–27 Viking hat

1. Fold the napkin in half diagonally, then fold corners A to B.
2. Fold the two flaps marked A up to B.
3. Fold the two flaps marked A out to the dotted lines at B.
4. Fold A to B, ensuring that the fold falls along the bottom dotted line.
5. Fold bottom edge A along dotted line marked B, then tuck ends marked C around the back to make the napkin stand up.
6. Finished fold.

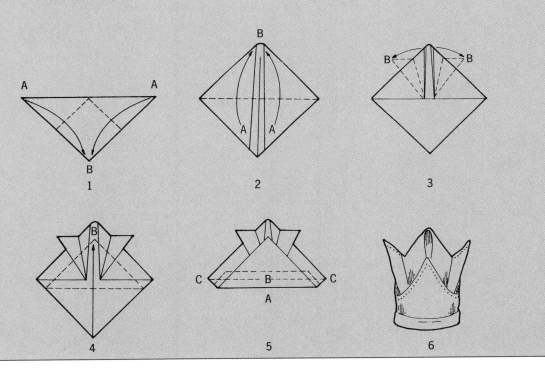

4

Coffee and Tea

4

Coffee and Tea

The word coffee *refers to the beans of the coffee plant as well as the beverage made from its roasted ground beans.*

Coffee

Coffee has become one of the world's most popular beverages, with over 25 million acres worldwide devoted to cultivating coffee trees. Worldwide, the coffee industry provides more than 20 million jobs. It is the second most traded commodity after oil. Unlike beer or wine, coffee's history, in the form that we would recognize, is a recent development. The coffee tree, whose foliage forms a rough pyramid and would grow more than 20 feet tall if not pruned, is native to Ethiopia in East Africa and has more than 25 known species. As is still done today, the coffee beans were crushed, mixed with lard, and chewed by nomadic tribes, because it was recognized to be a stimulant.

History of Coffee

- Circa A.D. **1000,** the coffee plant was cultivated in Yemen across the Red Sea on the Arabian peninsula, where it was brewed initially without roasting, yielding a tea-like beverage.
- In the late **thirteenth century,** Arabs began to roast and grind coffee beans before brewing. Coffee became their social beverage, as all alcoholic beverages were forbidden by the Islamic religion.
- Due to Islam's rapid proliferation and its tenet that all Muslims should perform a *hadjj,* or pilgrimage, to Mecca in the Arabian peninsula, coffee soon spread throughout the Middle East.
- Although the Roman Catholic Church's initial reaction to coffee was that it was the "devil's brew," coffee soon became popular with Europeans as trade with the Ottoman Empire grew.
- In **1616,** the Dutch obtained a coffee plant from Yemen and by 1658 had begun cultivation in the colonies of Ceylon and Java.

- In **1714,** the Dutch provided Louis XIV of France with coffee plants for his botanical garden.
- Java, one of the main Indonesian islands, was colonized by the Dutch, who planted coffee and turned it into such a successful major coffee center, that *Java* became synonymous with *coffee.*
- In **1720,** Gabriel Mathieu de Clieu, a French naval officer, took a seedling from Louis XIV's coffee plant to Martinique, a French colony in the Caribbean. This single plant became the progenitor of most Arabica coffee plants grown in the New World.
- Brazil, the world's largest coffee producer, began its coffee production with the introduction of a coffee seedling given to a Brazilian, Francisco de Melo Palheta, as a gift for arbitrating a dispute between the French and Dutch in Guinea.
- Coffee houses became popular all over Europe and were to play a significant role in the development of trading houses. The first coffee house in England was opened by a Turkish immigrant in **1650.** By the early **1700**s, London had over 2000 coffeehouses, several of which evolved into trading houses, such as Lloyd's, which became the famous London insurance conglomerate, or Jonathan's, which evolved into the London Stock Exchange. One interesting aspect was the English society's ban against women patronizing coffee houses, which spurred tea's popularity with English ladies.
- The word *tip* evolved from the custom of placing coins in brass boxes in coffee houses or "penny universities," as they were known in England. The boxes carried the inscription "**T**o **I**nsure **P**romptness."
- Cafes became the intellectual gathering places of French society. By **1843,** Paris had over 3000 cafes.
- Coffee's assimilation into Vienna's (Austrian) society began in 1683, following the defeat of the Turks at Vienna's doorstep. The green unroasted coffee beans left behind by the Turks were expropriated by Franz

Kolschitzsky, who opened a coffee house named the "Blue Bottle."
- Coffee became America's patriotic beverage as a response to the tax placed on tea, which led to the Boston Tea Party in **1773.***
- The coffee plant Robusta, native to West Africa, was recognized by major producers to be a hardier and more productive species and was cultivated in many parts of the world, including Brazil, beginning in the late nineteenth century.
- Coffee consumption in the U.S. has declined since its height in the early **1960**s when Americans were drinking over three cups per person a day. However, the emphasis has focused more on specialty coffee beverages which account for the more than 5,000 outlets in the U.S. and which is projected to total 10,000 specialty outlets by the turn of the century. This quite clearly demonstrates that upgrading coffee can be very profitable.

The Coffee Plant

Of the more than 25 wild species of coffee trees, only two have been cultivated on a commercial scale: **arabica** and **robusta.** Each has characteristics that should be considered when deciding which to purchase and serve.

Arabica

Coffea arabica is named for the Arabs, who first popularized coffee. Constituting 75% of the world's coffee production, this variety is predominantly grown in Central and South America and East Africa. It grows at an altitude of 3000 to 6000 feet above sea level. Arabica's characteristics include sweet aromas and winy flavors, balanced by much sought-after acidity that gives it freshness. Arabica produces the high-quality coffees that are sold in specialty coffee outlets. Arabica is more expensive because it is hand picked, it is more susceptible to disease, and its yields are lower. Arabica normally contains half the caffeine (an average of 1.1%) of robusta coffee beans.

* *See* Appendix C for update.

Robusta

Coffea canephora is most often called robusta, which refers to its hardy character. Unlike arabica, it grows well at sea level to altitudes of 2000 feet above sea level. Robusta also thrives in wet valleys and tropical forests. Its characteristics include a heavy, earthy aroma and flavor, and it is used by many to produce espresso beans that provide espresso with a syrupy texture. Robusta's lower costs are a result of the relative ease in mechanically cultivating and harvesting it. It is also more resistant to diseases and pests. Robusta is used by large commercial packagers to fill out their blends.*

The coffee plant matures in 4 to 6 years and can be expected to produce fruit for 40 years. As a self-pollinating evergreen, it produces 2000 **cherries** (or berries) from white flowers, enough to produce a pound to a pound and a half of roasted coffee beans. The cherries take from 7 to 8 months to ripen from green to yellow to red. Coffee trees that grow in areas with two distinct rainy seasons each year, such as Costa Rica, produce two harvests annually. The coffee beans are the inner seeds of the sweet cherries.

Coffee Production

Harvesting

There are three methods for harvesting coffee: **selective, strip,** and **mechanical.** The *selective method* is used for individual picking, made necessary by the terrain and by cherries that do not ripen simultaneously. A hand picker can harvest as many as 200 pounds of cherries daily, yielding about 40 pounds of roasted coffee. The *strip method* is used in areas, such as Brazil, where cherries ripen at the same time. The cherries are allowed to ripen on the branches and are harvested by one swift movement from the branch. *Mechanical harvesting* is the lowest-cost method but requires plantations where coffee trees are planted on relatively level soil and trees are planted in even rows. The harvester straddles the row of trees and agitates them, knocking the beans onto a conveyor belt.

* *See* Appendix C for update.

Processing

There are two methods for processing coffee to separate the beans from the cherries and reduce the moisture content of the beans: the **wet** and **dry** methods.

The **wet method** is used primarily for arabicas. The first part of the process is **depulping,** whereby the skins and pulp are removed from the cherries by machine, thereby exposing parchment-covered beans. The beans are then soaked in tanks and allowed to **ferment** so that the mucilage or pulp coating can come off easily. Fermentation has to stop at just the right point, so that it does not affect the bean itself. The next stage is for the beans to be **washed** off and **dried** in the sun from 7 days to 3 weeks. Some areas use drum dryers at 122° F to 140° F for 2 to 3 days. This drying-off process is critical, as the beans' moisture content drops from 70% to 11%. The beans are then given a **rest** period of a minimum of 20 to 30 days. The parchment is **peeled** by a hulling machine, which removes the parchment and silver skin when orders have been received. Beans that undergo the wet method tend to have the following characteristics:

1. Clean flavors
2. No undesirable characteristics
3. Greater acidity

The **dry method** is used primarily for robusta beans and in locales where there is an insufficient water supply, such as in Ethiopia. The cherries are allowed to partially dry on the tree and then are dried in the sun for 2 or 3 weeks. The dry pulp and parchment are removed by husking mechanically. The beans that undergo this dry process have the following characteristics:

1. A heavier body
2. Possible development of off-flavors

Sorting and Grading

Once the beans have been processed, they need to be sorted according to the bean's size, density, and color. The grading criteria is determined by the variety of coffee, altitude of the plantation, processing method, and age of the bean. The sorting is conducted both by hand and me-

chanically. The coffee beans are then packed in burlap or plastic bags and shipped throughout the world.

Coffee Classifications

The dried green beans are classified according to botanical variety, processing method, and altitude of growth.*

Colombian Milds

These are grown principally in Colombia, Kenya, and Tanzania. They constitute 16% of the world's production and are graded principally on bean size. Coffee produced from these beans is sweet in taste and high in aromatics and has a thick body.

Other Mild Arabicas

The majority of other arabicas are grown in Central and South America, They account for 26% of the world's production and are graded by altitude, density, color, and number of defects. The taste is typical of medium-altitude-grown coffee (2000 to 4000 feet), winy to sour, with a moderate level of aromatics and a smooth body.

Brazilian and Other Arabicas

Grown in Brazil and Ethiopia, these beans constitute 37% of global coffee production and are graded by the growing area, which determines taste characteristics and number of imperfections. The finished product is typical of Brazilian naturally processed arabicas grown at low-to-medium altitudes (sea level to 4000 feet) and has a winy-to-sour taste with a moderate level of aromatics and a smooth body.

Robustas

Produced primarily in Africa and Southeast Asia, robustas account for 21% of total coffee produced and are graded on density and size, as well as number of defects. Characteristics are a neutral-to-sharp taste, with pungent aromatics and a heavy body. However, robustas are generally

*See Appendix C for update.

priced from 10% to 40% below arabicas, which makes robustas an attractive filler.

Roasting the Beans

It is necessary to roast the coffee beans in order to bring out their full flavor and aroma. The beans are roasted for various lengths of time at high temperatures to achieve the desired level of caramelization. Many complex chemical changes take place during roasting: from the light "cinnamon" roast that is highly acidic; to the "full city" roast, in which the acidity is balanced with sweetness and bitterness; to the darker, more bitter flavors of the French and Italian roasts. Roasting generally takes from 8 to 16 minutes at approximately 500° F. As the beans are roasted, the level of acidity is reduced, while the level of bitterness is increased. This inverse relationship must be monitored by the roaster in order to control the flavor of the finished product. Coffee roasters provide many levels of roasted beans for specialty use. Most commercially available roasts, however, fall into three main categories: medium (caramelized), heavy (heavily caramelized), and dark (heavily caramelized, carbonized, slightly burned).

Cinnamon Roast

The lightest commercially available roast with no apparent oils on the surface of the beans, this type of roast is high in chlorogenic acid and is light in both body and flavor.

Full City Roast

Full City is considered a medium level of roasting. It is widely accepted by the bulk of American coffee drinkers and is, therefore, the most common degree of roasting used by commercial coffee companies marketing to the United States. The words *Full City* generally do not appear on the label.

Vienna Roast

This is a controversial name for a medium roast that is chocolate brown with dark speckles. It is also used as a term for a blend of different roasts.

French Roast

French roast involves heavy roasting to provide a full flavor with noticeable bitterness and a strong, distinctive flavor and aroma. Whole beans will display a slight oily coating, because extended roasting expels the natural oils in the beans. In the southern United States, the French roast is often called New Orleans roast due to the French cultural influence in that region.

Italian Roast

The last and darkest stage of roasting is generally referred to as Italian roast. Beans become heavily carbonized (with a coating of carbon) and secrete noticeable amounts of oils. This contributes to the very strong, bitter flavor of the coffee. Italian roast coffee beans are usually reserved for and best suited for **espresso** coffee.

Espresso

Espresso coffee requires a special espresso machine, as described in the section on hot beverage service in Chapter 1. Some establishments also may choose a wide variety of presentational styles, such as caffe fresco, espresso adagio, decaffeinated espresso, and decaffeinated Viennese blend, among others. The brewing process takes only about 15 seconds to complete, which enables each cup to be brewed to order, extracting the very heart from the bean. The flavors of espresso are intense, rich, caramel, and bitter. A *shot* of espresso is traditionally served in half cups, called *demi-tasse*. Sugar and a twist of lemon may accompany the coffee.

Also, espresso may be combined with ice, cold milk, steamed milk, foamed milk, whipped cream, and mocha syrup to create a wide range of recipes. The following is a list of classic recipes using espresso coffee.*

- *Cappucino* is made by combining one shot of espresso (for an 8-ounce serving) with equal parts of steamed milk and foamed milk.
- *Caffe latte* is made by combining one shot of espresso with steamed milk to one-fourth inch from the rim and topped with foamed milk.
- *Caffe mocha* or *Mochaccino* is made by adding one-half ounce of mocha syrup to the bottom of the serving cup or glass. Add one shot of espresso and steamed milk to one-fourth inch from the rim and top with whipped cream.

Decaffeinated Coffee*

Caffeine is a nitrogen compound found in many plants, including the beans of the coffee tree. Although research shows that caffeine can quicken the heart rate and cause sleeplessness and other side effects, its long-term effects remain inconclusive. The increased demand for decaffeinated coffee has led to the availability of numerous types of decaffeinated coffee products. "Decaf" can be purchased in ground or whole-bean form alongside caffeinated coffee. Brewed decaf can be obtained in most restaurants. The brewing process for decaffeinated coffee is the same as for caffeinated coffee. Currently, several processes are used to remove caffeine from coffee, although the amount of residual caffeine varies from producer to producer.

- *Water method:* The green beans are soaked in water for several hours. Chemicals may be used in this process.
- *Swiss water process:* This is similar to the water method, but charcoal filtration is used instead of chemicals.
- *Methylene Chloride:* The green coffee beans are soaked in a solution containing methylene chloride, which absorbs the caffeine. It is regarded as completely safe.
- *Supercritical carbon dioxide:* Carbon dioxide is lique-

*See Appendix C for update.

fied under great pressure and passed through the bean, extracting caffeine.

Degassing and Packaging

After the beans are roasted, they produce carbon dioxide gas in amounts equal to three times their volume. The carbon dioxide must be released prior to most commercial packaging as the gas would otherwise cause the can or brick package to burst. The unfortunate consequence of allowing the carbon dioxide to dissipate is that oxygen is absorbed by the coffee beans which become somewhat stale. Paper bags used for packaging beans immediately after roasting or valve-lock bags for longer termed storage avoid this problem. Obviously, coffee is enhanced by brewing it as soon as possible after roasting it. Since this is not always practical, one should examine briefly the storage conditions best suited for roasted beans.

Storage

Once the coffee beans have been roasted, they should be kept away from any light, sealed in a tight-fitting container and stored in a cool place other than a refrigerator. Coffee is best stored in a freezer, though, if already ground, it will absorb some unwanted odors and its oils will congeal, affecting the body of the brewed coffee, especially espresso.

Refer to the service chapter for a number of considerations that are important in the brewing of coffee.

Tasting Terms*

Acidity is the lively, palate-cleansing property that is characteristic of Arabica or high-altitude-grown coffees. Acidity is perceived primarily on the tip of the tongue and may range from low to high. Acidity should not be confused with bitter or sour.

Body is the feeling of weight of the coffee on one's tongue and mouth and can range from light to medium to

*See Appendix C for update.

full. Factors contributing to the body of a coffee are water, type of grind, percentage of coffee to the amount of water used, and the brewing method.

Flavor is the most important tasting term of all. It refers to the overall impression of aroma, acidity, and body. The flavor can be described in terms of its intensity ("This coffee has a strong flavor."). Also, for each variety of coffee that has a distinctive flavor, specific descriptors may be used ("This coffee reminds me of sweet choco- late.").

Crema is the amber foam that floats on the top of a well-made espresso. The foam is made of oils and colloids, suspended coffee particles that give the coffee the rich and desired feeling in the mouth.

Mocha is the original name of the port in Yemen on the Arabian peninsula, from which coffee was first traded. *Mocha* was a term used to describe coffee in Europe in the sixteenth century. When chocolate was brought from the New World to Europe, it was believed to be similar in flavor. *Mocha* is a term now used to describe a blend of coffee and chocolate.

Tea

The cultivation and consumption of tea has played a vital role in the history and development of human society and culture. In Chinese society, tea was (and is) at the heart of the culture. Chinese storytellers, writers, artists, mystics, politicians, and emperors all praised the dark green leaves. For the Japanese, tea and Buddhism are synonymous. The Buddhist temples cultivated the mystical leaves much the same as Catholic monasteries grew grapes to produce ceremonial wines in Europe. The Japanese tea ceremony is considered a mystical experience intrinsic to Japanese culture. In India, tea is brewed at dawn and served in unglazed clay bowls. The first sip of tea is often the first event of a new day. Tea tradition in India is also intricately tied to British culture and ritual. The railroads and grand hotels in India served tea to British patrons with customary formality.

Tea was brought to the Western world as early as the eighth century via Persia. It was not until the sixteenth century, when Portuguese, Dutch, and other traders began visiting the Orient, that the popularity of the beverage spread throughout Europe. The Dutch introduced tea to England, and by 1650 tea began to appear in coffeehouses as an alternative to coffee or chocolate.

"Tea Time" in the British tradition is served in a variety of ways with varied customs and teaware. Taking tea can be a casual affair, where two old friends meet to chat (tea for two), or an extremely formal event in a lavish hotel ballroom.

Dutch traders also introduced tea to North America in the seventeenth century. In 1773 the Colonists, in protest over a tax on tea levied by the British Government, dumped tea into Boston Harbor. The Boston Tea Party, as the event is known, set the stage for the American Revolution.

Tea Growing

The tea plant is a camellia, *Camellia sinensis* , and although all tea is primarily the same plant, there are many types which respond to a variety of soil conditions, climates, and cultivation practices. There are roughly 1500 different grades of tea and 2000 different blends. The variety of tastes and quality is due to the location where the bush is grown, the time of year the leaves are harvested, and the location of the leaves on the bush.

When harvesting and processing the leaves, called *shoots*, the weather on the day the leaves are harvested can effect the quality and character of the tea. On a very rainy day, tea harvesting is sometimes halted. The quality of the shoots harvested during strong rain is low, but on sunny warm days or slightly misty days, the harvest produces high-quality tea.

The shoots are handled with varying degrees of care, based on the daily quality. "Single Day" tea is of extremely high quality. All of the leaves are picked on a single day, which permits no blending of tea from previous days.

Processing the Leaves

There are three basic categories of tea, and they are defined by the level of *enzymatic oxidation* the leaves receive after harvesting. The leaves are tossed into a cylinder, which bruises their edges, releasing the tea enzyme for oxidation (a process sometimes mistakenly referred to as *fermentation*).

Green tea is not oxidized. Once picked, the leaves are steamed to destroy the enzyme needed for oxidation, then rolled gently to release their aromatic aroma and juices. Green teas are produced in China, Taiwan, Japan, and India. Green tea must be stored properly and served extremely fresh. Examples of green tea are

Gyokuro	The finest grade of exported Japanese tea
Imperial	A type of Ceylon, China, or India green tea
Tencha	The powdered tea used in the Japanese tea ceremony
Sencha	The most common Japanese tea, popular in restaurants and sushi bars
Shou Mei	China green tea known as "Old Man's Eyebrows"

Oolong tea is semi-oxidized. The leaves are partially oxidized before drying. The exact degree of oxidation is determined by the smell and appearance of the leaf, which requires experienced judgment. Too little oxidation causes the tea to taste raw and bitter, while too much oxidation destroys much of the flavor. The leaves are then fired to halt the oxidation process and then cooled before a second firing. Having been fired to the level desired, the leaves are rolled into compressed tea balls to extract more moisture and give the leaves their final shape. The tea is then sorted and packed. It takes about 4200 pounds of the green shoots to produce 1000 pounds of the finished product.

Examples of Oolong tea are

Black Dragon	A relative newcomer in tea production, developed in Formosa during the middle of the nineteenth century. It combines the fermented and unfermented processes. The leaves are picked when they reach their peak.
Formosa Oolong	Distinct in aroma and flavor, this semi-fermented tea is often referred to as the "Champagne of Teas."

Pouchong	Grown in China and Taiwan. The Chinese version has a brighter taste than the Taiwanese.

Black tea, known by the Chinese as red tea because of it's coppery red tones once it is steeped, is a highly processed, highly oxidized tea. The leaves are first placed on drying trays to wither and dry, either by the sun, in the shade, or by a gentle stream of warm air. Oxidation is the next step in the process, and then, like all styles of tea, the leaves undergo firing and then cooling which may be repeated several times.

After the final firing, the tea is sorted and graded according to size. Whole or *leaf* tea is superior to the broken leaves and dust that is used for tea bags. Black tea is used in most of the commercial teas served in the Western world.

Examples of black tea are

Assam	Grown in northeastern India
Ceylon	Produced in Sri Lanka (formerly called Ceylon)
China Black	Derived from the Anhui province of China
Darjeeling	Grown in the foothills of the Himalayas
Earl Grey	A blend of Darjeeling and China black teas
English Breakfast	A North American blend of India and Ceylon teas
Irish Breakfast	A blend of Assam and Ceylon teas
Lapsang Soochang	A smoky blend of South China black teas
Orange Pekoe	A grade of tea often confused with a flavored blend. *Orange* refers to the color of the Pekoe leaf following oxidation.
Russian tea	Originally grown during the mid-nineteenth century for the table of the Czar

Scented, Flavored, Spiced, and Herbal Teas

As mentioned previously, the term tea refers to the shrub *Camellia sinensis*, and the beverage is produced by infusing or steeping the leaves of the shrub in water. Many other "teas," however, are produced by infusing components such as roots, stems, seeds, berries, flowers, leaves, herbs, and spices in water. Throughout human history *teas* have been used as elixirs, tonics, medicines, remedies, and potions. The purpose of these beverages has been to calm the soul, to perhaps relieve pain and suffering, to ward off evil and disease, to enlighten the spirit, and to simply enjoy the flavor. The following are examples of various types of flavored infusions:

Scented teas are made by adding aromatic petals from flowers such as gardenia, jasmine, magnolia, habiscus, and lavender to tea leaves.

Flavored teas gain their distinct character by spraying the essence of citrus fruit, berries, vanilla, tree fruit, and other components onto processed tea leaves.

Spiced teas are produced by boiling flavoring agents such as cinnamon, nutmeg, coriander, and clove with their leaves and the leaves of *Camellia sinensis*.

Herbal teas are gaining in popularity and can be made from a wide variety of plants, such as saffron, basil, mint, chamomile, rosehip, spearmint, and peppermint, to name just a few. Complex herbal teas are made by combining aromatics and botanicals to produce distinct flavors.

The Tea Bag

Next to water, tea is the most popular beverage in the world. In the United States, it is the sixth most widely consumed beverage, trailing water, soft drinks, coffee, beer, and milk. This popularity is due to the convenience of the tea bag for hot tea, iced tea, and flavored iced teas.

Tea bags were originally designed as packaging for samples of tea used by merchants in an effort to control costs. Tins of tea samples were expensive, so in 1904, Thomas Sullivan of New York used small silk bags to deliver samples of his tea. To his astonishment, the receivers of his samples brewed the tea while it was still in the sample bags. When orders for tea in little bags came pouring in, a revolution in packaging was born.

Today, tea bags are made of paper and filled with "dust" or finely cut leaves. Merchants such as Twining, Tetley, and Dexter popularized the convenience of service of tea in a bag. The convenience of tea bags has dominated service in the United States to such an extent that over 50% of hot tea consumed is served in bags.

The quality of tea in a bag has been improved recently by small merchants. They are placing a higher quality tea (larger leaves) in a larger bag that is made with unbleached paper.

When serving tea in a bag, the water must be poured over the bag rather than the bag placed on top of the water. Preheat the teapot, add the bag, pour the water, and serve immediately.

5

*Wine
History and
Making*

Wine History and Making

Wine is a beverage that engages all of the senses.

The sound of wine being poured or the popping of the champagne cork creates a sense of anticipation; its myriad shades of beautiful colors engage our visual sense; the array of aromas and bouquets entices our sense of smell; the breadth of flavors delights our sense of taste; and the subtlety of textures teases or satisfies our palates.

In addition to being an enjoyable beverage, wine is a fascinating subject that has absorbed the efforts of not only wine makers and people in commerce, but also academics in many fields. Wine has been studied from a biologic and microbiologic as well as an organic chemical approach. Wine's effect on health and well-being has been the subject of numerous recent studies and is of considerable interest to those in the medical profession. These studies have demonstrated the benefits of moderate wine consumption (one to two glasses per day) on health and are now supported by the U.S. Food and Drug Administration (FDA).

The effects of elements such as climate, soil, and topography have absorbed those studying geography. The history of wine, which is a reflection of social and economic development, has been studied by archeologists, historians, anthropologists, economists, and social scientists. To gain a full appreciation of the role of wine in Western culture, it is necessary to review how wine became the beverage of choice to accompany food.

What is wine? **It is the fermented juice of grapes.** There are other sources of wine, made from other fruits, but they are referred to by their generic names. For example, a wine made from peaches is called a peach wine. This is a legal requirement in the United States.

Sugar + yeast → alcohol + carbon dioxide (+ heat)

Sugars are produced naturally in grapes. Yeast can be either wild, as part of the microflora of the **bloom** coating grapes while they are still on the vine, or commercial, with strains of *Saccharomyces cerevisiae* added by the wine maker. Alcohol can be as high as 15.5% as long as there is sugar to convert into alcohol. Carbon dioxide is either released into the atmosphere or trapped in the wine to produce sparkling wine.

The History of Wine

There are many species of grapes and thousands of varieties within each species. We are primarily concerned with the species **Vitis vinifera.** *Vinifera* means "wine bearing." Of the more than **5,000 varieties** of *Vitis vinifera*, wine enthusiasts are concerned with no more than 50. The origin of *Vitis vinifera* was most likely in the valleys of the Caucasus region, the present-day Republic of Georgia in Asia Minor. Wine making probably began by accident. It is important to understand that wine is a completely natural phenomenon. The skins of grapes have sugars that wild yeasts convert into alcohol. It was human intercession that produced the many different flavors of wine—by recognizing and developing characteristics of different varieties and matching these varieties to suitable environments to bring out their full potential. Humans have striven for millenia to find a way to prevent wine from spoiling. A byproduct of this struggle was the inadvertently added flavor of wood. It is only in the latter twentieth century that we have developed sufficient scientific understanding to control all aspects of wine making and prevent wine from spoiling. There is no longer an excuse for making a bad wine.

From ancient to modern times, wine has been associated with religion. Whether it was through Dionysus of ancient Greece or Bacchus of the Roman Empire, wine continues to be an integral part of the Jewish and Christian faiths. It is not difficult to envision early human's associating the euphoric and medicinal effects of wine with a mystical or religious experience.

The following is a chronology of major developments of winemaking:

- **6000 B.C.** This period marks the earliest traces of winemaking, in the Caucasus region. The earliest actual archeologic evidence was uncovered in 1996 in the Zagros Mountains of present-day Iran and is estimated to date back to 5400 B.C.
- **4000 B.C.–3000 B.C.** Wine making spreads to Mesopotamia, Babylon, and Egypt. Egyptian wines are stored with "labels" indicating the place of origin (i.e., the vineyard's location), the grape, the name of the wine maker, and the vintage, information still found on modern labels. There are written references to wine in the Gilgamesh, a text written in 1800 B.C.
- **2400 B.C.** One of the earliest *written* references is in the Bible, that Noah planted a vineyard. It should be pointed out that Noah's ark is said to have landed on Mount Ararat, which is in the Taurus mountains bordering Turkey and the Caucasus region.
- **2000 B.C.** Wine making spreads to Greece via the Phoenicians or Minoans of Crete. In this mostly inhospitable land, it is wine and olive oil that produced the surplus capital to create their great civilization.
- **750 B.C.** The Greeks settle and bring wine making to the southern coasts of Italy and call the area Oenotria, the land of the vine.
- **500 B.C.–A.D. 350.** The Roman Empire develops wine making to a more technologically advanced level. Pliny writes a definitive work on viticulture. There is a clear understanding of the importance of climate, soil, aging, storage temperatures, vintages, corks, and sulfur.
- Romans adopt the use of oak beer barrels of the Gauls (France) to use as wine barrels. One size of the barrel that is still used today is the **barrique** (225 liters). The Rhone valley is settled first, in 500 B.C., followed by Spain and Portugal.
- **50–150.** Romans introduce wine making to the Bordeaux, Burgundy, and the Loire regions.

- **150–350.** Romans introduce wine making to Champagne and the Mosel of Germany.
- **350–1200.** Wine-making knowledge is preserved by Monastic orders, especially the Benedictine, Cistercian, and Carthusian. The further development and growth of vineyards under monastic orders flourishes after the eleventh century. The need for sacramental wine was an underlying cause for this growth. As the only literate class of people, monks were employed by the ruling lords of the feudal system. As payment for their services, monastic orders were granted lands. They cultivated the same viticultural areas that the Romans had developed. Wine became a principal source of income and prestige for many monasteries.
- **1100.** Leif Ericson ostensibly travels to New England and names it Vinland.
- **1100–1400.** The English crown rules Aquitaine in southeastern France, developing wine trade with the Cahors and Bordeaux regions.
- **1400–1700.** Dutch and English commercial trading impacts on the exportation of French wine. The addition of spirits or brandy to fortify and stabilize wine becomes more prevalent. The practice of using sulphur in wine as a preservative is rediscovered in the fifteenth century in Germany. Until this time, medieval wines would usually last only a year before spoiling. The practice of sulphuring wine slowed down the oxidation process and was used profusely until the 1960s.
- **1700.** Dom Pérignon, as the cellar master of the monastery at Hautvilliers at Épernay (the modern site of Moët et Chandon), is a major contributor to the development of fine wines of Champagne through his understanding of the different characteristics of varietals, the role of **terroir**, the **cuvée,** the **blending** of different varietals, and the role of temperature in fermentation and cellaring.
- **1600–1700.** The development of sufficiently strong glass bottles for commercial use (by the Englishman Digby in 1622) does not become prevalent until the mid-seventeenth century. This type of glass replaced leather "jacks" and stoneware. Although the Romans

had used corks as a stoppers, they did not become commonplace until the middle of the sixteenth century. Premier wine estates, such as Haut Brion of Bordeaux, differentiate themselves from other claret producers to sell their wines in developing markets, such as in England.

- **1500–1800.** Western nations begin settlement of the New World, bringing viticulture and wine making to the Americas, South Africa, and Australia.
- **1789–1815.** The French Revolution destroys the power of monastic orders by expropriating their land holdings. Vineyards are distributed to supporters of the revolution. The Napoleonic Code of Law regarding inheritance grants equal distribution of estates to all offspring. This causes wine estates in many regions to diminish greatly in size and increase in number, thereby giving rise to **négociants.**
- **1855.** Napoleon III asks the Chamber of Commerce of Bordeaux to provide a listing of its best producers as its contribution to the *Paris Exposition Universelle.* This listing was created by the wine brokers, beginning in the eighteenth century, to determine which estates produced the best wine. The **Classification of 1855 of Bordeaux** wines, rating the best 61 wines primarily of the **Médoc** region, survives to this day, relatively unchanged.
- **1851. Oidium,** a powdery mildew fungus, devastates the vineyards of France, particularly Bordeaux. Sulphur and lime was and is still used to combat this problem.
- **1862.** Napoleon III invites Louis **Pasteur,** France's premier scientist, to find a solution to the spoilage of wines, which was proving to be a major problem, affecting France's export income. Pasteur's contribution to science was his discovery of different bacteria that are present in wine, particularly **Acetobacter,** which was responsible for converting wine into vinegar. He discovered that bacteria need oxygen to thrive. Very slight amounts of air coming into contact with the wine over time would slowly change but not destroy the wine. If the contact with oxygen was greater, however, it would allow *Acetobacter* to grow

rapidly enough to change the wine into vinegar. Pasteur presented the following solutions to the spoilage of wine. First, wine bottles should be filled as much as possible, to the exclusion of oxygen. Second, wine should be placed in colored glass bottles to protect it from bacteria that react to light. Third, wine bottles should be laid on their sides to prevent corks from drying out and allowing wine to come into contact with oxygen at a fast rate. Fourth, wine should be stored in a cool environment (50° F) to prevent premature aging, because bacteria in the wine react to heat. He also recommended the process of applying a temperature of 142° F to145° F for 20 to 30 minutes to kill all bacteria in the bottle. This process is known as **pasteurization** (also used in milk production). Pasteur demonstrated that this could be done without giving the wine a cooked taste.

- **1863.** One year after Pasteur's solutions were presented, France's vineyards are stricken by a microscopic louse called **Phylloxera vastatrix,** which was native to New England. *Phylloxera* was imported to France accidentally in **Vitis labrusca** Concord grape vines. It has been suggested that American vines were imported because the French were looking for alternatives to native *Vitis vinifera,* which were suffering in the severe winters of Europe in the 1850s. *Phylloxera* was able to survive the trans-Atlantic trip due to the advent of fast steamships, which could make the trip in 10 days. *Phylloxera* became so widespread that by 1880, the infestation became known as the Blight of Europe. Once introduced into Europe, this insect, which has a remarkably complicated life cycle, devastated vineyards by attacking the root system of the vines. The defense mechanism of the vine is to produce root galls or swellings, which prevent it from absorbing the sap and nutrients that it needs to survive. It took 40 years for France and the rest of Europe to resolve this crisis. **Jules-Emile Planchon** arrived at a solution of **grafting** the rootstocks of New England *Vitis labrusca* variety to European *Vitis vinifera.* Almost all of the vineyards of the world use this system of grafting, because *Phylloxera* is still a problem. *Phyl-*

loxera also devastated California vineyards and continues to be a major problem. Chile is the only major wine-producing country in the world that has remained *Phylloxera*-free.

- **1880–1890.** In their efforts to combat *Phylloxera,* the French develop a number of **hybridized** varietals, crossing American *Vitis labrusca* with French *Vinifera.* This solution was not deemed effective because the French realized that the quality of these wines was not equal to their predecessor. However, these hardy hybridized varieties, such as **Seyval Blanc** or **Vidal Blanc,** are still used, especially in New England, to make wine.
- To implement the solution of grafting, huge quantities of American rootstock were required. This brought blight to Europe, particularly Bordeaux, called **downy mildew,** which weakened the vines and drastically reduced the wine crop and subsequent quality of the wine. It took 4 years to arrive at the solution of spraying copper sulphate to prevent this mold; this procedure is still used. The devastation caused by these blights resulted in France's permanently losing 30% of its vineyards.
- **1920.** Another "blight" impacts American wine production, **Prohibition.** Temperance and prohibition have always been recurring themes in the American political scene. In 1846, Maine is the first state to prohibit production and sale of alcoholic beverages. The **Volstead Act,** which was the enforcement tool for the **Eighteenth Amendment,** stated that no alcoholic beverages could be produced or sold. It was passed and became law in January of **1920.** The effect of this law devastated many wineries, because they were able to produce wine only for sacramental or medicinal purposes. However, this law had a loophole that enabled each American to make up to 200 gallons of "non-intoxicating cider and fruit juices for use in his home." This loophole was a boon to vineyards, whose production increased by 50% during the 13-year period of Prohibition. These vineyards planted inexpensive grape varieties with high yields to maximize their profits. Although Prohibition was repealed in December of 1933, it left the legacy of Americans

grown accustomed to second-rate wine. It would take 40 years to change that legacy.

- **1920–1930s.** France develops the **Appellation Contrôlée** system. This system was first adopted for Roquefort cheese, for which the area of production was delimited to the mountains of Aveyron. This system not only delimited the name of a wine to a particular region (e.g., a Pauillac wine to the commune of Pauillac), but also determined which grape was best suited to the particular environment of that region *in order to achieve authenticity.* Thus, the concept of **terroir** was born. It refers not only to the soil, but also to the complete ecosystem of an area, including the climate, wind, temperature, rainfall, sunlight, topographic features, and soil composition.
- **1950–1970.** The development of fine wines in the United States is boosted by the owner of Hanzell winery, James Zellerbach, who replicated a Burgundian cellar down to the type of oak used for aging his Chardonnay. The flavors that this wine produced were a revelation to premier winemakers, such as J. Heitz and Robert Mondavi. These and other winemakers gained an understanding of the importance of varietals when visiting Europe. Plantings of top-quality *vinifera* become more prevalent. The University of California–Davis School of Oenology became a world leader in the study of viticulture and wine making, matriculating many graduates that have become some of the world's top winemakers.
- **1970–1990s.** In 1976, California wineries are judged better at an international wine tasting than their French counterparts, destroying the latter's smug self-confidence. Due to tax advantages, many heavy investments in vineyards and wineries were made, leading to the construction of over 240 wineries in the Napa Valley alone. Major European investments in Californian and American wineries have become extensive. Beginning in 1981, certain geographic areas have become identified as **American Viticultural Areas (AVA),** such as Napa Valley, although there are currently nine AVAs in the Napa Valley. This system is beginning to mirror the appellation system of Europe. Through technology, wine-making knowledge has de-

veloped to the point that its every aspect can be controlled. Wines can now be designed.

The Making of Wine

There are four critical elements to producing a good wine: the **grape,** the **climate, growing conditions,** and **wine making.**

The Grape

Before discussing the varietals of grapes, the categories and composition of the grape should be discussed briefly, because the grape is the heart and soul of wine.

Grape Categories

There are four different categories of grapes:

- First, there are wild vine grapes from the United States, such as *Vitis labrusca.* An example of this category is the Concord grape, which gives a very **"foxy"** flavor and does not pair well with food.
- Second, there are *Vitis vinifera* grapes that produce an indistinct and undistinguished quality. These grapes are used to make the *vins ordinaires* of Europe or many of the jug wines of the United States. This category includes table grapes (e.g., Thompson Seedless) that are sometimes used in the blending of these bulk wines.
- The third category is that of *Vitis vinifera* wines, which will be a focus of discussion, because they can provide the consumer with distinct character and refreshing acidity.
- The fourth category is French-American hybridized grape varietals, which were developed as a response to the *Phylloxera* blight and also will be discussed briefly.

The Grape's Composition

Wine has over 300 organic compounds, 200 of which have distinct odors. We will refer to odors that derive from the grape as **aromas,** and odors that develop due to fermentation and the aging process as **bouquets.** Highly complex bouquets develop over years, as the wine slowly oxidizes and changes its chemical composition.

What is the composition of a grape?

- Water constitutes between 70% and 85%.
- Sugars and extracts constitute 15% to 30%.
- Acids constitute 0.3% to 1.8%.
- Tannins constitute 0% to 0.2%.

What produces the *aromas?*

- There are several hundred aromatic components, which include acids, alcohol, aldehydes, and cetones. These compounds are found in all fruits.

What produces the taste of *sweetness?*

- Sweetness can remain in wine if all sugars have not been fermented into alcohol.
- Ethanol, which is the main form of alcohol that is produced by fermentation, also gives the perception of sweetness.

What causes the taste of *bitterness?*

- Bitterness is mainly a result of tannins and phenolics, which come from the skins, stems, and pipes (seeds) of the grape.
- **Tannin** provides an astringent feeling in the mouth, as if it has been dried out and that the tongue has been lightly sand-papered.
- Tannins are found in other foods and beverages and can best be exemplified for a wine novice by the experience of drinking a cup of overly steeped tea or a glass of very young Cabernet Sauvignon.
- The amount of tannin found in white wine is negligible but can be significant in flavor and texture in red wines, depending on the varietal used and the process of vinification adopted.
- Tannins also act as a preservative and suppress bacterial growth.

- Tannins and pigmentation in wine are **anthocyanins,** which precipitate (form crystals) and form sediment in the barrel or bottle over time. This is the cause of sediment in red wine.

Where do *acids* originate?

- Wines have tartaric, malic, citric, and lactic acids.
- Tartaric acid is very acidic in flavor and is not very common in fruits and vegetables.
- Tartaric acids will precipitate in alcohol, which is why one may find crystalline structures attached to the cork in a bottle of wine or floating in the wine. Although these crystals do not detract from the quality of the wine, other than its aesthetics, they are far less common today because the wine is cold-stabilized. **Cold stabilization** causes the tartaric acid to precipitate and be strained from the wine prior to bottling.
- Tartrates are scraped out of the insides of emptied vats or tanks and are sold to bakers as cream of tartar, which is used as a stabilizer in baking.
- Malic acids are found in Granny Smith apples and can also contribute to the perception of bitterness. Malic acids are frequently converted to lactic acids in wines to soften the tartness. (This will be detailed in the section on wine making.)
- Citric acids are found only in traces, because they disappear during vinification.

Wine Varieties

Vitis vinifera is considered to be the wine vine. This species is genetically unstable and has produced over 5000 identified varieties and hundreds of different clones of each variety. For example, there are more than 1000 clones of Pinot Noir. Each grape variety has specific flavors and can create different styles of wine. Most oenophiles (devotees of wine) are concerned with only 50 or so varieties. Varieties are divided into two categories: white grape and black grape.

White Grape Varieties
Chardonnay.   Chardonnay is used for white **Burgundies,** such as Chablis, Montrachet, Meursault, and Pouilly

Fuissé. It is favored by wine makers because it is so malleable. For example, its flavors can develop enormous complexity by interacting with oak barrels. Chardonnay can provide a firm, full, strong wine with great aromas and character. In chalky soils, it becomes almost luscious without being sweet. It can have good acidity, which allows it to age well, and is usually made dry. It is also a primary grape in the making of **Champagne.** Chardonnay is the leading grape variety of **California** and produces some of the best white wines of Napa and Sonoma in Northern California. It is widely planted in **Washington State** and is thriving in **Australia,** where it is frequently blended with Semillon.

Sauvignon Blanc.   Sauvignon Blanc, the principal white grape of **Bordeaux,** along with Semillon and Muscadelle, makes a dry Graves with an herbaceous and gravelly character. In the Sancerre and Pouilly Fumé regions of the **Loire,** it makes a very acidic, clean, and sometimes spicy herbaceous wine. In warmer climates, such as **Chile,** the grapes can have a tropical melon and fig aroma and flavor. In **California,** it is often referred to as **Fumé Blanc.**

Riesling.   Riesling is considered by many to be the most noble white grape. It can have searing acidity but be balanced by luscious fruit flavors and alcohol. Riesling has beautiful floral aromas, especially a rose quality with hints of apples or peaches. Riesling is grown in **Germany,** its homeland, where it represents only 20% of total production but makes the best quality wine. It can be produced both dry or very sweet. On the banks of the Rhine in Germany, it is very susceptible to the fungus **Botrytis cinerea,** called *Edelfäule* in Germany, *la porriture noble* in France, and noble rot in the United States. This mold dehydrates and causes the grape to shrivel, so that the grape's sugar becomes very concentrated, producing a luscious and complex wine. Riesling is also grown in **Alsace,** where it is made into a delicate and bone-dry wine. It is used successfully in **California** and particularly in **Washington State,** where it tends to be made semi-dry. Riesling is also cultivated in other European countries and is grown extensively in **Australia.**

Chenin Blanc. This is a universal grape, as it is found in **Europe,** the **United States, Australia,** and **South Africa.** Its origin is the **Loire Valley** of France, where it is also known as the Pineau de la Loire. It can be made both bone-dry or very sweet. Chenin Blanc has high acidity, which is balanced by apricot and honey aromas and flavors. Its best expression is found in the wine of **Vouvray** in the Loire and the luscious long-lived dessert wines of the Cotes de Layon.

Gewürztraminer. This grape is native to the Pfalz of **Germany** and has spread to neighboring **Austria** and **Alsace.** *Gewürz* is German for "spicy," as wine made from this grape can be. It has a very distinct aroma, which is jasmine-scented and also reminiscent of lychee fruit. The richness of flavor is supported by a rich, almost oily texture and by average acidity. Gewürztraminer is the only white wine that has a slight bitterness in the finish. This wine can be made both bone-dry, as it is in Alsace, or off-dry, as it is in Germany, **California,** and **Washington State.** It is also susceptible to noble rot (*Botrytis*) and can be made into a luscious dessert wine. The wine of this grape is very underappreciated and, although considered an "aromatic" wine, makes a perfect complement to both Alsatian cuisine and some spicy cuisines of the Orient. It is one of the most adaptable existing wines for pairing with food.

Semillon. Semillon is one of the principal grape varieties of **Bordeaux.** Although it is in decline in that region, it is the basis of the rich and complex *Botrytis* dessert wines of Sauternes. It is often blended in Bordeaux with Sauvignon Blanc. Semillon lacks distinct aromas but develops a wonderfully rich, honeyed, complex bouquet after it has aged 5 or more years. This grape is successfully grown in **Australia,** where it is frequently blended with Chardonnay. It is also produced successfully in **California** and, particularly, **Washington State.***

Pinot Gris. Pinot Gris is a derivative of the Pinot Noir and is known as Pinot Grigio in **Italy,** Ruländer in **Germany,** and Tokay in **Alsace,** where it finds its finest expression. For the most part, it is made into a fairly light-bodied wine
* See Appendix C for update.

with moderate acidity and a floral character (if it has any aroma). When produced in Alsace and **Oregon,** Pinot Gris develops into a more full-bodied and complex wine.

Pinot Blanc. Pinot Blanc also is a mutation of the Pinot Noir grape. Known as the Klevner in **Alsace,** it is similar to Chardonnay but has less complexity of aroma, flavor, and texture. Pinot Blanc is grown in **Northern Italy,** where it is made into a "prosecco" sparkling wine.

Silvaner. Grown in **Germany, Austria, Alsace,** and **Northern Italy,** Silvaner lacks acidity and, for the most part, is not an interesting wine.

Müller-Thurgau. The most prevalent white wine grape in **Germany,** Müller-Thurgau was developed as a hybrid of Riesling and Silvaner. It was developed as a hardier variety that matures earlier and produces higher yields than Riesling and is highly aromatic but lacks the acidity of Riesling. Its best expression is found when made sweet.

Palomino. This grape is used for Sherry production in **Spain.** It yields large crops in a hot climate, producing a neutral tasting wine with low acidity, and oxidizes easily.

Muscat. This aromatic grape has several varieties. Muscat's origin was in ancient Greece, from which it spread to areas around the Mediterranean. Most Muscat is made semi-sweet or sweet, with the exception of **Alsace.** The best Muscats are from **Beaunes de Venise** in the **Rhône** valley of France, and included the most sought-after wine of the eighteenth century, Constantia of **South Africa.** **Italy** uses this grape for the sparkling wines of **Asti. Australia** uses it to produce "liqueur muscats," as do **Oregon** and **California,** where Bonny Doon produce similar liqueurs. Its aromas are very recognizable and reminiscent of fruit salad and orange blossoms.

Ugni Blanc-Trebbiano. This grape variety originated in **Italy** and is the most widely planted white variety in **France** and **Italy.** It produces a low-alcohol wine with little character but high acidity. It forms the basis of **Cognac** and **Armagnac** brandies in France and the **balsamic vinegar** of Modena in Italy.

Muscadet. Otherwise known as the Melon de Bourgogne, it originated in Burgundy but was transplanted in the sixteenth century to the Nantes region of the **Loire Valley.** Muscadet makes a light delicate wine with **floral aromas** and leaves a musky flavor in the mouth, which accounts for its name. It should be drunk young because it does not age well.

Hybridized Varieties. Two of the most frequently used hybrids, especially in **New England,** are Vidal Blanc and Seyval Blanc (alias Seyve-Villard 5/276). They are hardy varietals that can thrive in colder climates. They tend to have good fruit characteristics and good acidity. These hybrids do not make complex wines but can be enjoyed with much of the regional fare of New England.

Black Grape Varieties

Pinot Noir. This black grape's origin is in **Burgundy,** where it has found its greatest expression. Many believe this grape produces the finest reds of the world. Pinot Noir is known for its longevity, complexity of flavors and aromas, and suppleness of texture. The aromas can range from bright berry aromas to earthy, truffle-like bouquets. Pinot Noir has low tannin and good acidity. It is the only black grape allowed in the Appellation Contrôlée of the Côte d' Or of Burgundy. Pinot Noir is a difficult grape to grow successfully, because it is thin-skinned, which makes it prone to poor climatic conditions and pest infestations. Pinot Noir is a primary grape in the production of Champagnes. It is only in the past decade that Pinot Noir has been made into excellent quality wines in **California** and **Oregon.**

Gamay. Its origin is in Burgundy, but it was banished from the Côte d'Or in 1395. Gamay is found in the southern Burgundy region of Beaujolais, where it has adapted well to the granite soil. Gamay makes excellent wines, primarily in the ten **cru** villages of Beaujolais. Gamay wines tend to be light and fresh, with good berry and mint aromas. Beaujolais should, for the most part, be drunk young, especially those produced by **carbonic maceration** fermentation. This grape should not be confused with Gamay Beaujolais, which is the nomenclature for a Pinot Noir clone that is also grown in **California.**

Cabernet Sauvignon. The *Biturica* vine, originally known as the *Balisca,* may have been brought from the Adriatic to the Rioja region of Spain during Roman times and then taken to Bordeaux and became known as Cabernet Sauvignon. This grape variety is found not only in **Bordeaux,** but also in **Italy, Spain, California, Washington State, Chile,** and **Australia.** Cabernet Sauvignon is a tiny grape with a higher ratio of skin to pulp, producing a very astringent wine. It produces a wine that has aromas of cassis, mint, eucalyptus, and very often vegetal (green bell pepper) characteristics. Cabernet Sauvignon is full bodied and has good acidity, which gives it the ability to age well and develop into a supple and complex wine. It is blended with Merlot and its cousin Cabernet Franc, especially in the Médoc region of Bordeaux, for mellowing. When blended in this manner in California, it is frequently called **Meritage.** The better Cabernet Sauvignon–based wines need aging to be fully appreciated.

Cabernet Franc. Cabernet Franc is a cousin to Cabernet Sauvignon but is overshadowed by the latter's power. It is used in **Bordeaux** and is the primary grape for some wines of **St. Emilion,** such as Chateau Cheval Blanc, although it is always blended. Cabernet Franc is the primary grape of many **Loire** reds, such as Chinon and Bourgeuil, and is flourishing in the North Fork region of **Long Island** (NY) and in **California.** Cabernet Franc contains fewer tannins but has a showier **"nose,"** having aromas of violets, blackberries, and licorice.

Merlot. Another cousin to Cabernet Sauvignon, Merlot is grown in the **Bordeaux** region, particularly as the principal grape of St. Emilion and Pomerol. Merlot produces a less tannic wine that is soft but full bodied. It has cherry and earthy flavors that complement Cabernet Sauvignon, with which it is frequently blended. Merlot also is grown in **Northern Italy, California, Washington State, Long Island, Chile, Australia,** and **South Africa.** This wine is increasingly popular because it is less astringent and can be appreciated upon release.

Syrah. Also known as **Shiraz** in **Australia,** Syrah may have originated in Persia. Grown in the Rhone **Valley,** Syrah finds its most splendid expression in Côte Rôtie and Hermitage wines. It is used as the basis for Australia's finest red wine, Grange, and also as a blend with Cabernet Sauvignon. Syrah has aromas of black pepper, violets, and black currants. The finest expressions are full bodied, high in alcohol, and tannic and can age over decades. There has been increasing demand for Syrah cuttings in **California,** particularly in Mendocino, Napa, and Sonoma.

Grenache. Its origin is Spain, where it is known as Garnacha. Grenache is grown in the **southern Rhone** Valley and in southern France. It is a sweet grape that makes a strong-flavored and alcoholic wine, and it is the basis for many **Châteauneuf-du-Pape** wines. Tavel wines are France's premier rosé wines, made exclusively from Grenache. Grenache is also one of the principal varieties used in the making of Rioja wines in **Spain.** There has been increasing demand for Grenache in **California,** where it has been used primarily for making rosé wines.

Tempranillo. Its origins may be southern France, but it has established itself as the premier grape for making Spanish wines. Tempranillo is the key varietal for making Spain's Rioja, Catalan, and Ribera del Duero wines. It has good color and fruit flavors, relatively low acidity, and good tannins and is well suited to oak aging.

Zinfandel. There has been much speculation as to its origin, because its name appears in no country other than the United States. It has been conclusively proven that it is related to the Primitivo grape of Italy, but it may well have arrived via Hungary. Zinfandel is one of the most widely planted varietals in **California,** where it can be vinified in very different styles. From the huge, tannic, alcoholic, smokey, black pepper, and blackberry styles of Ridge or Ravenswood to the fruity, simple, semi-sweet blush wines such as **White Zinfandel** from Sutter Home, this varietal demonstrates its adaptability to the winemaker's art. The best quality comes from cooler areas of Amador and Sonoma counties, and it can age for decades.

Sangiovese. Grown in Tuscany, **Italy,** and used as the principal grape in the production of **Chianti,** Sangiovese has good acidity and makes a dry wine, although is very susceptible to climatic changes from year to year. In hot years, it makes a rich, alcoholic, and long-lived wine, whereas in cool years, it tends to be overly tannic and acidic. **Californians** have demanded more Sangiovese cuttings, and it is probable that the vintners will blend Sangiovese with Cabernet Sauvignon in the same manner as Supertuscan red producers. Sangiovese is also known as **Brunello di Montalcino,** which can age for decades.

Nebbiolo. Dating possibly back to ancient Roman times, this varietal is found primarily in the Piedmont region of **Italy.** Nebbiolo, which is named after the mists that sweep down from the mountains, produces the great wine of Barolo, Barbaresco, and Barbera. These wines tend to be tannic, quite austere, and high in alcohol, but they mature into remarkably fine and elegant wines. Their aromas have a haunting iris floral quality, and their bouquets develop into a very earthy, truffle-like character. **Californians** have shown greater interest in this varietal and are expected to produce quality wines in the near future.

Hybridized Varieties. Many were developed mostly as a response to *Phylloxera,* while some occurred by chance, such as **Catawba,** which became the basis of **Ohio's** sparkling wine industry in the mid-1800s. Many hybrids, such as **Chancellor** and **Baco Noir,** are used, particularly in **New England, New York,** and **Canada.**

The Climate

Climate refers to the prevailing weather in a region, including:

- Temperature
- Wind
- Rainfall
- Sunshine

Temperature

Growing seasons vary with climates, so it is important to understand that the grape's amount of sugar and acidity is directly correlated to the climate in which it grows. Professors Maynard Amerine and Albert Winkler, at the University of California–Davis School of Oenology, developed a model that demonstrated that different grape varietals develop at their best in different climates. Geographic areas were designated as Heat Summation Areas, in which the average temperature of each area was calculated during the growing season. The climatic zones were divided into five areas:

Region I   Less than 2500° F
Region II   2501–3000° F
Region III   3001–3500° F
Region IV   3501–4000° F
Region V   4001–4500° F

The growing season in the northern hemisphere begins on April 1, because the average temperature must exceed 50° F for the vine to awaken from winter dormancy. New shoots develop from the dormant buds. This is referred to as bud-break. Flowering occurs from mid-May to June, and tiny berries appear and develop but remain green until mid-July. The onset of ripening is called **véraison** (French for "true season"), when the berries develop color and begin to soften. The fruit is harvested beginning in mid-September but varies from region to region, due to weather conditions of the particular vintage and the grape varietal used.

Temperatures are very important to wine making. Higher temperatures elevate the amount of sugar in the grape. Conversely, acidity declines faster, and it is this inverse relationship that concerns the winemaker who is looking to balance alcohol and acidity in wine. The development of the varietal's characteristics is the other principal factor that the winemaker must monitor carefully. Usually the winemaker works in tandem with the vineyard manager to harvest the optimum quality of grape to ferment into wine.

Ancient Romans recognized that there is a correlation between fine wines and cooler climates, which yield smaller quantities but a higher quality of fruit. Cooler regions provide an environment for the flavors and color of the grape to develop more fully while retaining good acidity. Acidity is the component in wine that makes it refreshing. This is the reason the world's best wines are found in cool regions.

Rainfall

Rainfall is ideal during winter, because the vines' deep root systems can extract the moisture during the growing season. Rainfall during the growing season, however, can be troublesome, because it causes fungal diseases and fruit bunch rot. Too much rain in the summer can bloat the grapes and reduce the sugar content.

Wind

Winds are significant in that they can affect the heat that is trapped between the vines, resulting in sudden changes in temperature. Wind stress is produced, particularly in young vines, and can reduce the yield and ripening process of the vines. To diminish the effects of winds, windbreaks of all types are used, such as fast-growing trees or tall shrubs.

Sunlight

Sunlight is essential to the life of the plant, because part of its energy is used by the vine to combine carbon dioxide from air with water from the soil. This process of photosynthesis forms sugar in the grape. The amount of direct sunlight on the grapes themselves also plays a significant role in their health and condition.

Growing Conditions

Growing conditions include

- Soil or terroir
- Irrigation
- Weather in the particular vintage

- Viticultural practices of pruning, pesticide use, yield management, age of vines, and harvesting.

Terroir

Terroir is a French term that has been greatly misunderstood in the United States. It has been the contention of Californian oenologists that the soil merely supports the vine and is a reservoir for water and nutrients. They do not believe, as do the French, that the soil contributes to the flavors of grapes. *Terroir* encompasses not only the composition of the soil, but also climate, sunlight, topography, geology, and hydrology.

Irrigation

Irrigation, which is used in California and the Northwest, Australia, and Chile, can result in consistently high quality yields of grapes if used judiciously. Drip irrigation is more prevalent because it is more cost effective than boom irrigation. Irrigation is not allowed in fine-wine regions of Europe, resulting in significant differences from vintage to vintage.

Vintage

Vintage from the French word *vendange*, meaning "harvests," but it also refers to the year in which the wine is made. Weather conditions can be ideal or detrimental to the development of grapes and determine the quality of the vintage year. Vintage years that are deemed "great" are usually exceptions to the rule in Europe. The implication of a great vintage is the winemaker's ability to take advantage of the grape's full flavor development and balance its alcohol and acidity.

Some wines can be made without a vintage year indicated on the bottle. These nonvintage wines are usually a blend of different vintages, such as many Champagne wines. See Figure 5–1 for generalized assessments of vintages in different regions.

Viticultural Practices

The grape grower can influence considerably the development of the grape's flavor and composition by manipulating the vine in different ways. The selection of rootstock and clone will affect the result. The age of the vine has considerable impact on the flavors of the fruit. The vine does not provide sufficiently high enough yield or quality of fruit until its fourth year. Many vines do not attain their peak quality until their tenth year. There are many areas with vines that are 100 years or older. For the most part, vines are productive for about 25 to 40 years.

The size and shape of the vine is controlled by **training, trellising,** and **pruning.** The training and trellising of vines impact the canopy management of the vine. Canopies are the leaves of the vine that absorb sunlight for photosynthesis. In the New World (i.e., the United States and Australia), canopy management encourages leaf growth to limit yields. **Pruning** not only determines the growth of the vine, but also the number of buds, which will affect the number of clusters and, therefore, the yield of the fruit.

The number of vines per hectare (2.47 acres) can vary enormously but are limited by appellation laws in European countries. There is currently considerable controversy regarding correlation between high vine density and good quality.

Yield Management

Different varietals produce different yields. Those high-yielding varietals such as Colombard or Carignan produce undistinguished wines that may be deemed "jug" wines or *vin ordinaire.* These varietals tend to do well in warm climates and have high alcohol but less acidity.

Fine wine varietals can be manipulated further to offer greater flavor by reducing the yield via pruning and crop thinning or the *vendange vert* (green harvest). This occurs either before flowering or after fruit set. One can under-

Figure 5–1 Assessment of vintages from various regions

White Wine and Champagne

Vintage	France/Burgundy	France/Champagne	France/Sauterne	Germany/Riesling	California/Chardonnay
1976				19	
1977				16	
1978				14	
1979		18		18	
1980	15	16		13	17
1981	16	17		16	17
1982	17	19		16	16
1983	17	17	19	19	16
1984	16	16	14	15	17
1985	19	19	17	17	18
1986	18	17	18	17	18
1987	17	16	16	17	17
1988	18	18	19	19	18
1989	18	18	20	18	17
1990	18	18	20	19	18
1991	17		15	17	18
1992	19		14	18	19
1993	16			18	18
1994	17			17	

Scale:
Superior 20
Excellent.........19
Very Good 18
Good..............17
Average..........15-16
Poor...............13-14

stand why some fine wines are so expensive when up to 50% of the crop is thinned and discarded.

Appellation Contrôlée laws limit the maximum amounts of yield per hectare to ensure that quality standards are maintained. There has long been a consensus among experts that low yields are synonymous with high-quality wines. Production under 225 cases per acre seems to be the limit for top-quality wine production.

Harvesting

The decision to harvest is made jointly by the vineyard manager and the winemaker. In the United States, the

Figure 5–1 Assessment of vintages from various regions *(continued)*

Red Wine and Port

	France		Italy			Portugal	California
Vintage	Bordeaux	Burgundy	Brunello di Montalcino	Chianti and Tuscan Wines	Piedmont	Vintage Port	Cabernet Sauvignon
1945						20	
1947						19	
1948						20	
1955						19	
1960						17	
1961	20						
1962						16	
1963						20	
1964	16					16	
1965						16	
1966	18					19	
1967						18	
1968						15	
1969		19				14	
1970	18	16				19	
1971	16	18					
1972	12					16	
1973	14	14					
1974	12	13				15	18
1975	17	13				16	17
1976	16	17				15	15
1977	12					19	16
1978	17	18				17	19
1979	17		18			15	18
1980	16	16	16			17	17
1981	16	15	16				17
1982	19	16	17		18	17	16
1983	17	16	18		15	18	16
1984	14	15	14		16	16	19
1985	19	19	19	19	19	19	19
1986	19	16	17	17	17	16	19
1987	15	17	16	16	17	18	19
1988	19	18	19	19	18	16	16
1989	20	19	16	16	19	16	17

(continued)

Figure 5–1 Assessment of vintages from various regions *(continued)*

Red Wine and Port

| Vintage | France | | Italy | | | Portugal | California |
	Bordeaux	Burgundy	Brunello di Montalcino	Chianti and Tuscan Wines	Piedmont	Vintage Port	Cabernet Sauvignon
1990	19	20	20	20	19	16	19
1991	14	17		16	16	19	19
1992	14	16		15	14	19	19
1993	17	18		16	17		17
1994	17						19

Scale:
Superior 20
Excellent.........19
Very Good 18
Good 17
Average..........15-16
Poor...............12-14

sugar level is measured by using a refractometer indicating the Brix measurement. The Brix scale measures the density of sugar in the grape juice, which accurately reflects the potential alcohol level of the wine.

Most of the harvesting is done mechanically, because it is less labor intensive than hand harvesting and grapes can be brought to the winery expeditiously, before oxidation takes place. As soon as the grape is picked, **oxidation** begins. Oxidation is the chemical reaction that occurs when oxygen comes into contact with the juice of the grape. For example, if you cut an apple and leave it exposed to room temperature, it will turn brown and mushy. If you place that apple in a refrigerator, it will not turn color as quickly and will remain crisp.

To prevent oxidation, which occurs at a faster rate in warmer climates, harvesting might take place at night, and refrigerated trucks might be used to replicate a cooler climate. Grapes may be sprayed with sulphur dioxide to neutralize the natural yeast on their blooms. Sulphur dioxide also acts as a retardant to oxidation.

For the finest of wines, such as in Champagne and Bordeaux, pickers hand-sort through the grapes to allow only

the best quality to be used. This process, called **triage,** is very expensive because it is labor intensive.

Pesticides

Pesticides destroy, repel, or reduce the impact of bacteria, fungi, and insects. Due to the greater awareness of environmental issues, however, vineyard managers are rethinking the use of chemical pesticides and their long-term impact on human beings. Integrated Pest Management (IPM) is a system encouraged by the U.S. federal government to minimize chemical usage. For example, instead of spraying an entire vineyard, only affected areas are sprayed. IPM encourages a more thorough knowledge of pests and their life cycles, monitoring their activity, and allowing insect predators. Those predators in turn might be limited by the inclusion of birds of prey, such as owls. Thus, the natural food chain is restored.

Many vineyard managers are moving away from the monoculture of the vine and are growing such plants as mustard greens, which may attract some pests away from the vines and fertilize the soil naturally. Birds are a major pest, because they *enjoy* harvesting the fruit. Netting is used in many parts of the world to protect the vines.

Wine Making

Wine can be divided into five classifications:

- Table wine
- Dessert wine
- Sparkling wine
- Fortified wine
- Aromatized or Apéritif wine

Although all are a result of the winemaker's decision, they are determined largely by the ability of the grape to develop best into these different classifications. In this way, winemakers are no different than chefs who make decisions based on type and quality of ingredients.

Table Wine

Although the procedures for making white wine vary from those for red wine, most of the steps are similar enough to discuss in tandem. Table wines range in alcoholic strength from 6.5% to 15.5%. These wines are made dry or off-dry (semi-sweet) for the most part, and the normal alcoholic range is from 10% to 12%. The wines can be pale white to amber, crimson to tile brick red, or just a shade of salmony pink for rosé or blush wines.

The steps for making white and red wines are

1. Destemming
2. Pressing or crushing
3. Chaptalization
4. Maceration
5. Fermentation
6. Malolactic fermentation
7. Fining and racking
8. Blending and aging
9. Finishing and bottling

Destemming

Once the grapes are harvested, they are transported to the winery. Most grapes then go through a process to remove the stalks and stems, by a machine called a crusher destemmer. Although with some mechanical harvesters, the grapes are already removed from the stalks and stems.

White grapes are pressed and strained in various types of machines to extract the juice (**must**), with minimum amounts of solids present. Black grapes may or may not be destalked. The stalks of Pinot Noir or Merlot can make a positive contribution to the final quality to the wine by adding tannins. Grapes such as Cabernet Sauvignon or Syrah have sufficient tannin extract from their skins without requiring the addition of stems.

Pressing (White Wine)

White grapes are gently pressed in a horizontal or balloon press, which squeezes out their juice without extracting tannins by crushing the pips. The first pressing by a mechanical press may extract up to 75% of the juice. This juice may be used for better quality wine. Subsequent pressings will be of lower quality, while the final 10% to 15% will be high in tannins, iron, and color. The remaining solids, consisting of the last 10% to 15% of juice with stems, pipes, and skins, is called **marc** in French and **pomace** in the United States. Marc can be used to make inexpensive brandies (e.g., Marc de Champagne) or vinegars, or can be composted to be used as fertilizer for the vineyard.

The must is generally treated with sulfur dioxide to prevent oxidation and inhibit fermentation. It is then pumped into a holding tank where it can be cold-sterilized to precipitate as many solids out of the must as possible before fermentation.

Crushing (Red Wine)

The oldest method of crushing is to place the grapes in a vat or other large holding container and stomp on the grapes with one's feet. This still occurs in a few areas but is becoming increasingly rare.

Black grapes are now crushed in a mechanical grape crusher, unless the winemaker is making a clear wine such as a champagne. The grapes in this case would be pressed in the same manner as white grapes. The **must** is then treated with sulfur dioxide and then pumped into a fermenting or maceration vat or tank. If **must** is **chaptalized,** it needs to be prior to fermentation.

Chaptalization

Chaptalization is the process of adding sugar to must before fermentation. It usually gives wine a rounder, softer texture, making it more appealing in a shorter amount of time. The term was coined after Chaptal, the Minister of Interior under Napoleon. He wrote a treatise advocating the addition of beet sugar to strengthen the alcoholic content of wine.

Chaptalization is prevalent in northern Europe, the Northeast of the United States, and Canada, where the climates are often insufficient to allow the grapes to mature sufficiently. Although it is allowed in Burgundy, it is tightly controlled by the Institute National des Appellations d'Origine and varies in use depending on the vintage. It is not allowed in Bordeaux, the Rhone Valley, California, or the Northwest. In Germany, the use of chaptalization is forbidden for any quality wines labeled *Qualitätswein mit Prädikat*.

Maceration (Red Wine)

The color of wine is extracted from the skins of grapes. Although many winemakers continue the time-honored approach of extracting color during the fermentation process, others macerate the semi-liquid mass of must with the grape skins and stems prior to fermentation.

To macerate without fermentation, the winemaker needs to keep the must cold (below 48° F). This process, which is referred to as cold maceration, may last 2 to 3 days. **Rosé** or **blush** wines are made by allowing brief contact to occur between the must and the skins of the grapes.

Fermentation

White Wine   For fermentation to occur, not only do yeast and sugar need to be present, which has been discussed, but the temperature needs to be controlled. Fermentation is a violent process. Heat, which is a byproduct of fermentation, can reach temperatures over 100° F if left uncontrolled. At that temperature, the yeast would die. Before the advent of current technology, in northern Europe, temperatures were often too cold to allow fermentation to occur naturally. The temperature needs to exceed 48° F

for the yeasts to be active. Fermenting rooms (*cuverie*) were often warmed. In California and Australia, the temperature of the room or the fermenting tank needed to be cooled. Technology, however, has allowed the winemaker to control fermentation precisely via the use of stainless steel vats, which have cooling "jackets." Small wood barrels (**barriques**) are still used for the finest of wines, but research has demonstrated fairly conclusively stainless steel's advantage at every other level of wine making.

Fermentation normally takes place between 50° F and 59° F. The warmer the temperature, the shorter the fermentation time. At this normal range, fermentation will last 1 to 3 weeks. Cooler fermentation temperatures result in more refreshing, fruitier, and faster-maturing wines. While warmer temperatures can be detrimental to most white wines, the best Chardonnays from Burgundy, for example, are fermented in oak barrels at 77° F to gain further complexity and longevity.

Red Wine.   Black grapes are fermented with their skins and pips. The grapes are fermented in vats called *cuves*, which are usually made of wood but also concrete, stainless steel, or glass-lined plastic tanks.

Fermentation occurs at higher temperatures (65–86° F) than for white wine. If temperatures are allowed to climb above 86° F, the fruitiness and delicacy of the wine may be diminished.

Red wines can be fermented at cooler temperatures to extract greater fruit flavors. During fermentation, carbon dioxide and heat force the skins and stems to the surface, which will cause a cap, or *chapeau,* to form. This cap needs to be punched down to prevent it from forming a hardened skin, which will trap the heat in the wine.

Many winemakers "bleed" (*saigner*) their tanks early in the fermentation process. This process involves the releasing of some of the must to concentrate the flavors in the remaining must in the vat. This run-off can also be sold as a light rosé, which in Bordeaux is called *Clairet.*

Inverse osmosis is another process that is used, particularly in poor vintage years. This process concentrates the must by removing water from it. Fermentation can last from a few days to 6 weeks, but 1 to 3 weeks is the normal range. It ends when all sugars are eaten by the yeast, or when the alcohol level reaches 14% and, in a very few cases, 15%.

Fermentation can be *prematurely* arrested for a number of reasons:

First, a **stuck fermentation** can take place. This can be a result of temperatures exceeding 98° F (killing the yeast), insufficient nitrogen in the must, or insufficient aeration during fermentation. If wild yeast is used, the fermentation can become stuck due to the yeast's lower tolerance to alcohol. *Second,* **alcohol** in the form of brandy or neutral spirits is added to the must, raising the alcohol content above the range for yeast. This is done to leave residual sugar in the wine, such as is done in port wines. *Third,* **pasteurization** is applied. This not only neutralizes all harmful bacteria in the wine, but also yeast. Wines are usually flash-pasteurized by heating the wine to 185° F for 1 minute. This process is opposed by many who believe that the wine is stripped of flavor components, and it is, therefore, not used for wines requiring bottle aging. *Fourth,* **sulphurization** takes place. This practice is more prevalent in making sweet dessert wines, because residual sugar results from stopping fermentation. The use of sulphur, however, is far more constrained today than in the past due to legislation limiting its use. *Fifth,* **filtration** can be used to filter yeasts out of wine. A rough filter followed by a sterile filtration process prevents harmful bacteria or yeasts from remaining in the wine during clarification and final bottling stages.

Malolactic Fermentation

Malolactic fermentation occurs in almost all reds and in many whites after the alcoholic fermentation. It is caused by bacteria present in the wine, not by yeasts. The lactobacteria convert the malic acids in the wine into lactic acids. This transforms acidic wine into a softer, *buttery* wine. Wines from the cooler climates are often subjected to this treatment to modify their acidic nature.

Malolactic fermentation, however, can have the undesirable effect of leeching out or masking the fruit flavors from the wine. To prevent malolactic fermentation from occurring, the wine has to be centrifuged or filtered and the storage vessel has to be sanitized.

Lees and Batonnage

Once fermentation has ended, the solids in the wine precipitate and fall to the bottom of the tank or wine cask, forming a sediment. This sediment consists mostly of dead yeast cells and is referred to as **lees.** Some wines are left on the lees (*sur lie*) to add complexity to the wine (e.g., Muscadet, high-quality Chardonnays from Burgundy or California, and Champagne wines). Most wines are fined without lees treatment.

Lees is stirred in a process called **battonage** to help spread the flavor components throughout the wine. It adds a certain creamy quality to white wine, in addition to acting as a natural disinfectant and promoting malolactic fermentation.

Fining

Fining is the process for clarifying the wine. This involves adding a protein substance such as gelatin, egg whites, caseine, bentonite clay, and isinglass. Fining is applied to almost all still wines. It can remove compounds such as tannins, which are desirable in wine, if it is not applied with care. If given sufficient aging time, wine will eventually clarify itself.

Racking

Normally, wines are drawn off the lees once fermentation has occurred. The process is referred to as racking. The young wine is drawn from one vat, cask, or barrel to another, leaving the lees behind. This operation involves the loss of 2% or 3% of the wine's volume. All fine wines are racked a minimum of twice, while the finest wines are racked four times the first year and twice more in the second. Racking also is used to aerate the wine.

Blending and Aging

Wines can develop greater complexity through the process of aging, or *élevage.* The medium in which this process takes place is critical. Maturation will take place only if wood is used as the medium. **Oak** is used because it is both supple, hard, and sufficiently porous to allow slow and minute interaction with oxygen to add flavor to wine without losing its water-tight qualities. The source of the oak, its treatment, age, and size all contribute to the amount of flavor it imparts to wine. Oak from different regions of France— **Limousin, Tronçais, Allier, Nevers,** and **Vosges**—tend to be tighter grained than American oak, which is more porous, giving wine more distinct vanillin and tannic flavors. Oak barrels from these French forests are very expensive, averaging over $600 for a barrique in 1995, compared to comparably sized American oak barrels at $180 each.

The science of making good barrels is quite complex and performed by a **cooperage** firm. The degree to which the oak is **"toasted,"** or charred, by fire in the making of the barrel affects the amount of toastiness there is in wine aged in wood. The smaller the barrel, the more the oak is in contact with the wine. The small barrique holding 225 liters gives considerably more oak flavors than some barrels holding 40,000 liters. The newer the oak, the more extract will be contributed to the wine. Oak barrels that are used longer than 4 years become mere storage vessels, contributing little flavor to the wine. Other woods can be used, but they do not complement wines in a similar manner.

During the first few months the wine is aging in wood, it will evaporate and be absorbed by the wood. The air space created by this evaporation in the cask is referred to as **ullage.** Ullage must be filled with the same wine to prevent oxidation. Casks are sealed loosely with glass bungs (stoppers) during this period of **topping off** and are later replaced with wooden bungs. These are tightly fitted and the barrels are turned 30 to 40 degrees to submerge the bung so that oxygen cannot seep into the cask at a faster rate. During aging, wine will throw off impurities, which will fall to the bottom of the cask. The wine is then racked to another cask.

Many wines cannot stand up to 100% oak aging. For example, a winemaker might blend three lots of Chardonnay from the same vintage and vineyard; the first 100% oak-aged in new casks, the second aged in older wood, and the third lot aged in stainless steel.

Blending also takes place in the cellar. The process of blending, or **assemblage,** is the opportunity for the winemaker to create the style of wine desired. The percentages of different blends will vary slightly from year to year, depending on the characteristics of the wines for that particular vintage.

Aging takes place both in the **cellar** (*chai*) and in the bottle. Some winemakers age their wines so that they reach perfect maturity at the cellar (e.g., tawny port or *Vega Sicilia Unico*). Most release their wines with the recognition that they need bottle aging to reach their peak (e.g., the great white and red wines of California, Bordeaux, Burgundy, or Rhône). These winemakers generally release their wines within 2 years of the vintage.

Finishing and Bottling

Prior to bottling, wine is often centrifuged or filtered. Centrifuging wine allows solids to be removed, but this can lead to a dilution of flavors and is not used for fine wine.

As has been mentioned, wine is generally filtered twice. The first is a rough filtration, while the second is a sterile filtration carried out immediately prior to bottling. This is to prevent any yeast or harmful bacteria from entering the bottle.

Fine wines, particularly reds, do not go through a filtration, because many winemakers believe it will cause wines to lose flavor components that add complexity to the wine. Many fine red wines are sold as *unfiltered* and may not have the clarity of other reds.

Winemakers can correct a wine's balance by finishing or correcting the balance of the wine. Generally, this applies to adjusting the acidity of the wine by adding ascorbic acid. This is a practice that is not uncommon in warmer climates, where wines lack acidity.

Bottles are sterilized before filling. Once the bottle is filled, the neck may be filled with nitrogen or carbon dioxide to prevent oxidation. The bottle is corked, and the wine is stored upside down to keep the cork moist. (Bottling machines can fill more than 55 bottles per minute.)

Cork is the bark taken from a species of oak tree prevalent in Spain and Portugal. It is stripped from the oak once it is 25 years old and can be harvested from a tree every 9 to 15 years. Cork is the perfect stopper or seal because it is impervious to liquids. It will last about 25 years before it needs to be replaced.

Note: Wine is not usually shipped for sale until it is allowed to rest for several weeks, due to **bottle shock.**

Special Wine-Making Method

Carbonic Maceration

Carbonic maceration is a red wine–making method prevalent in the Beaujolais area of Burgundy, France, northern Italy, and California for Gamay Beaujolais. The purpose of this method is to extract a fruity, light-bodied, aromatic wine such as Beaujolais Nouveau. Grape bunches are hand picked and left whole when placed in a sealed fermenting vat. The weight of the grapes crush the grapes at the bottom, and fermentation begins. Carbon dioxide is released by fermentation and is trapped in the sealed vat. The fermentation takes place inside the upper grapes, resulting in a less tannic and fruitier wine.

Dessert Wine

Dessert wines are made from grapes with a minimum of 24° Brix. There are four methods for making a dessert or sweet wine:

1. **Mutage** is the adding of alcohol or sulphur dioxide to prevent the yeast from continuing to convert sugar into alcohol. This method was first applied by Arnaud de Villeneuve in the thirteenth century.
2. **Late harvest** wines. Generally, grapes are harvested a minimum of 1 week after the regular harvest to allow them to ripen further. There is an inherent risk in leaving the grapes on the vine, as both climate and pests can become more of a danger to them.
3. The development of **Botrytis cinerea** on the grapes. As has been discussed previously, this mold causes the grape to dehydrate and allows the sugar content to increase dramatically and proportionately to the water in the grape. The best examples of this type of wine are from Sauternes in France, Trockenbeerenauslese in Germany, the Neusiedlersee in Austria, Tokay wines of Hungary, and late-harvest Rieslings of California and the Northwest.

4. **Ice wine.** This process originated in Germany and is known as *eiswein*, whereby the grapes are left on the vine until frozen by cold weather. The grapes are then quickly harvested and pressed. The sugar is more concentrated in the must because much of the iced water crystals remains in the press. This process has been replicated artificially in California by harvesting and freezing the grapes artificially.

In the United States, the producer must declare the Brix level on the label, both prior to harvesting and after the wine is fermented. The German model for classifying different levels of sweetness is used by American producers:

Late Harvest	24° Brix
Select Late Harvest	28° Brix
Special Select Late Harvest	35° Brix

Sparkling Wine

There are five major methods for producing a sparkling wine, the most famous of which is named for the region in which it originated: **Champagne,** France.

- **Champagne method,** or methode champenoise (also known as classic method)
- **Transfer method**
- **Dioise method**
- **Charmat** or **bulk method**
- **Carbonation** or **injection method**

Champagne Method

With the champagne method, a second fermentation takes place in the bottle, and the carbon dioxide produced by it is trapped in the bottle. Three grape varietals are used: Chardonnay, Pinot Noir, and Pinot Meunier. The grapes are harvested and undergo a triage system. They are carefully pressed to avoid contact with skins and pips. The best juice is called the **cuvée** and is reserved for premium champagne. The second pressing is called *première taille*, which is also used for making less distinguished but still excellent sparkling wine. The wines are fermented dry, resulting in 10% to 11.5% alcohol, and may be stored in steel tanks or aged in wood.

There are three levels of quality in Champagne:

1. **Prestige** Cuvée or Premium Champagne that is made from a specific vintage year and uses the best **must,** or *tête de cuvée,* from the best vineyards. A premium champagne is generally known for the name given it by the champagne house, such as Dom Pérignon of Moët et Chandon.
2. **Vintage** champagne, because the wine is made from a particularly good vintage. Vintage champagnes may be made only three times in a decade. The vintage year is printed on the label.
3. **Non-vintage or *multi-vintage champagne,*** which is a blend of wines from different vintage years and is crafted to represent the style of a producer so that it appeals to the consumer on a consistent basis.

The wines are then blended for flavor and consistency to form the base wine, called **assemblage.** This is a difficult process because not only do the varietals but also the different vintages need to be blended to create balance, style, and consistency, blends of varietals affect the style of the wine. For example:

Blanc de Blancs	100% Chardonnay
Blanc de Noirs	100% Pinot Noir and Pinot Meunier
Rosé	Short skin contact or addition of up to 5% red Pinot Noir from Bouzy
Crémant	A sparkling wine with half the pressure; light, delicate, and creamy

To create a **second fermentation,** a solution of wine, sugar, and yeast, called **liqueur de tirage,** is added to the wine and bottled, The bottle is sealed with a stainless steel cap, or **agraffe,** so that the carbon dioxide cannot escape. This is the **prise de mousse,** or capturing of the bubbles. There may be more than 70 million bubbles in a bottle of Champagne. The pressure of the carbon dioxide is equal to 6 atmospheres or 90 pounds per square inch.

The bottles are then stored on their sides in a dark cool cellar, or **cave.** It takes 3 to 4 weeks for the second fermentation to be completed and all the remaining sugar to

be converted into alcohol. This process adds an additional 1% to 1.5% alcohol, bringing the total to 12% or 12.5%.

The next stage is **remuage,** or **riddling.** The remaining lees is stuck to the side of the bottle and needs to be moved down to the neck of the bottle. Classically, this was accomplished manually by a remueur or riddler who could shake and turn as many as 30,000 bottles a day. With this method, an A-frame wooden rack, called a **pupître,** is used. The sides of the frame are extended wider during these weeks so the necks of the bottles point in a more vertical position. Gyropalettes, or automated riddling machines, are used currently by most large producers. Additionally, there have been successful developments of "beads" and membrane cartridges, which contain the yeast cells but allow them to continue converting sugars into alcohol and carbon dioxide. The use of these modern techniques will make riddling redundant (see Figure 5–2).

Bottles are placed upside down and stacked on top of each other (*sur pointe*) to allow the wine to age.

The aging requirements for Champagne is 1 year; for classic-method (CM/CV) sparkling wine in the United States, it is 9 months. During this time, the lees (dead

Figure 5–2 Wine bottles on a pupître

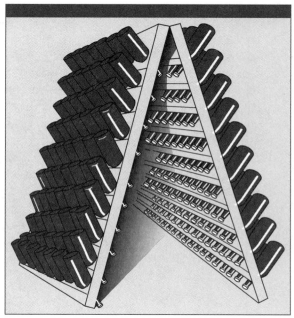

yeast cells) is partially absorbed by the wine through a process called **autolysis,** giving it added flavor and complexity. For vintage Champagne, the aging time is 3 years, and for many super premiums it is as long as 13 years.

Once the lees has been worked down the neck of the bottle, it needs to be expelled. This is done through the process of **dégorgement,** or disgorging. The neck of the bottle is placed in a solution to freeze the top inch or two of wine and trapped lees, forming a plug. The cap is removed and the carbon dioxide expels the plug. The bottle then needs to be filled with additional wine to replace the missing contents. A **liqueur d'expedition,** or **dosage,** consists of the same wine with a possible addition of sugar syrup. The amount of sugar determines the style and sweetness of the wine. The various sweetness levels of wines are as follows:

Brut Sauvage or extra brut	Bone dry, with no trace of sugar
Brut	Very dry, with up to 1.5% sugar but no noticeable sweetness
Extra-dry or Extra-sec	Slightly sweet, up to 2% sugar
Sec or dry	Noticeably sweet, up to 3.5% sugar
Demi-sec	Very sweet, up to 5% sugar
Doux	Extremely sweet, more than 5%

Champagnes are filled in a variety of bottle sizes:

Size	Metric Equivalent
Split	187 milliliters
Half-bottle	375 milliliters
Bottle	750 milliliters
Magnum	1.5 liters (2 bottles)
Jeroboam	3 liters (4 bottles)
Rehoboam	4.5 liters (6 bottles)
Methuselah	6 liters (8 bottles)
Salmanazar	9 liters (12 bottles)
Balthazar	12 liters (16 bottles)
Nebuchadnezzar	15 liters (20 bottles)

Champagne bottles have four special characteristics that other wine bottles do not share:

- They are made of **heavier gauge** glass.
- They have an indentation at the base of the bottle, called a **punt** or kick, which is needed when the wines are stacked upside down, or *sur pointe.*
- The cork is **mushroom** shaped. It is larger in diameter than that used for still wines and is usually made with an agglomerate of two or three disks glued to the end that is in contact with the wine.
- The wire hood, **cage,** or muzzle that keeps the cork in place needs to be turned five times counterclockwise to loosen it.

Transfer Method

The transfer method is very similar to the classic Champagne method until the riddling and disgorgement after the second fermentation in the bottle. To save expense, producers age the wine on the lees and empty the chilled wine into a stainless steel pressure tank, where the wine is filtered of the sediments and a dosage is performed prior to rebottling. The wine will lose some carbonation, and the texture will generally not have the finesse of Champagne-method wines. By law, producers in the United States may label wines that are made using the transfer method as "fermented in *the* bottle"; wines that are made in the classic method are labeled "fermented in *this* bottle" or with the initials CM/CV which is an abbreviation for classic method/classic varietals.

Dioise Method

This method is similar to the transfer method. It is a single fermentation process by which the wine is fermented in steel tanks at very low temperatures. The wine is then filtered and bottled. The fermentation continues in the bottle until the alcohol content reaches 7.5%. The wine is then disgorged before being transferred to new bottles. Asti (Spumante) of Italy is an example of this process.

Charmat or Bulk Method

In the charmat method, the wine is fermented in bulk the first and second time and is bottled only after the wine is given the dosage. This method is faster and less expensive than the transfer or classic methods The quality of sparkling wine is considerably less: The bubbles are larger and the carbonation will dissipate faster.

Carbonation or Injection Method

Carbon dioxide is injected into a tank of wine and bottled under pressure in a method very similar to that used for soft drinks. This method produces the least expensive and least desirable of sparkling wines, because the wine is coarse and the carbonation dissipates quickly. This category represents fewer than 10% of sparkling wines.

Fortified Wines

Fortified wines are those that have had neutral spirits or brandy added, raising the alcohol level to 16% to 22%. This is done to stop fermentation and retain sweetness or simply to ensure the stability of the wine. The most common of the fortified wines are

Type of Fortified Wine	Country of Origin
Port	Portugal
Sherry	Spain
Madeira	Portugal
Marsala	Italy
Vin Doux Naturel	France

Port Wine

Port wine originally comes from the Douro Valley in northern Portugal. It is made from a blend of six varietals. The complete extraction of color was done by foot in a **lagar** (a low-sided stone or concrete trough) but now is done mostly in fermentation vats. The must is fortified when it has fermented to approximately 6% alcohol, and it is then added to barrels filled one fifth with *aguardiente* or brandy (at 77% alcoholic strength). The wine is then aged in used wood, depending on the basic type of port desired.

There are two basic types of port wines: **wood** and **vintage.** They are differentiated by whether they are aged mostly in wood or in the bottle.

Wood Port.   There are different styles of wood ports but all are aged in wood and are meant to be consumed once bottled. The most common styles are **tawny** and **ruby.** Ruby ports are aged in large wood casks for 2 to 3 years. They are deep ruby, have a very full sweet fruit flavor, and are best consumed as an after-dinner beverage. They are

one of the few wines that can stand up to chocolate without being overwhelmed. Tawny ports are aged in wood for 6 or more years. The longer the wines age in wood, the more they lose their color. Tawnys can be blended from wines indicated by the age on the label, such as 10, 20, 30, and 40 years old. The French, who are the largest importers of port, prefer this lighter style of port, which has delicate fruit aromas and a silky texture. The French tend to drink tawny as an apéritif usually chilled.

Consumers should check the date of bottling on tawny ports as they lose their delicate fruit aromas and flavors quickly.

Vintage Port.   Vintage port is the most expensive and represents less than 1% of total production. These ports are made from the best grapes of the best region and from a single vintage year. Generally there are fewer than three vintages out of ten that are "declared." A year after harvest and after repeated tastings, a producer submits samples to a Portuguese governmental agency for approval.

Vintage ports are aged between 2 and 3 years in wood and should then be bottle-aged for 15 or more years by the consumer. These ports can age 50 or more years. They have a great deal of tannins and color, which are turned into sediment with bottle aging. There is so much sediment after a couple of decades that it is referred to as "throwing a crust."

Therefore, vintage port needs to be properly decanted.

Its character becomes softer with age but is still full bodied, with excellent berry and nutty flavors and aromas. Vintage ports are wonderful accompaniments to pears and Stilton cheese. Some of the best vintages of the past three decades are 1994, 1992, 1991, 1985, 1983, 1977, 1970, 1966, and 1963.

To attract new markets, other styles of port wines have developed. One that has become quite prevalent is **Late-Bottled Vintage** (LBV), which is aged 4 to 6 years in wood. It should be bottle-aged another 5 years and needs to be decanted. LBV ports are made from single vintage years that are of lesser quality than vintage ports.

Ports are produced by companies from their own *quintas* (estates) and shipped from their lodges, some of which include Cockburn Crofts, Delaforce, Dow, Ferreira, Graham, Niepoort, Sandeman, Taylor Fladgate, and Warre. Excellent port wines are also produced in Australia, South Africa, and more recently California.

Sherry

Sherry wines are produced in the southern region of Spain, known as Andalucia. The grapes are grown in a triangle delineated by the towns of Jerez de la Frontera, Sanlucar de Barrameda, and Puerto de Santa Maria.

Sherry is the English corruption of the word *Jerez. Xérès* is the French word for sherry. All bottles from this area of Spain are labeled Jerez-Xérès-Sherry. Jerez has an ancient history, settled 3000 years ago by Phoenicians and then by Carthaginians Romans, Visigoths, and Arabs. With the Arab invasion of Spain in the seventh century and their knowledge of distillation, wines made in this area were fortified and thereby stabilized, making them ideal for exporting to England. This practice and that of blending became more prevalent with the loss of South America as a market for these Spanish wines, to preserve the wines that had accumulated.

The soil in this Spanish triangle is distinct in that it is very chalky, and called *albariza*. The hot weather is moderated by cool ocean breezes. The principal grape grown is the **Palomino. Pedro Ximénez** is grown to make a very rare sweet wine known as PX, but it is also added to certain dry sherries to make cream sherries.

Unlike port wines, sherry is fortified after fermentation. The Palomino grapes are harvested, pressed, fermented, and then fortified.

To understand sherry, one has to comprehend the two fundamental processes that make sherries unique:

1. Partial oxidation (through the yeast flor development)
2. Fractional blending (through the solera system)

After the wine is fortified to 15.5% to 17% and placed in American oak casks, a **yeast flor** develops on the wine, forming a crust that prevents the wine from totally oxidizing and that gives it its unique yeasty quality. The yeast flor is naturally present in the air and feeds off the alcohol in the wine. Not all casks, however, are equally affected by a flor, but the development of flor determines the style of sherry.

Once the sherry is classified, it is sent to a warehouse, or **bodega,** where it is aged for a minimum of 3 years and goes through a continuous fractional blending process. The barrels of wine are stored in a tiered system (**criaderas**) in which no more than one third of the wine of 1 year is blended with that of the previous year. This feeding of the older wine with newer wine keeps the flor alive (for as many as 10 years) by providing it with the necessary nutrients.

Typically, there are nine to 14 criaderas in a **solera** system, and soleras can be a blend of more than 50 harvests. The solera system ensures that the style of sherry is consistent and explains why there are no vintages. When a year appears next to the solera, it indicates the year of the earliest harvest. Fino sherries are fined using egg whites.

There are two basic types of sherry wine from which all styles are derived: fino and oloroso. Fino sherries are affected by flor and can vary in style, depending on the locale and aging processes. The principal styles include:

Fino
Amontillado
Manzanilla
Palo Cortado

Fino sherries are the driest category of sherries. They are pale and medium bodied and have a fresh-baked-bread aroma. **Amontillado** is Spanish for "in the style of Montilla." These sherries are darker, almost amber in color, fuller bodied, and nuttier in flavor. They acquire these flavors from aging in the solera system. **Manzanilla** sherries are the lightest and most delicate fino sherries, coming from the coastal town of Sanlucar de Barrameda, where the local flor and sea air give the wine a special tang. **Palo Cortado** starts as a fino , but the flor dies and it becomes an oloroso when its alcohol percentage needs to be augmented to 18% to 20%. It is rare and therefore expensive.

Oloroso sherry never develops a flor. To prevent it from oxidizing, it is fortified to 18% alcohol, an environment that will prevent any flor from developing later and stabilizing the wine. There are two aging processes that olorosos can undergo: baked or long barrel aging. The application of heat speeds up the maturation process. True oloroso is dry, full bodied, and rich. Oloroso sherries are best known when sold as **cream sherries.** Traditionally, this was accomplished by adding a sweet wine made from Pedro Ximénez, but now sweet Palomino grape must is usually used.

Producers of sherry include Gonzalez Byass, Croft, Pedro Domecq, Harvey, Emilio Lustau, Sandeman, Williams and Humbert.

Sherries are generally enjoyed as an apéritif, but in Spain they are viewed as an accompaniment to meals. Fino sherries are best appreciated with food. Fino and Manzanilla should be served chilled (45° F). They are a superb accompaniment to consommes and spicy seafood dishes. Olorosos are best served at room temperature and, if sweet, are a good accompaniment to desserts.

Sherries are served in sherry glasses called **copitas.** They are a very good value, and some have the advantage of not fully oxidizing or losing their aromas quickly. Finos should be treated like fine wines, while olorosos, particularly cream sherries, last in an opened bottle for months before losing their appeal.

Sherries also are produced in South Africa, where a natural yeast flor also exists. California produces a sherry that does not have the same degree of complexity of flavor.

Madeira

Madeira wines are named after the Portuguese volcanic island of Madeira. As with port and sherry, there is a close historical link with England. The Portuguese have long enjoyed close diplomatic relations with the English, who used the island as a port-of-call to replenish supplies on the trans-Atlantic crossings to Charleston, South Carolina, and Savannah, Georgia.

Madeira wines were found to improve with age and with the heat of a transequatorial journey. They were the best wines to be found easily in the American colonies, and it was the beverage toasted at the signing of the Declaration of Independence.

Madeira wine production and reputation were severely affected by *Oidium* and *Phylloxera*. It was only after the Portuguese joined the European Economic Community that quality grapes were replanted on the island.

There are four types of Madeira wines that are named after the grape varietals used:

1. **Sercial** is tart, tangy, and very dry, with almond-like aromas.
2. **Verdelho** is medium dry and develops a wonderful smoky character.
3. **Bual** is medium sweet and rich textured and has prune and nutty aromas.
4. **Malmsey,** an English corruption of Malvasia, is the sweetest type but is balanced by wonderful acidity with hauntingly rich, dark, fruit aromas.

After the wine is fermented, it is fortified. In the case of Bual and Malmsey, fortification occurs prior to complete fermentation. Madeiras are unique in that they undergo a process of heating called the **estufa** system. The wines are heated for a minimum of 3 months if done by direct application of heating coils to the wine, and 6 months if barrels of wine are placed in a room that is heated by steam pipes. The best Madeiras are not artificially heated at all but are placed under the eaves of buildings to allow the sun to heat the wine.

The best madeiras are special reserve, extra reserve, and vintage madeiras:

1. Special reserve Madeiras are a blend of wines, the youngest being 10 years old, all aged in casks without using the estufa system.
2. Extra reserve Madeiras are a blend of minimum 15-year-old wines.
3. Vintage Madeiras are from a single vintage and must be aged a minimum of 20 years in casks and 2 years in the bottle. These wines can age in the bottle for not just decades but well over 150 years.

Vintage Madeiras can throw a little sediment and should be decanted to allow the wine to breathe. Once decanted, the wine will last almost indefinitely. Sercial and Verdelho Madeiras are best served slightly chilled (55° F), while Bual and Malmsey are best served at room temperature. Dry Madeiras can accompany such dishes as consommé and game birds such as quail and pheasant. Bual and Malmsey are best accompanied by biscotti and nuts.

Marsala

Marsala is named after the city of Marsala in western Sicily. It was originally produced in 1770 by John Woodhouse, an English merchant who dealt in sherry, port and Madeira.

Marsala is fortified by alcohol and by concentrated must of overripe grapes to 17% to 19% alcohol. The Grillo grape is considered the quality grape for Marsala. Marsala comes in three colors: oro (golden), ambra (amber), rubino (ruby). Each color comes in three sugar levels: secco (dry), semi-secco (semi-dry), dolce (sweet).

There are five types of Marsala, depending on the amount of oak aging:

Fine	1 year
Superiore	2 years
Superiore Riserva	4 years
Vergine	5 years
Stravecchio	10 years

Due to the proliferation of less well made, inexpensive brands, Marsala has a tarnished reputation, which has resulted in a steep decline in its popularity other than its use in the kitchen. The most innovative makers of Marsala are producing their wines under the label of **Vino da Tavola** (table wine) without mentioning the name Marsala, a fact that hardly bodes well for its future.

Vin Doux Naturel

Vin Doux Naturel (VDN) is French for "naturally sweet wine" but denotes the use of mutage, the arresting of fermentation by adding alcohol during fermentation. The best known white (VDN) wines are made from the Muscat de Frontignan varietal and come from the village of **Beaumes-de-Venise** in the Côtes du Rhône area of France. These wines are golden, rich, and very sweet.

The other appellation for Vin Doux Naturel is Rasteau, where the red Grenache is used to produce complex port-like wines, such as **Banyuls** produces 20- and 30-year-old wines in any significant numbers. Banyuls are matured in wood casks for a minimum of 30 months. The Banyuls Grand Cru develop enormous complexity. This is done in

part by deliberately exposing the wine to oxygen and topping it off with new wine every 6 months. This enables the wine to develop the prized bouquet of **rancio,** which is also found in old cognac. Banyuls are often tawny and have a rich, nutty, pruny flavor and a particularly long, dry finish.

Aromatized or Apéritif Wines

An aromatized wine is usually known as an apéritif wine. Federal regulations define *apéritif wine* as being a minimum of 15% alcohol. It can be flavored with herbs, spices, roots, flowers, bark, and other aromatic and bitter ingredients. Aromatized wine was and still is used as a stimulant and an aid to digestion. As opposed to cocktails and spirits, which deaden the taste buds, an apéritif wine should be offered prior to an especially well prepared meal to stimulate the appetite. Italians use wines and spirits made with bitters as a *digestivo*, or aid to the digestion, after the meal.

Wines were aromatized by the ancient Romans and Greeks to help preserve and camouflage the flavors of wine that had oxidized. There are both dry and sweet aromatized wines, such as Vermouth, Punt e Mes, St. Raphael, Dubonnet, Lillet, and Kir.

Vermouth

Vermouth stems from the German *vermut*, meaning "wormwood." This is an herb that was used frequently in beverages and found its fullest expression in absinthe, an addictive and hallucinogenic liqueur that was outlawed in France in 1915.

Vermouth is made in both a dry white and sweet red style. The French and the Italians make both styles. The wine base is made from inexpensive varietals. A white wine base is used; it is fermented dry, infused with aromatics, and fortified with brandy to 19% alcohol. By law, the French must bottle and age the vermouth 3.5 to 4 years before shipping.

Sweet Vermouth is made from sweeter white varietals that are fermented, fortified to 17% alcohol, and infused with aromatics and quinine. After filtering, caramel coloring and sugar is added. It takes 2 years for an Italian vermouth to be made and aged prior to release.

Dry vermouth is served chilled. It is also used as a substitute for dry white wine in cooking. Sweet vermouths tend to be served on the rocks with a splash of soda. Vermouths tend to be used in the United States to make cocktails such as martinis and manhattans.

The most famous producer of vermouth in France is Nouilly Prat, and in Italy it is Cinzano and Martini & Rossi. Punt e Mes (France) and St. Raphael (Italy) are also brand names for vermouths.

Dubonnet

There is both dry and sweet versions, which are white and red, respectively. Its origin is French, and it is best served chilled or on the rocks with a twist of lemon.

Lillet

Also from France, Lillet is both white or red and dry or off-dry. It is infused with citrus fruit and is best served chilled or on the rocks with a twist or zest of lemon or orange.

Kir

Kir is named after Canon Kir, a mayor of France's second largest city, Lyon. It was originally made with the highly acidic Aligoté white varietal of Burgundy with 2 tablespoons of Crème de Cassis, a black currant liqueur.

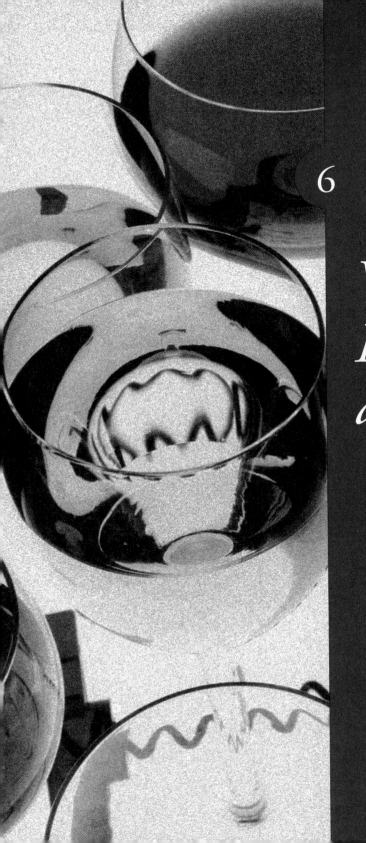

6

Wine
Purchasing
and Tasting

6

Wine Purchasing and Tasting

Wine Purchasing

Now that we have examined the factors that go into the production of wine, we need to investigate how the consumer, in this case the establishment, can make a sound decision in selecting appropriate wines for a wine list. All too often the establishment abdicates this responsibility and leaves the decision making to a wine distributor, the primary goal of which is to sell as much of its wine as is possible to the establishment. This is not to imply that distributors cannot be of great assistance in selecting wines for a wine list, but there are a number of factors that should be taken into consideration when selecting wine.

- Most wines are purchased from distributors, who in turn source their wines from *négociants,* wine merchants or importers. Although it is possible for a food service establishment to purchase directly from vineyards, it is contrary to most state laws.
- It was not so long ago that *négociants* were responsible for aging, bottling, and selling wine for the wineries. The négociants of Europe had better underground cellars, providing superior aging conditions. It is only since the 1920s that fine wine began being aged and cellared at the winery.
- Today, the words *mis(e) en bouteille au Château,* or *estate bottled,* are synonymous with quality. It would be rare to find a fine wine that is not estate bottled.
- It is worth noting that many négociants have become producers of wine in their own right (e.g., Louis Latour or Louis Jadot of Burgundy). This is becoming increasingly common, especially in certain regions of France, where the role of the *négociant* has changed.

Wines are purchased on the basis of **brand name** recognition; **place of origin; varietal** of the wine; the **reputation** of the **négociant,** importer, or distributor; and **cost.**

- By **brand name** recognition, we are referring to the name of the producer, such as Château Lafite Rothschild, the Domaine de la Romanée-Conti, Robert Mondavi, or Opus One. Those purchasing by brand are less interested in the place of origin or the varietal blend that is used.
- As we have seen, France is oriented toward the concept of **place of origin.** While this is somewhat true of American marketing, such as Napa Valley or Sonoma, it is usually the wine producer (i.e., Robert Mondavi, Château Ste. Michelle) or brand name that receives greater attention.
- The marketing of wines by **varietal** is again a fairly recent phenomenon, given the greatest impetus in the United States by Frank Schoonmaker. In response to the very mediocre wines that were being sold under **generic** labels, such as Hearty Burgundy in the 1930s, he suggested to the Californian producers who were attempting to produce fine wines that they label the wines under varietal names. Many consumers make the varietal the primary factor in their purchasing decision (e.g., Cabernet Sauvignon).
- Another factor that is important in purchasing wine is the **reputation of the négociant, importer, and distributor.** The conditions in which wine is transported, especially internationally, should be of concern to the consumer. Some wines are transported in temperature-controlled containers, while others might be exposed to extreme heat or freezing temperatures. Many négociants and importers have built reputations on their abilities not only to purchase fine wines but also to deliver them under optimum conditions.
- **Cost** is a factor in any purchasing decision. The establishment must ensure that the cost of wine falls within the price framework of the food menu. Generally, establishments look for a 100% to 300% return on the cost of the wine. Discount purchasing is usually

possible if buying sufficient volume. The highest price does not equate necessarily with the highest quality; it is more a reflection of supply and demand.

Decoding the Wine Label

The ability to read a wine label is essential because there is much information to glean from it. Unfortunately, for the purchaser, not all areas observe the same laws in using terminology on a label. Terminology is determined in large measure by the legal requirements and limits of the producing country. (See section on labeling requirements.) The information that is of greatest concern to the purchaser is:

- The place of origin
- The quality level
- The vintage year
- Varietal, generic or proprietary labeling

Place of Origin

The place of origin is determined and guaranteed by the official state or regulatory agency of each country. The entire appellation system is based on the primacy of the concept of "place of origin." The wine may be labeled primarily after the location in which the grapes were grown, especially for some quality French and Italian wines. In Europe, if a geographic area is stated on the label, 100% of the grapes have to be grown in that area. In Australia, however, the requirement is that 80% of the grapes have to be grown in that area, and in the United States, 85%.

When determining the place of origin, one needs to examine the geographic level that is given on the label. In general, the more defined the area, the higher the quality of the wine. As the following examples demonstrate, there are four levels, from the broadest to the narrowest geographically defined areas:

The country	France	U.S.A.
The region	Burgundy	California
The village or district	Beaune	Napa
The field or vineyard	Clos des Mouches	Martha's Vineyard

Quality Level

There is no consistency between all countries, but with the development of the European Economic Community (ECC), all European producers have to conform to certain standards. This has led to a common hierarchy of quality.

Each country has a governmental or regulatory agency to oversee viticultural and wine-making practices. These agencies qualify the level of each wine based on place of origin, viticultural practices, and wine-making processes. As will be discussed in greater detail in the next chapter, the quality ratings fundamentally designate three levels of:

1. Table wine in the European sense (lowest)
2. Wine from a designated region
3. Quality wine (highest)

There may be some permutations between one country and another.

The United States also has a federal regulatory agency, the Bureau of Alcohol, Tobacco and Firearms (ATF), as well as state regulatory agencies to oversee the wine industry. The United States, Australia, and other wine-producing New World countries do not have as defined a hierarchical system as does Europe, giving their wine producers greater freedom to experiment.

The brand name or name of a producer may be as significant a designation as the quality rating given by a regulatory agency. For example, Angelo Gaja of Piedmont in Italy produces wines of the highest quality, even though they have been designated by the Italian regulatory agency as *Vino da Tavola,* or table wine. In addition, the purchaser should be aware of the reputation of the *négociant,* wine merchant, or importer reputation (e.g., Frederick Wildman and Sons, Neal Rosenthal, or Kobrand Corporation).

Vintage Year

A vintage, as has been detailed, is a reflection of the weather for a particular year. Thanks to scientific developments, vintages matter a great deal less today than in the past. Winemakers are able to manipulate wines to extract the most flavor possible. However, there are limits to what the winemakers can achieve. They may be able to make a good wine in an "off" year, but not a great wine.

Vintages are assessed by many wine organizations, societies, and publications and are recorded on vintage charts. These may prove useful, but the purchaser should be cautious because charts are notoriously unreliable. One must consider, for example, the sampling of wine for a designated region and when the sampling was tasted. One should check on the frequency with which the chart is updated, because wine changes as it ages.

A great vintage will indicate the potential for a quality wine to develop greater complexity and last longer than those from a mediocre or poor vintage. Vintages have the most impact on fine wines, because they are made to evolve and last. In disastrous vintage years, the producer may not sell wine under his own label in order to protect the integrity of the name.

In Europe, vintages may not appear on the label for a table wine, but the wine must contain a minimum of 85% of a particular vintage if specified on a label. In the United States, however, it is 95% from that year.

Varietal, Generic, or Proprietary Labeling

Wines can be labeled by varietal, generic, or proprietary names.

Varietal

There are very specific laws governing the use of varietal names, whether in the United States, Australia, or Europe. Many wines from France or Italy do not include varietal names, but there is a presumption that the consumer knows what varietals are used in specific regions for quality wines. In Australia and Europe, a wine whose label specifies a varietal must comprise a minimum of 85% of that varietal. In the United States, the minimum is 75%, with the exception of Oregon, where it is 90%.

Generic

Generic labels are used primarily by U.S. and Australian wine producers, but they are less popular than in the past because of their association with poorer quality wines.

Generic terms are named after famous European wine regions, but they do not even approximate the styles of wine produced in those regions. There is no law regulating the grape varietals used. For example, American Chablis is made with Thompson Seedless grapes.

There are 14 legally acceptable generic labels in the United States:

Burgundy (France)	Malaga (Spain)
Chablis (France)	Moselle (Germany)
Champagne (France)	Port (Portugal)
Chianti (Italy)	Rhine (Germany)
Claret (France)	Sauterne (France)
Hock (Germany)	Sherry (Spain)
Madeira (Portugal)	Tokay (Hungary)

Proprietary

Proprietary or brand names are created by wine producers to market their wines under an exclusive name. It is a means for promoting their wines under a brand name versus a varietal name, or place of origin. These wines do not reflect any single quality. Some proprietary labels reflect European table wines, such as Blue Nun from Germany, while others represent the highest quality, such as Opus One from the United States or Sassiciai from Italy.

Labeling Requirements

Having discussed the factors that should be considered in purchasing wine, it is now necessary to distinguish the

U.S. Labeling Terms	
Vintage	95% of grapes from that vintage year
Estate bottled	100% grown, made, and bottled at the winery
Produced by	75% or more crushed, made, and bottled at the winery
Made by	10% to 75% crushed, made, and bottled at the winery
Cellared and bottled by	10% or less crushed, made at the winery
Vineyard name	95% or more grown at the particular vineyard

labels, labeling terms, and laws of major wine-producing countries.

United States

In the **United States,** seven items are legally required to be on a wine label (see Figure 6–1).

1. Brand name: The name of the producer or proprietary name
2. Type of wine: Generic, table (red, white, rosé), sparkling wine
3. Name and address of the bottler
4. Alcohol content: For table or still wines, a 1.5% variance allowed
5. Sulfite statement: Whether wines contain sulfites
6. Health warning: To advise pregnant women and those operating heavy machinery not to consume alcoholic beverages
7. Net contents: The amount of wine in the bottle

Figure 6–1 Wine label identification

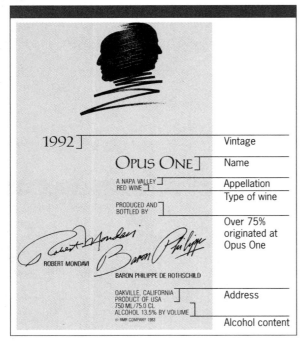

1992	Vintage
OPUS ONE	Name
A NAPA VALLEY RED WINE	Appellation / Type of wine
PRODUCED AND BOTTLED BY	Over 75% originated at Opus One
ROBERT MONDAVI BARON PHILIPPE DE ROTHSCHILD	
OAKVILLE, CALIFORNIA PRODUCT OF USA 750 ML/75.0 CL	Address
ALCOHOL 13.5% BY VOLUME	Alcohol content

Australia

Australia has a regulatory agency called the Wine and Brandy Corporation that enforces laws governing labels through an annual audit through the Label Integrity Program (LIP). The LIP enforces laws and regulations that include the following:

1. A minimum of 85% of the wine has to be of that variety if its name is on the label.
2. A minimum of 80% of the wine has to be from a region if it is named on the label.
3. A minimum of 95% of the wine has to be from a stated vintage.
4. If more than one varietal is named, it must be labeled in descending amounts. For example, a wine that is labeled Cabernet - Shiraz must be composed of more Cabernet Sauvignon than Shiraz.
5. Generic labels that are named after European locations, such as Port or Champagne are being phased out.
6. Clear geographic delineation is becoming more prevalent as an appellation system evolves from its nascency in 1963.

France

The content of labels is determined by the Institute National des Appellations d'Origine (INAO), the French regulatory

French Labeling Terms	
Récolte or Millésime	Vintage year; a minimum of 85% of that year
Mis en bouteille au Château/domaine	Estate bottled; 100% grown, made, and bottled
Mis en bouteille dans nos caves	Bottled in our cellars; a term used by négociants
Négociants	A wine merchant who sells to distributors
Négociants-eleveurs	Responsible for cellaring, aging, and selling wine
Château	Estate
Cuvée	Blend
Mousseux	Sparkling
Moelleux	Sweet

Agency governing wines. French wines are classified broadly into four categories which are included on the label:

1. Appellation d'Origine Contrôlée (AOC): The best classification of wines, representing 43% of the total wine production of France
2. Vin Delimité de Qualité Supérieure (VDQS): Superior quality wines, representing regions that aspire to be AOC regions
3. Vin de Pays (country wines): created to inspire regional pride
4. Vin de tables: Ordinary table wine, equivalent to jug wine

The INAO regulates the wine industry comprehensively, including the following factors under AOC laws:

1. Geographic limits to production areas or place of origin
2. Wine varietals
3. Minimum alcoholic strength
4. Yields
5. Viticultural practices
6. Wine-making practices

Place of Origin
As has been explained, place of origin is the cornerstone of French laws. It is based on the concept of *terroir,* which the French believe determines the character of the wine. The laws protect the integrity of the place name to ensure that if a customer purchases a wine from Pauillac, the grapes were grown in that area.

Wine Varietals
The AOC controls which grapes may be sold under the geographic name. Over the centuries, the French have been able to determine which grape varietals do best in the dominant wine-growing regions. There is some controversy that this is not the case for wines in secondary areas, where the most cultivated grape, Carignan, was planted as an expedient response to the *Phylloxera* blight.

Minimum Alcohol Content
The AOC specifies the minimum alcohol content for each area to ensure minimum sugar levels, which also reflect the development of flavor components. Chaptalization is allowed in some regions (e.g., Burgundy) and is widely practiced, but it is tightly controlled by the AOC.

Yields
To maintain standards, the AOC prescribes the maximum allowable production in terms of hectoliters per hectare.

Viticultural Practices
The AOC controls such practices as banning irrigation, defining the allowable density of vines per hectare, and controlling the pruning methods allowed.

Wine-making Practices
The AOC controls many aspects of wine-making practices, such as destemming and rosé wine making, although it grants considerable leeway by allowing local practices. Within AOC wines there are different classifications that are unique to each region. Most AOC regions have a four-tier system that is defined by the geographic area. In sequence of quality, from lowest to highest, they are

1. The region
2. The village
3. Premier cru (1er cru), meaning first growth
4. Grandcru (grand cru classé), meaning "great growth"

The term *cru* means "growth" but refers to a specific classification level.

Italy

Since 1963, the Italian wine industry has been regulated by the rigid rules of the Denominazione di Origine Controllata

(DOC). Despite this rigidity, there is often a paucity of information on an Italian wine label. It can be very frustrating to the consumer to purchase a bottle that merely has the name of a small village. There are three ways that an Italian wine can be labeled generically:

1. The name of a region, town or village (e.g., Barolo)
2. The name of a varietal (e.g., Pinot Grigio)
3. The name of a varietal plus a region (e.g., Brunello di Montalcino)

There are four categories of Italian wines, one of which must be included on the label. In sequence of quality from lowest to highest, they are:

1. **Vino da Tavola** (VDT) (table wine representing 88% of total production)

Italian Labeling Terms	
Vendemmia	Vintage
Azienda agricola, fattoria, tenuta	Estate (each)
Imbottigliato al castelo	Estate bottled
Imbottigliato all' Origine	Estate bottled
Classico	From the center of a DOC wine region
Riserva	A DOC (G) wine with additional aging
Superiore	A DOC (G) wine with 0.5% or more alcohol than required
Bianco	White
Rosso	Red
Nero	Dark red
Rosato	Pink
Secco	Dry
Abboccato	Semi-dry
Dolce	Sweet
Spumante	Sparkling
Frizzante	Sparkling
Cantina Sociale	Wine growers' cooperative
Marchio Nazionale	These words appear on a red seal on the neck of a wine bottle, indicating compliance with government controls for wines exported to the United States.

2. **Indicazione Geographica Tipica** (IGT) (country wines similar to the Vins de Pays)
3. **Denominazione di Origine Controllata** (DOC) (equivalent to AOC in France)
4. **Denominazione di Origine Controllata e Garantita** (DOCG) (the highest rating; not just controlled, but guaranteed)

The DOC rigidly controls numerous factors, which has limited the number of areas that have attained this designation to 250. The aspects of viticulture and wine making that are regulated include the following:

1. Geographic limits of each area
2. Grape varietals that can be grown or used
3. Percentage of each grape varietal in blends
4. The yield
5. Minimum alcoholic content
6. Aging requirements in wood or the bottle prior to release

Due to the tight controls that are placed on Italian winemakers for DOC or DOCG, many have refused to abide by the regulations and are producing some of Italy's finest and most expensive wines under the lowest-quality category of Vino da Tavola (VDT). This anomalous situation precipitated changes in the Goria law of 1992 that took effect in 1995. Under the law, DOC and DOCG wines are subject to closer analysis and tasting panels. Fine-quality wines that do not fall under the prescribed regulations fall under the IGT category. VDT wines no longer are allowed to carry a vintage year.

Germany

As opposed to Italian labels, German labels reveal more information than any other wine-producing country. German wines are classified according to the ripeness of the grapes at the time of harvest. Strict laws and regulations dictate the degree of sugar the grapes must have at harvest to qualify for the different quality categories.

German wines are divided into two main categories:

German Labeling Terms	
Rotwein	Red wine
Weissherbst	Rosé QbA or QmP wine made from a single variety of black grapes
Rotling	Rosé made from a blend
Schillerwein	QbA or QmP rosé wine from Württemberg
Perlwein	A red or white wine with a light sparkle, usually by carbon dioxide (CO_2) injection
Deutscher Sekt	A quality sparkling wine with less alcohol than champagne
Trocken	Dry
Halbtrocken	Semi-dry
Erzeugerabfüllung	Estate bottled
Gutsabfüllung	Estate bottled
Winzergenossenschaft	Wine growers' cooperative

Tafelwein (table wine) and *Qualitätswein* (quality wine). Tafelwein has three subcategories that are rarely seen in the United States: *Tafelwein, Deutscher Tafelwein,* and *Deutscher Landwein.* Tafelwein is usually made from imported grape must or wine and is bottled in Germany. Deutscher Tafelwein comes from a German growing region, and Landwein connotes a higher quality, similar to Vin de Pays or country wine. German wines that concern the American consumer are those of the category, Qualitätswein which can be divided into two subcategories:

Qualitätswein bestimmter Anbaugebiete *(QbA)* Quality wines from one of 13 specified regions. They form the largest category of German wines.

Qualitätswein mit Prädikat *(QmP)* Quality wines with special distinction

QbA wines are imported in the United States, and many are known by their brand names, such as Blue Nun or Black Tower. However, QmP wines are the primary focus for U.S. consumers. There are six levels of QmP wines, which are listed here in ascending order of ripeness at the time of the harvest:

Kabinett   Normal harvest time; light wines with excellent acidity

Spätlese   Late harvest (1 week after normal harvest); more intense and richer in flavor

Auslese   Hand-selected grapes, intensely flavored and usually sweet; may be affected by *Botrytis cinerea*

Beerenauslese   Overripe and often botrysized grapes, individually selected; a rare sweet wine that is very rich and flavorful

Eiswein   Literally means "ice wine"; must have ripeness of Beerenauslese and be harvested and pressed while frozen; very high in acidity and sweetness

Trockenbeerenauslese (TBA)   Grapes dried into raisins and individually picked; are affected by *Botrytis* and make a very rich, sweet, honey-like wine

All Tafelwein (table wine) and QbA wines are allowed to be chaptalized, but QmP wines are not.

German wines are differentiated from French and Italian wines by their tendency to be sweeter or have discernible residual sugar. This is due to the winemakers adding *Süssreserve* (sweet reserve) made of unfermented must of the same or equal quality back into the fermented wine to add flavor and enhance its aromas.

In response to changing tastes, many German winemakers have been making wines with the designation of *trocken* (dry) or *halbtrocken* (semi-dry). Both of these designations can be made for wines in ripeness categories up to Auslese.

There are eight items that are on QmP wine labels:

1. Appellation or place of origin
2. The official control number (AP Nr)
3. The town and the vineyard in which the grapes were grown
4. The grape variety
5. The quality category (e.g., Kabinett)
6. The vintage
7. The grower, producer, and bottler (not necessarily the same person)
8. The style of wine (dry or off-dry)

In addition to the label, a German wine bottle may have seals and awards placed on it. The seal indicates that a sensory panel has qualified the wine as exceeding minimum standards for a particular category. The gold seal on the neck denotes *trocken,* or dry; the green seal denotes *halbtrocken,* or semi-dry; and the red seal indicates that the wine is sweet.

Storage of Wine

As discussed previously, wine has living microorganisms that can be enhanced or retarded in their development depending on the wine's storage. Additionally, the organization of a wine cellar is important to any purchaser, especially a foodservice establishment that purchases wine in volume. It is worth noting that most wines are made to be consumed within 2 to 3 years and will not improve with aging. There are five factors that should be considered when storing wine which will prevent bacteria from developing and allowing wine to age properly:

1. The storage area should be well ventilated. A 60% to 75% level of relative **humidity** is necessary to prevent corks from drying out.
2. There should be a constant temperature level. The optimum temperature is 50° F to 55° F. The constancy of temperature is more important than the temperature level, because variations will cause certain bacteria to become active. The lower the **temperature** (down to 50° F), the slower the maturation process of the wine. No wine should be stored under refrigeration for an extended period of time, because doing so will cause the cork to dry out and cause precipitation of tartrates.
3. Direct **light,** be it artificial or sunlight, should be avoided. Direct sunlight also will heat the wine, which will cause quick deterioration.
4. The wine also should be free of agitation or **vibration,** which also will cause rapid deterioration.
5. Wine bottles should be **stored on their sides** to keep the corks moist, only allowing minuscule interaction with oxygen. Wines that are stored upright will result in dried-out corks, causing the wine to oxidize. If wine is stored upside down, the purchaser should

be cognizant that any sediment that forms will most likely stay attached to the neck of the bottle. This will prove to be problematic when serving.

To organize a wine cellar, one needs an inventory system that includes recording the name, vintage, price, amount purchased, distributor, shipper, and any other pertinent information. The wines should be stored in numbered bins so that they are easily found and inventoried.

Wine Tasting

Wine tasting can be both simple and complex. It is simple to quaff wine and enjoy its attributes without contemplating its subtleties. However, one will not appreciate wine fully unless one develops an ability to distinguish the subtle characteristics of color, aromas, bouquets, flavors, and texture. For a professional wine taster, all of these characteristics must be recognized, identified, and recorded. There are three types of wine consumers: novice, appreciative, and professional. By *professional,* we are referring to people who taste wine for a livelihood (e.g., tasters at the winery who blend decisions).

There are basically four **types** of wine tastings:

1. General wine tastings
2. Horizontal tastings
3. Vertical tastings
4. Blind tastings

General tastings are often conducted in the wine trade, whether by distributors or retailers or at such events as the Wine and Food Experience. Tasters walk from table to table, perhaps in a sequentially organized manner, starting with dry whites to full-bodied reds and finishing with dessert or fortified wines.

Horizontal tastings are conducted to evaluate wines that are usually from a particular region and from the same vintage. For example, tastings from 1990 from Pauillac might include Château Latour, Château Lafite-Rothschild, Château Mouton-Rothschild, and Château Pichon-Longueville-Lalande. This allows the taster to focus on and differentiate between the styles of different producers from a single region.

Vertical tastings are conducted to evaluate wines that are usually of a single producer from different vintages. This allows the taster to evaluate factors that differentiate vintages as well as determine how the wine matures and develops.

Blind tastings are the most complex form of tasting. No information is given about the wine. The wine is generally of the same varietals or blend. Blind tastings are a very effective way for tasters to hone their tasting and evaluative skills. Some of these tastings are partially blind in that the taster is informed of the varietal or the place of origin.

When conducting a professional wine tasting, the following procedures should be observed:

- The room should be lit with nonfluorescent lighting or natural daylight to evaluate the color accurately.
- The glassware should be clean and free of odors imparted by detergents.
- The size and style of glass should be taken into account, because it will affect the taster's ability to differentiate subtle characteristics.
- Wine glasses should be placed on a white background. In professional tastings, wine glasses are often placed on white paper mats that have numbered circles for each glass.
- All tasters should have a writing implement and a tasting (scoring) sheet to record their thoughts and scores.
- Tasters should not be wearing colognes or perfumes, which interfere with wine tastings.*
- Water should be served as a palate cleanser.
- Foods other than flavorless water biscuits should be avoided.
- Two-ounce portions of wine should be served.
- Spit buckets or **spittoons** should be provided. Tasters should be silent during the tasting process so as not to distract each other.
- Wines that are grouped together are described as a **flight.**
- If tasting different styles of wine, the **order** of the

* See Appendix C for update.

wines tasted is critical. Tasters should begin with light-bodied and dry whites to full-bodied whites, proceed to rosé and red wines, and finish with sweet wines, whether dessert or fortified.
- White wines can be served at slightly warmer than optimum temperatures to help the taster distinguish certain characteristics.

The Six S's of Wine Tasting

The six S's of wine tasting are see, swirl, sniff, sip, swallow or spit, and savor.

See

Although sight is the least accurate of the senses with which to evaluate wine, it provides clues and anticipation of what is to come. The **disc** is the upper surface of the wine. The outer edge of the wine is called the **meniscus.** As a red wine matures, it will change significantly. Its meniscus will be clear, and one will discern **discing** or gradation of colors like the rings of a tree. At this point, the taster is examining the clarity of the wine.

The **robe** is the color or hue of the wine. For example, a white wine with little or no color will indicate that the fruit was immature, and the wine will probably lack aroma and flavor. Pale and light-colored white wines come from cooler climates. The majority of white wines tend to be straw yellow and light yellow wines. As white wine matures, it develops more color. Medium yellow and light gold wines tend to be sweet dessert wines. Wines that are brown either are fortified, such as Madeira, or have oxidized.

Dark purple indicates immaturity in red wines. Lighter reds indicate varietals such as Pinot Noir and Gamay. The majority of red wines are medium cherry red but with age develop a red tile or brick color. Red wines lose color as they age. The taster is now examining the depth and intensity of the color, which are clues to the flavors.

Swirl

Swirling is the act of holding the glass by the stem and spinning the wine so that it coats the upper level of the glass. It is not necessary to swirl for more than a couple of revolutions. The wine evaporates off the sides of the glass, allowing the flavor components to be released.

Swirling also causes **tears, arches,** or **legs.** These three terms refer to the residual stripes of wine that cling to the sides of the glass. They are caused by the alcohol level in the wine. As the alcohol evaporates off the sides, the residual wine streaks the glass. The more alcohol, the denser and more pronounced the legs.

Swirling aerates the wine, allowing it to **breathe.** As a wine is exposed to air, the flavor components are released and the wine "**opens up.**" Red wines open up with more difficulty because they have less volatile acids. Some red wines require up to half an hour in the glass to breathe to fully expose their aromas and bouquets. Many evaluators enjoy observing the changing development of the aromas and bouquets. There are no set rules on how long wine should be opened prior to serving, because the length of time varies considerably according to type, varietal, style, and age.

Sniff or Smell

Smell is the most important of the senses. The tongue is able to discern only four components, but the olfactory sense enables us to differentiate smells. The flavors in the mouth are vaporized by the body's heat and travel up the retronasal passageway to the olfactory bulb. Humans collectively can identify up to 10,000 different odors, but any one individual is able to be trained to detect up to 1200. Wines have approximately 200 detectable odors. The taster should differentiate between **aromas,** which are odors that come from the fruit, versus **bouquets,** which are odors that develop from the fermentation and aging processes.

Aroma descriptors fall under different categories, such as fruity, spicy, floral, and vegetative. Bouquet descriptors include nutty, caramelized, woody, earthy, petroleum, and microbiologic. There is a third set of odors that is a result of bad wine, such as a sulphurous smell when too much sulphur dioxide is used (see Figure 6–2).

When sniffing wines, the taster should follow these guidelines.

- Swirl the wine and, tilting the glass toward oneself, place the nose right into the glass.
- Take short sniffs without inhaling deeply. Inhaling wines deeply will quickly tire one's sense of smell.
- Record the initial impression. This first impression is often termed the **attack** or **first nose.** Very often this will be dominated by aromas.
- Pause at least 30 seconds before sniffing a second time. The odors that are noted, the **second nose,** may be different, but that should not be taken as an invalidation of the first sniff. More complex wines will offer more bouquets.
- Sniff the wine one more time before sipping to verify or add to the earlier impressions.

Sip

The tongue is able to discern only four tastes: sweet, sour, salty, and bitter. It is argued by some that the tongue is also able to taste **umami,** the best example of which is monosodium glutamate (MSG). Most sensory evaluators, however, view umami as amplifying other tastes or flavors. There is another controversy regarding the taste map of the tongue. It has long been held that the taste buds are differentiated in the mouth, with sweet-focused taste buds located on the tip of the tongue. Recent studies dispute these long-held views, contradicting the differentiation of taste buds. Most taste buds are concentrated on the tip and sides of the tongue, not on the roof of the tongue. When tasting wine, it is important to roll it on and around the tongue to coat these taste buds. Of the four flavors, saltiness is not a typical or common component of wine (see Figure 6–3).

Sweetness
- Ethanol, the alcohol in the wine, enhances the apparent sweetness in wine. Wines high in alcohol give the appearance of being sweet.
- Tannins tend to reduce the perception of sweetness.
- Sweetness reduces the perception of sourness or acidity.
- Without sufficient acidity, sweet wines taste unctuous and cloying but not refreshing.

Figure 6–2 The wine aroma wheel. (Copyright American Society for Enology and Viticulture. Noble, A.C. et al. Am J Enol Vitic 38:143–146, 1987.)

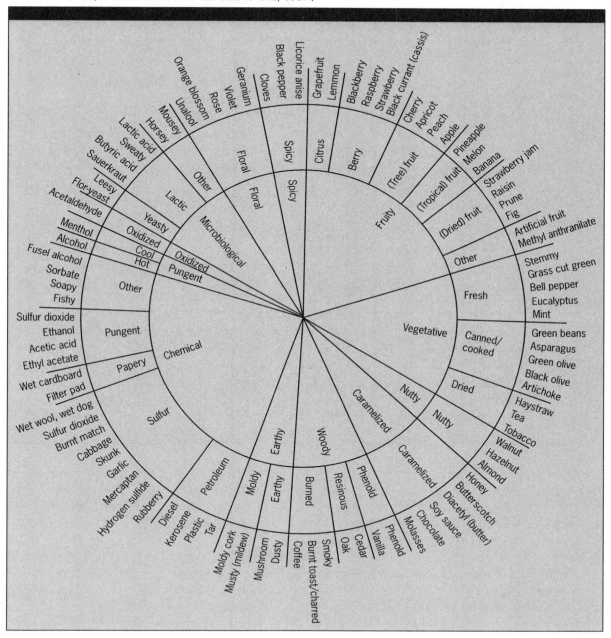

Figure 6–3 Sensory evaluation card

WINE INFO (Points)	WINE #__: Observations	WINE #__: Class Notes	WINE #__: Observations	WINE #__: Class Notes:
Type Vintage Appellation Producer Cost/Other				
Clarity (1)				
Color (2)				
Off Odors				
Aroma Association Descriptors Intensity Varietal (4)				
Bouquet (2)				
Flavors (2)				
Components: Sweetness, Acidity, Bitterness - Balance (3)				
Body (1)				
Astringency (1)				
Finish (2)				
Overall Quality (2)				
Total Points:				
Questions raised by this testing				
Food Pairing				

DATE _____   **SENSORY EVALUATION CARDS**

- Sweetness gives a pleasant mouth feel.
- Sweetness enhances desirable aromas (e.g., fruits).
- Descriptors should include **dry** (for absence of sugar), **off-dry** or **semi-sweet, sweet,** and **very sweet.**

Sourness
- The tart taste of wines is due to their tritable acidity or low pH.
- The order of decreasing sourness of the principal organic acids is: tartaric, citric (lemons), malic (Granny Smith apples), and lactic (milk). Buttery wines are a result of malolactic fermentation.
- Acidity seems to be most apparent along the sides of the tongue.

- The following terms are used to describe wines that have low, normal, or high acidity: **flat** for insufficient acid, **fruity** for normal acidity, and **acidulous** for wine that has excessive acidity.

Bitterness
- Bitterness is often confused with astringency and sourness. Black coffee or aspirin is a good example of bitterness.
- Bitterness is not usually associated with white wines. An exception is Gewürztraminer from Alsace.
- Red wines high in tannins also tend to be bitter.
- The palate is most sensitive to bitterness, which causes it to linger.

- Descriptors for wines that have bitterness include **slightly bitter, moderately bitter, bitter,** and **very bitter.**

Tactility

In addition to flavors, tactile sensations are perceived when tasting wines. These sensations include the wine's **texture, body,** and **viscosity.**

- The texture of wine can be smooth, silky, or astringent. *Astringent* is a term used to describe the rough sandpapered feeling that one experiences when tasting a wine that is high in tannin. As red wines age, they become far less astringent and can develop an extraordinary richness. Astringency is not a major factor in white wines.
- The body of the wine can be thin like water or full-bodied, reflecting a satisfying richness. One of the pleasures of sparkling wine is the way the bubbles tingle on the mouth and tongue.
- Wines made from some varietals can also have an element of viscosity or oiliness, such as Pinot Gris.
- Additionally, wines high in alcohol give the taster a hot tactile experience.
- The temperature of the wine is important because of its effect on smell, taste, and touch. For example, the cold sensations of a white wine make it pleasant and refreshing.

Swallow or Spit

Spitting, while seemingly awkward, is a necessary process for proper evaluation at a wine tasting. A taster cannot remain alert and maintain a discernable palate if consuming the wine. Swallowing, however, allows the taster to fully savor the wine.

Savor

Savor refers to the taster's appreciation and evaluation of the wine by focusing on the way it lingers in the mouth. The lingering sensations, flavors, and tastes are referred to as the **finish.** The finish should be balanced and integrated in its various components, flavors, and texture. No one element should stand out, or the wine will be considered unbalanced. A wine can be described as having a **short, medium,** or **long** finish. Wines described as having a short finish are those that do not leave any lingering flavors after 15 seconds. Great wines are those that have finishes that linger from 1 to several minutes.

Wine-Tasting Terminology

One of the problems that tasters have is their lack of ability to communicate with each other. Wine terms have been developed over the centuries and are applied on a consistent basis, but there are hundreds of adjectives that many mean very little. The aroma wheel (see Figure 6–2), developed by Professor Anne Noble at the University of California at Davis, was designed to constrain the use of poetic terms and limit adjectives to a more scientific level. The following terms, however, have universal acceptance within the wine trade:

Austere	Unyielding, perhaps too young
Baked-burned	Lack of freshness and acidity, as if baked in the sun
Big/Full	Full-bodied and full-flavored
Buttery	Soft, round whites with evident malolactic fermentation (MLF) bouquets
Coarse	Lacking finesse; inexpensive wines
Complex	Multilayered and multifaceted in flavors and components
Creamy	Denotes richness (e.g., Champagne)
Crisp	Refreshing, with good acidity
Dense	Packed with flavor and color
Dried-out	Fruit flavors have dissipated
Earthy	Aromas remind one of soil or mineral
Elegant	Great finesse and balance
Fat	Full-bodied, but lacking necessary acidity; usually sweet
Finesse	Great balance and harmony
Firm	Structure backed by tannins or acidity
Flabby	Lacking acidity
Flat	Lacking acidity and freshness
Fragrant	Flowery
Green	Young or unripened grapes

Hard	Tannins perhaps too young and unforgiving
Heavy	Overly alcoholic and full-bodied
Herbaceous	Aromas of grass and herbs
Hot	Overly alcoholic; typical of hot-climate wines
Jammy	Overly ripe fruit; typical of hot-climate wines
Lean	Limited in flavor
Long	A lingering finish
Mouth-filling	Satisfying and richly textured
Penetrating	Intense flavors and aromas
Perfumed	Fragrant and flowery
Petillant	Spritzy, tingly
Rich	Deep and satisfying flavor
Robust	Full-bodied
Rough	Coarse and unpolished
Round	Lacking hard edges
Sharp	High acidity
Short	Lacking finish
Silky	Smooth texture
Simple	Lacking any distinction
Smooth	Tannins or acidity in harmony
Soft	Mellow flavors
Solid	Integrated and hardy
Sour	Overly acidic or vinegary
Spritz	Prickly from CO_2
Stalky/stemmy	Bitter, vegetal taste
Steely	Good acidity, with a firm quality
Supple	Sensuously smooth
Tangy	Piquant
Thin	Lacks body and flavor
Vegetal	Aromas of vegetables (e.g., green beans, bell peppers)
Velvety	Rich silkiness
Watery	Weak and thin
Woody	Old cask odors
Zesty	Crisp and fresh

The following terms are used for wines that are spoiled:

Acetic	Vinegary
Corked	Wine affected by a cork mold
Maderized	Baked, flat, partially oxidized wine
Moldy	Smells of mold

Oxidized	Partially exposed to air and producing **acetaldehyde**
Sulphurous	Bad egg smell from overabundance of sulphur dioxide

Wine and Food Pairing

The time-honored method of pairing wine and food was based on a French approach of matching specific dishes to specific wines. From this approach stemmed generalities such as pairing white wines with white meats and fish, and red wines with red meats. Americans challenged this methodology in the 1970s and 1980s. The underlying reasons for why certain wines pair well with certain foods were investigated. The result was the Americans' challenge to the premise that there is a single right wine for a particular dish. The cause and effect of wine on food can be discussed and defined, but personal tastes and preferences in wine and food are subjective. It is worth noting that contemporary Western cuisine has evolved over the past three decades due to cultural assimilations, by combining unusual ingredients, herbs, and spices, thereby creating lighter and healthier sauces. The following are guidelines for wine and food pairings (see also Figure 6–4):

- Match the intensity of flavors in both food and wine. For example, pairing a full-bodied tannic red wine with a light poached sole would overpower the sole's flavor. Conversely, a grilled steak would overwhelm the flavors of a light dry white wine.
- Match and contrast wines to the dominant flavors of a dish. The main food item may not be the dominant flavor. One needs to take into account the method of preparation, the seasoning, and the sauce. For example, the flavors of a poached darne of salmon are significantly different from those of a grilled salmon steak. The latter will stand up to wine with more intense flavors, such as a Pinot Noir.
- Match or contrast components of both food and wine. Having similarities in components (sweet, sour, salty,

Figure 6–4 Food and wine pairing chart

Wines:	Sparkling Brut	Blanc de Blanc	Demi-sec, Doux or Asti Spumante	Sauvignon Blanc/Fumé Blanc	Semillon	Pinot Grigio and Italian Whites	Light Chardonnay	Full-bodied Chardonnay	Chenin Blanc	German and U.S. Riesling and Gewürztraminer	Alsatian Riesling, Gewürztraminer and Pinot Blanc	Dry Rosé: e.g., Tavel, Vin de Mistral Rosé	Gamay and other Nouveau/Novello style wines	American Pinot Noir	Pinot Noir	Merlot	Cabernet Sauvignon	Zinfandel	Nebbiolo	Chianti Riserva	Valpolicella/Bardolino	Sauternes, Special Select Late Harvest, TBA	Port
Acidic, tart foods																							
Citrus-based sauces	X	X		X		X	X		X	X			X							X			
Lemon, garlic and parsley						X	X		X				X							X			
Marinated foods				X		X	X		X	X	X	X	X										
Tomato sauces						X												X	X	X	X		
Salty, smoked food																							
Ham, proscuitto	X	X		X	X	X			X	X	X	X	X							X	X		
Oysters	X	X		X	X		X																
Sausages									X	X	X	X	X	X	X	X		X		X			
Smoked chicken	X	X		X	X																		
Smoked/cured fish	X	X		X	X				X	X	X	X	X										
Rich, fatty foods																							
Beef								X		X	X		X	X	X	X	X	X	X	X	X	X	
Cream sauces				X	X	X	X	X					X										
Duck, goose						X	X	X	X		X		X		X	X		X	X	X		X	
Fried foods				X	X	X	X	X	X		X	X	X							X		X	
Pâté				X	X	X				X	X	X	X					X		X		X	
Salmon and tuna				X			X	X		X	X	X	X	X	X					X	X	X	
Spicy foods																							
Caribbean				X					X	X	X	X	X	X				X				X	
Indian				X					X	X	X	X	X	X									
Pacific Rim				X		X	X		X	X	X	X	X					X					
Southwest				X		X			X	X	X	X	X	X		X		X		X	X	X	
Sweet foods																							
Desserts			X																			X	X
Leek and onion-based foods									X	X	X												
Fruit-based sauces									X	X	X		X										
Scallops and lobster	X	X		X	X		X		X	X	X	X											
Tropical fruits									X	X													
Delicately flavored foods																							
Chicken	X	X		X	X	X	X	X	X	X	X	X	X	X	X	X		X		X	X		
Light appetizers	X	X		X	X				X	X	X	X	X							X	X		
Poached	X	X		X					X	X	X												
Lean fish, e.g., sole	X	X		X	X	X	X		X	X	X												
Veal/pork	X			X	X	X	X	X	X	X	X		X	X	X	X		X		X	X		

(continued)

Figure 6–4 Food and wine pairing chart (continued)

Wines:	Sparkling Brut	Blanc de Blanc	Demi-sec, Doux or Asti Spumante	Sauvignon Blanc/Fumé Blanc	Semillon	Pinot Grigio and Italian Whites	Light Chardonnay	Full-bodied Chardonnay	Chenin Blanc	German and U.S. Riesling and Gewürztraminer	Alsatian Riesling, Gewürztraminer and Pinot Blanc	Dry Rosé: e.g., Tavel, Vin de Mistral Rosé	Gamay and other Nouveau/Novello style wines	American Pinot Noir	Pinot Noir	Merlot	Cabernet Sauvignon	Zinfandel	Nebbiolo	Chianti Riserva	Valpolicella/Bardolino	Sauternes, Special Select Late Harvest, TBA	Port
Intensely flavored foods																							
Barbequed meats								X				X	X	X	X	X	X	X	X	X	X		
Game								X	X	X	X			X	X	X	X	X	X	X			
Grilled meats								X						X	X	X	X	X	X	X			
Lamb														X	X	X	X	X		X			
Roasted meats						X			X	X	X			X	X	X	X	X		X			
Mild cheeses																							
Brie, Muenster	X			X	X	X	X		X	X	X	X	X	X						X	X		
Goat cheese				X																			
Strong cheeses																							
Pont L'Eveque								X							X	X	X	X	X				
Roquefort, Blue cheeses																						X	
Stilton																							X

and bitter) may be a safer approach but not necessarily an interesting one. For example, sweet food with sweet wines match perfectly as long as the wine is sweeter than the food. A sweet wine like a Sauternes, however, provides a wonderful pairing with Roquefort cheese, the primary component of which is saltiness.

- Consider the effect of acidity. Acidity makes food and wine interesting. Acidic food and acidic wine go well together, such as Sauvignon Blanc and cool-climate Chardonnays. High-acid food, however, will wash out low-acid wines. Acidic wines also pair well with salty and oily food. This is the same reason for pairing citrus fruit such as lemon with fish.
- Modify bitterness. Bitter food and bitter wine will rein-

force the bitterness of each. Bitterness can be modified by sweetness. For example, a mixed green salad with grilled chicken might be paired with an off-dry white wine such as White Zinfandel or Chenin Blanc.
- Match or contrast flavors of both food and wine. Herbs, spices, and seasonings can be used to enhance flavors in a wine. For example, judicious use of thyme or basil in a dish will bring out the herbaceous character of a Sauvignon Blanc. Contrasting flavors can be more interesting (e.g., a smokey with a floral flavor).
- Match the intensity of textures. A balance of intensity must be found to ensure that one does not overpower the other. Lightly textured foods should be paired

with light-bodied wines, and rich foods with full-bodied wines (e.g., a young Californian Cabernet Sauvignon with a grilled sirloin steak).

- Remember that tannins can be bound by fat. For example, a hard tannic Cabernet Sauvignon will not be astringent if accompanied by beef, duck, or strong cheese.
- If serving a fine older wine, accompany it with simpler foods that will act as a foil.
- Use good-quality wine for cooking.
- Use the same style of wine in cooking as is being served. This creates better harmony.
- Be cognizant of the effect that certain foods have on wines, especially certain vegetables, such as artichokes, which will compete with the acidity of the wine. Additionally, foods that are high in umami, such as anchovy, soy sauce, bonito, or smoked salmon, will cause the taster to perceive less fruitiness in the wine and leave a metallic flavor on the palate. Corn is also a difficult food to pair with wine because of its sugars and starch.
- Be aware that mixed green salads tend to be difficult because they are bitter and often served with a vinaigrette. Avoid using vinegar by substituting a citrus juice and serve with a slightly off-dry white with good acidity (e.g., Chenin Blanc).
- Be alert to the difficulty of pairing egg dishes if they prepared without other flavor components. For example, a poached egg will coat the tongue and palette, preventing the taster from enjoying the wine. A western-style omelet, however, has flavor components such as onions, tomatoes, peppers, and cheese, all of which are very compatible.
- Consider the intensity of chocolate. Chocolate is difficult to pair if very sweet or the only dominant flavor.
- When serving very hot and spicy foods, avoid serving wine, if possible, because its flavors will be overwhelmed.

One can explain the effects of food on wine and vice versa, but that is not to imply that one wine is better than another. The best wine is the wine that the taster most enjoys. Many psychological factors are also important to consumers when making a wine selection, and they have little to do with the gustatory senses:

- *Seasonality.* Most people enjoy light and white wine in warm seasons and full-bodied red wines in cold weather.
- *Prestige.* Consumers often want to pair fine quality food with the most expensive wines regardless of its suitability.
- *Ethnicity.* Consumers enjoy pairing regional wines to the same cuisine.
- *Occasionality.* There are some wines such as Champagne which are associated with celebrations.

If serving more than one wine at a dinner, a few general guidelines should be observed:

- Serve dry wine before sweet wine.
- Serve light-bodied wines before full-bodied ones.
- Serve whites before reds.
- Serve young wines before older ones.

7

Wine Regions of the New World

Wine Regions of the New World

The United States

The United States is the fourth largest wine producer in the world after France, Italy, and Spain. Although wine is produced in 48 states, the focus of this section is the major wine-producing areas of California, Washington, Oregon, and New York. Wine making developed independently on the East and West Coasts. Since early colonial times, attempts were made to make wine from the *Vitis labrosca* and subsequently from the imported *Vitis vinifera*. Thomas Jefferson, one of the leading wine connoisseurs of the late eighteenth and early nineteenth centuries, was unable to produce fine wine because of *Phylloxera*. Thus, wine making in the East was centered around *Vitis labrusca* (Con-

cord grapes) and hybrids such as Catawba. The first *vinifera* grape was planted in California by a Franciscan monk, Junipero Serra, in 1769 (see Figure 7–1).

California

California produces over 90% of the total U.S. wine production. California's wine industry was boosted by the importation of 100,000 European vine cuttings by Colonel Agoston Haraszthy in 1861. Unfortunately, many of the vines were not identified correctly and were planted in the wrong climatic areas, The focus of University of California at Davis School of Oenology was to correctly identify the vines and prescribe the areas best suited for each varietal.

Figure 7–1 Map of the wine-producing regions of the United States

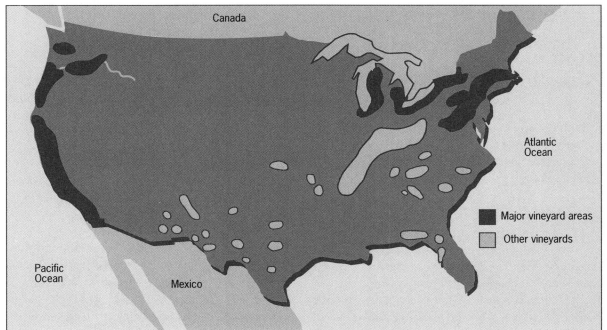

Huge investments in the wine industry have had an international appeal, resulting in joint U.S. and foreign ownership of wineries such as Opus One and Dominus. The international influence has been felt particularly in the sparkling wine industry. The dominance of Cabernet Sauvignon and Chardonnay is being challenged by newly introduced varietals (Rhone and Italian) and new blends. The Bureau of Alcohol, Tobacco and Firearms (BATF) regulations effective as of January 1, 1983, that requires that a wine must consist of 75% of a varietal for it to be so named. This resulted in the trademarked name of Meritage (rhymes with heritage), which denotes a traditional Bordeaux blend.

California can be divided into five wine-producing regions (see Figure 7–2):

North Coast
North Central Coast
South Central Coast
South Coast
Central Valley (San Joaquin Valley)

North Coast

The **North Coast** has become preeminent since the 1960s. It is divided into four counties:

Napa County
Sonoma County
Mendocino County
Lake County

Napa County

Napa has become synonymous with the development of fine wines. The Napa Valley is the Mecca of California's wine producers; it has more than 240 wineries and continues to develop further. Charles Krug, a pioneer winemaker, was the first to build a modern commercial winery in Napa County. It was here that Robert Mondavi gained his knowledge of wine and early experiences before starting his own winery in 1966.

Napa is an ideal wine-producing area because the valley acts as a conduit for the cool jet streams that come off of the San Pablo Bay. This jet stream acts as a kind of super air conditioner, resulting in three distinct climatic zones within the Napa Valley itself. As discussed previously, the development of an appellation system in the United States resulted in the naming of nine American Viticultural Areas (AVAs) within Napa itself, each differentiated from the other by soil type, climate, and topographic landmarks. These areas are

Atlas Peak
Carneros
Howell Mountain
Mount Vedeer
Oakville
Rutherford
Spring Mountain
Stag's Leap
Wild Horse Valley

The best known varieties for this district are Chardonnay, Sauvignon Blanc, Johannisberg Riesling, Chenin Blanc, Gewürztraminer, Pinot Noir, Merlot, Cabernet Franc, Cabernet Sauvignon, and Zinfandel.

Top producers include Acacia, Burgess, Caymus, Cakebread, Chappelet, J. Heitz, Robert Mondavi Winery, Beringer, Rutherford, Domaine Chandon, Mumm, Schramsberg, Villa Mt Eden, Far Niente, Sterling, Dunn Vineyards, La Jota Vineyard, Grgich Hills, The Hess Collection, Beaulieu Vineyards, Niebaum Coppola Estate, Opus One, Clos du Val, Stag's Leap, Chimney Rock, Shafer, Silverado, Duckhorn, Saintsbury, Schug Winery, and William Hill.

Sonoma County

Sonoma County, which borders Napa on the western side of the Mayacamas Mountains, competes with Napa for wine preeminence. Due to its longer wine history, Sonoma County, a bastion of wine making, has been divided into more AVAs than has Napa. This is not to suggest that differences in the tastes and styles of wines are as significant as these subdivisions would make it appear.

The Sonoma County AVAs include

Figure 7–2 Map of the wine-producing regions of California

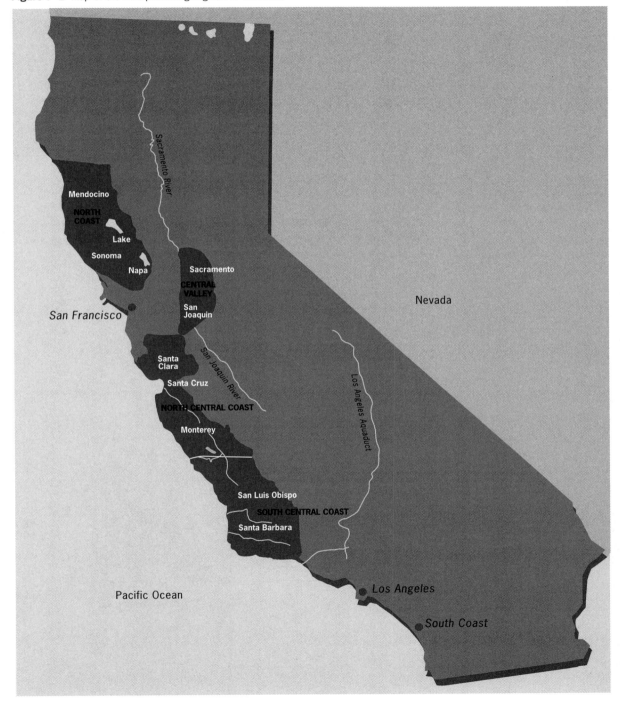

Napa Valley Varietals

Sonoma County Varietals and Styles

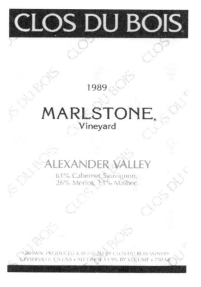

Alexander Valley
Chalk Hill
Dry Creek Valley
Knights Valley
Northern Sonoma
Russian River Valley
Sonoma-Green Valley
Sonoma Coast
Sonoma Mountain
Sonoma Valley

The principal grape varieties grown include Chardonnay, Sauvignon Blanc, Gewürztraminer, Pinot Noir, Cabernet Sauvignon, and Zinfandel. There have been increasing plantings of Rhone varietals such as Grenache and Syrah as well as the Italian Sangiovese.

Top producers include Jordan, Simi, Alexander Valley Vineyards, Geyser Peak Winery, Dry Creek Vineyards, Ferrari-Carano, Quivera, Preston Vineyards, Dehlinger, De Loach Vineyards, Iron Horse, Sonoma Cutrer, Rodney Strong Vineyards, Château St Jean, Hanzell Vineyard, Kenwood Vineyards, Landmark Vineyards, Laurel Glen, Gauer Estate, Clos du Bois, and Seghesio.

Mendocino County

Mendocino is the largest and most diverse wine-producing county of the North Coast. Its historical isolation allowed it to continue growing fine wine varietals during Prohibition. This area is divided into four AVAs:

Mendocino
Anderson Valley
McDowell Valley
Potter Valley

The principal grape varietals grown are Chardonnay, Gewürztraminer, Riesling Sauvignon Blanc, Cabernet Sauvignon, Grenache, Petit Sirah, Pinot Noir, Syrah, and Zinfandel.

The principal producers include Fetzer, Parducci Wine Cellars, Greenwood Ridge, Handley, Hidden Cellars, Jeopson Vineyards, Husch, Lazy Creek, McDowell Valley Vineyards, Navarro, Roederer, and Scharffenberger; Roederer and Scharffenberger are producing two of the best premium sparkling wines in California.

Lake County

Lake County is the smallest of the North Coast appellations. This district is divided into two AVAs: Clear Lake and Guenoc Valley.

The principal varietals grown include Sauvignon Blanc, Cabernet Sauvignon, Petite Sirah, and Zinfandel.

The principal producers include Konocti, Kendall-Jackson, Guenoc, and Steele.

North Central Coast

The North Central Coast is divided into four districts:

Monterey
Santa Clara
Livermore
Santa Cruz Mountains

Monterey

Monterey is one of the most heavily cultivated areas of the North Central Coast. However, its climate is such that without irrigation, grapes could not be grown. Monterey has five AVAs:

Monterey
Arroyo Secco
Carmel
Chalone
San Lucas

The principal grape varietals include Chardonnay, Riesling, Sauvignon Blanc, Semillon, Pinot Blanc, Pinot Noir, Cabernet Sauvignon, and Zinfandel.

The principal producers include Jekel Vineyard, Estancia, Mirassou, Chalone Vineyards, Durney Vineyards, and Monterey Vineyard.

Santa Clara County

Santa Clara County is south of San Francisco and has been a casualty of urban development. It is also known as Silicon Valley. Its principal AVA is San Ysidro. This county attained fame as the home of Almaden and San Martin.

**California Regional Label Variations—
increasingly specific appellation**

Central California Varietals

The principal grape varietals include Chardonnay, Semillon, Sauvignon Blanc, Cabernet Sauvignon, Merlot, and Zinfandel.

The principal producers include J. Lohr, Mirassou Vineyards, Fortino Winery, and Jory Winery.

Livermore Valley

Livermore Valley is located east of San Francisco Bay and has been producing grapes for more than 100 years. Wente Brothers has been an established winemaker in the area since 1883. The gravelly soil is particularly conducive to growing Sauvignon Blanc and Semillon. Livermore Valley is the only AVA.

The principal grape varieties are Sauvignon Blanc, Semillon, Chardonnay, Cabernet Sauvignon, and Merlot.

The principal producers are Wente Brothers, Concannon Vineyards, Fenestra Winery, and Ivan Tamas Winery.

The Santa Cruz Mountains

Located just south of San Francisco, the Santa Cruz Mountains is a dynamic area that is in the process of establishing itself as a premium wine-producing area. The Santa Cruz Mountains, one of California's coolest wine-producing regions, is its own AVA.

The principal grape varieties include Chardonnay, Marsanne, Rousanne, Cabernet Sauvignon, Pinot Noir, Zinfandel, and Syrah.

The principal producers include Ahlgren Vineyard, Bonny Doon Vineyard, David Bruce Winery, Byington Winery & Vineyards, Cinnabar Vineyard & Winery, Cronin Vineyards, Mount Eden Vineyard, Ridge Vineyards, and Storrs Winery.

South Central Coast

Although this designation is not recognized by the BATF, it is used to encompass a number of AVAs that stretch from Paso Robles to Santa Barbara. The South Central Coast is divided into two major districts: San Luis Obispo County and Santa Barbara County.

San Luis Obispo County

San Luis Obispo County has different climatic areas, from the boiling hot sun beating down on Paso Robles to the cool coastal plain of Edna Valley. San Luis Obispo has four AVAs:

Paso Robles
York Mountain
Arroyo Grande
Edna Valley

Paso Robles and York Mountain. Midway between San Francisco and Los Angeles, these neighboring AVAs have dramatically different climates. York Mountain is at an elevation of 1800 feet and is affected by the maritime influence of the Pacific Ocean, with heavy fogs keeping the temperatures cool. The Paso Robles area is generally much warmer, depending on elevation.

The principal grape varieties grown are Chardonnay, Sauvignon Blanc, Cabernet Sauvignon, Zinfandel, Merlot, Petit Sirah, Nebbiolo, and Pinot Noir.

The principal producers are Adelaide Cellars, Arciero Winery, Creston Vineyards, Eberle Winery, Justin Winery and Vineyard, Martin Brothers Winery, Meridian Vineyards, Wild Horse Winery, and York Mountain Winery.

Arroyo Grande. The area of Arroyo Grande is twice the size of Edna Valley (see next section) and just to the south of it along the coast. Arroyo Grande has produced less distinguished wines to date, with the exception of Maison Deutz. Maison Deutz produces high-quality sparkling wines in a joint American-European venture.

The principal grape varieties include Chardonnay, Pinot Blanc, Pinot Noir, and Zinfandel.

The principal producers are Maison Deutz Winery, Sausalito Canyon Vineyard, and Talley Vineyards.

Edna Valley. Although Edna Valley is a small AVA, it gained quick prominence with the quality of its Chardonnays in the 1980s.

The principal grape varieties include Chardonnay, Gewürztraminer, and Pinot Noir. The principal producers are Chamisal Vineyard, Corbett Canyon Vineyards, Edna Valley Vineyards, and Windemere Wines.

Santa Barbara County

Santa Barbara County is one of the most ideal and temperate climates for growing grapes. Its cool climate is proving

Central California Varietals

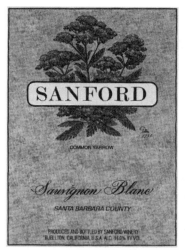

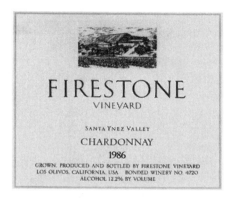

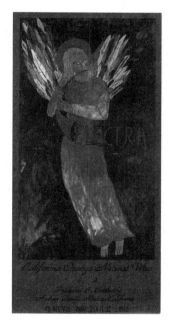

to be an ideal setting for successful viticulture of Pinot Noir. Many of its vineyards are located along the coastline, while others are situated at high elevations. Santa Barbara became a serious wine-producing region in the 1970s and currently has two AVAs:

Santa Maria Valley
Santa Ynez Valley

Santa Maria Valley. Santa Maria Valley is located at the foothills of the Sierra Madre mountain range. The first vineyards since Prohibition were planted here in 1964. The Santa Maria Valley has developed a reputation for producing some of California's best Chardonnay and Pinot Noir.

The principal grape varieties include Chardonnay, Sauvignon Blanc, Riesling, Pinot Noir, Cabernet Sauvignon, Merlot, and the newly introduced Syrah.

The principal producers include Au Bon Climat, Byron Vineyard and Winery, Cambria Winery, and Qupe Cellars.

Santa Ynez Valley. The Santa Ynez Valley is sheltered from maritime air flow by the Santa Rita Hills and has innumerable canyons that considerably differentiate the temperatures of vineyards, which tend to be moderate.

The principal grape varieties include Chardonnay, Riesling, Chenin Blanc, Sauvignon Blanc, Gewürztraminer, Cabernet Sauvignon, Pinot Noir, and Merlot.

The principal producers include Austin Cellars, Babcock Vineyards, Brander Vineyard, Fess Parker Winery, Firestone Winery, Gainey Vineyard, Sanford Winery, Santa Barbara Winery, and Zaca Mesa Winery.

South Coast

Although the South Coast is considered the birthplace of modern viticulture in California, the amount of acreage under viticulture has dissipated since its heyday in the 1870s and early 1880s. The climate in this area is much warmer than in Santa Barbara, even though maritime influences are still effective. The only significant wine-producing area is the **Temecula** AVA, which is located between Los Angeles and San Diego.

The principal grape varieties include Chardonnay, Sauvignon Blanc, Semillon, Riesling, Pinot Blanc, Cabernet Sauvignon, and Zinfandel.

The principal producers are Callaway Vineyard and Winery, Culbertson Winery, Hart Winery. and Mount Palomar.

Central Valley

The Central Valley is the largest wine-producing area of California, with over 55% of its vineyards and 75% of its wine. The largest wine companies are located in the Central Valley, such as E&J Gallo Winery, whose annual production equals 78 million cases. The Central Valley is divided into the Sacramento Valley in the north and the San Joaquin Valley in the south.

Sacramento Valley
The Sacramento delta is known for three AVAS:
Lodi
Clarksburg
Solano

Lodi. The viticultural improvements made over the past decade have led to much improved "jug" wine and good quality table wine. The Lodi AVA enjoys a cooler climate than much of the Central Valley, with areas falling under Heat Summation regions II and III.

The principal grape varieties grown are Chardonnay, Chenin Blanc, Sauvignon Blanc, Cabernet Sauvignon, and Zinfandel.

The principal producers are Guild Winery, Lucas Winery, and Mondavi Woodbridge.

Clarksburg. Clarksburg's one claim is that it produces excellent Chenin Blanc. The principal producers include Bogle Winery and R&J Cook.

Solano. Solano is known for one estate, the Château de Leu, which has been developing an extraordinary reputation with its Sauvignon Blanc and other blends, although much of its grapes are brought in from other regions.

San Joaquin Valley
Known as the center of production for jug wines, one needs to appreciate the improvements made since the 1960s, when Thompson Seedless represented 50% of the grapes grown. Many large producers have not used this variety for wine making since the early 1970s. The San Joaquin Valley is also a major supplier of Zinfandel for the production of White Zinfandel (Sutter Home). Two notable producers, Ficklin Vineyards and Quady Winery, have developed some of California's best fortified wines. The Ficklin property grows the principal traditional Portuguese varieties

plyinburgplyokayply

to make decent ports. Quady has developed the Orange Muscat, with the label Essencia, and Electra, which has developed a popular following among cognescenti.

The principal grape varieties include Chenin Blanc, Chardonnay, Sauvignon Blanc, Carignan, Cabernet Sauvignon, Petit Sirah, and Zinfandel.

The principal producers include J F J Bronco, Delicato Vineyards, Ficklin, Franzia, E&J Gallo, Giumarra Vineyards, and Quady Winery.

The Pacific Northwest

The Pacific Northwest comprises Oregon and Washington. The recent viticultural growth and development in these states have differed significantly from each other. It was believed that *vinifera* could not be successfully grown north of Mendocino County in California, because there was no natural barrier to the maritime winds, causing high humidity and high rainfall. It took entrepreneurs from California, such as Richard Sommer, David Lett, and Dick Erath, who ignored the University of California–Davis contention that *vinifera* could not be transplanted successfully, to develop the wine industry of Oregon in the 1960s (see Figure 7–3 on page 186).

Oregon

Oregon's wine country lies to the west of the Cascade Mountains and Washington's lies to the east. The climate is in many ways similar to Burgundy's, with its cool climate, considerable rainfall, and greater variability of weather from year to year. Pinot Noir, which had been unsuccessfully grown in California through the late 1970s, found a more inviting environment in this area.

The wine world first took notice of Oregon's potential as a wine region with the showing of David Lett's Pinot Noir at a wine tasting in Paris in 1979. The success of this was not lost on Joseph Drouhin, a major négociant and producer of Burgundy wines, who proceeded to invest substantially in Oregon. Oregon also has attracted the attention of winemakers such as William Hill from California and Brian Croser from Australia. By the mid 1990s there

Oregon Varietals

were 115 wineries in Oregon, although this still represents less than 2% of the viticultural area in California.

Oregon has banned the use of generic labeling (e.g., Chablis for a dry white wine). Additionally, Oregon requires that a wine contain a minimum of 90% of a varietal grape before its name can appear on the label, and that the origin of the grapes also be stated on the label. The stricter regulations ensure Oregonians' commitment to quality and the likelihood that their wines will be in high demand throughout the United States.

Figure 7–3 Map of the wine-producing regions of Oregon and Washington

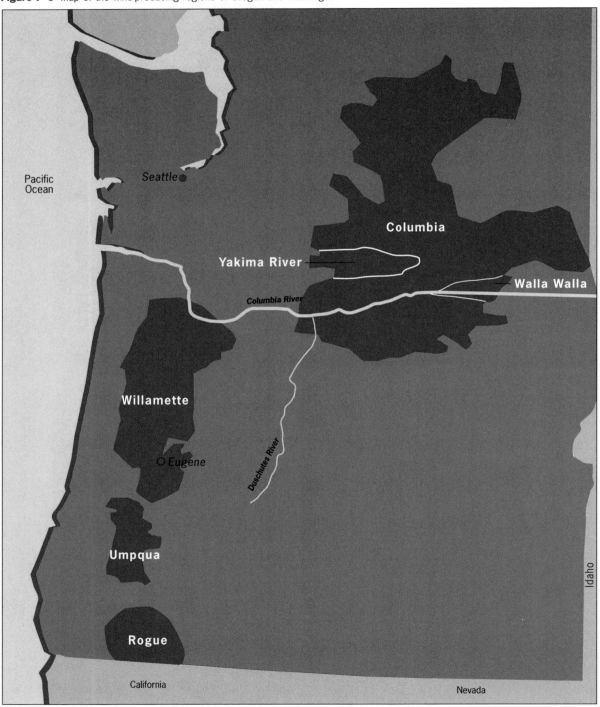

Oregon has five AVAs, two of which are shared with Washington:

Willamette Valley
Umqua Valley
Rogue Valley
Columbia (shared)
Walla Walla (shared)

Willamette

The Willamette Valley runs parallel to the coast, from Portland south for 150 miles to Eugene, and is protected by the Coast Range. The soils are not particularly fertile, frost is rarely a problem, and summer temperatures vary considerably. As a result, the characteristics of the wines differ substantially from year to year.

The principal grape varieties include Chardonnay, Gewürztraminer, Riesling, Pinot Gris, and Pinot Noir.

The principal producers include Amity Vineyards, Adelsheim Vineyard, Argyle, Bethel Heights Vineyard, Domaine Drouhin, Eyrie Vineyards, Knudsen Erath, Oak Knoll Montinore, Ponzi Vineyards, Tualitin, and Sokol Blosser.

Umqua Valley

The Umqua Valley is located south of the Willamette Valley, extending down to Roseberg, and benefits from drier and warmer weather.

The principal grape varieties are Chardonnay, Gewürztraminer, Riesling, Cabernet Sauvignon, and Pinot Noir.

The principal producers are Callahan Ridge, Henry Estates, Hillcrest Vineyards, Lookingglass, Girardet, and La Garza.

Rogue Valley

The Rogue Valley runs south of the Umqua Valley, from Wolf Creek to the California border. Its climate is warmer and drier than the northern AVAs, allowing more Cabernet Sauvignon to thrive.

The principal grape varieties are Chardonnay, Gewürztraminer, Riesling, Cabernet Sauvignon, Merlot, and Pinot Noir.

The principal producers include Ashland Vineyards, Bridgeview, Foris, Valley View, Rogue River, and Weisinger's.

Washington

Washington has overtaken New York as the second largest wine producer of the United States, although still only one thirtieth of California's total. It has the second largest plantings of *vinifera*, after California. In contrast to Oregon, vineyards were established to the east of the Cascade

Washington State Varietals

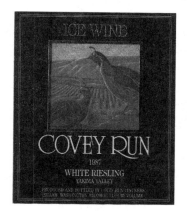

Mountains in desert areas along the Columbia River, which irrigates them. The vineyards are planted on south-facing slopes to capture as much sun as possible. The growing season is marked by long sunny days accompanied by chilly nights, which allow grapes to maintain their acidity while fully developing. This is one of the reasons that Riessling is so widely planted.

Vinifera was first planted in 1967 by Associated Vintners, now known as Columbia Winery and Château Ste. Michelle, which was guided by the great Californian oenologist Andre Tchelischeff. Unlike Oregon, Washington's eight largest wineries produce 95% of its wines.

Washington has four principal AVAS:

Columbia Valley
Walla Walla Valley
Yakima Valley
Puget Sound

Columbia Valley

The Columbia Valley is the primary AVA, with almost 60% of the state's *vinifera*. The close proximity to the Columbia River and its tributaries, the Snake and Yakima Rivers, moderate the climate, but cold nights allow the grapes to preserve good acidity.

The principal grape varieties are Chardonnay, Gewürztraminer, Sauvignon Blanc, Riesling, Semillon, Cabernet Sauvignon, and Merlot.

The principal producers include Arbor Crest, Columbia Winery, Chateau Ste. Michelle, Covey Run, The Hogue Cellars, Latah Creek, Preston Cellars, Quarry Lake, and Chateau Gallant.

Walla Walla

Walla Walla is a small appellation at the eastern end of the Columbia River bend and is in the Columbia Valley AVA. It has greater humidity and fewer temperature extremes than Yakima. It crosses over into Oregon with Seven Hills Vineyard and Canoe Ridge Vineyard. Walla Walla's principal grape varieties are Chardonnay, Sauvignon Blanc, and Cabernet Sauvignon.

The principal producers include Woodward Canyon, L'Ecole No 41, Waterbrook, and Leonetti Cellar.

Yakima Valley

The Yakima Valley is on the same latitude as Burgundy, running along the Yakima River from Franklin to the town of Yakima. Its summers are rainless, and its nights are cool. In the past, the vineyards were irrigated by great booms, but drip irrigation is increasingly employed because it is more effective. This area is likely to become well known for sparkling wines.

The principal grape varieties are Chardonnay, Sauvignon Blanc, Gewürztraminer, Riesling, Semillon, Cabernet Sauvignon, and Merlot.

The principal producers include Covey Run, Eaton Hill, Washington Hills Cellars, Tucker Cellars, Yakima River, Kiona, Chateau Ste. Michelle, Porteus, Stewart Vineyards, Hogue Cellars, and Staton Hills.

New York and The Eastern States

New York has a long history of viticulture. After early attempts at planting *vinifera* failed, attention was focused on the development and use of *Vitis labrusca* and hybrids that were resistant to *Phylloxera* and could survive frosts and winters more easily. The grapes traditionally used were primarily Concord, which are still used in the making of many kosher wines. The hybrids that became preeminent were Catawba, Aurora, Delaware, Seyval Blanc, and Vidal Blanc for whites, and Baco Noir, Chambourcin, and Chancellor for reds. The traditional areas developed in the nineteenth century were Lake Erie, the Finger Lakes region, and the Hudson Valley (see Figure 7–4).

Two recent developments have had a significant impact on New York's and subsequently New England's, wine industry. First, Dr. Konstantin Frank, a Ukrainian immigrant, developed experimental clones for vinifera varieties such as Riesling and Chardonnay. These clones were able to withstand severe winters and became the grapes of choice for New York vintners. Second, the Farm Winery Act of 1976 lowered licensing fees and allowed small wineries (fewer than 20,000 cases) to sell directly to the public. This provided enough impetus to create 73 of the current 97 wineries.

When American tastes shifted away from labrusca wines,

Figure 7–4 Map of the wine-producing regions of New York and the Eastern States

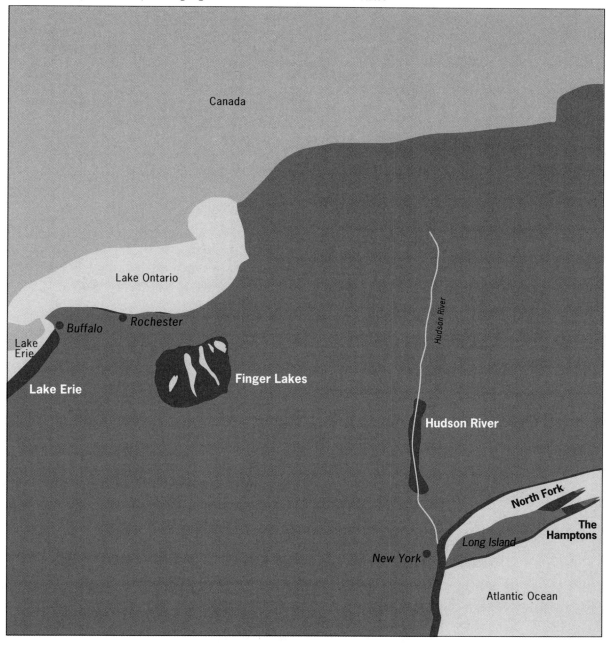

New England Varietals

a precipitous drop occurred in the price wineries were willing to pay for *labrusca* and hybridized varieties. This also gave impetus to grape growers to plant *vinifera* and produce their own wines, especially in the Finger Lakes region.

New York currently has five AVAs:

Finger Lakes (including the Lake Cayuga AVA)
Lake Erie
Hudson River
North Fork (Long Island)
The Hamptons (Long Island)

Finger Lakes

The picturesque region of the Finger Lakes includes Lake Canadaigua, Lake Keuka, Lake Seneca, and Lake Cayuga, which are large enough and deep enough to moderate the climate. This AVA has 40 wineries and produces 85% of the state's grapes.

The principal grape varieties include Cayuga White, Seyval Blanc, Chardonnay, Gewürztraminer, and Riesling.

Major producers include Taylor, Great Western, Gold Seal, Canandaigua Wine Co., Chateau Frank, Glenora Wine Cellars, Knapp Vineyards, and Wagner Vineyards.

Lake Erie

The Lake Erie AVA includes three states around the Chautauqua region of New York, Ohio and Pennsylvania. Lake Erie moderates the climate of the vineyards that line its edge. The principal grapes grown are Catawba and Concord, but as they are being cleared, *vinifera* is replacing them.

The principal grape varieties include Chardonnay, Gewürztraminer, and Riesling.

The principal producers include Woodbury Vineyards, Johnson Vineyards, and Firelands.

Hudson River

The Hudson River Valley is located 60 miles south of Albany between Poughkeepsie and New York City. The vineyards are located on both sides of the river on its steeply sloped, palisaded banks. There are more than 20 wineries, most of which still plant and use the hybrid Seyval Blanc, although there are increasing plantings of Chardonnay and Cabernet Sauvignon.

The principal grape varieties include Seyval Blanc, Chardonnay, Riesling, Vidal Blanc, Pinot Noir, Cabernet Sauvignon, Cabernet Franc, and Baco Noir.

The principal producers include Benmarl Wine Co., Clinton Vineyards, Riverdale Winery, and Millbrook.

North Fork and The Hamptons

The eastern end of Long Island is surrounded by the Long Island Sound to the north, Peconic Bay to the south, and the Atlantic Ocean to the east, providing this wine-producing region with a temperate and moderate climate. The growing season is 3 weeks longer than in other AVAs in New York. The first pioneers were the Hargraves, who, in 1973, purchased a potato farm in the North Fork region and grew *vinifera* successfully.

The principal grape varieties are Chardonnay, Gewürztraminer, Riesling, Sauvignon Blanc, Cabernet Franc, Cabernet Sauvignon, and Merlot.

The principal producers are Bedell Cellars, Bridgehampton Winery, Hargrave Vineyards, Palmer Vineyards, and Pindar Vineyards.

The Eastern States

There has been an explosive growth of small vineyards and wineries extending from Massachusetts to Virginia. Connecticut has six wineries, including Chamard Vineyards and Stonington Vineyards; Rhode Island has three vineyards, including Sakonnet Vineyards, which provides the best expression of Vidal Blanc; Massachusetts has 10 wineries, the best of which is Westport Rivers Winery, producing exceptional sparkling wines comparable to California's best. New Jersey, Pennsylvania, Maryland, and Delaware produce hybrid and *vinifera* wines. Virginia may be the most exciting wine-producing area in the East, with the exception of Long Island. There are currently five AVAs

that have been designated, the most notable being the Monticello AVA. Prince Michel, Rapidan, Horton, and Blenheim are all estates that are located near Charlottesville, where the climate and the soil are able to produce the best quality grapes, such as Cabernet Sauvignon, Riesling, Chardonnay, and Sauvignon Blanc.

Australia

Australia's emergence as a significant wine-producing region occurred in the mid-1980s and led to the erroneous conclusion that its entry into the foray of wine making is recent. Australia has a long history of wine making, dating back to the first plantings of South African cuttings in Sydney Cove in **1788,** and its first wine to be exported was in 1823. Vine cuttings were brought from France, Germany, Spain, Portugal, Italy, and South Africa during the nineteenth century. George Brown, Thomas Hardy, Henry Lindeman, Christopher Penfold, and Joseph Seppelt were all prominent winemakers at that time, and their names are still synonymous with Australia's leading wine-producing houses.

By **1870,** southeastern Australia was producing 8.7 million gallons of wine. However, *Phylloxera* devastated the wine industry, beginning in 1875, and although it quickly recuperated by grafting vines onto American rootstocks, the trend shifted away from dry wines to the fortified styles that were favored by Victorian England, its primary export market. By the mid-1930s, nearly 75% of Australian wine was being produced in South Australia, with the Barossa Valley becoming the center of production. Much of Australia's viticulture moved from cooler to warmer climates, which affected the types of grapes grown and the resulting styles of wine.

In the 1950s Australia's path to making fine wines began with the pioneering use of stainless steel refrigeration and fermentation. The result was a spectacular increase in first red and then white wine consumption. The large wine producers purchased lands in cooler climatic regions, such as the Coonawarra and Padthaway, all the while focusing on

Australia Varietals

making finer quality wines. The use of nighttime harvesting, refrigeration, and temperature-controlled fermentation led to white wines that were more refreshing, and had more fruit aromas and flavors and a cleaner finish. It is ironic that the Australians' thirst for wine was enhanced by the development of "bag-in-box" packaging of wine, which, to a certain degree, prevents the wine from oxidizing once it is opened. Australians currently have the highest per capita consumption of wine among English-speaking peoples: 17 liters per person.

Another major factor that differentiates the development of Australian viticulture is the heavier use of mechanization. Mechanization not only has lowered the relative cost of Australian viticulture, compared with either Europe or the United States, but also has led to the practice of minimal pruning and new canopy management systems.

Australia's land mass is very similar to that of the United States, and, therefore, it is difficult to generalize about its climate. The climate of Australia is similar to California's, because most of its vineyards lie between 32 and 43 degrees south latitude, but it is not affected as much by cooling maritime influences. Because Australia lies in the Southern Hemisphere, the growing season is inverted, with the harvest beginning in January and ending in March in cooler regions. This has allowed Australians, such as the Australian "Flying Wine-makers," to become a worldwide influence involved in wine production in France and the United States.

All of Australia's six states—**New South Wales, South Australia, Victoria, Western Australia, Queensland,** the **Northern Territory**—and the island of **Tasmania,** produce wines, but the vast majority are made in the southeast corner of the continent, and it is this region that will receive most of the focus (see Figure 7–5).

The principal *white* grape varieties include Chardonnay, Riesling, Semillon, Muscat Gordo Blanco, and to a lesser extent, Sauvignon Blanc. Chardonnay wines are quite distinctive, offering luscious tropical fruit aromas and flavors while balanced by oak spiciness and complexity. Semillon is very successful as a varietal. Classically its magic was woven by bottle aging, but today it is barrel fermented and aged. Riesling is also vinified into a wonderfully fruity

Figure 7–5 Map of the wine-producing regions of Australia

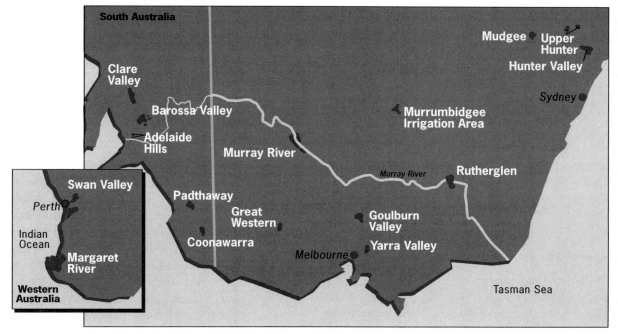

but dry style that, although unique, is clearly reminiscent of that noble variety.

The principal *black* grape varieties include Shiraz, Cabernet Sauvignon, and Pinot Noir. Shiraz (Syrah) is the most widely planted black grape variety and produces Australia's most magnificent red wines. The Shiraz of the Barossa Valley is reminiscent of spicy opulent Rhone wines, although with greater fruit and anise flavors, and is considered among the world's best red wines. Shiraz is much less tannic, often blended with Cabernet Sauvignon to add body and spice. The best of Shiraz can be aged for decades to reach their peak.

Cabernet Sauvignon is the second most widely planted variety and produces wine with a definite herbaceous and even minty quality, while retaining plum and blackberry flavors. Often blended with Shiraz, it is more frequently blended with typical Bordeaux varieties, such as Cabernet Franc and Merlot, which is the fastest proliferating variety in Australia.

Pinot Noir's plantings have doubled in the past 5 years,

although it ranks well behind the other two leading varieties. It is producing some exciting wines in the cool climate regions of Victoria, Adelaide Hills, and Tasmania. As in Champagne, it is also being used in the production of premium sparkling wines.

New South Wales

New South Wales has 11 wine zones, the most significant of which are Lower Hunter Valley, Upper Hunter Valley, Mudgee, and the Murrumbidgee Irrigation Area. Although it produces only 28% of Australia total harvest, New South Wales is disproportionately important due to its proximity to Sydney, Australia's, largest population center. The Hunter Valley has a long history of wine making, dating to 1825, and developed a reputation that made it preeminent in Australia's viticultural lore. Hunter Valley's volcanic soil and irrigation mitigate what might otherwise be considered an inhospitable climate, although modern technology seems to be able to overcome most potential barriers. This region often suffers from rainfall during the growing season. The wines do not share the diversity or quite the opulence of wines from Victoria and South Australia. Furthermore, the Hunter Valley no longer is the most productive region; it has been supplanted by the Murrumbidgee Irrigation Area.

The principal grape varieties include Semillon, Chardonnay, Shiraz, Cabernet Sauvignon, and Pinot Noir. The Semillon has been vinified as perhaps nowhere else, developing into a rich, honeyed, and nutty wine if allowed to age sufficiently well. Chardonnay has also developed a merited reputation, with concentrated tropical and tree fruit aromas and varying degrees of butteriness and charred oak.

Lower Hunter Valley

The **Lower Hunter Valley** contains approximately 50 of Australia's 650 wineries, many of which have become well known to the American consumer. The most notable include Lake's Folly, Lindeman's, McWilliam's Mount Pleasant, The Rothbury Estate, Tyrrells Wines, and The Wyndham Estate.

Upper Hunter Valley

The **Upper Hunter Valley** has a recent history of viticulture; Penfolds established new vineyards and a winery in 1960. There are only nine major wineries in this region, the most significant being Rosemount Estate, and all focus most of their efforts on Chardonnay and Semillon.

Mudgee

Mudgee is located west of the Hunter Valley on the western side of the Great Dividing Range, providing it with a more stable summer season. Although Mudgee has enjoyed brief and sporadic periods of viticultural accomplishment, it has only been in the past 20 years that it has enjoyed a renaissance. The principal wines are Cabernet Sauvignon, which has plenty of berry and minty flavors and is combined with sufficient tannins to allow the wines to develop for a decade; Shiraz, which has leathery and earthy qualities,

is not long lived, and is frequently used as a blend; and Chardonnay, which is produced very successfully and ages very well into a complex Burgundian-style white wine. Mudgee has 23 wineries, mostly small producers, the most significant of which include Craigmoor, Huntington Estate, and Montrose.

Murrumbidgee Irrigation Area

This region is located several hundred miles southwest of Sydney, along the Murrumbidgee River. The hot summer climate makes it an unlikely candidate as the region with the most acreage under viticulture. Until 1960, this region, centered around Griffith, was dedicated to making fortified wines but since then has led the way in using modern technology to produce good table wines. As its name suggests, its viticulture is entirely dependent on irrigation. The principal grape varieties are Semillon, Trebbiano, Chardonnay, Shiraz, and Muscat Gordo Blanco. Botrytized wines are a significant factor in the area's overall production and reputation. The principal wineries include De Bortoli Wines, McWilliam's, Miranda, and Raced.

Victoria

The southern state of Victoria has been at the forefront of Australian viticulture since in the 1840s. *Phylloxera* struck this region first, and it has only been in the past 30 years that serious wine making has been practiced on a significant level. Victoria has 12 wine-producing regions, the most significant of which are the Yarra Valley, Goulburn Valley, the Murray and North Goulburn Riverland regions, Great Western, and Rutherglen.

Yarra Valley

The **Yarra Valley** is located just east of Melbourne, the capital city of Victoria, and has been growing at a phenomenal rate, commensurate with the international reputation of its wines. The Yarra Valley's style of wine making was heavily influenced by the Swiss, who were the first immigrants to develop viticulture in this region. The infusion of

Australian Wine Regions

new wineries is reflected in the establishment of Domaine Chandon Australia, which has been producing premier sparkling wines since 1989. The principal wine varietals are Pinot Noir, Cabernet Sauvignon, Chardonnay, and Riesling. The principal producers include Coldstream Hills, De Bortoli, Lillydale Vineyards, and Yarra Ridge.

Goulburn Valley

Although the **Goulburn Valley** is not a large producing area, it is significant as the site of Australia's oldest winery, Chateau Tahlbilk, which produces wines of uncompromising quality. This region is recognized primarily for its full-bodied red wines, Shiraz and Cabernet Sauvignon, although it is also a producer of Riesling, Chardonnay, and Marsanne, the varieties native to the Rhone Valley. The principal producers include Chateau Tahlbilk, Michelton, and Mount Helen.

Murray and North Goulburn Riverland Regions

The wines of this arid region, which is irrigated from the waters of the great Murray River, are for the most part straightforward, bland, bulk wines.

Great Western

This small wine-producing region has gained fame from its sparkling wines, although it also produces some of Australia's finest still wines and is the only region of Australia to have a tradition of French influence on its wine making. Shiraz is this district's finest wine varietal, followed by Chardonnay, Cabernet Sauvignon, Riesling, and Pinot Noir. The sparkling wines are made from Chardonnay, Pinot Noir, and Pinot Meunier, which are sourced mainly from other districts, and are cellared underground in old gold mine shafts. The most notable producers include Best's, Montara, Mount Langi Ghiran, and Seppelt Great Western.

Rutherglen

The **Rutherglen** in northeastern Victoria is the site of some of Australia's finest fortified wines, Tokay, Liqueur Muscats, and Ports, which can age 50 years or more. The principal grape varieties are Chardonnay, Riesling, Muscadelle, Muscat a Petits Grains, Shiraz, and Cabernet Sauvignon. Tokay is made from Muscadelle, while Muscats are made from the Muscat à Petits Grains. The wines are harvested late but are not affected by *Botrytis*. Some producers allow some fermentation to take place prior to fortification, but others do not. The wines are fortified to 17% or 18% alcohol and aged in small barrels. With 10 to 20 years of aging, the wines develop enormously complex bouquets and a superb syrupy yet uncloying texture. The most prominent producers include All Saints Estate, Bailey's, Brown Brothers, Campbells, Chambers Rosewood, Morris, and St. Leonard's.

South Australia

South Australia produces over 50% of Australia's wines, and its seven wine-producing districts are located to the north and east of the city of Adelaide. Its climate is the most like that of the Mediterranean, and it has had a wine-producing tradition dating back to 1838. Its most famous wine districts include the Barossa Valley, Coonawarra, Padthaway, Clare Valley, and the Adelaide Hills and surrounding area. The principal grape varieties are Riesling, Chardonnay, Sauvignon Blanc, Cabernet Sauvignon, Shiraz, Pinot Noir, and Merlot.

Barossa Valley

The Barossa Valley is internationally famous, although it produces less than 9% of Australia's grape crush. It is the headquarters of Australia's largest producers, which account for over 50% of Australia's production. The Barossa Valley is home to some of Australia's and, by some accounts, the world's greatest red wines, such as Penfolds' Grange Hermitage (now labeled Grange) made from Shiraz. Its Rieslings are quintessentially Australian, with very pronounced tropical and citric fruit flavors and the ability to undergo considerable bottle aging. The Cabernet Sauvignon is most often blended with the same variety from Coonawarra or McLaren Vale. The principal producers include Basedows, Chateau Yaldara, Grant Burge, Krondorf, Leo Buring, Orlando (Jacob's Creek), Penfolds, Peter Lehman, Saltram, Seppelt, Tollana, Wolf Blass, and Yalumba.

Coonawarra

Coonawarra is the preeminent red wine region of Australia. Its cool climate and famous thin red-clay soil (terra rosa) overlying a bed of limestone are conducive to viticulture. It is a wine district that has been in the forefront of viticultural changes, with the practice of minimal pruning introduced in the 1980s. Coonawarra produces Australia's greatest Cabernet Sauvignon, with rich, ripe fruit intensity and modest tannic strength. The principal producers include Lindeman's, Mildara, Penfolds, Petaluma, Rosemount, Seppelt, and Wynns Coonawarra Estate.

Padthaway

Padthaway has a very recent history of viticulture and a climate very similar to that of Coonawarra. Although it has a higher heat summation than its counterpart, Padthaway suffers from spring frosts that can be devastating. Padthaway is to white wine what Coonawarra is to red wine. The principal varietals are Riesling, Chardonnay, Sauvignon Blanc, Cabernet Sauvignon, Shiraz, and Pinot Noir. The principal producers include Lindeman's Padthaway, Padthaway Estate, Seppelt, and Thomas Hardy.

Clare Valley

Clare Valley produces much of Australia's finest Riesling, which is, for the most part, long lived and able to develop extraordinary complexity. The Clare Valley also produces excellent Cabernet Sauvignon and Shiraz. The other dominant varietals are Chardonnay and Semillon. The principal producers include Eaglehawk Estate, Jeffrey Grosset, Leasingham, Mitchell, Petaluma, Taylor's, and Tim Knappstein.

Adelaide Hills and Surrounding Areas

This area is defined in part by its consistent altitude of 1200 feet above sea level and its cool-to-very cool climate. This region has a viticultural history dating back 100 years, with a heavy Silesian influence. The principal varietals are Riesling, Chardonnay, Gewürztraminer, Cabernet Sauvignon, Shiraz, and Pinot Noir. The principal producers include Henschke, Petaluma, and Pewsey Vale.

Western Australia

Western Australian wines are not well known in the United States or in Europe, because the remoteness of the locale from major population centers has stunted its potential. The first vineyards were planted in 1842. Wine production has been limited to a few regions, the most important being the Swan Valley, which has accounted for almost 70% of total production. Recent enormous capital investments will make other districts, such as the Margaret River, more prominent.

Margaret River

The Margaret River district is located primarily between Cape Naturaliste and Cape Mentelle on the Indian Ocean. There are over 30 wineries, the most prominent being Leeuwin Estate, which used Robert Mondavi as a consultant in the 1970s. The principal varietals include Chardonnay, Semillon, Sauvignon Blanc, Riesling, Cabernet Sauvignon, Shiraz, and Merlot. The principal producers include Cape Mentelle, Evans and Tate, Leeuwin Estate, Moss Wood, Sandalford, and Vasse Felix.

Swan Valley

The Swan Valley is almost synonymous with Houghton, one of Australia's largest wineries, which produces Australia's largest-selling white wine, Houghton White Burgundy. Swan Valley has a history of viticulture that has been influenced significantly by Yugoslav immigrants. Chenin Blanc is the dominant variety but others include Chardonnay, Verdelho,

Shiraz and Cabernet Sauvignon. The principal producers include Evans and Tate, Houghton, Moondah Brook Estate, Sandalford, and Talijancich Wines.

Other regions of Australia produce wines on a smaller or less notable basis. The island of Tasmania has two growing regions, and although there has been an infusion of both capital and experience, the results in this coolest of Australian wine regions have been disappointing. The central problem seems to be a lack of understanding concerning which variety is best suited to the terroir. Once this is resolved, however, this region should be able to produce great wines.

New Zealand

Until recently, New Zealand's reputation as a wine-producing country was unknown outside of Australia or its borders. New Zealand has a history of viticulture dating back to 1836, when James Busby, considered the father of New Zealand viticulture, planted his vineyard in Waitangi. *Oidium* and *Phylloxera* had a devastating effect, as the vines that were replanted were entirely American varieties, not *vinifera* grafts. Additionally, due in no small measure to its English heritage, beer has been and continues to be the country's most prevalent beverage, exceeding 100 liters per-capita consumption annually.

New Zealand's wine industry, as it is today, developed in the past 25 years. The quality of its Sauvignon Blanc has been extraordinary and has received accolades from around the world. All of New Zealand's wines have improved enormously over the past 15 years, and one should expect other varietals such as Chardonnay to reach a similar quality level.

New Zealand is divided into two main islands (see Figure 7–6). The **North Island** has four wine districts: **Auckland area, Hawke 's Bay, Gisbourne/Poverty Bay,** and **Martinborough.** The North Island contains 70% of New Zealand's population, and it is here that the exceptional vineyards produce the particularly excellent Sauvignon Blanc, Chardonnay, and Cabernet Sauvignon. However, Müller-Thurgau is New Zealand's dominant grape varietal,

made in a Germanic style with considerable residual sugar. New Zealand's wine production is dominated by **Montana,** which crushes over 50% of the total harvest. It should be noted that the majority of New Zealand's grapes is grown on the South Island, much of which is shipped to the North Island wineries to be vinified. The four wine regions of the **South Island** include **Nelson, Marlborough, Canterbury,** and **Central Otago.** It is from the Marlborough region that the wineries Montana and Cloudy Bay have produced the Sauvignon Blancs that have gained worldwide attention.

The most notable producers of New Zealand wines include Kumeu River, Matua Valley, Corbans, Martinborough Vineyard, Montana, Villa Maria, Te Mata, Vidal, Cooks, Cloudy Bay, and Hunters.

An overview of New World wines would not be complete without some discussion, however brief, of Chile, Argentina, and South Africa, all major wine-producing countries (see Figure 7–7 on page 200).

Chile

Chile is only the world's sixteenth largest wine-producing country but is the most significant South American producer in the export market. Chilean wines have become so prevalent in America's retail stores and restaurant establishments, it is hard to imagine that in the early 1980s Chilean wines were basically unknown outside of its borders. The cause for this explosive growth and development is simply that Chilean wines provided reasonably priced and good quality wines at a time when both French and Californian wines were becoming increasingly expensive and perceived to be less than good value for everyday drinking.

The Spaniards introduced the **País** variety in the mid-sixteenth century, but the Chilean wine industry owes more to French rather than Spanish influences. Claudio Gay, originally French, persuaded the Chilean government to establish a nursery of vines of imported French cuttings in the 1830s. The Chilean landowner, Echazarreta, traveled

Figure 7–6 Map of the wine-producing regions of New Zealand

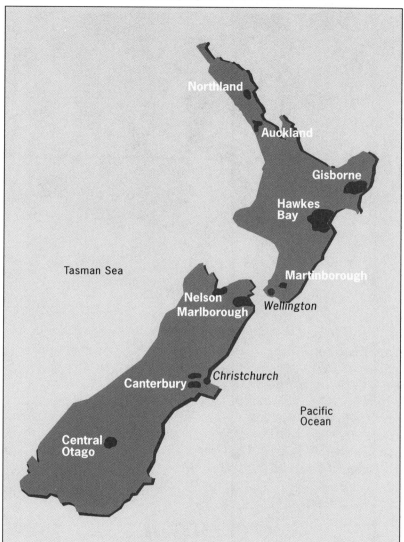

to France in 1851 and returned to Chile with cuttings of classic Bordeaux varieties. Chile is fortunate to be the only country that has not suffered the ravages of either *Oidium* or *Phylloxera,* thereby maintaining a very successful wine tradition.

As in other Latin countries, consumption of wine declined precipitously in the 1970s and 1980s forcing wineries to adopt a different marketing strategy. The most prevalent grape was and continues to be the Pais. Chilean wine producers took a two-track policy in the 1980s: making premium wines strictly for the export market and continuing to produce very ordinary, somewhat oxidized wines for domestic consumption. The producers invested heavily in updating their facilities to employ modern vinification techniques, such as temperature-controlled stainless steel fermentation and aging in American oak or French bar-

Figure 7–7 Map of the wine-producing regions of Chile, Argentina, and South Africa

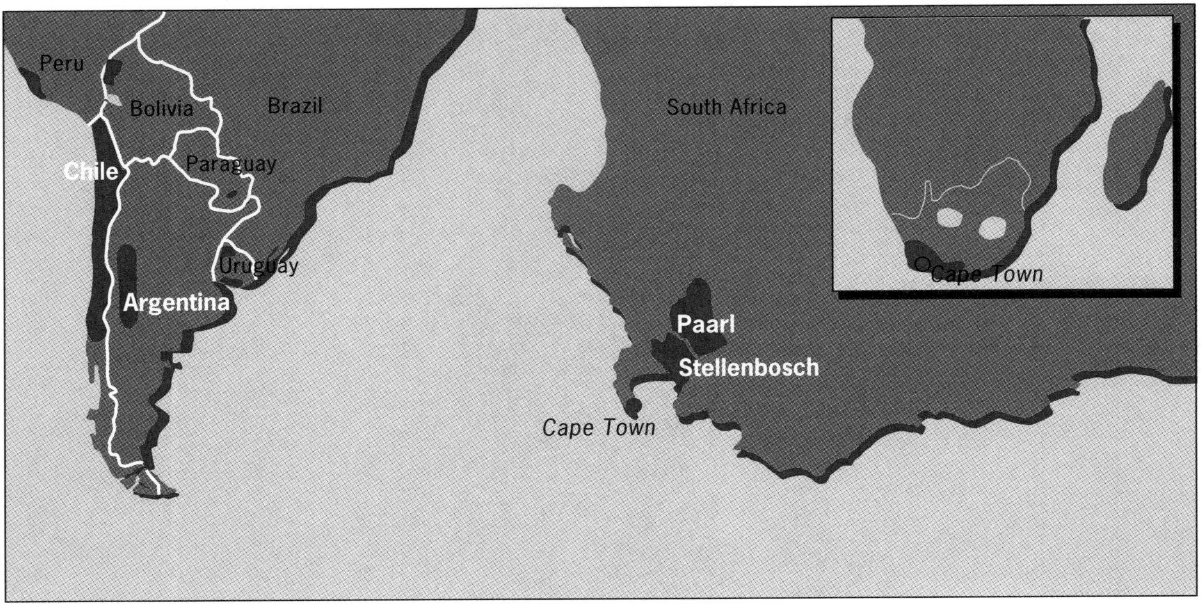

riques. At the same time, nearly 30,000 acres of premium vines were planted, including Cabernet Sauvignon, Merlot, Chardonnay, Sauvignon Blanc, and Semillon. Chileans have been able to produce wines at very reasonable prices because the cost of land and labor is so much less than its competitors and the growing conditions are ideal.

Chile is blessed with ideal climatic conditions, with most of its vineyards located in the 320-mile-long **Central Valley.** Plentiful water from the Andes Mountains is used to irrigate during long dry summers. Chile's most famous wine region, **Maipo,** is in close proximity to the capital, Santiago. As land prices have begun to climb, other regions, such as **Casablanca, Curico, Rapel,** and **BioBio,** are being developed more fully. These cooler wine-producing regions hold great promise for the varietals that are being made. The Rapel region is divided into two subregions, Cachapoal and Colchagua, where some of Chile's best Cabernet Sauvignons are being produced, many with the cooperation of foreign capital and expertise. For example, Chateau Lafite-Rothschild is in partnership with a local winery at Los Vascos, and the winemaker at Carmen is French. Although most exported wines are perceived as good quality, none are accorded the prestige of being great. It is expected, however, that excellent wines will be produced in the decades to come.

The most notable producers include Caliterra, Canepa, Carmen, Concha y Toro, Errazuriz, Cousino Macul, Montes, La Playa, San Pedro, Santa Carolina, Santa Rita, Miguel Torres, Undurraga, Valdivieso, Los Vascos, Vina del Mar, and Walnut Crest.

Argentina

Argentina is the fifth largest producer of wine in the world, although its exports have been negligible until recently because its wine basically met only the needs of its domestic market. However, that market has changed considerably during the past two decades with a precipitous drop in red wine consumption. The result has been a decrease by almost 40% since 1977 in amount of acreage under viticulture. Three fourths of all Argentine wines is produced in the Mendoza region at the foothills of the Andes, which

Chile and Argentina Varietals by Region

that make white or blush wines and are sometimes blended with Argentina's leading black grape, **Malbec.** Malbec has produced Argentina's finest red wines, so it is somewhat paradoxical that Malbec was being pulled out during the 1980s, with the clamor from Argentinians for more white varietals and Cabernet Sauvignon.

During the past decade, dramatic efforts have been applied to modernize viticultural techniques and vinification processes. Plantings of classic *vinifera* such as Chardonnay, Sauvignon Blanc, Semillon, Cabernet Sauvignon, and Merlot have increased significantly. There has been an upsurge in foreign investment of capital and technological assistance. The next decade will show to what degree Argentina has been successful in developing and marketing its wines and to what degree they are unique.

The most notable producers include Etchart, Catena of Vina Esmaralda, Penaflor, San Telmo, and Bodegas Weinert.

South Africa

South Africa is one of the oldest wine-producing regions in the Southern Hemisphere. Vines were first planted in **1655,** and the first wine was made in 1659. Although they are included in the New World category, South African wines are more European, being leaner and more austere. Due their higher tannins and acidity, these wines take well to bottle aging.

Wine making in South Africa was decidedly influenced by the arrival of the Huguenots (French Protestants) in 1688 and their establishment of communities in the area called Franschoek. The emigration of Huguenots was a result of the rescinding of the Edict of Nantes, which caused them to be persecuted. Huguenots also settled in Savannah, Georgia, and Charleston, South Carolina, in the United States for the same reason.

By the early eighteenth century, one of South Africa's wines, called Constantia, was the most prized in Europe. Trade with Europe and particularly Britain flourished until *Oidium* and *Phylloxera* struck in 1885. The wine industry collapsed, especially as the British removed preferential tariffs.

in turn provides the region with ample water for irrigation. Even though all of the climatic conditions are well suited for viticulture, the reason for Argentina's less-than-notable presence in the international wine trade is a lack of quality.

The principal grape variety is the **Criolla** grape, a pink-skinned variety first brought over by the Spanish conquistadors in the sixteenth century that is similar to the País grape of Chile and the Mission grape of California. The Criolla and the Cereza are high yield–producing varieties

South Africa Varietals and Appellations

Today, South Africa is the world's eighth largest producer, with 6000 growers but only 70 cooperatives and 110 private producers. The basis for South Africa's reemergence is the Ko-operatiewe Wynbouwers Vereniging (KWV), which was established in 1918 as a government-sponsored cooperative, whose function it was to set quotas and administer price controls on the wine industry. The KWV's role is beginning to change, because its influence has been to slow the growth and development of the South African wine industry. Loose laws governing labeling were introduced in 1973 and included the minimum percentage necessary for a wine to be labeled as a varietal: 75% of the total if domestic and 85% if exported. South Africa's wine makers are embracing the viticultural and vinification techniques used throughout the modern wine-making world and are producing some very exciting wines. With the lifting of sanctions against South Africa, it is expected that exports to the United States will climb considerably from the 70,000 cases exported in 1995.

South Africa's wine-producing region is located primarily along the Cape, especially where the Atlantic and Indian Oceans meet. The climate is very Mediterranean, and the soil in this rugged land is ideal because it is schistous in some areas and sandstone combined with granite in others. There are 14 wine-producing regions, the most significant being **Paarl** and **Stellenbosch,** which is the largest.

Most of South Africa's wines are white (80%), although fortified wines are an important part of its tradition. The most widely planted variety is Chenin Blanc, locally called the Steen, which can be vinified in the same styles of the Loire Valley in France, from bracingly dry to lusciously sweet. Sauvignon Blanc wines are very reminiscent of Bordeaux, and Chardonnay, which had been banned by the KWV, is being planted in increasing quantity. The main black grape variety is Cinsaut, native to southern France, which was cross-bred with Pinot Noir in 1926 to produce a very interesting variety called Pinotage. There is increasing production of Cabernet Sauvignon, Cabernet Franc Merlot, and Pinot Noir.

The principal producers include Backsberg, the Bergkelder, Boschendal, Delheim, Grangehurst, Groot Constantia, Kanonkop, Meerendal, Meerlust, Nederburg, Rusten Vrede, Schoongezicht Rustenberg, Stellenbosch Farmers's Wineries, Villiera, Wegemeend, and KWV.

8

Wine Regions of the Old World

Wine Regions of the Old World

France–Various Appellations

France

France is one of the two largest producers of wines. France has an ideal combination of soil, climate, and grapes and a long tradition of dedicated wine making and, as a result, over the centuries has created excellent wines that are the standards against which other wines are judged. It is the internationalization of French *vinifera* that is commonplace in our age, be it in Australia, the United States, South America, Italy, or Eastern Europe. Wine consumption has been a way of life, but this is now being challenged by the pressures of modern society.

Until the 1960s, the average consumption of wine was 150 liters per person. The past 30 years has seen a precipitous drop to 60 liters per person. (This amount is still significant, however, when compared to the U.S. rate of 7.2 liters per person.) Wine has always been seen as an intricate part of the meal in France, and this drop in consumption merely reflects the changing role of the meal in France. Luncheon used to be the primary meal of the day, but due to the pressures and demands of modern business, 3-hour lunch breaks are no longer the norm in Western Europe. (The precipitous drop in wine consumption is also reflected in the rest of Western Europe.) This decline in consumption has resulted in greater discrimination in what is being consumed. The consumption of fine wines has increased, while that of *vin ordinaire* has dissipated.

The French tend to be very systematic as a people, prone to classifying and controlling many aspects of life. This is reflected in the system of Appellation d' Origine Contrôlée (AOC), which was discussed previously.

Most districts south of the fiftieth latitude are wine-producing regions (see Figure 8–1 on page 206). We are concerned with the principal AOC wine regions, because they produce the best quality wines which are most likely to be seen in the export market, including the United States. The six most important wine regions are:

Figure 8–1 Map of the major wine-producing regions of France

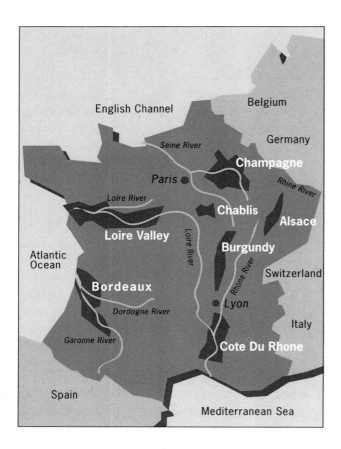

Bordeaux
Burgundy
Rhône Valley
Loire Valley
Champagne
Alsace

Bordeaux

Bordeaux developed into an important wine region while under the domain of the English, which ruled this part of France for 300 years until 1453. The strong connections made at that time continue to the present. The red wines of Bordeaux, called clarets from the French *clairet,* were and are still favored by the English. Bordeaux's development was more recent than that of the region of Burgundy, because Bordeaux was primarily swampland and forests.

The development of Bordeaux as an important trading port led to the growth of a new wealthy mercantile class, which, from the mid-seventeenth century, invested in vineyards on the best possible lands. Dutch engineers were hired to drain swamps by building *jalles,* or narrow canals, which had the effect of lowering the water table under the best areas.

It was in the late seventeenth century that the best vine-

Bordeaux Appellations

yards differentiated their products from generic Bordeaux claret wines. For example, the name of Haut Brion was well known in London in the 1660s as an exceptionally fine wine. During the eighteenth and first half of the nineteenth century, the wines of Bordeaux became classified according to the highest price and presumably best quality. As has been discussed, this classification became formalized in 1855 at the request of Napoleon III, and it holds mostly true to this day as an indicator of which wines are most likely to be of the best quality.

Quality Levels

There are four qualitative levels under which Bordeaux wines are sold. In order of ascending quality, they are

- **Regional.** The wine is made by a négociant or producer who will purchase the grapes from a number of appellations, all within the region of Bordeaux. Some wine may be given a brand name, such as Mouton Cadet, while others might be given a regional appellation, such as Médoc.
- **Communal.** The wine is made by a négociant or producer who purchases grapes from growers all within the geographic bounds of a district, such as Pauillac.
- **Château.** The wine is estate bottled with wine made from grapes grown entirely on the vineyards of a single estate and is vinified, aged, and bottled at that estate.
- **Cru classé.** Classified growth wines. Sixty wines from Médoc and one from Graves were classified into five classifications. Graves had its own classification in 1959. Sauternes and Barsac has a two-tiered classification, dating to 1855. St. Emilion's classification dates back to 1955 and was revised in 1969, 1975, and 1995. The only region of Bordeaux that is not classified is Pomerol. In addition to the cru classé, there is a cru bourgeois classification in Médoc representing viticultural and vinification standards that usually exceed AOC minimum requirements. The cru bourgeois is particularly significant in the Listrac and

Moulis communes. All classified wines are estate bottled, with the wine vinified, aged and bottled at the Château.

Classified Bordeaux red wines need at least a decade in which to mature for good vintages. These red wines also seem unharmonious and unyielding, lacking proper balance during their fourth to eighth years.

Grape Varieties

Although all red wines of Bordeaux are restricted to five grape varieties, each region uses blends differently due to the terroir of each area, which enables the characteristics of these grapes to show differently. The five grape varieties for red wines in Bordeaux are:

Cabernet Sauvignon
Merlot
Cabernet Franc
Malbec
Petit Verdot

Cabernet Sauvignon and, to a lesser extent, Cabernet Franc give the wine tannic structure and longevity. Merlot provides spice, softness, body, and suppleness. Malbec and Petit Verdot provide added complexity, color, and aromas and are used to a limited extent, if at all, to provide balance.

The major grape varieties grown for Bordeaux white wines are:

Sauvignon Blanc
Sémillon
Muscadelle

Sauvignon Blanc provides the acidity, while Sémillon provides body and floral aromas and is prone to *Botrytis*. Muscadelle is used to a minimal degree for good-quality dry whites and primarily in blends of the sweet botrytized wines of Sauternes.

Bordeaux is French for "water's edge." It is located off the Atlantic Ocean, protected by forests that range from the coast to the wine-producing region of the Médoc. These forests act as a wind breaker, which enables the grape-growing regions to thrive. Bordeaux is dominated by its rivers, beginning with the broad estuary of the Gironde down to the Dordogne and Garonne Rivers.

Bordeaux has six principal regions

Médoc
Graves
Pessac-Léognan
Sauternes
St. Émilion
Pomerol

Médoc

The Médoc is located on the east side of the large Gironde estuary and is divided into two appellations: Médoc (formerly known as Bas-Médoc) and Haut-Médoc. Haut-Médoc includes six communes that are entitled to their own appellation. The following is a list of all appellations of the Médoc:

Médoc
Haut-Médoc
St. Estèphe
Pauillac
St. Julien
Margaux
Moulis
Listrac

Médoc

The most northern promontory is called the Médoc, formerly referred to as the Bas-Médoc. Good-quality red wines and a few whites are produced in the Médoc, but they are not of the same caliber as those produced in the Haut-Médoc or the other six communes. Many wines from this area are sold under the label of Cru Bourgeois, which is a league of quality producers. The wines are a very good value but do not have the aging capabilities of the finer Haut-Médoc wines.

Some of the best producers include Château Greysac,

Château Livran, Château Loudenne, Château La Cardonne, and Château Potensac.

Haut-Médoc

The Haut-Médoc is an appellation that runs on the eastern side of the most notable communes and is a type of catch-all appellation. Its wines vary in quality from excellent to mediocre. The six most important communes in the Haut-Médoc are allowed their own appellations: **St. Estèphe, Pauillac, St. Julien, Margaux, Listrac,** and **Moulis.** All other wines from the Haut-Médoc are labeled with the broader appellation.

The most significant producers are Château La Lagune (third growth), Château Cantermerle (fifth growth), Château de Camensac (fifth growth), Château La Tour Carnet (fourth growth), and Château Belgrave (fifth growth, although it has not lived up to its reputation in the past few decades). Other important producers from this area include Château Larose-Trintaudon (the biggest producer in all of the Médoc), Château Malecasse, and Château Peyrabon.

St. Estèphe

St. Estèphe lacks gravelly soil characteristics and has more concentration of the clay of its southerly communes. The deep-colored wines are a little coarser, more austere, have more acidity and tannins, and lack the finesse of those of its southern neighbor, Pauillac. The 1980s saw a change in style, with many producers opting for a greater proportion of Merlot to soften their wines. The best of St. Estèphe wines, however, maintain traditional high Cabernet Sauvignon blends, leaving wines that are austere but very long lived.

St. Estèphe has five classified growths, the most esteemed being Château Cos d'Estournel (second growth), Château Montrose (second growth), Château Calon-Ségur (third growth), Château Lafon Rochet (fourth growth), and Château Cos Labory (fifth growth). Other significant producers include Château Beau Sité, Château Haut-Marbuzet, Château de Marbuzet, Château Les-Ormes-de-Pez, Château de Pez, and Château Phélan-Ségur.

Pauillac

The commune of Pauillac produces the quintessential red wine of Bordeaux. It is the only commune that can boast that it is home to three of the five Premier Grand Cru Classé: Château Lafite-Rothschild, Château Latour, and Château Mouton Rothschild, the only revision to the 1855 classification, when, in 1973, it was officially upgraded from a second growth to a first growth. The wines are made primarily of Cabernet Sauvignon, producing powerful and long-lived wines with the soft, almost sweet flavors of blackberries and cedar wood, balanced with dusty tannins that give the wine not only structure and depth, but also youthful vigor. These wines develop over decades, producing nuances of bouquets and fruit as they mature.

Pauillac is home to 18 classified wines:

1st growth

Ch. Latour
Ch. Lafite-Rothschild
Ch. Mouton-Rothschild

2nd growth

Ch. Pichon-Longueville Baron
Ch. Pichon-Longueville-Comtesse de Lalande
Comtesse de Lalande

4th growth

Ch. Duhart-Millon-Rothschild

5th growth

Ch. d'Armailhac
Ch. Batailley
Ch. Clerc-Millon
Ch. Croizet-Bages
Ch. Grand-Puy-Ducasse
Ch. Grand-Puy-Lacoste
Ch. Haut-Bages Liberal
Ch. Haut-Batailley
Ch. Lynch-Bages
Ch. Lynch-Moussas
Ch. Pédesclaux
Ch. Pontet-Canet

St. Julien

St. Julien is a small commune of the Médoc, occupying one of the prime areas along the Gironde River. St. Julien is a highly underrated commune, in part because it lacks a first-growth classification like its neighbors Pauillac to the north and Margaux to the south. St. Julien, however, has a higher percentage of classified growths than any other commune (11 of 40 Châteaux). The wines of St. Julien are Cabernet-based, and deep-colored with hard tannins when young but more subtle than Pauillac's when allowed to mature.

2nd growth

Ch. Ducru Beaucaillou
Ch. Gruaud-Larose
Ch. Léoville Barton
Ch. Léoville Las-Cases
Ch. Léoville Poyferré

3rd growth

Ch. Lagrange
Ch. Langoa Barton

4th growth

Ch. Beychevelle
Ch. St Pierre (-Sevaistre)
Ch. Talbot

In addition, there is Château Gloria, which is not a cru classé but attains the quality level of a third or fourth growth.

Margaux

Margaux is larger than its famous neighboring communes, with more classified growths than any other. The soil is the most gravelly of the communes, allowing good drainage and resulting in wines that can be silkier in texture and the most perfumed. The wines of Margaux failed to meet expectations in the 1970s and 1980s and were slower to utilize available modern techniques. A resurgence is expected in the future.

1st growth

Ch. Margaux

2nd growth

Ch. Brane-Cantenac
Ch. Durfort-Vivens

Ch. Lascombes
Ch. Rausan-Segla
Ch. Rauzan-Gassies

3rd growth

Ch. Boyd-Cantenac
Ch. Cantenac-Brane
Ch. Desmirail
Ch. Ferriere
Ch. Giscours
Ch. d'Issan
Ch. Kirwan
Ch. Malescot-St-Exupéry
Ch. Marquis d'Alesme-Becker
Ch. Palmer

4th growth

Ch. Pouget
Ch. Marquis-de-Terme
Ch. Prieuré-Lichine

5th growth

Ch. Dauzac
Ch. du Tertre

Moulis

Moulis is the smallest commune in the Haut-Médoc. Its wines vary considerably due to differences in topography and soil composition. The best vineyards are located on a gravelly dune. None of the wine is classified as a growth wine, but several attain a high level of quality comparable to many fifth or fourth growths. These wines represent good purchasing value. The best producers include Château Chasse-Spleen, Château Maucaillou, and Château Poujeaux.

Listrac

Listrac is the commune regarded with the least respect of all in the Haut-Médoc. Higher yields of grapes are permitted in Listrac than the other communes. The wines represent good value, although the wines are tannic when young. More Merlot has been planted in Listrac to mellow this

characteristic of the wines. The best producers include Château Clarke and Château Fourcas-Hosten.

Graves

The appellation of Graves was subdivided in 1987 with the creation of Pessac-Léognan, which included the best properties. This has somewhat devalued the name of Graves, although excellent wines continue to be made there. *Graves,* which is the French term for "gravel", is considered by many to be a white wine–producing region, although it produces more red wines than white. Its white wines have recently gained a better reputation, but it is its reds that are of consistent high quality. The reds are lighter and less tannic and mature faster than their Médoc counterparts. Due to the good drainage from the layers of gravel, Graves wines are more consistent from vintage to vintage than are other wines of Bordeaux. Although Cabernet Sauvignon is the major black grape variety, as much as 40% Merlot is used, giving the wine not only suppleness but also an earthy flavor. The white wines have improved enormously in the last two decades, however, with a few reaching great finesse and complexity.

The top 40 Châteaux are entitled to the appellation of Pessac-Léognan, the most famous of which is Château Haut-Brion, which was included in the 1855 classification. The principal producers of Graves include Château d'Archambeau (red), Château Le Bonnat (white and red), Clos Bourgelat (white and red), Château de Chantegrive (white and red), Château Constantin (white), Château L'Étoile (red and white), Clos Floridene (white), Château de Landiras (red and white), Château Magneau (white), Château Montalivet (red and white), Château de Portets (white), and Château Rahoul (white).

Pessac-Léognan

Pessac-Léognan includes 10 communes closest to the city of Bordeaux. The AOC regulations are more stringent than for Graves, allowing for smaller yields at harvest. The wines that are part of this appellation were associated with Graves before the break-up and include not only the great

Château Haut-Brion, but also 22 estates that were given the classification of Cru Classé.

Château Haut-Brion	Red & white
Château Bousaut	Red & white
Château Carbonnieux	Red & white
Domaine de Chevalier	Red & white
Château Couhins	White
Château Couhins-Lurton	Red & white
Château de Fieuzal	Red
Château Haut-Bailly	Red
Château La Mission-Haut-Brion	Red
Château La Tour-Haut-Brion	Red & white
Château La Tour-Martillac	Red & white
Château Malartic-Lagravière	Red & white
Château d'Olivier	Red & white
Château Pape-Clément	Red
Château Smith-Haut-Lafitte	Red

Sauternes

Sauternes is the appellation for the district further south of Graves that is bound by the Garonne and Ciron rivers, which provide the ideal humid conditions for the development of *Botrytis cinerea,* or noble rot. The appellation comprises five communes: Sauternes, Barsac, Preignac, Bommes, and Fargues. Sauternes is dedicated to the making of sweet unfortified white wines. The AOC regulations are very strict, requiring a minimum alcoholic strength of 13%, with residual sugar to make an additional 6% alcohol, and approval by a tasting panel to ensure its character. Sauternes develop into sweet, golden, luscious, honeyed, floral, and powerful wines that can age over decades.

These wines are very expensive to produce, requiring great care in the vineyard and in the cellar. *Botrytis* affects vineyards unevenly, requiring several harvests (as many as 11) from the vineyards over a period lasting weeks, because only botrysized grapes may be used. The yield is often less than a fourth of regular wine production, and new barrel fermentation and aging is required for top-quality wines.

The demand for Sauternes declined in the 1960s and

1970s, resulting in many producers cutting corners, with a concomitant drop in quality. With the production of the great vintages of the mid- and late-1980s, however, demand has again grown, resulting in better overall quality, though top producers maintained their standards throughout these decades.

Barsac is the only commune to be able to use either the appellation: Sauternes or Barsac. Due to its terroir, the wines are lighter and have more finesse.

In 1855, the wines of Sauternes were classified as Château D'Yquem, achieving the singular status of First Superior Growth (Premier Cru Superieur), with 12 estates being awarded First Growth and 14 wines accorded the title Second Growth. It is only recently that some of these producers have deserved the status they have been accorded.

First Great Growth

Ch. D'Yquem

First Growth

Ch. La Tour Blanche
Ch. Lafaurie-Peyraguey
Clos Haut-Peyraguey
Ch. de Rayne-Vigneau
Ch. de Suduiraut
Ch. Coutet (B)
Ch. Climens (B)
Ch. Guiraud
Ch. Rieussec
Ch. Rabaud-Promis
Ch. Sigalas-Rabaud

Second Growth

Ch. de Myrat (B)
Ch. Doisy-Daëne (B)
Ch. Doisy-Dubroca (B)
Ch. Doisy-Vedrines (B)
Ch. d'Arche
Ch. Filhot
Ch. Broustet (B)

(B) denotes wines from Barsac.

Ch. Nairac (B)
Ch. Caillou (B)
Ch. Suau (B)
Ch. de Malle
Ch. Romer du Hayot
Ch. Lamothe
Ch. Lamothe-Guignard

St. Émilion

St. Émilion is located on the right bank of the Dordogne River in a region called the Libournais. St. Émilion produces more wine than any other appellation on the right bank and has a much longer history and tradition of wine making than does the Médoc. The best wines of St. Émilion have extraordinary suppleness and rich fruit flavors, but it is hard to pinpoint a particular St. Émilion style because there are different terroirs and a plethora of producers. Rather than the large estates of the Médoc, St. Émilion has over 900 growers, who produce only red wines. The soil tends to be divided into two types: (1) the sandy, gravelly soil of the low-lying plain between the Dordogne River and the plateau and (2) the limestone plateau, which produces the longer-lived and best-quality wines. The predominant grape is Merlot, known as the Bouchet, followed by the early maturing Cabernet Franc. Little Cabernet Sauvignon is grown, although its presence is obvious in the longer-lasting style of Château Figeac.

The wines of St. Émilion were classified into two categories: First Great Growths and Great Classified Growths. The classification has undergone three revisions, the most recent in 1996.

First Great Classified Growths

Ch. L'Angélus	Ch. Clos Fourtet
Ch. Ausone	Ch. Figeac
Ch. Cheval Blanc	Ch. La Gaffelière
Ch. Beau Séjour-Bécot	Ch. Magdelaine
Ch. Beausejour	Ch. Pavie
Ch. Belair	Ch. Trottevieille
Ch. Canon	

In addition, there are 55 Great Classified Growths.

Pomerol

Pomerol is a tiny appellation abutting St. Émilion to the east and the town of Libourne to the west. This appellation comprises 1800 acres of vineyards and owes its current prominence to the efforts of a single individual, Jean-Pierre Moueix, whose family owns many of Pomerol's premier properties, including Château Pétrus, Château La Fleur Pétrus, Château Trotanoy, and the négociant firm of Établissements Jean-Pierre Moueix.

The preeminent grape variety is Merlot, with Cabernet Franc a distant second. Cabernet Sauvignon is almost insignificant. Not surprisingly, Pomerol wines mature faster and are ready to drink within 5 or 6 years, although wines from good vintages have the ability to age for decades like their Haut-Médoc counterparts. The wines characteristically have a full, rich, plummy flavor with spicy undertones.

Pomerol is the only appellation not to have any classification system, yet the top producers fetch the same or higher prices than the great premier crus of the Haut-Médoc. This is a result of the tiny production of the better known Châteaux, the most notable being Château Le Bon Pasteur, Château Bonalgue, Château Certan de May, Château Clinet, Château La Conseillante, Château L'Eglise Clinet, Château l'Enclos, Château L'Evangile, Château LaFleur-de-Gay, Château LaFleur-Petrus, Château LaFleur, Château Latour a Pomerol, Château Nénin, Château Petit Village, Château Le Pin, Château Trotanoy, and Château Vieux-Château-Certan.

Other Appellations of Bordeaux

There are a number of AOC appellations in which modern viticultural and vinification techniques have vastly improved the quality of wines. These wines tend to be reasonably priced and should be considered to fill a useful role in moderately priced dining establishments.

Entre-Deux-Mers

This is an area located between the Dordogne and Garonne rivers, producing both red and white wines. It is the whites, by such producers as Château Bonnet, that seem to have attracted more attention of late.

Fronsac and Canon Fronsac

Located near Pomerol on the right bank, this area is known for its reds. The wines from these appellations were well known in prior centuries. It is only recently that some producers, such as Château de La Dauphine, Château de La Rivière, and Château Junayme, have made wine with greater finesse, giving them a broader appeal.

Côtes de Castillon and Côtes de Francs

These appellations adjoin St. Émilion and produce red wines reminiscent of St. Émilion but without their depth and complexity. Producers include Château des Demoiselles and Château de Pitray.

Côtes de Bourg and Côtes de Blaye

The Bourg and Blaye appellations lie north of where the Garonne meets the Dordogne on the right bank. Between the two appellations, there are 34,000 acres of vineyards. The wines of Bourg are mostly Merlot and Cabernet Franc reds, while those of Blaye are whites, the latter not being very distinct. The most famous producers include Château Le Menaudat, Château Segonzac, Château Bourdieu and Château Barbe of the Blaye, Château de Barbe, Château de Thau, Château Falfas, Château Mendoce, Château du Bousquet, Château Labarde, and Château Rousset.

Premières Côtes de Bordeaux

The Premières Côtes is sandwiched between the west bank of the Garonne and the Entre-Deux-Mers appellation. This region produces almost two-thirds red wines and one-third white. The wines tend to be easy to drink and pleasant, if somewhat rustic. There has been renewed interest in this area, with modern techniques being applied. On the whole, the wines of the Premières Côtes de Bordeaux are good value wines. Notable producers include Château Beau-Sité, Château du Juge, and Château Reynon.

Burgundy (Bourgogne)

Burgundy's history of producing fine wines dates back to the second century A.D., although there is archeologic evidence to suggest that the Celts who inhabited this region in the sixth century B.C. were engaged in wine consumption if not winemaking. In his history of the Franks, Burgundy

was recognized by Gregory of Tours in the late sixth century A.D. to produce wines comparable to the legendary "first growth" Falernian of ancient Rome. It was during the late sixth century A.D. that the Franks began giving vineyards to monastic orders as payment for their services. Monastic viticulture developed over the following 1200 years, creating the rich wine-making heritage that Burgundy continues to enjoy. Two monastic orders dominated viticulture after the tenth century: the Benedictines centered at Cluny and the Cistercians centered at the great monastery of Citeaux. Their holdings were enlarged by the land grants of the dukes of Burgundy as well as by donations from the wealthy.

After the defeat of the Duchy of Burgundy by the French king in the early fifteenth century, the power of the Church declined, forcing the monastic orders to sell some of their holdings to the growing class of wealthy nobility. The two defining events that transformed Burgundian viticulture were the French Revolution and the Napoleonic code of inheritance. The French Revolution destroyed the power base of the monastic orders by expropriating their lands and selling them to its supporters. The Napoleonic code ensured equal apportionment of inheritance. This caused landholdings to be so fragmented, it is very difficult for the consumer to be familiar with the hundreds of different producers of wine. One has to be familiar not only with the merits of each village and of specific vineyards but also, potentially, with the scores of different owners and producers of each vineyard. Due to economies of scale, nearly all Burgundian wine has been sold by négociants. In 1960, only 15% of wines were bottled by producers, whereas today this number exceeds 50%. This trend has been reinforced by négociants becoming producers as they purchase more vineyards.

Quality Levels

There are five quality levels under which Burgundy wines are sold. In ascending order of quality, they are

1. **Generic.** White wines are allowed to be sold under the generic appellation of Bourgogne Blanc and Bourgogne Grand Ordinaire, which contain Chardonnay Aligoté and Pinot Blanc. Generic red wines are sold under the label of Bourgogne Rouge or Bourgogne Grand Ordinaire, which are made from Pinot Noir.

Burgundy Region Appellations

2. **District.** Wines with the appellation of a district, such as Macon-Villages, can be made from several villages within one district.
3. **Communal or village.** The wines are made from one delineated village or communal area with its own appellation (e.g., Gevrey-Chambertin).
4. **Premier Cru.** Certain villages have the vineyard names on the label, with the designation of a "first growth."

5. **Grand Cru.** This is the highest designation given to certain vineyards of a few villages in the heart of Burgundy and Chablis. The vineyard's name is placed on the bottle without further elaboration (e.g., La Tache or Le Montrachet). The words *Grand Cru* are not mentioned.

Burgundy is the most restrictive region of France in terms of which grape varieties are allowed. For white wines, *only*

Chardonnay is used for AOC wine. Aligoté, which makes a highly acidic wine, is sold under the label of Bourgogne Aligoté. For red wines only the **Pinot Noir** is allowed in the heart of Burgundy. Most oenophiles tend not to consider Beaujolais as part of Burgundy, which it is, and Gamay is the only black grape grown in that district.

Burgundy stretches from the town of Chablis, located 70 miles southeast of Paris, and extends 225 miles south to the city of Lyons (see Figure 8–1). Burgundy is divided into **five distinct wine regions.**

> **Chablis**
> **Côte d'Or** (The Gold Coast)
> **Côte Chalonnaise**
> **Maconnais**
> **Beaujolais**

Chablis

Chablis has become well known internationally due in no small measure to the misuse of the term *chablis* to denote dry white wine. Chablis in its true sense is named after the small town of that name and produces very austere dry white wines that develop an almost mineral flavor as they mature. The climate is cool, and vineyards are prone to damage from spring frosts. The soil is part of a limestone and clay ridge consisting of fossilized shells, which provide good drainage. Chablis is classified into four categories:

> **Petit Chablis**
> **Chablis**
> **Chablis Premier Cru** (First Growth)
> **Chablis Grand Cru** (Great Growth).

Petit Chablis

Petit Chablis is a designation for outlying vineyards of the Chablis appellation. It is not commonly seen in export markets, and there have been efforts to remove it as an appellation.

Chablis

The Chablis appellation represents the bulk of the wine produced and provides the consumer with a good, dry, clean taste. These wines compete with the Chardonnay wines of the Mâconnais in terms of price.

Chablis Premier Cru and Grand Cru

The premier and grand cru Chablis have greater structure, depth of flavor, and character than does simple Chablis. Many producers prefer not to use oak or new oak in making their wines. The premier crus are best consumed after 3 years of aging, while the Grand Crus fully develop after 8 to 10 years of aging.

Grand Crus	Chablis Premier Crus
Blanchots	Bauligneau
Les Clos	Les Beauregards
Valmur	Beauroy
Grenouilles	Berdiot
Vaudésir	Chaume de Talvat
Preuses	Côte de Jouan
Bougros	Côte de Lechet
	Côte de Vaubarousse
	Fourchaume
	Les Fourneaux
	Mont de Milieu
	Montée de Tonnerre
	Montmain
	Vaillons
	Vaucoupin
	Vaudevey
	Vosgros

Top producers include René Dauvissat, Jean-Paul Droin, Jean Durup, William Fevre, Domaine Laroche, François Raveneau, Long-Depaquit, and Robert Vocoret.

Côte d'Or

Côte d'Or is the true heartland of Burgundy, running 30 miles in a southwesterly direction from the outskirts of Dijon at Marsannay-la-Côte to the town of Santenay. *Côte d'Or* means "gold coast," and although the name is believed to be representational of the golden colors of autumn vine leaves, it is an abbreviation of Côte d'Orient, or eastern slope—the vineyards only face east to catch as much sunlight as possible. Côte d'Or rests on a geologic fault where an escarpment has caused limestone and marl to lie close to the surface. The limestone is made of shellfish deposits dating from the Jurassic era. The best vineyards are those that are planted directly over the marl stratum. Côte d'Or is divided into two subregions, called Côte de Nuits and Côte de Beaune.

Côte de Nuits

Côte de Nuits is located in the northern half of Côte d'Or and is dedicated to the production of red wine made entirely from Pinot Noir. There are nine communal appellations of Côte de Nuits, which are listed from north to south:

Marsannay-la-Côte
Fixin
Gevrey-Chambertin
Morey St. Denis
Chambolle-Musigny
Vougeot
Flagey-Échezeaux
Vosne-Romanée
Nuits-St. Georges

Marsannay-la-Côte.   This most northern commune is famous for its excellent rosés, but its reds are not of the same finesse as those to the south.

Fixin.   The true "Côte" begins in this appellation, with a number of Premiers Crus. The wines are full bodied and long lived. The first-growth vineyards include Arvelets, Clos du Chapitre, Cheusots, Hervelets, Meix-Bas, La Perrière, and Queue de Hareng. The principal producers include Domaine Bart, Denis Berthaut, Bruno Clair, Clemency Frères, Pierre Gelin, Philippe Joliet's Domaine de la Perrière, and Domaine Morion.

Gevrey-Chambertin.   Gevrey-Chambertin is the largest of Côte d'Or communes and has a diverging quality, because it is here that the Grands Crus begin to be located, while some of the wines from the lower plain are of mediocre quality. The following eight Grand Crus need to be laid down for aging to be fully appreciated.

Chambertin
Chambertin Clos de Bèze
Chapelle-Chambertin
Charmes-Chambertin
Griotte-Chambertin
Latricières-Chambertin
Mazis-Chambertin
Ruchottes-Chambertin

There are 26 Premier Cru vineyards, including Cazetiers, Combottes, Fonteny, Perrière, and Clos St. Jacques. Chambertin is said to have been the only wine that Napoleon drank.

The best producers include Pierre Amiot et Fils, Denis Bachelet, Bruno Clair, Pierre Damoy, Joseph Drouhin, Domaine Dujac, Maison J. Faiveley, Louis Jadot, Philippe Leclerc, Domaine les Perrières, Charles Quillardet, Rossignol-Trapet, Joseph Roty, Armand Rousseau, Christian Serafin, Domaine Tortochot, and Domaine des Varoilles.

Morey St. Denis.   Morey St. Denis lacks the recognition of its sister communes. It produces some of the finest red wines and maintains overall high standards. It has five Grand Crus, the most notable being the Clos de la Roche and Clos St. Denis:

Bonnes Mares (partial)
Clos de Lambrays
Clos de la Roche
Clos St. Denis
Clos de Tart

Morey St. Denis has 21 premier cru vineyards, including Bouchots, Clos de la Bussière, Chabiots, Les Charmes, Riotte, Ruchots, and Clos Sorbe.

The most notable producers include Pierre Amiot et Fils, Georges Bryczek, Domaine Dujac, J Faiveley, Robert Groffier, Georges Lignier, Mommesin, Domaine Ponsot, and Armand Rousseau.

Chambolle-Musigny.   Chambolle-Musigny produces red wines that are among Burgundy's best. They can be elegant, floral, and subtle and without the tannins of a Morey St. Denis or a Gevrey-Chambertin. Chambolle-Musigny has two Grand Crus: Bonnes Mares and Le Musigny. There are 21 Premiers Crus, which include Les Amoureuses and Les Charmes, which are made to the same standard as the Grand Crus.

The most notable producers include Pierre Amiot, Château de Chambolle-Musigny, Maison Joseph Drouhin, Robert Groffier, J Faiveley, Hubert Lignier, Georges Mugneret, Maison Georges Roumier, Domaine des Varoilles, and Comte de Vogue.

Vougeot.   Vougeot evokes the historic Clos de Vougeot, built by the Cistercian monks in the fourteenth century, although its divided ownership of more than 80 growers has resulted in wines of different caliber. The vines on the highest slopes abutting Le Musigny and Grand Échezeaux are the best, but it is most important for the consumer to be aware of the best producers. The best-made wines show good fruit, are powerful and develop a silky texture with long aging. Vougeot has only one Grand Cru: Clos de Vougeot. There are two Premiers Cru vineyards that produce red wine: Cras and Petit Vougeot.

The most notable producers include Domaine Bertagna, Maison Joseph Drouhin, J Faiveley, Jean Grivot, Jean Gros, Maison Leroy, Alain Hudelot-Noellat, Domaine Mongeard-Mugneret, Georges Roumier, and Domaine des Varoilles.

Flagey-Échezeaux.   This appellation does not have a village or commune and is located near the village of Vosne-Romanée. There are two Grand Cru vineyards and no Premier Cru. These wines are powerful, with heady aromas, and need a decade to mature. They are Grand-Échezeaux and Les Échezeaux.

The best producers include Maison Joseph Drouhin, Rene Engel, Henri Sayer, Mongeard-Mugneret, Domaine de la Romanée-Conti, and Robert Sirugue.

Vosne-Romanée.   The appellation of the Vosne-Romanée has become so world renown that its land as well as its wines are exorbitantly expensive. There are six Grand Crus, whose wines can be described as rich, fiery, velvety, intense, and perhaps incomparable. They are

made with the intention of being aged over many years. The six Grand Crus are:

> La Romanée
> Romanée-Conti
> Romanée-St-Vivant
> Richebourg
> La Tâche
> La Grande Rue

The most significant producer is the Domaine de la Romanée-Conti, which is the sole owner of Romanée-Conti and La Tâche and a major owner of Richebourg, Romanée-St. Vivant, Grand-Échezeaux, and Échezeaux. These wines have gained such fame that the 13 Premier Crus wines are often overlooked. The Premiers Crus include Les Chaumes, Croix Rameau, Clos Parentoux, Overeaux, Gaudichots, Malconsorts, Petits Monts, Clos de Reas, Orveaux, Raignots, Rouges du Dessus, and Les Suchots.

The principal growers include Robert Arnoux, Maison Albert Bichot, Bruno Clair, Cathiard-Molinier, Rene Engel, Jean Grivot, Jean Gros, Henri Jayer, Leroy, Lamarche, Méo-Camuzet, Moillard, Mongeard-Mugneret, Mugneret-Gibourg, Mugneret-Gouachon, Bernard Rion, Pernin-Rossin, Domaine de la Romanée-Conti, Robert Sirugue, and Charles Vienot.

Nuits-St. Georges.   The reputation of the appellation of Nuits-St. Georges is due in large measure to its status as the second most important town for négociants in Burgundy. There are no Grand Crus wines that are perceived as meriting the label of Grand Cru. There are 40 Premiers Crus, many of which are full flavored and robust, needing a minimum of 10 years to develop subtlety and complexity. Of the Premiers Crus, the most notable include Les-St. Georges, Les Vaucrains, Les Cailles, Les Porrets, and Clos de la Maréchale.

Principal producers include Jean-Claude Boisset, F Chauvenet, Robert Chevillon, Dufouleur Frères, J Faiveley, Henri Gouges, Jean Grivot, Jean Gros, Labouré-Roi, François Legros, Hospices de Nuits-St. Georges, Domaine de la Poulette, Henri et Gilles Remoriquet, Daniel Rion, Charles Vienot, and Alain Verdet.

Côte de Beaune

The southern half of Côte d'Or begins at Pernand-Vergelesse just north of the beautiful medieval town of Beaune and continues for 15 miles to the plain at Santenay, just west of Chagny. Côte de Beaune includes 20 villages, each with its own appellation, but the appellations do not always coincide with commune boundaries. Although this area produces mostly red wines, it is its white wines that have provided a benchmark for the making of dry white wine.

The 18 communes, listed from north to south, are

Ladoix-Serrigny
Aloxe-Corton
Pernand-Vergelesses
Savigny-Lès-Beaune
Beaune
Chorey-Lès-Beaune
Pommard
Volnay
Monthélie
Meursault
Blagny
Auxey-Duresses
St. Romain
Puligny-Montrachet
Chassagne-Montrachet
St. Aubin
Santenay
Maranges

There are eight Grand Crus appellations, all of which are white except for the Corton:

Grand Cru Appellation

Bâtard-Montrachet
Bienvenues Bâtard-Montrachet
Chassagne-Montrachet
Charlemagne
Chevalier-Montrachet
Corton
Corton-Charlemagne
Criots Bâtard-Montrachet
Montrachet

Principal Village

Puligny-Montrachet/Chassagne-Montrachet
Puligny-Montrachet
Aloxe-Corton
Puligny-Montrachet
Aloxe-Corton
Aloxe-Corton
Puligny-Montrachet/Chassagne-Montrachet

Ladoix-Serrigny.   Ladoix-Serrigny has the smallest part of the Corton hill, which harbors the magnificent Chardonnays of Burgundy. This nearly forgotten appellation is allowed to sell its best wines from the Corton under the Grand Cru appellation of Corton Charlemagne and may sell its red Premier Cru wines under the Aloxe-Corton appellation. The wines produced in this area are mostly reds.

The Grand Crus are only white wines: Basses Mourettes, Hautes Mourettes, and Le Rognet-Corton.

The principal producers include Bouchard Père et Fils, Michel Mallard, Prince Florent de Merode, and Serrigny.

Aloxe-Corton.   This is one of the most important villages of Côte de Beaune. Among the finest Chardonnays of the world, the Corton-Charlemagne can age over 15 years for good vintages. It has a wonderful nutty and spicy quality that develops only with aging. The only Grand Cru reds come from the vineyards of Corton. These wines need several years of aging for their truffle-scented bouquets to develop.

The Grand Crus are Le Charlemagne for red wines and Corton Charlemagne for white wines. The vineyards within the appellation are also attached to the names of these Grand Crus and indicate a further differentiation (e.g., Corton Les Bressandes, Corton Clos du Roi, and Corton les Renardes). The Premier Crus of the Aloxe-Corton appellation include Les Chaillots, Les Fournières, Les Guerets, Les Valozières, Les Vercots, Marechaudes, and Les Meix.

The principal growers include Adrien Belland, Bonneau du Martray, Bouchard Père & Fils, Maison Doudet-Naudin, Maison Joseph Drouhin, Joseph Faiveley, Antonin Guyon, Maison Louis Jadot, Louis Latour, Lucien Leroy, Moillard, Rapet Père et Fils, Daniel Senard, Serrigny, Tollot-Beaut & Fils, and Michel Voarick.

Pernand-Verglesses.   The Grand Crus of these villages are labeled under the Corton-Charlemagne label. The Premier Crus are red wines.

The Grand Cru comes from one vineyard: En Charlemagne. The Premiers Crus include Basses Vergelesses, Caradeux, Creux de la Net, Fichots, and Ile des Hautes Vegelesses.

The principal producers include Bonneau du Martray, Daudet-Corcelle, Jacques Germain, Louis Latour, Lucien Leroy, and Michel Voarick.

Savigny-Lès-Beaune.   The red wines of Savigny-Lès-Beaune do not have the international cache of other appellations, but they are well made and more reasonably priced. There are a number of Premiers Crus, which include Basses Vergelesses, Charnières, Clous, Fourneaux, Guettes, Hauts Marconnets, Narbantons, Petits Godeaux, Peuillets, Serpentières, and Talmattes.

The principal producers include Bouchard Père & Fils, Chanson Père & Fils, Bruno Clair, Girard-Vollot, Antonin Guyon, Lucien Leroy, Jean-Marc Pavelot, Pierre Seguin, and Henri de Villamont.

Beaune.   Beaune is not only a beautiful medieval town but also an important wine center that houses a number of négociants. Beaune has the largest area of Premier Cru vineyards in Côte de Beaune. Most of the wines are red and are softer and more straightforward than the wines of Côte de Nuits.

Of the 36 Premier Crus, the most notable reds include Les Grèves, Les Fèves, Cras, Champimonts, and Clos des Mouches. The most notable white wines include Chouacheux, Marconnets, and Teurons.

The principal producers include Besancenot-Mathouillet, Bouchard Aine & Fils, Bouchard Père et Fils, Chanson Père & Fils, Joseph Drouhin, Hospices de Beaune, Maison Louis Jadot, Michel Lafarge, Maison Louis Latour, Albert Morot, Patriarche Père & Fils, and Remoissenet Père et Fils.

Chorey-Les-Beaune.   This appellation has no Grand or Premier Crus and provides good value and very approachable wines when young.

Pommard.   Pommard's wines are all reds, are surprisingly tannic and are perceived as almost coarse compared with those of its neighbor Volnay. With 10 years' aging, the best Premier Crus soften considerably and offer concentrated fruit and earthen flavors. Of the 28 Premier Crus, three are particularly outstanding: Les Epenots, Les Rugiens, and Clos de la Commaraine.

The principal producers include Robert Ampeau & Fils, Jean Marc Boillot, Bouchard Père & Fils, Domaine de Courcel, Maison Leroy, Andre Mussy, Patriarche Père & Fils, Château de Pommard, Ropiteau-Mignon, Serrigny, and Joseph Voillot.

Volnay.   The appellation of Volnay evokes the delicate, silky, strawberry-scented, soft red wines of Côte de Beaune. There are 24 vineyards entitled to Premier Cru appellation, the best of which include Les Caillerets, Champans, Clos de Chenes, Clos des Ducs, and Santenots.

The principal producers include Robert Ampeau, Marquis d'Angerville, Bouchard Père & Fils, Antonin Guyon, Michel Lafarge, Rene Monnier, Jacques Prieur, and Ropiteau-Mignon.

Monthelie.   This neglected appellation has seen considerable investment in the past two decades, which should result in better recognition. There are 10 Premier Crus, which produce red wines similar to those of Volnay. The best of these are Les Champs Fuillot and Sur la Velle.

The principal growers include Jean-François Coche-Dury, Monthelie-Donhairet, Ropiteau-Mignon, and Robert de Suremain.

Meursault.   Meursault is one of the most significant appellations of the Côte de Beaune, producing white wines that have a sharp edge counterbalanced by mild, almost bland, nutty flavors. The Premier Cru whites of Meursault need 4 or 5 years of aging to allow them to round out. Although there are no Grand Crus, Meursault has 18 Premier Crus, the best of which are Les Perrières, Les Charmes, and Les Genevières.

The principal producers include Robert Ampeau, Pierre Boillot, Bouchard Père & Fils, Antonin Guyon, Michel Lafarge, Lafon, Joseph Leflaive, Maison Leroy, Mazilly Père et Fils, Rene Monnier, Ropiteau Frères, Guy Roulot, Etienne Sauzet, and Joseph Voillot.

Blagny. This small commune has no Côte de Beaune appellation of its own and sells only red wines. White wines take the name of Meursault or Puligny-Montrachet.

Auxey-Duresses. The appellation produces two-thirds red wine and one-third white wines. There are seven Premier Crus, with the best whites comparable in style to Meursault and the best reds comparable to Volnay, though lacking the depth. The best red Premier Crus are Les Duresses and Clos du Val.

The principal producers are Robert Ampeau, Maison Leroy, Duc de Magenta, Henri Potinet-Ampeau, Guy Roulot & Fils, and Roland Thevenin.

Puligny-Montrachet. This appellation straddles the border between the villages of Puligny and Chassagne and produces the most famous and expensive white wines of Burgundy. Puligny is dedicated to making white wines, producing four Grand Crus: Le Montrachet, Chevalier-Montrachet, Bienvenues-Bâtard Montrachet, and Bâtard-Montrachet. In addition, there are 11 Premier Crus, some of which (e.g., Le Cailleret and Les Pucelles) nearly attain the quality of the Grands Crus. The wines are defined by the concentration of flavor, backbone of acidity, and richness of texture. The wines are best consumed with several years of aging and can last for more than 10 years if from exceptional vintages.

The principal producers include Robert Ampeau, Bouchard Père & Fils, Maison Joseph Drouhin, Maison Louis Jadot, Maison Louis Latour, Domaine Leflaive, and Etienne Sauzet.

Chassagne-Montrachet. Half of the wines of the Grand Crus Montrachet and Bâtard-Montrachet are grown in this appellation. Unlike Puligny-Montrachet, most of Chassagne wine is red. The red wines are frequently overlooked but present good value, because they are powerful and reminiscent of Corton or Côte de Nuits wines and have comparable aging ability.

Chassagne-Montrachet's third Grand Cru is Criots-Bâtard-Montrachet. Additionally, it has 15 Premier Cru vineyards, the best of which are Abbaye de Morgeot, Cailleret, Grandes Ruchottes, Maltroie, and Clos St. Jean.

The principal growers include Bachelet-Ramonet Père & Fils, Louis Carillon, Jacques Gagnard-Delagrange, Vincent Leflaive, Duc de Magenta, Château de la Maltroye, Albert Morey & Fils, Ramonet-Prudhon, and Etienne Sauzet.

St. Aubin. St. Aubin, like St. Romain, is located behind the main Côte and produces some premier crus, mainly for red wines. The bulk of its wines are sold under the Côte de Beaune appellation.

Santenay and Maranges. The Santennay and Maranges appellations are at the southern-most end of Côte de Beaune, and it is here that red wines predominate. The wines are straightforward and rather earthy and, for the most part, will not improve with aging. There are eight Premier Crus, the best of which are Les Gravières, La Comme, and Le Clos de Tavannes.

The best producers include Adrien Belland, Château de la Charrière, Fleurot-Larose, and Lequin-Roussot.

Côte Chalonnaise

Côte Chalonaise runs 15 miles, from Chagny to Montagny, and incorporates four villages, which have their own appellations: **Mercurey, Givry, Rully,** and **Montagny.** The wines of Mercurey and Givry are basically red; those of Rully are both red and white; and the wines of Montagny are 100% white.

The wines are impossible to generalize because the terroir varies enormously, but one still gets a semblance of what Burgundian Pinot Noir and Chardonnay wines offer without having to pay the high price. The red wines from good vintages still age nicely for 4 to 5 years.

The principal producers include Château de Chamirey, Domaine Chanzy-Daniel, Jean-François Delorme, Paul & Henri Jacqueson, E. & X. Noel-Bouton, Domaine Ragot, Antonin Rodet, Domaine Château de la Saule and Hugues de Suremain.

Mâconnais

Mâconnais is named after the town of Mâcon and is a wide band of territory running 20 miles alongside the Saone River. Mâconnais has developed a reputation of producing good-quality Chardonnay wines. Because the climate is warmer than Côte d'Or, the wines are rounder, with tropical fruit flavors. The levels of quality are reflected in the appellations of Mâcon Blanc at the lowest end of the spectrum, Mâcon-Superieur, **Mâcon-Villages,** which is limited to nine villages, and the appellations of specific communal areas, at the highest end of the spectrum: **Pouilly-Fuissé, Pouilly-Vinzelles,** and **St. Véran.**

Mâcon-Villages wines present better value than Mâcon Blanc or Mâcon Superieur and may include the name of one of its villages, such as Mâcon-Lugny. **St. Véran** is an appellation for the eight southernmost communes. The wines produced here represent good value and are less expensive than Pouilly-Fuissé. **Pouilly-Fuissé** is an appellation that includes the communes of Pouilly, Fuissé, Chaintre, Solutre, and Vergisson. These wines became very fashionable and popular in the United States, beginning in 1960s. For the most part, the wines are made by co-ops and négociants and certainly do not deserve the prices often commanded. The exceptions are small independent producers who make rich and heady wines that can develop over 2 or 3 years. The best producer is Château Fuissé.

Beaujolais

The Beaujolais area comprises 12 individual appellations covering 55,000 acres and producing over 13 million cases of wine each year. Beaujolais runs south of the Mâconnais to the outskirts of Lyons. As opposed to the rest of Burgundy, the Gamay grape is grown in Beaujolais, where it thrives in the granite soils.

There are three quality levels of Beaujolais:

1. Beaujolais including Beaujolais Supérieur
2. Beaujolais-Villages
3. Cru Beaujolais

Beaujolais wines attain their fresh and fruity characteristic from carbonic maceration (see Chapter 5). Much of this category of Beaujolais is released as Beaujolais Nouveau, a wine that, by law, has to be vinified and bottled by the third Thursday of November. The minimum alcohol content has to reach 9%. This wine should be consumed within 6 months of bottling.

Beaujolais-Villages is the appellation in the warmer northern half of Beaujolais, which includes 39 villages. Its minimum alcohol content is 10%. These wines can last 1 to 2 years and represent good-value uncomplicated wines.

There are ten villages at the most northerly point of Beaujolais which produce **Cru Beaujolais** and are entitled to use their own village names. They do not include the appellation Beaujolais so that they cannot be confused with the other categories. The ten villages are

Brouilly
Chénas
Chiroubles
Côte de Brouilly
Fleurie
Juliénas
Morgon
Moulin-à-Vent
Régnié
St. Amour

Cru Beaujolais has the capability of developing into richly textured, full-bodied wines and a few can be aged for 10 years. The wines of Morgon are particularly rich, developing exotic fruit flavors.

Most of the grapes in Beaujolais are grown by small producers who sell them to large négociants. The principal négociants include Joseph Drouhin, Georges Duboeuf, Pierre Ferraud, Louis Jadot, Mommessin, Lorin & Fils, Thorin, and Trenel & Fils.

Rhône Valley

The Rhône Valley is located in southeastern France, beginning just south of Beaujolais and continuing 140 miles to Avignon. The Rhône Valley is divided into two regions: Northern Rhône and Southern Rhône. Its viticultural history is said to date back to Phocaeans (Ancient Greeks) at

Rhône Region Appellations

the time they established the city of Massilia (Marseilles), around 600 B.C. The Romans planted vineyards further north, and it is believed that pilgrims returning from Spain in the Middle Ages introduced Spanish grape varieties such as Mourvedre and Grenache, which is predominant in Southern Rhône.

Northern Rhône

Northern Rhône extends 60 miles from Vienne to Valence. The climate is continental, with hard winters and hot summers. The vineyards are planted mostly along the steep, terraced slopes of the Rhône River. The region is dedicated to the monoculture of the **Syrah** variety to make robust red wines that need several years of aging to round out and develop into exotic wines. There is limited white wine, which is made from the currently fashionable Viognier grape, as well as wines of lesser quality made from the **Marsanne** and **Roussanne** varieties, especially in St. Peray. Northern Rhône is divided into eight appellations:

Côte-Rôtie
Hermitage
Crozes-Hermitage
Cornas
St-Joseph
St-Péray
Condrieu
Château Grillet

Côte-Rôtie

Côte-Rôtie, French for "roasted slopes," has recently been expanded to include some of a westerly plateau above the river banks. Its main concentration is on two disparate sections of a slope, Côte Blonde, which is chalky, and Côte Brune, which is darker, with schistous soil. The wines are hard, tannic, and unforgiving when young, but with 10 or more years of aging, they develop wonderful spicy and dark fruit aromas and bouquets. In the past, most wines were blended from both Côte Blonde and Brune, but recent trends strive to accentuate the differences between the two terroirs.

The principal producers include Bernard Burgaud, Marcel Guigal, Joseph Jamet, Rene Rostaing, Jaboulet Aîné, Chapoutier, and Gilles Barge.

Hermitage and Crozes-Hermitage

Hermitage was accorded great stature in the late seventeenth century. The blights of *Oidium* and *Phylloxera* had a devastating impact on the region. It is only in the last two decades that its wine making has attained a quality level to match its former reputation. The wines of Crozes-Hermitage have not attained their former distinction because the appellation was enlarged to include alluvial land.

The principal producers include Chapoutier, Gerard Chave, Delas Frère, and Paul Jaboulet Aîné.

Cornas

The quality of Cornas wines was recognized in the early nineteenth century, but it is only recently that they have become fashionable in the international marketplace. These wines are very dark and tannic in their youth but develop into velvety wines with earthy and spicy bouquets when aged at least 10 years.

The most notable producers include Auguste Clape, Robert Michel, and Paul Jaboulet Aîné.

St. Joseph

With the addition of the alluvial plain to the original appellation of the granite slopes of St. Joseph, the overall quality and reputation of its wines have diminished considerably. There have been considerable efforts by a few producers to replant on the original slopes, and time will tell if their efforts are successful.

St. Péray

St. Péray produces only white wines, both still and sparkling, made from the Marsanne and Rousanne varieties. The wines are quite heavy and are rarely seen outside of France.

Condrieu and Château Grillet

These two appellations are located at the northern end of the valley by Côte Rôtie. Château Grillet, which is one of the smallest appellations of France, is an enclave surrounded by Condrieu. The wines are made from the Viognier grape and aged 18 months in oak. The wines of Château Grillet are able to age for two decades or more while improving and developing complexity. Château Grillet was appreciated by the likes of Thomas Jefferson in the late eighteenth century.

Condrieu, which is also made from the Viognier grape, is not traditionally aged in oak and is not long lived; it should be consumed within 4 years. Viognier has lovely floral and apricot and peach aromas.

The principal producers include Cuilleron, Guigal, Délas Frères, Alain Paret, and Georges Verney.

Southern Rhône

The Southern Rhône region begins at Bourg-Saint-Andreol and continues along the Rhône for 50 miles, to Avignon. The vineyards are planted along hillsides high in limestone and clay, with areas that are covered with small rocks and pebbles. Warmer than the Northern Rhône the climate is ideal for the principal grape varieties used in this region: Grenache, Syrah, Cinsault, and Mourvèdre. Ninety-nine percent of Rhône wines are red or rosé wines. The hot summers allows the grape to develop high sugar concentration, resulting in high-alcohol wines.

There are 11 AOC appellations in the Southern Rhône:

Châteauneuf-du-Pape
Gigondas
Vacqueyras
Tavel
Lirac
Côtes du Vivarais
Côteaux du Tricastin
Côtes du Ventoux
Côtes du Lubéron
Côtes du Rhône
Côtes du Rhône-Villages

This section focuses on only the best appellations of the region or the ones most likely to be seen in the U.S. market.

Châteauneuf-du-Pape

This appellation means "new palace of the Pope." Jacques Duez, a Frenchman, was elected Pope Clement V and moved his papal court to Avignon, the city at the southern end of the Rhône appellation. Châteauneuf-du-Pape owes its name to the new palace built by John XXII, who rebuilt the destroyed papal palace after the Second World War. Châteauneuf-du-Pape wines are made from as many as 13 varieties, the principal varieties being Grenache, Mourvèdre, Syrah, and Cinsaut.

The wines are deep-colored, with ripe, dark berry character, and are drinkable sooner than Northern Rhône wines. The best producers make wines that drink well within 6 years and can last for as long as 25 years.

The most notable producers include Château de Beaucastel, Clos des Papes, Château Fortia, Château Rayas, and Domaine du Vieux Télégraphe.

Tavel

Tavel is the appellation that produces one of France's best dry rosé wines. This wine has a lovely berry aroma and is crisp and full bodied. The wines in general are very food-friendly and adaptable and have become very popular in France. They should be consumed while young, because they tend to oxidize quickly. The most notable producer is Château d'Aqueria. Lirac produces both reds and rosés but has not acquired the same reputation.

Côtes du Rhône and Côtes du Rhône-Villages

Both of these appellations are visible in the U.S. market. The quality of Côtes du Rhône wines varies enormously from one producer to another. The wines are Grenache-based and are meant to be drunk when young. The most notable producers are Jaboulet's Parallèle 45, Guigal, Chapoutier, and Vidal-Fleury.

The Côtes du Rhône-Villages appellation consists of 16 communes. The best wines have a higher concentration of Syrah and Mourvèdre and are more satisfying than those of Côtes du Rhône. The best producers include Domaine St. Anne, Domaine de la Soumade, Domaine des Gourberts, Château de Couranconne, and Domaine des Grand Devers.

Loire Valley

The Loire Valley takes its name after the 600-mile-long Loire River, which flows 350 miles east to west before emptying into the Atlantic Ocean. The viticultural area stretches over such a distance that to make generalizations about its soil and topography is impossible. The Loire has a long history of wine making, dating back to the fourth century and perhaps earlier, but its wines have never gained the reputation of those of other French regions outside of France. It is the Loire's white wines that are best known, although excellent red wines are also produced. The discussion in this section focuses on four of its most prominent regions:

Loire Region Appellations

Muscadet
Anjou-Saumur
Touraine
Sancerre and Pouilly-Fumé

The principal white grape varieties are Chenin Blanc, Muscadet (alias Melon de Bourgogne), and Sauvignon Blanc. The principal black grape varieties include the predominant Cabernet Franc, Cabernet Sauvignon, and Pinot Noir.

Muscadet

Muscadet and Muscadet de Sèvre et Maine are appellations at the mouth of the Loire River by the Atlantic Ocean. The area is known for its white wines made from the Muscadet grape. The wines are fresh and crisp with a touch of spritz, which results from the wines' being made *sur lie,* or on the lees without racking the wine before bottling. The best wines are *mis en bouteille au Château* or *domaine,* because wines bottled by négociants are racked before bottling and will have lost this particularly refreshing characteristic. With very few exceptions, the wines should be drunk when young and are an excellent accompaniment to white seafood dishes, particularly shellfish.

The best producers include Marquis de Goulaine, Guy Bossard, Claude Branger, Robert Brousseau, Chereau-Carré, Bruno Cormerais, Château de la Galissonière, Guilbaud Frères, Pierre et Joseph Landron, Louis Metaireau, Marcel Sautejeau, and Sauvion et Fils.

Anjou and Saumur

These appellations are in the eastern section of the central Loire Valley and produce many different styles of wines. The soil of the Central Valley is *tufa,* a soft limestone that is volcanic in origin and allows not only good drainage but also the creation of innumerable **caves** or cellars, which have been carved underground.

The wine for which Anjou is best known is the **Rosé d'Anjou,** a light, pink, refreshing wine with raspberry aromas, made from Cabernet, Merlot, Gamay, and the local Groslot. The best rosés are labeled **Cabernet d'Anjou** and are made wholly from Cabernet Franc; they are more full bodied and drier. The most notable producers include Albert Bescombes' Moc Beril and Rémy Pannier.

The white wines from Anjou are made from **Chenin Blanc,** known locally as the Pineau de la Loire. The styles vary immensely, from the extremely dry and highly acidic white wine of **Savennières,** which needs a minimum of 5 years' aging to appreciate the concentrated floral and honey characteristics of the wine, to the rich full-bodied wines of the **Côteaux de Layon, Bonnezeaux,** or **Quarts de Chaume** appellations. These appellations border a tributary of the Loire called the Layon River. The vineyards are susceptible to noble rot, and in good vintages, the sweet honeysuckle-scented wines are reminiscent of German Beerenauslese and can age longer than any other white wine. The most notable producers of Savennières include Clos du Papillon Domaine de Baumard, Domaine du Closel, and Château d'Epire. The most notable producers of Côteaux de Layon, Bonnezeaux, or Quarts de Chaume are Clos de St. Catherine, Château de Fesles, A. Laffourcade, Jacques Lalanne, Rene Renou, Pierre Tijou, Moulins Touchais, and Les Vignes Touchais.

The **Saumur** appellation is known primarily for its white wines, which are made both dry, off-dry, and sparkling. The wines are usually a blend of Chenin Blanc and Sauvignon Blanc. If a vintage yields a highly acidic wine, the best option for the winemaker is to transform it into a sparkling wine. Saumur is the largest producer of sparkling wine, other than Champagne. The most notable producers of sparkling wines include Ackerman-Laurance, Maison Veuve Amiot, Bouvet-Ladubay, and Gratien Meyer & Seydoux.

The best-made red wines of the Saumur appellation are produced in the commune of Champigny. These red wines are made from Cabernet Franc and are sold under the appellation of **Saumur-Champigny.** The most notable producers include Clos de l'Abbaye, Château de Chaintre, Jean-Pierre Chene, Claude Daheuiller, Paul Filliatreau, and Château de Targe.

Touraine

The Touraine appellation is divided into many individual appellations, the most famous of which is **Vouvray.** Vou-

vray's white wines are made from Chenin Blanc and, as in Saumur, can be dry, off-dry, or sweet. The wines of Vouvray are crisp and lively, due to the acidity, and have great versatility in pairing with food. Great vintages, such as 1989, will be able to age for decades. The most notable producers include Marc Bredif, Philippe Brisbarre, Domaine Bourillon d'Orleans, Gaston Huet, Château Moncontour, Clos Naudin, and Prince Poniatowski.

Two other appellations of the Touraine are well known as producers of red wines: **Chinon** and **Bourgeuil.** The grape used is primarily Cabernet Franc with a possible small percentage of Cabernet Sauvignon. The wines of these two appellations are reminiscent of some wines of St. Emilion, although lighter bodied and more aromatic. The wines of Chinon are made in two styles: One is light bodied while the other, made from the vineyards on the tuffeau plateaux and more similar to the wines of Bourgeuil, is more full bodied. The most notable producers include Bernard Baudry, Couly-Dutheil, Château de la Grille, Charles Joguet, Jacques Malibeau, Jean-Maurice Raffault, and Olga Raffault.

Sancerre and Pouilly Fumé

The region of the Upper Loire lies south of where the Loire River bends to a north-south axis near the city of Orléans. This region comprises two AOC appellations, which have developed a worldwide reputation. These are Sancerre and Pouilly-Fumé, which are located on opposite sides of the Loire River. Their reputations are built on a single grape varietal: **Sauvignon Blanc.** In large measure, it is the chalky soil that has allowed the Sauvignon Blanc to develop this supreme expression. The wine has a smoky, almost gunflint aroma and an herbaceous grassy character that sometimes provides gooseberry and black currant flavors backed by bracing acidity.

The wine of Sancerre has more body and higher acidity than that of Pouilly and consequently can be aged for 2 or 3 years to allow it to reach its peak. The wines of this region helped to create a worldwide trend of vinifying Sauvignon Blanc, whether in California, New Zealand, South Africa, or Chile.

Sancerre also produces red wines that are made from

Pinot Noir, but they seldom reach the depth and intensity of a Burgundian wine.

The most notable producers of Sancerre include Pierre Archambaud Clos la Perrière, Cotat, Lucien Crochet, Andre Dezat, Gitton Père et Fils, Lucien Picard, Paul Prieur & Fils, and Domaine Vacheron. The most notable producers of Pouilly-Fumé include Bernard Blanchet, Dagueneau, Paul Figeat, Château du Nozet (Patrick de Ladoucette), Michel Redde & Fils, Guy Saget, and Château de Tracy.

Champagne

Champagne has become synonymous with the sparkling wine that it produces. Located 30 miles northeast of Paris, Champagne is at the most northerly climatic limit for the successful cultivation of *vinifera* grapes. The area of Champagne has produced wines for 1500 years, but it is only since the early eighteenth century that it has produced the sparkling style from which it has gained fame.

Dom Pérignon's role in the development of the fine wines that helped augment Champagne's reputation is incontestable, but he did not create the *product* that we know as Champagne. Due to Champagne's northerly climate, fermentation would cease during the winter months as the yeast became dormant. The following spring, with temperatures above 45° F, the fermentation process would restart, often when the wine had already become bottled. It was the English court and aristocracy who were introduced to Champagne wines by the banished Marquis St. Evremond, who had business interests in the region. It was the English who took such a liking to the fizzy wines. (They were disparaged by self-respecting French.) It was not until the mid-nineteenth century that producers discovered the correct formula for making sparkling wines that did not cause their bottles to explode. The growth of Champagne consumption has proliferated to such an extent that there is enormous pressure to expand the delineated areas of Champagne to meet the rising demand.

The appellation of Champagne is divided into three main areas: the **Vallée de la Marne,** the **Montagnes de Reims,** and the **Côte des Blancs.** There is a fourth delimited area known as the Aube. The soil is high in chalk,

Champagne Styles

allowing better heat retention and excellent drainage. The soil is so poor in nutrients, however, it needs constant fertilization, which includes the finely ground garbage of Reims and Paris. Due to its geography, there is greater variation in vintages, which has led not only to the blending of vintages but also to the blending of wines made from different villages.

The grape varieties are restricted to three types: **Chardonnay, Pinot Noir** and **Pinot Meunier.** Pinot Noir is not as predominant as in the past, but it is still the variety that provides the structural backbone and fruit flavors of the wine. It is the varietal planted in the Montagne de Reims, while Chardonnay, which provides finesse to the wines, is planted in the Côte des Blancs.

Only one tenth of the vineyards are owned by the large négociants-manipulants. The remaining 90% are owned by 20,000 growers who sell their grapes to more than 140 cooperatives and producers. There are more than 4000 different labels made for the growers by cooperatives in addition to the major producers. The most famous producers are known as Grandes Marques.

The history of Champagne has been rife with struggles between growers and négociants-manipulants. It has only been since the 1970s, under the leadership of **Moët et Chandon,** that the stranglehold on grape prices was broken. The turbulent 1980s and 1990s have resulted in the top seven Champagne houses producing 70% of Champagne wines. Sales have reached 240 million cases worldwide, with almost 150 million cases consumed in France. There is a hidden classification system that is generally not revealed on the label. There are 17 Grand Cru vineyards, whose grapes are distributed under the auspices of the Comité Interprofessionel du Vin de Champagne. Côteaux Champenois is an AOC designation for the very small quantity of still wines that are produced in Champagne.*

Although there are many styles of Champagne, as was discussed previously, there is a notable difference between the Champagnes made from Epernay, situated by the Côte des Blancs, and Reims, which is located by the Montagnes de Reims. The style of Epernay tends to be less full bodied, although with plenty of finesse, while the Champagne of Reims has more depth and more noticeable fruit flavor.

*See Appendix C for update.

Notable Champagne Producers

Producer	City	Style
J. Bollinger	Ay	Full, rich
Deutz	Ay	Light to medium
Gosset	Ay	Medium
Charles Heidsieck	Reim	Medium
Henriot	Reims	Medium to full
Krug	Reims	Full, rich
Lanson	Reims	Full, rich
Laurent-Perrier	Tours-Sur-Marne	Light to medium
Moët & Chandon	Epernay	Medium
G.H. Mumm	Reims	Light to medium
Perrier-Jouët	Epernay	Light to medium
Piper Heidsieck	Reims	Medium
Pol Roger	Epernay	Light
Pommery & Greno	Reims	Light to medium
Louis Roederer	Reims	Full, rich
Ruinart Père et Fils	Reims	Light to medium
Taittinger	Reims	Light to medium
Veuve Clicquot-Ponsardin	Reims	Full, rich

Alsace

Alsace is a region in northeast France that is bordered by the Vosges Mountains to the west and the Rhine Valley to the east. Alsace has had a tumultuous history, with frequent

Alsace Region Varietals

struggles between France and Germany disputing their claims over this region. Alsace has its own identity, with a separate dialect. The wine-producing region extends along a narrow 1.5-mile band west of Strasbourg, from Marlenheim south 62 miles to Thann. The climate provides a long and cool growing season, and Alsace is surprisingly one of the driest regions of France. Most of the vineyards face south and southeast to catch as much sun as possible.

Alsace is unusual as a French growing region because it produces mostly (95%) white wines, and the wines are labeled for the grape varietal. Although there are over 2000 growers who bottle and sell their own wines, more than 80% of the wines are produced by 170 négociants. Some producers, such as Trimbach, have histories dating back to the mid-seventeenth century.

Alsace was granted appellation status in 1962. The appellation laws require that wines have 8.5% alcohol, but most Alsatian wines are chaptalized to bring the level up to 11%. Wines with the label Grand Vin or Grand Cru must have a minimum of 11% alcohol. Beginning in 1975, the Appellation recognized Grand Cru vineyards. There are two criteria for a grand cru wine: It must come from a single designated vineyard, and it must be made from one of four varieties—Riesling, Muscat, Gewürztraminer, or Pinot Gris. By 1983, there were 25 Grand Cru appellations, and this figure was doubled by 1993.

With the exception of **Vendange Tardive** dessert wines, Alsatian wines are fermented dry. Winemakers avoid fermenting or aging their wines in new wood, because the flavors of oak would compete with those of the varietals. The wines do not undergo malolactic fermentation, again to preserve the integrity of the varietal aromas and flavors.

The principal grape varieties include Riesling, Gewürztraminer, Pinot Gris, Muscat, Sylvaner, and Pinot Blanc.

Riesling

Riesling is one of the most noble white-wine grapes, producing graceful wines with fruit and floral aromas balanced by searingly refreshing acidity. Rieslings develop very complex diesel, gunflint, and mineral bouquets while maintaining their fruit flavors and acidity.

Gewürztraminer

Gewürztraminer is usually made dry and, infrequently off-dry. It tends to have a high glycerol content, giving it a heavier textural quality. The wine has intense jasmine or orange blossom aromas and a spiciness with lychee and grapefruit flavors. Due to the high sugar level, this wine has a high alcohol content, providing the perception of sweetness, but it lacks acidity. Poorly made Gewürztraminers appear to be flat and flabby. Gewürztraminers are very adaptable to many different food styles.

Pinot Gris

Pinot Gris is a very underrated wine, combining the best characteristics of Gewürztraminer with those of Riesling. This wine has gentle apricot and faint peach aromas, with the wonderfully bracing acidity of Riesling. It also ages well, developing a smoky, buttery flavor.

Muscat

Muscat is unusual in Alsace in that it is fermented dry, leaving a fresh, grapey flavor in the taster's mouth. Muscat develops into good wines only if the weather is exceptional.

Edelzwicker

Edelzwicker is German for "noble blend." It is a term that is seen less frequently than in the past. This blend is usually made from Chasselas and Sylvaner.

Vendange Tardive

Vendange Tardive is French for "late harvest" and is the equivalent of German Auslese. The wine must come from a single vintage and be made from one of the following four varieties: Riesling, Gewürztraminer, Pinot Gris, or Muscat. The wine may be bone dry or sweet, depending on the vintage, varietal, and producer.

Selection des Grains Nobles

These are wines made from grapes harvested after the Vendange Tardive and usually are affected by *Botrytis* to further enhance the sugar content of the grapes. The same grape varieties allowed for Vendange Tardive are used. This style of wine is made in warmer years and, if made correctly, will be sweet with extraordinary rich complexity.

The most prominent producers are J. Becker, Leon Beyer, Domaine P. Blanck, Dopff 'Au Moulin', Dopff & Irion, Heim, Hugel & Fils, Jos. Meyer, Andre Kientzler, Kuentz-Bas, Maison Michel Laugel, Domaine Ostertag, Domaine Schlumberger, F.E. Trimbach, and Domaine Zind-Humbrecht.

Other Wine Regions of France

A number of wine regions that produce prodigious amounts of wine should not be entirely overlooked, even though much of the wine may simply be for quaffing or are not sold in the U.S. market.

Many regions have AOC status, while others have VDQS or Vins de Pays appellations. Together, they contribute to France's reputation of being the world's most prolific wine producer. Those regions that are not upgrading their wines are finding decreasingly available markets. The lesser known regions include:

The Midi
The Southwest
Bergerac
Cahors
Madiran
Gaillac
Jurançon
Jura
Savoie

The Midi

In the Midi region are the appellations of Roussillon, Corbières, Minervois, Blanquette de Limoux, and Languedoc. Many of these districts have received AOC appellations in the past decade, and this proving to be an exciting one after a long history of producing very ordinary wine. Much of the vineyards are planted with Grenache, Syrah, Mourvèdre, and the ubiquitous Carignan for red wines, and with

Marsanne, Roussane, Picpoul, Bourboulenc, and Clairette for white wines.

The Southwest
The southwest corner of France, between the Pyrenees Mountains to the south, the Atlantic Ocean to the west, and Bordeaux to the north, has a number of appellations with distinct grape varieties and a style quite dissimilar to other regions. These appellations include **Bergerac, Cahors, Madiran, Gaillac,** and the **Jurançon.**

Bergerac
The appellation of Bergerac, located on the Dordogne River inland from Bordeaux, is probably best known for the sweet wines of Monbazillac, although red and dry white wines are also produced in this area. The grape varieties are from Bordeaux ,such as Merlot, Cabernet Sauvignon, Cabernet Franc, Sauvignon Blanc, and Sémillon. The red wines tend to be lighter in style but are a good value compared to many of the Bordeaux wines.

Cahors
In terms of fame, Cahors' wines preceded those of Bordeaux. The red wines were known as the "black wines" of considerable alcoholic and tannic constitution made from Malbec. Cahors' medieval status was undermined by the rise in Bourdeaux stature and wealth, and Cahors is only beginning to recover from the devastation caused by *Phylloxera* in the 1880s. The black grape varieties include Auxerrois (Malbec), Tannat, and Merlot. The wines improved steadily during the 1980s and deserve the AOC status the appellation received in 1971.

Madiran
Located just south of Armagnac country, the Madiran is considered by many to be producing the best wines of the southwest region. The red wines are made from a local grape, the Tannat, which, as the name suggests, offers a great deal of tannins, Cabernet Sauvignon, and Cabernet

Franc. Additionally, a white wine is made both dry and off-dry from a local grape, the Pacherenc. The leading producers have invested considerable effort and capital, which will no doubt be repaid in high-quality wine.

Gaillac
Gaillac has a long history of wine production dating back to the Romans in the first century A.D. Many of its varieties can be traced to ancient origins and are seldom seen elsewhere, such as, Mauzac and Loin de l'oeil for white wines, and Duras and Fer Servadou for reds. More standard Bordeaux varieties now predominate though are blended with these indiginous varieties to make unique blends.

Jurançon
Located in the Pyrenees foothills south of Pau, the Jurançon appellation produces a highly alcoholic white wine whose reputation goes back to the sixteenth century. The wine is made from three local grapes: the Gros Manseng, the Petit Manseng, and Courbu. The wine has spicy cinnamon and tropical aromas when allowed to mature. It is usually made in a sweet moelleux style and less frequently in a dry style.

Jura
The Jura appellation lies east of Burgundy and west of the border shared with Switzerland. The Jura produces white, rosé, red, and sparkling wines as well as two wines unique to France: the *vin jaune,* or yellow wine, and the *vin de paille,* or straw wine. Vin Jaune, which is made best in the appellation of Château Chalon, is aged a minimum of 6 years in small barrels that are not completely filled, allowing significant ullage. A flora yeast develops, remarkably like that which occurs in Sherry, creating a film that prevents total oxidation. The wine is very similar to a first-rate fino sherry and provides an excellent apéritif.

The **Vin de Paille** is similar to **Vin Santo** in Italy and stems from an ancient practice of drying out grapes on straw mats to allow them to dehydrate and even become botrytized. This results in a more intensely flavored wine, with rich texture that usually has residual sweetness.

Arbois and L'Etoile are communal regions noted for rosé-style wines and very good sparkling wines made from local grapes such as Savignin (Traminer) blended with Chardonnay.

Savoie

Located in the foothills of the French Alps, from the south shore of Lake Geneva west to the Italian border, the Savoie appellation is known for delightful white and sparkling wines. Three-fourths of the wine in this mountainous region is white. The best-known still whites are from Crépy, made from the Chasselas grape. Seyssel produces one of the most sought-after sparkling wines next to Champagne. It is made from the Molette and full-flavored Rousette grape varieties.

Germany

Germany has a wine history dating back at least to the first century B.C., when the Romans conquered and settled in the Mosel region. It is important to understand that Germany is located in a borderline climatic region, where there is barely sufficient sunshine for the grapes to mature. Southern Germany's latitude is parallel to Labrador (50 degrees). Germany's history of viticulture reflects a preoccupation toward finding those slopes that could absorb the most sunshine. Additionally, the vineyards are almost always located on the banks of major rivers, such as the Mosel, Rhine, and Elbe, or their tributaries, because the waterways moderated the climate and provided, until the 1960s, the principal mode of transporting the wine from the vineyards to urban areas. The only viable regions that allow grapes to mature are almost all located in the southwest corner of Germany. Due to the borderline nature of the climate, there are wide variations of wine production from year to year, and the wines always remain low in alcohol (see Figure 8–2).

In many ways, Germany's historical development of wine making mirrors that of France. Monastic orders developed and operated the best vineyards until their lands were

German Regions—Quality Designations

expropriated by Napoleon in 1803. These vineyards were divided and sold to individual owners. A few large estates remained intact but were given to the state. Today, there are 260,000 acres of vineyards, owned by almost 80,000

German—Designation According to Sweetness/Ripeness at Harvest

individual growers. A third of Germany's wines are produced by cooperatives, but the best wines are estate bottled (Erzeugerabfüllung or Gutsabfüllung).

Germany produces primarily white wines (82% of the total), the best of which are made in 13 wine regions, or *Anbaugebiete.* Six of these regions are located on the slopes of the Rhine: **Baden, Hessische Bergstrasse, Pfalz, Rheinhessen, Rheingau,** and **Mittelrhein.** Four regions are named after other rivers and their tributaries: the **Ahr, Nahe, Mosel-Saar-Ruwer,** and **Saale-Unstrut. Franken**'s vineyards lie on the Main River; most of **Württemberg**'s vineyards are on the slopes of the Neckar River; and **Sachsen**'s vineyards are located along the banks of the Elbe. The wine regions are further divided into 39

districts, or *Bereiche,* with each district having a number of *Einzellagen,* or single vineyard sites, which are very similar to the Grand Cru vineyards of France. Unfortunately, a law was passed in 1971 grouping many of these traditional sites into *Grosslagen,* depriving consumers of the ability to differentiate the wines of one particular site from another. Thus, it has been necessary for consumers to become familiar with producers' names to accurately determine the quality of the wine.

Quality levels were discussed in Chapter 6 in the German labeling section, so the focus of this section is only on Qualitätswein mit Prädikat (QmP) wines: Kabinett, Spätlese, Auslese, Beerenauslese, Eiswein, and Trockenbeerenauslese. One point that needs to be examined is

Figure 8–2 Map of the wine-producing regions of Germany

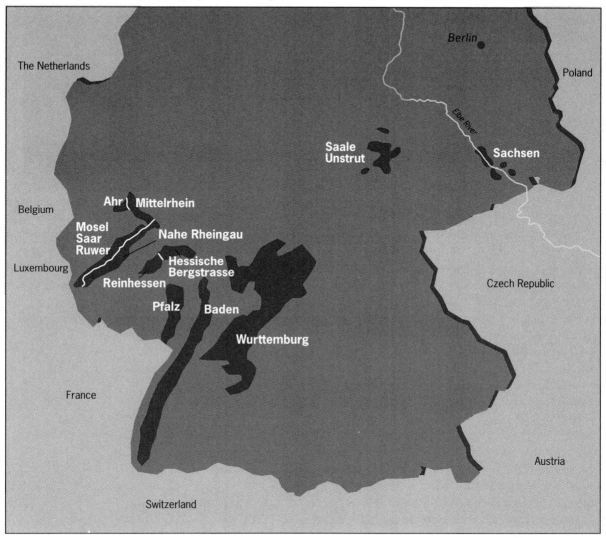

the frequently repeated axiom that the sweeter the wine, the better the quality. It is the sugar level of the grape, however, not the sweetness of the wine that is the criterion for determining quality. The amount of residual sugar in a wine is left to the winemaker's discretion. The objective of the winemaker is to find an harmonious balance between the acidity of the wine and its sugar level. German winemakers ferment wines in categories up to and including Auslese until they are dry and then add *Süssreserve,* or unfermented **must,** back into the wine to give it sweetness. The worldwide demand for dry wines has encouraged German winemakers to produce their wines *trocken* (dry) or *halbtrocken* (off-dry).

The principal white grapes grown in Germany are Riesling, Müller-Thurgau, Silvaner, Gewürztraminer, and Kerner.

Riesling, the premier white-wine grape variety of Germany, is considered by many as capable of producing the world's finest wine. It has racy acidity, which gives it a refreshing quality and compatibility with a wide cross-section of cuisines and enables it to age for many years. Riesling, when planted in the best vineyards and harvested late, will develop incomparable fruity aromas, such as peach and apple flavors. Riesling is most widely planted in Mosel-Saar-Ruwer, the Rheingau, and the Pfalz and represents 20% of Germany's total harvest.

Müller-Thurgau represents 26% of Germany's harvest. It is a hybrid crossing of Riesling and Silvaner that was developed in 1882 by Professor Müller of Thurgau, Switzerland. Müller-Thurgau has become more predominant because it can ripen sooner, offers significantly higher yields, yet maintains good quality with floral aromas and much of Riesling's acidity.

Although the *Silvaner* grape was once dominant in German viticulture, it now represents 7% of the total harvest. Silvaner is an early-ripening grape that produces a fuller-bodied but neutral-flavored white wine. Although the Silvaner is associated with the Franken wine region, it is most widely planted in Rheinhessen.

Very little *Gewürztraminer* is planted, because it needs a long growing season. The wines have the familiar aromas of the Gewürztraminer varietal of Alsace but are often made with some residual sugar.

Kerner is a cross-bred variety of Riesling and Trollinger that produces high yields and ripens early. It is a Riesling-style grape with pronounced acidity and good fruit aromas and flavors. Kerner is the third most widely planted grape in Germany.

Other white wine varietals include Rülander (Pinot Gris), Weissburgunder (Pinot Blanc), Elbling, Gutedel (Chasselas), Scheurebe, Bacchus, and Morio-Muskat.

Although Germany is known for its white wines, it does produce both sparkling *Sekt* and red wines. There has been an increasing demand for red wines within Germany, resulting in a doubling of the acreage of black grape varieties in the past 40 years. Black grape varieties are grown principally in the Ahr, Baden, Pfalz, and Württemberg wine regions. The red wines are lighter in color and body and with fewer tannins than their French or Italian counterparts. For the most part, these wines are consumed within their own wine-making regions. The three principal black grape varieties are Spätburgunder (Pinot Noir), Portugieser, and Trollinger. Much of the black grape production is used for making a rosé wine called Weissherbst.

Germany's wine regions can be divided into three wine groups: those of the Mosel region, whose Rieslings are noted for their "nervy" or acidic style; those of the Rhine heartland (Rheingau, Rheinhessen, Pfalz, and Nahe); and those from less climatically fortuitous areas that depend on less notable varieties, such as Franken, Baden, and Sachsen.

Mosel-Saar-Ruwer

The Mosel region is the most easterly area, with a long history of viticulture dating back to Roman settlements. Mosel's style of wine is reflected when young by light acidic Riesling wines that can develop with aging into enormously complex wines balancing fruit and acidity. Until the 1960s, Mosel vineyards were planted only on steep river banks. However, the viticultural area has since nearly doubled as flat areas away from the banks have been planted with lesser quality varieties. The best vineyards plant only Riesling.

The Mosel-Saar-Ruwer is divided into five districts, three

of which have developed far-reaching reputations: the Bereich Zell in the Lower Mosel, Bereich Bernkastel in the Middle Mosel, and Bereich Saar-Ruwer in the Upper Mosel.

Bereich Zell is named after the village of Zell and produces light and refreshing white wine. Riesling has difficulty ripening in this area, and while the overall quality is good, little of its wine attains the level of Mittel Mosel.

Bereich Bernkastel includes nine Grosslagen, whose names are not used for the best estates. Most wine estates use their Einzellage appellations, making it necessary for the consumer to learn not only the names of producers but also individual estates. The most famous villages have become household names in the wine world: Piersport, Brauneberg, Wehlen, Zeltingen, Urzig, and Erden.

Saar wines can reach the apogee of white-wine making after the infrequent good vintage years (usually three vintages out of ten). Saar Rieslings have apple and floral aromas, delicate honey flavors, and a steely finish. The most well-known villages are Serrig, Wiltingen, Kanzem, Oberemmel, and Ockfen.

The principal wine producers of the Mosel-Saar-Ruwer region include Verwaltung der Bischöflichen Weingüter Trier, Weingüter Dr. Fischer, Stiftung Staatliches Friederich-Wilhelm-Gymnasium, Weingut Forstmeister Geltz Zilliken, Gutsverwaltung Farthäuserhof, Weingut Reichsgraf von Kesselstatt, Weingut J.J. Prüm, Weingut Max Fer. Richter, Herman Freiherr von Schorlemer Weingüterverwaltung GmbH., C. von Schubert, Maximin Grünhaus, Verwaltung der Staatlichen Weinbaudomänen, Weingut Wwe Dr. H. Thanisch, Güterverwaltung der Vereinigten Hospitien, and Gutsverwaltung Wegeler-Deinhard.

Ahr

It is ironic that the most northerly and smallest wine region produces mostly red wines from the Spätburgunder and Portugieser grapes along steep slopes on the Ahr River. The wines are traditionally pale and thin and often made semi-sweet, although rosé Weissherbst also is a specialty of the Ahr. There are currently some producers who are trying to make a more substantial wine using French vinification methods.

Mittelrhein

The Mittelrhein has 11 Grosslagen running along a thin band for 60 miles from Bonn to Bingen on the eastern banks of the Rhine. The river banks are so steep in stretches, they are considered cliffs, resulting in less than a total of 1800 acres of planted vineyards. Riesling is the principal grape variety, and austere but vibrant wines are produced here. The best Bereichs include Bacharach, Boppard, Königswinter, Mühlental, and Lahntal.

Rheingau

The Rheingau is synonymous with quality wine, which is produced from grapes grown along the Rhine from Lorchhausen to Schierstein. The 12-mile heart of the Rheingau runs along the north bank of the Rhine River, is protected by the Taunus Mountains, and has the famous Bereich name of Johannisberg. Riesling is traced to this region, with the first recorded references made in 1435. The region is filled with historical and grand names comparable to those of the Côte De Nuits of Burgundy, such as the Kloster Eberbach and Johannisberg, producing sensuous, floral, and spicy Riesling wines, which, when produced in hot years, can age for decades. Rheingau has 10 Grosslagen, including the villages of **Rüdesheim, Geisenheim, Johannisberg, Winkel, Mittelheim, Hattenheim, Erbach, Eltville,** and **Hochheim.**

Some of the most notable producers include Verwaltung der Staatsweingüter Kloster Erbach, Schloss Groenesteyn, Schloss Johannisberg, Weingut Freiherr zu Knyphausen, Schloss Reinhartshausen, Balthasar Ress, Domänenweingut Schloss Schönborn, Schloss Vollrads, Gutsverwaltung Wegeler-Deinhard, and Weingut Robert Weil.

Nahe

The Nahe is named for the Nahe River, a minor tributary of the Rhine that joins it in Bingen. Nahe is divided into two Bereiche: Bereich Schlossböckelheim and Bereich

Kreuznach. Although it is one of the smaller wine regions, it has a wide variety of soil types and is able to produce a diverse number of wines. Riesling only represents 25% of the total harvest, with Müller-Thurgau and Silvaner being the dominant varieties. Schlossböckelheim is also the name of a village that is the site of one of the premier vineyards, the Kupfergrube. **Bad Kreuznach,** in the lower Nahe region near Bingen, is an equally famous wine center that produces more full-bodied Riesling with some of the "nervy" acidity of Mosel wines.

Some of the more notable producers include Weingut Paul Anheuser, Weingut Dr. Josef Hofer Schlossmühle, Staatsweingut Weinbaulehranstalt, Prinz zu Salm-Dalberg'sches Weingut, and Verwaltung der Staatlichen Weinbaudomänen.

Rheinhessen

Rheinhessen is Germany's largest wine-producing region, with a 20×30-mile region nestled between the Rhine and Nahe rivers and framed by the cities of Kreuznach, Bingen, Mainz, and Worms. This wine region is known for its soft, pleasant, semi-sweet, and easy-to-drink wines, such as the well-known Liebfraumilch. Müller-Thurgau represents almost 25% of the harvest, and, with the world's largest planting, Silvaner represents almost 14%. Rheinhessen is divided into three Bereich names: Nierstein, Bingen, and Wonnegau. The most famous and best wine-producing villages include **Nierstein, Oppenheim,** and **Ingleheim,** all of which can produce superlative Riesling wines.

Worms, located in the Bereich Wonnegau, is the birthplace of **Liebfraumilch,** originally named for the wine made from grapes grown in the vineyards surrounding Liebfraukirche (Church of Our Lady). This designation has been extended to any wine from Rheinhessen, Pfalz, Nahe, or the Rheingau. It must be a QbA wine with at least a 70% blend of Müller-Thurgau, Silvaner, Riesling, or Kerner varieties.

The most notable producers include Weingut Gunderloch, Weingut Freiherr Heyl zu Herrnsheim, Weingut Rappenhof, Gustav Adolf Scmitt'sches Weingut, Heinrich Seip

Kurfürstenhof, Staatsweingut der Landes-Lehr-und Versuchsanstalt.

Pfalz

Known as the Palatine in English, the Pfalz stretches 50 miles, from Bockenheim to Schweigen in the south. It is the second largest region but the biggest producer of wine. Pfalz is divided into two Bereiche: **Mittelhaardt** and **Weinstrasse,** the former possessing villages producing the region's best wines. The most significant Grosslagen are Hollenpfad, Mariengarten, Hofstück, and the Bereiche Südliche Weinstrasse. The best wines are made predominantly with Riesling and present very good value.

The principal producers include Weingut Dr. von Bassermann-Jordan, Weingut Dr. Bürklin-Wolf, Weingut Müller-Catoir, Gutsverwaltung Wegeler-Deinhard, and Gebiets-Winzergenossenschaft Deutsches Weintor.

Hessische Bergstrasse

The tiny region of Hessische Bergstrasse is nestled between the Main, Rhine, and Neckar rivers. The region is divided into two Bereiche: Umstadt and Starckenburg. The wines are not particularly distinctive, with the Müller-Thurgau predominating in Umstadt and the Riesling more frequently cultivated in Starckenburg. These wines are unlikely to be exported.

Franken

Franken is a region to the east of the Hessische Bergstrasse that lies on both banks of the winding Main River. Franken is divided into three Bereiche: the Steigerwald in the east, the Maindreieck by the city of Würzburg, and Mainviereck in the west. The wines are 95% white and are made from Müller-Thurgau. The wines of Franken tend to be fuller bodied, drier, and less aromatic, with an earthy character. Most wines are bottled in a unique, squat, green or brown flagon called a **Bocksbeutel.** The best wines of Franken are made in the region around Würzburg.

The best producers include Bürgerspital zum Heiligen Geist, Juliusspital-Weingut, and Staatlicher Hofkeller.

Baden and Württemberg

These two wine regions are located along the Rhine and Neckar rivers, respectively, in southern Germany, extending as far south as Lake Constance on the Swiss border. Baden is more prolific, but the reputation of Württemberg exceeds that of its sister region. Very little of its wines are exported, because they are consumed by the gastronomic Württembergers themselves. Most of the Württemberg wines are red and are planted with the native Trollinger variety.

Baden, which is Germany's third largest wine region, produces mostly white wines but has significant Pinot Noir production as well. Nearly all of the wines are produced by huge cooperatives, including Badischer Winzerkeller, the largest cooperative in Europe. The consumption of wine by local inhabitants is 40% higher than the German national average, resulting in very little exported wine.

The principal producers of Württemberg include Weingut Graf Adelmann, Weingut Robert Bauer, Freiherrlich von Gemmingen- Hornberg'sches Weingut, and Schlosskellerei Graf von Neipperg. The principal producers of Baden include Staatliches Weinbauinstitut, Staatliches Weinbauinstitut Freiburg Blankenhornsberg, Schloss Istein, Schloss Staufenberg, Weingut Bercher, Weingut Dr. Heger, and Weingut Rudolf Stigler.

Saale-Unstrut and Sachsen

Located in the former East Germany, these two wine regions are located farthest northeast, where climate variations have more detrimental impact on viticulture. Sachsen's wine history dates back to 1161 and parallels much of Germany's historical wine-making developments. Müller-Thurgau predominates in this region, with 40% of the total harvest. The wines of Saale-Unstrut and Sachsen are rarely seen outside of the region, because they are both made by small producers.

Italy

Italy's wine history dates back at least to 1000 B.C. with the settlements of ancient Greeks on its southern coastal region. The Greeks named the area Oenotria, or Land of the Vine. The names of several grape varieties, such as Aglianico or Greco, and the names of 10% of Italians living today in this region are testament to the influence of the Greeks so many centuries ago. Although the origin of the Etruscans in the Tuscany region is not fully known, their role in viticulture, particularly the use of a **pergola** system, is recognized as also being significant. The Romans were later to incorporate the viticultural techniques of both civilizations and spread them throughout Europe during their conquests (see Figure 8–3).

Wine has always been a central part of the Italian diet. Wine is viewed by Italians as part of the sacred trinity of foods: bread, olive oil, and wine. Wine, however, was not viewed as a product that could become especially refined, particularly by aging it. Wine was a beverage to be consumed with the appropriate foods of the region in which it was made. In many ways, the wines of Italy are a reflection of the people of each region, and there is a remarkable symbiosis between the wines and foods of each particular geographic region.

With the exception of Chianti and some Piedmontese wines, most wines in Italy were made and transferred to consumers in bulk, with little regard to the effects of bottle aging and maturation of fine wine. There were efforts dating back to the turn of the twentieth century by Tuscan producers to prevent other regions of Italy from using Chianti on their labels. In 1936 the central government took the first measures to protect the appellations of certain wines, including Chianti. It was not until after the Second World War, however, that the growth of a large indigenous middle class created sufficient demand for high-quality wines. The past 30 years has seen a meteoric rise in the stature of many Italian wines.

It is important to note that economic developments in Italy have brought to it the most modern viticultural and vinification techniques, which has led to conflicting ap-

Figure 8–3 Map of the wine-producing regions of Italy

Italian Quality Designations

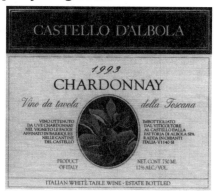

Cabernet Sauvignon. His wines are considered to be extraordinary, and the prices fetched for these wines match their reputations accordingly. Many of his wines, however, cannot be sold under DOC appellation, because the system has incorporated the traditionalists' methods for wine making. As previously discussed, the DOC system is responding slowly to the challenges posed by modernists.

Italy often surpasses France's position as the world's leading wine producer. Each of its 20 regions produces wine. The temperate climate and volcanic soils are ideally suited to producing the hundreds of different grape varieties. As was discussed in the section on Italian label laws

proaches to making wines: traditionalists versus modernists. For example, Angelo Gaja among others in Piedmont is not only using French barriques (small 225-liter barrels), but also planting French *vinifera* such as Chardonnay and

(see Chapter 6), it wasn't until 1963 that the **Denominazione di Origine Controllata** (DOC) system, which in many ways parallels the appellation system of France, went into effect. There are approximately 250 DOC and 13 DOCG (guaranteed by the government) zones, which are delineated geographically and represent only 12% of all Italian wines. The 13 DOCG zones include 10 red wines and three white wines.

Regions	DOCG Wines
Piedmont	Barbaresco, Barolo, Gattinara, and Moscato d'Asti or Asti (Spumante)
Tuscany	Brunello di Montalcino, Carmignano, Chianti, Vernaccia di San Gimignano, and Vino Nobile di Montepulciano
Emilia-Romagna	Albana di Romagna
Umbria	Torgiano Rosso Riserva and Montefalco Sagrantino
Campania	Taurasi

Within the DOC and DOCG zones, there are more than 900 types of wines, differentiated by the grape varieties used, method of vinification, and aging. To minimize the potential confusion the plethora of Italian wines can create for the reader, the major focus in this chapter is on Italy's three most significant producing areas and their grape varietals: Piedmont, Tuscany, and Veneto.

Piedmont

Piedmont, or Piemonte in Italian, has the largest vineyard area in Italy, although almost half of the region is covered with mountainous terrain leading to the Alps. Piedmont has the largest number (38) of the DOC and DOCG zones of Italy. Its geographic isolation and close proximity to France enabled it to develop and define its viticultural practices more extensively than any other Italian region. Piedmont is famous not only for its red wines made from the **Nebbiolo** grape but also for the famous sparkling wine made from **Moscato** (Muscat Blanc à Petits Grains), named for the appellation of Asti.

The principal black grape varieties of Piedmont include Nebbiolo, Barbera, and Dolcetto. Each variety will be discussed with its accompanying DOC(G) appellation.

Nebbiolo

The Nebbiolo, named for the fog that rolls off the Langhe hills of Piedmont, was referred to in the thirteenth century as making extraordinary wine. It may have been the out-standing varietal wine that Pliny the Elder cited in the first century A.D. The Nebbiolo was traditionally vinified by being macerated with its skins for up to 2 months. The wine was then aged a minimum of 2 years in large oak or chestnut *botti* or barrels, and 1 year in the bottle before being released. The resulting wine needed 10 years to age and allow its massive tannic structure to dissipate. Many "modern" producers limit skin contact but compensate by fermenting and aging the wine in *barriques* to give the wine structure. The wines made in this fashion can be enjoyed within 5 years, but it is questionable how well the wine will continue to mature. Wines made in good vintages by top producers will develop into a perfumed, vinous, full-bodied wine with bouquets of iris or violets, chocolate, tar, truffles, spices, and smoke. This is not a wine for neophytes.

Nebbiolo is produced in several DOC appellations, but it reaches its full majesty in three DOCGs: **Barolo, Barbaresco,** and **Gattinara.**

- Barolo offers its most famous expression with wines that can last for decades.
- Barbaresco tends to be a little lighter in style but has just as much perfume and acidity as Barolo.
- Gattinara from northern Piedmont produces Nebbiolo's most austere expression and is the most long-lived.

Barbera

The Barbera is the mainstay of the region but until recently did not have the recognition of the Nebbiolo grape. Barbera

Piedmont Region Varietals and Appellations

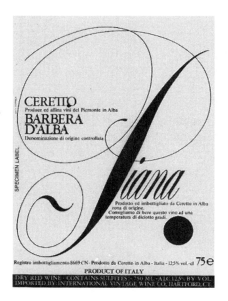

is being vinified in many cases in a more French manner, and the fuller versions have been recognized as fine wine. It has very distinct aromas of blackberries and licorice and has excellent acidity but does not have the maturation capability of the Nebbiolo. The three DOCs associated with Barbera are the regions of **Alba, Asti,** and **Monferrato,** with the Barbera d'Asti producing the most full-bodied and fragrant expression.

Dolcetto

Dolcetto is grown almost exclusively in the provinces of Cuneo and Alessandria in the southeastern region of Piedmont. The wines produced are soft and full of fruit and licorice flavors. They are meant to be drunk within 2 or 3 years and are reminiscent of Beaujolais cru wines. Dolcetto is produced in seven DOCs, the preeminent being **Dolcetto d'Alba** and **d'Asti.**

Other black grape varieties include **Grignolino** and **Brachetto,** the latter used in making a delightfully sweet sparkling red wine. The principal white grape varieties include Moscato, Arneis, and Cortese.

Moscato

The Moscato grape is used in making spumante (sparkling) and still white wines from the region around the town of **Asti.** Over 50 million liters of Asti are produced each year, making it one of the world's best-known sparkling wines. In 1994, Asti gained DOCG status, allowing its wines to be labeled without the word *spumante* to differentiate it from all other regions producing similar spumante wines. The dioise method for making this single-fermentation sparkling wine is described in Chapter 5. The wine should be consumed within 2 years, before it loses its inherently refreshing aromas.

Arneis

Arneis is indigenous to Piedmont and can produce a delightfully soft, full-textured, and herbaceous wine that, due to its low acidity, does not age well. It attained DOC status in 1989 under the appellation of **Roero Arneis.**

Cortese

The Cortese variety provides the basis of DOC **Gavi,** one of Italy's most coveted dry white wines. The wine is very crisp, with a tendency to have a little spritz, and has delicate citrus fruit aromas. The wine should be consumed within 2 or 3 years of the vintage.

The principal producers of Piedmont include Elio Altare (Barolo), Antoniolo (Gattinara), **Villa Banfi** (Asti, Brachetto d'Acqui, Dolcetto d'Acqui, Gavi), Marchesi di Barolo (Barolo, Asti, Barbaresco, Barbera d'Alba, Dolcetto d'Alba, Gavi), Bersano (Barbareso, Barolo, Barbera d'Alba, Docetto d'Alba, Asti, Gavi), Ceretto (Arneis, Barbaresco, Barbera d'Alba, Barolo, Dolcetto d'Alba), Pio Cesare (Barbaresco, Barbera d'Alba, Barolo, Dolcetto d'Alba, Gavi), Fontanafredda (Asti, Barbaresco, Barolo, Barbera d'Alba, Dolcetto d'Alba), Gaja (Barbaresco, Barolo, Barbera d'Alba, Dolcetto d'Alba), Bruno Giacosa (Arneis, Barbaresco, Barbera d'Alba, Barolo, Dolcetto d'Alba), Martini & Rossi (Asti), Castello di Nieve (Barbaresco, Barbera d'Alba, Moscato d'Asti), Alfredo Prunotto (Barbaresco, Barbera d'Alba, Barolo, Dolcetto d'Alba), and Renato Ratti (Barbaresco, Barbera d'Alba, Barolo, Dolcetto d'Alba).

Tuscany

Tuscany, which is located in Central Italy, typifies Italian wines for most consumers who, when asked to name an Italian wine, will respond **"Chianti."** Tuscany's history flourished during the Renaissance when its two major cities, Florence and Siena, became the banking, literary, and artistic centers of Europe. Leading contemporary wine-making families, such as Antinori, were established at that time. Despite the depth of traditions that exist in Tuscany, it has become a leader in the Italian wine-making revolution of the past 30 years. It is here that **supertuscan** wines such as **Sassicaia, Ornellaia,** and **Tignanello,** names for Cabernet Sauvignon or Sangiovese blended wines, have been made. These brilliantly made wines have been heralded throughout the wine world but remained until 1994 Vini da Tavola, because they did not follow the prescribed DOC formulas. Antinori's Sassicaia di Bolgheri was the first to receive DOC appellation.

Tuscan Region of Italy

Tuscany's rolling hillsides are home to five DOCGS, four of which are red wines made from the same grape variety, Sangiovese. The four are Chianti, Brunello di Montalcino, Carmignano Rosso, and Vino Nobile di Montepulciano. The fifth DOCG wine was Italy's first white wine to attain this level, Vernaccia di San Gimignano.

Chianti

Chianti is the appellation for a region that includes seven zones, including Chianti Classico, which was first delineated by the Medici Grand Duke Cosimo in 1716. The consortium of producers from the Classico area differentiate their wine labels by adding their symbol of a black rooster. Chianti is confusing to the consumer, until one realizes that there are three distinct quality levels and styles, despite the fact that all are made primarily from the Sangiovese grape:

- **Chianti:** A wine that is soft, fresh, and fruity with discernible traces of bitterness. This is a wine that is aged only 1 year and frequently bottled in *fiaschi*, straw-covered bottles.
- **Chianti Classico:** A wine made from the heartland of Chianti, which has improved its quality, by reducing yields and the amount of other varieties in the blend. This wine has good acidity and distinct black cherry aromas and flavors.
- **Chianti Classico Riserva:** The best-quality Chianti, which, by law, is required to age an additional year. These wines have greater depth and tannic structure, requiring further bottle aging before they achieve their peak. The wines have a citrusy, minty, and spicy quality.

Chianti has traditionally been made by blending 80% **Sangiovese** with the black grape variety of Canaiolo and *passito* white grapes of Malvasia and Trebbiano. The traditional *Governo al'uso* system of making Chianti was adding the **must** of passito or very sweet dried white grapes to the fermented wine, allowing the wine to referment, thereby boosting its alcoholic content, giving the wine smoothness and lessening the perception of tannins.

Riserva wines do not benefit from this age-old system of vinification, and most producers are ignoring these laws by adding other black varieties, if blending at all. There has also been a recent (1999) change in the aging requirements to 2 years and 4 months for Riservas.

The most prominent producers include Fattoria di Ama, Antinori, Villa Banfi, Brolio Barone Riscasoli, Castello di Cacchiano, Tenuta Capezzana, Castello di Fonterutoli, Castello di Gabbiano, Isole e Olena, Melini, Monsanto, Ruffino, Castello di Uzzano, Castello Vicchiomaggio, Vignamaggio, and Castello di Volpaia.

Brunello di Montalcino
Brunello is a Sangiovese clone that produces a very powerful, dark, tannic, and concentrated wine. Riserva is aged 5 years in wood and needs 10 years of bottle aging to allow it to reach its peak. This 100% Sangiovese wine was created by the Biondi-Santi family in the late nineteenth century. They continue to be one of the leading producers, who include Altesino, Biondi-Santi, Tenuta Caparzo, Tenuta Il Poggione, and Villa Banfi.

Carmignano
Carmignano is a small appellation located west of Florence and is made of Sangiovese and 10% Cabernet Sauvignon or Franc, which are alleged to have been introduced to the area in the nineteenth century. The most notable producers include Tenuta di Capezzana and Artiminio.

Vino Nobile di Montepulciano
The beautiful town of Montepulciano has been recognized as the center for fine red wine since the eighteenth century, hence the epithet of *nobile,* or noble. The wines are made from a Sangiovese clone called Prugnolo, which constitutes 60% to 80% of the blend, with the addition of **Canaiolo Nero.** The wines must be aged 2 years in wood and require a further 6 or more years of bottle aging to reach their peak. The Vino Nobile is a leaner wine than its counterparts and develops a lovely sandalwood and spicy nose. The most notable producers include Avignonesi, Poderi Boscarelli, and Melini.

Vernaccia di San Gimignano
Vernaccia is one of Italy's few substantial white wines when vinified in a traditional manner (by fermenting and aging it in wood). Most winemakers, however, have opted for modern techniques, which make Vernaccia somewhat indistinct. Vernaccia has good acidity and offers honeyed bouquets when given a little bottle aging.

The most notable producers include Brolio Barone Ricasoli, Fattoria di Cusona, Ricardo Falchini-Il Casale, Melini, Conti Serristori, and Teruzzi & Puthod.

There are other notable styles of wine made in the Tuscany region, which merit mention: Vin Santo, Capitolare, and Supertuscan wines.

Vin Santo
Vin Santo is a wine made from passito grapes, which have traditionally been hung to dry from rafters in the lofts of houses or barns until January. The resulting grapes are shriveled and very sweet and may be botrytized. These grapes are usually white, from the Malvasia or Trebbiano varieties, but can also be red. The wine is sealed in *caratelli,* or small barrels, and aged 3 to 6 years. The resulting wine can be dry or sweet. Vin Santo is one of Italy's outstanding wines.

Capitolare Wines
Capitolare wines, formerly known as Predicato wines, are a recognized new category of white or red wines made from untraditional grape varieties, such as Chardonnay. Although Capitolare wines do not have DOC appellation, they are still prestigious, and there is a possibility of their being granted DOC status. There are four categories of Capitolare wines:

Capitolare del Muschio: A Chardonnay- or Pinot Blanc–based white wine that is blended with no more than 20% Riesling, Müller-Thurgau, or Pinot Grigio

Capitolare del Sevante: A 100% Sauvignon Blanc–based wine

Capitolare di Biturica: A Cabernet Sauvignon–based wine that is blended with no more than 30% Sangiovese and 10% other red grape varieties.

Capitolare di Cardisco: A Sangiovese-based wine that is blended with no more than 10% other red grape varieties.

Supertuscan Wines
A number of Bordeaux-blended style of wines have emerged from Tuscany in the past 20 years that carry all

of the prestige of a Premier Cru. The story of Supertuscan wines is a reflection of the Antinori family's efforts at wine making and experimentation. The primary Supertuscans are Sassicaia, Solaia, and Ornellaia.

Tignanello

Tignanello does not fit the paradigm that is being discussed because it is basically a Sangiovese blend. It is mentioned here, however, because it is a wine that is made by the Antinori family and has achieved great fame as a premier wine. Tignanello is a wine that does not merit the Chianti DOC appellation because it includes 10% Cabernet, although this blend is quite acceptable in Carmignano for a DOCG appellation.

Sassicaia

The -*aia* suffix of *Sassicaia* is a geographic reference. *Sassicaia* means "a place of many stones." This Cabernet Sauvignon wine was first released in the 1940s and was ill-received by local producers. Sassicaia is vinified as though it were a Bordeaux wine, and it certainly achieves the stature of First Growth wines.

Solaia

Solaia means "place of the sun." This wine is also produced by Antinori. It began as 100% Cabernet Sauvignon, but more recent vintages include 20% Sangiovese and Cabernet Franc.

Ornellaia

Ornellaia means "place of the ash trees," and it is the most recent addition to the Antinori Supertuscan collection. The red wine is a Médoc blend of Cabernet Sauvignon, Cabernet Franc, and Merlot. The wines all have concentrated flavors and are rich in tannins (crying out for bottle aging) and demand a place among a wine collector's choice Cabernet Sauvignon wines.

Veneto

Veneto is Italy's largest wine-producing region for DOC classified wines. Veneto is located in northeastern Italy

Venice Appellations

and is geographically the most diverse of Italy's regions. The area is subdivided into three climatic and geologic zones: the western region around Verona and Lake Garda, the hilly region of Central Veneto, and the eastern seaside region around Venice and Treviso. The region to the east (e.g., the Piave) has more internationally recognized varietals, such as Merlot, Pinot Noir, and Cabernet Sauvignon, which have improved immensely in the past decade. The area around Verona has become known internationally for the appellations of **Soave, Bardolino,** and **Valpolicella.** It is these appellations which we will focus on. There are three principal indigenous wine varieties grown in this region: Garganega (white), Trebbiano di Soave (white), and Corvina (black).

Soave and Recioto di Soave

This appellation is Italy's best-known white wine. It is made with the Garganega and Trebbiano varieties. Soave, like Chianti, has an appellation of Classico, but there is little in the quality of the wine to differentiate it from the rest of the Soave appellation. The wine is simple, straightforward, light, and very refreshing when young. Recioto di Soave is a concentrated rich and sweet wine made from semi-dry grapes.

The most notable producers include Bertani, Bolla, Masi, Pieropan, and Cantina Sociale di Soave.

Bardolino

Bardolino is named after one of the 16 villages in the appellation by Lake Garda. It is produced primarily from the Corvina variety blended with Rondinella and Molinara. Bardolino is a soft, uncomplicated red wine that should be drunk a year after its harvest. Bardolino also can be produced in a pale, almost rosé version called Chiaretto.

The most notable producers include Bolla, Guerrieri-Rizzardi, Lamberti, Masi, Tommasi, and Zonin.

Valpolicella and Recioto della Valpolicella-Amarone

Valpolicella is a delightfully brisk, easy-to-drink wine made from the same varieties as Bardolino. Valpolicella has a strong cherry aroma and flavor and always seems to finish with a bitter almond flavor. The best Valpolicella comes

from the Classico area and should be drunk young like its Bardolino counterpart.

The Recioto della Valpolicella can be produced in a sweet style or in a very powerful, dry style called Amarone. Amarone is considered by many to be Italy's finest red wine. The dried passito grapes are fermented beginning in January or February and require 45 to 50 days to ferment. The wine is still sweet at this point and requires another 2 years in barrels to ferment to 15.5% alcohol. The wine is aged for 3 years in wood before bottling. Amarone, with sufficient bottle aging, is a very rich, full-bodied, and velvety wine.

The most notable producers include Allegrini, Bertani, Bolla, Lamberti, Masi, Le Ragose, Serego Alighieri, Fratelli Tedeschi, and Tommasi.

Other Wine Regions of Italy

The Northwest

Valle d'Aosta

Valle d'Aosta is positioned between Piedmont and France and produces 21 types of wine, which are given names in both Italian and French. These wines are rarely seen outside of their own appellation.

Liguria

Liguria is a crescent-shaped area along the Tyrrhenian Sea and is the link between France and Tuscany. The city of Genoa, the region's capital, provides the demand for good-quality wines. There are four DOCs, the most notable of which is Cinqueterre, a dry and sweet white wine.

Lombardy

Lombardy, which borders Switzerland and Piedmont, produces no wine of international repute. This region produces both reds and whites, the most notable produced in the Valtellina DOC, which makes a Nebbiolo-based red wine.

Emilia-Romagna

Emilia-Romagna is divided into two provinces (as its name suggests), with its capital, Bologna, intersecting it in the middle. Lambrusca is the wine for which this region is best known. Lambrusca is a pink or red *frizzante* or fizzy wine, made from Malvasia, Trebbiano, or Ortrugo grapes. The region is home to one DOCG, Albana di Romagna, and 14 DOCs. Albana di Romagna is usually a dry white wine that lacks much individual character. The region produces a number of different varieties, including Chardonnay, Pinot Grigio, Barbera, Cabernet Sauvignon, Sauvignon Blanc, Pinot Noir, Trebbiano, and Sangiovese.

The Northeast

Trentino–Alto Adige

This region borders Austria and Switzerland and is the most northerly of Italy's regions. Only 15% of its land is cultivatable, so the emphasis is on quality rather than quantity. Sixty percent of its wines are classified as DOC, 35% of which are exported.

There are eight DOCs, the most notable of which are the Alto Adige and Trentino. Culturally, the region is very Germanic, particularly in the northern province of Alto Adige. The Alto Adige produces mainly crisp dry whites, the most notable of which are Pinot Bianco, Chardonnay, Pinot Grigio, Gewürztraminer, Riesling, Sylvaner, and Sauvignon Blanc. The Trentino province is the largest cultivator of Chardonnay in Italy. Red wines are made in both provinces from the Schiava, Lagrein and Teroldego native varieties, as well as from international varieties such as Pinot Noir. The red wines are refreshing and smooth but finish with a slightly bitter, almond flavor.

The most notable producers are Cavit, Ferrari, Giorgio Gray, Kettmeir Alois Lageder, Vinicola Santa Margherita, and Roberto Zenni.

Friuli-Venezia Giulia

This region borders Austria, Slovenia, and Croatia to the east and has developed a noteworthy reputation with its international varietal wines. The Friuli-Venezia Giulia is divided into six zones, the largest of which almost incorporates the entire region, the Grave del Friuli. The **Grave del Friuli,** the neighboring **Collio Goriziano,** and the **Colli Orientali del Friuli** are the most significant DOC regions.

The Collio Goriziano is so diverse that wine authors state that it calls California to mind. It is the white wines made from Tocai Friulano, Pinot Bianco, and Pinot Grigio, however, that provide the best and most assertive wines. The Colli Orientali del Friuli produces similar white wines, with two other varieties of note: the Verduzzo, a delicate, light dessert wine; and the Picolit, which was a favored dessert wine of the Hapsburg emperor's court.

The Grave di Friuli is best known for its Merlot, which accounts for more than 50% of its production. The Grave also produces a notable indigenous red called Refosco. Its white wines can be as well made as those of the Collio.

Central Italy

Central Italy includes, other than Tuscany, the regions of Umbria, Marche (the Marches), Abruzzi, Molise, and Lazio (Latium). Although this region accounts for less than a fourth of Italy's wine production, it harbors a disproportionately high number of DOCs.

Umbria

In the past, Umbria, located southeast of Tuscany, was known only for Orvietto, a DOC appellation for a white wine made in dry and *abboccato* styles. The modern, crisp, pale style of today's Orvietto, however, is quite different from the former traditional golden and somewhat oxidized wine. The principal grapes used in the making of Orvietto are Trebbiano and Malvasia. The best wines to date are the two that have been accorded the status of DOCG: **Torgiano Rosso Riserva** and **Montefalco Sagrantino.** Furthermore, there are a number of excellent French grape varieties, such as Sauvignon Blanc and Merlot, that are being vinified into commendable wines.

Torgiano Rosso Riserva is a red wine made from 70% Sangiovese blended with Canaiolo and Trebbiano Toscano. The appellation is a tribute to an individual producer, Dr. Giorgio Lungarotti, whose Rubesco Riserva has reached the apogee of the Torgiano appellation.

Montefalco Sagrantino Riserva is a native black grape

grown in the Montefalco hillside town near Assisi. Sagrantino produces a wine that is rich in color and texture, with unmistakable aromas and flavors of blackberries, and the Riserva, which is aged 3 years in wood, is exceptional.

Marche

The Marche is best known for its dry white wine with the appellation **Verdicchio,** which is shipped in distinctive green amphora-shaped bottles by one of its premier producers, Fazi-Battaglia. The best Verdicchio comes from the Castelli di Jesi appellation. The wine is crisp and clean, making it a perfect foil for many Adriatic Italian seafood dishes. The region of Marche is also developing a reputation for the reds made from the Montepulciano grape.

Abruzzi

Abruzzi, which borders Marche to the north and Molise to the south, also is on the Adriatic coast. Although located in close proximity to Rome, albeit on the eastern side of the Apennine mountains, it has only two DOCs: **Montepulciano d'Abruzzi** and **Trebbiano d'Abruzzo.** There has been considerable and successful effort by modern producers, such as Valentini or Masciarelli, to develop the finest characteristics of the Montepulciano variety. The Riserva is aged 2 years in wood; with 4 years of aging, it develops a full, meaty bouquet to complement the blackberry and blueberry aromas and flavors.

Molise

Often viewed as a southern appendage of Abruzzi, this small Adriatic region of Italy has two DOC appellations: **Biferno** and **Pentro di Isernia.** Because most of the wine is consumed within Molise, there is little need to classify it for the benefit of others. The exceptions are the DOC Biferno wines and the red wine named Ramitello from the estates of Masseria Di Majo Norante. These wines are made from the Montepulciano and Aglianico grapes and are aged 3 years in wood.

Lazio

The region of Lazio hosts the capital of Italy, Rome. Lazio, also called Latium, is known for its white wines, particularly

Frascati, Est! Est! Est! di Montefiascone, Marino, and Montecompatri-Colonna. Frascati is made from the Trebbiano and Malvasia varieties, and nearly 20 million liters of it are produced each year. Unfortunately, due to the modern wine-making approach, Frascati is now somewhat neutral in flavor if refreshing and crisp, and it should be drunk very young. Traditional Frascati had far more color, aromas, and flavor, which married well to the cuisine of Rome.

Est! Est! Est! derives its name from the actions of a steward of a twelfth-century German Bishop, who was traveling to Rome for the coronation of the new pope. The steward, who was sent ahead of the traveling party, was instructed to mark the doors of taverns where good wine could be found with the word *Est*, meaning "This is it!" After tasting the wine at a tavern in the small town of Montefiascone, the steward was so enthused by it, he chalked Est! Est! Est! on the tavern door. Ironically, current wines of this region bear little resemblance to the wines made during the twelfth century. That wine was made primarily sweet, using the Malvasia variety, whereas it is now made primarily dry, using Trebbiano.

The South and the Islands

The South incorporates the area the early Greeks named Oenotria. It was into this region that the Greeks introduced their grape varieties and viticultural practices. The Romans recognized the potential of the volcanic soil, temperate climate, and cooling mountainous terrain and produced their First Growth wines of Falernum, Caecubum, and Mamertinum. This area incorporates six wine-producing regions: Campania, Apulia, Basilicata, Calabria, Sicilia, and Sardinia.

Campania

The region around Naples has not been noted for making fine-quality wines in the modern era. Through the efforts of producers such as Mastroberardino, however, Campania has one DOCG appellation, **Taurasi,** and 13 DOCs. Campania produces three noteworthy wines: the red Taurasi, the white Fiano di Avellino, and the white Greco di Tufo, all of which are produced by Mastroberardino.

Taurasi DOCG is made from the Aglianico black grape, producing a full-bodied, firm, and aggressive wine that is aged 3 years in wood and requires 6 or more years of bottle aging to reach its peak. *Fiano de Avellino* is a fine white wine with aromas and flavors reminiscent of nuts. It gains complexity with 3 or 4 years of bottle aging. *Greco di Tufo* is a white wine named after the grape variety and gains considerable complexity with 3 to 4 years of bottle aging.

Other wines of note are those of **Lacryma Christi del Vesuvio,** "the Tears of Christ," which can be red, white, or rosé. The reds are made from the indigenous Piedirosso, Sciacinoso, and Aglianico grape varieties. These wines are quite capable of aging 6 years and have found a niche in the U.S. market.

The red and white wines of the island of Ischia are worth heeding, especially those produced by D'Ambra Vini d'Ischia and Perrazzo Vini d'Ischia.

Apulia

Apulia is Italy's most prodigious producer, with much of its wine sent to the north to be converted into vermouth. Some of the better wines come from the Salento peninsula. The most successful wines are reds, which are made from the **Negroamaro** and Primitivo grape varieties. Apulia has 24 DOCs, the most notable of which are Aleatico di Puglia, producing a port-like fortified red wine; Brindisi; Castel del Monte; and Salice Salentino. These wines tend to be powerful, dark, alcoholic, and spicy, with less finesse than northern Italy's great reds. Modern techniques, however, are enabling producers such as Taurino, Rivera, and Leone de Castris to make better-balanced and more refreshing styles of wine.

Basilicata

Basilicata, located to the west of Apulia, has the advantage of providing a cool climate in the higher altitudes away from the coastline. Basilicata has arguably the south's greatest red wine, grown in its only DOC, **Aglianico del Vulture.** The Aglianico grape variety is grown on the slopes of the extinct volcano Vulture and offers a dark, rich, and flavorful red wine.

Calabria

Calabria forms the toe of the Italian "boot" and is a very mountainous region with varying climatic zones. There are two prominent, indigenous grape varieties whose origins date back to the Greek settlement: the Gaglioppo for reds and the Greco di Bianco for sweet whites. Calabria produces mostly red wines; the most significant is **Ciro.** Its reputation may be a reflection of the wine itself (i.e., somewhat exaggerated), but, with modern techniques, its almost pruny character may become more restrained and balanced.

Sicilia (Sicily)

Sicily is the largest island in the Mediterranean and has a history of wine making dating back to the Greeks in the fifth century B.C. The western province of Sicily is dedicated to making wine produced in prodigious amounts, making it one of the largest producing regions of Italy. Sicily is known for one of the world's great fortified wines, **Marsala,** but it is also a producer of many white and red table wines made from local grape varietals. The proportion of its wines that are classified as DOC is very small (2.5%) and includes Marsala. The noteworthy white varietals include Grillo, Inzolia, and Catarratto, and the black varietals include Calabrese (Nero d'Avola), Nerello Mascalese, and Frappato di Vittoria. The internationally best-known wine, **Corvo,** is not one of the region's 10 DOCs. The most satisfying wines come from the appellations of Etna, Faro, and Regaleali with its elegant reds and brisk whites, and the Moscato di Noto which is considered one of the world's most sumptuous, though rare, dessert wines.

Sardinia

Sardinia has a history of isolation coupled with the influences of formers invaders, particularly the Spanish, which has helped to shape its viticultural history. Current wine-making practices reflect very clearly the conflict between traditionalists and modernists. Much of Sardinia's wine, especially within the 18 DOCs, is made from indigenous varieties or varieties that were imported centuries ago.

The principal varieties include the red **Cannonau,** Monica, and Giro and the white Nuragus, Vernaccia di Oristano, Nasco, and Torbato. One of Sardinia's most distinctive wines is Vernaccia di Oristano, which develops a flor, as occurs in sherry, and becomes partially oxidized. It has many of the similar bouquets and refinements of a good sherry. The Giro, Monica, and Cannonau (which is related to Garnacha from Spain) were traditionally made with residual sugar left in the wine, even though the alcohol level would naturally reach 13.5%. Modern winemakers, such as Sella & Mosca, are producing wines that are more refined and better balanced, with cleaner finishes. Sardinian wines are becoming more commonplace in the U.S. market and represent good value.

Spain

Spain is the world's third largest producer of wine, though it has more acreage under viticulture than any other country. This apparent anomaly is due to the grape varieties used, the methods of viticulture, and the drier climatic conditions, which limit yields because irrigation is forbidden. Spanish viticulture did not develop fully until the past two decades because of its overall economic condition. Spain was one of the few countries that did not receive economic support from the United States under the Marshall Plan after the Second World War. There was insufficient domestic demand for fine-quality wines, and until the last few years of Franco's reign, Spain remained protectionist and somewhat isolated. During the past two decades, however, a transformation occurred, both economically and viticulturally (see Figure 8–4).

As in the rest of Europe, Spanish domestic consumption has fallen precipitously to 42 liters per person. This has forced Spanish growers and producers to react in the same way as their counterparts in other countries: They are cultivating better-quality varieties and employing modern vinification techniques. Gone are the days of heavily oxidized white wines.

Spain has an ancient wine history, dating back at least to the Phoenicians, who founded Cadiz in 1100 B.C. The Phoenicians' successors, known as Carthaginians, expanded their territories in Spain, especially during the Punic

Spain and Portugal

wars against the Roman Empire in the third century B.C. The Romans, who had settled in the areas east of the Ebro River, had established their own viticulture in the area now known as Rioja. There is much literary and archeological evidence to demonstrate the increasing wine trade from

Figure 8–4 Map of the wine-producing regions of Spain

Spain to Rome, once Spain had been conquered and settled under Roman rule. The wines of Spain have been recognized throughout the centuries as low in quality, with the exception of sherries.

Although Spain claims to have over 600 grape varieties, only 20 of them are grown in significant amounts. The most widely planted variety is the Arien, which provides the basis for Spain's significant brandy industry and for the plonk served at Spanish bars. The second most prevalent grape is the Garnacha (Grenache), followed by Monastrell (Mourvedre), Tempranillo, Macabeo (also known as Viura), Palomino, and Pedro Ximenez.

Spain has seven climatic zones and 17 regions, but this discussion is concerned with only four regions: **Rioja, Penedes** (in Catalan), **Ribera del Duero,** and **Jerez-Xérès-Sherry** (discussed in Chapter 5).

Although the European Community recognizes two basic qualities of wine—table wines and quality wines—Spain subdivides and classifies its wines further. In ascending order of quality, they are

Vino de mesa: Table wine

Vino de la tierra: Country wine similar to the French Vin de Pays

Denominacion de origen (DO): Comparable to AOC or DOC in Italy

Denominacion de origen calificada (DOCa): Comparable to DOCG

Additionally, wines can be labeled according to their aging status.

Vino joven (young wine): Intended for immediate drinking after bottling

Vino de crianza (wine of breeding): Aged a minimum of 6 months in oak and is released its third year

Reserva whites: Must be aged 6 months in oak; are released their third year

Red wines: Must be aged a full year in oak; released in their fourth year

Gran Reserva: Allowed only in good vintages; must spend a minimum of 2 years in oak; released in its sixth year for reds, and aged for 4 years with 6 months' oak aging for whites

Rioja

Rioja located in the upper Ebro Valley along the river Oja, has a wine-making tradition dating back over 2000 years. Its modern manifestation began in the 1850s when the Marqués de Riscal traveled to Bordeaux and returned with Cabernet Sauvignon and Merlot vines and, more importantly, ideas regarding vinification. He and the Marqués de Murrieta planted these vines and applied the techniques to their local variety, Tempranillo, with spectacular results. French influence was further felt when *Phylloxera* struck Bordeaux, and many Bordelais winemakers traveled and worked in Rioja for a decade or more.

Rioja is divided into three subregions:

Rioja Alta
Rioja Alavesa
Rioja Baja

The best red wines come from the Rioja Alta and Alavesa, which enjoy cool climates at altitudes of approximately 1500 feet. Riojas are made primarily from the **Tempranillo** grape blended with **Garnacha Tinta** and a smaller percentage of Mazuelo and Graciano. White riojas are made primarily from the Viura grape and are oak aged.

The most notable producers include Bodegas Marqués de Cáceres, CVNE (Compania Vinicola del Norte de Espagna), Bodegas Muga, Bodegas Marqués de Murrieta, and Marqués de Riscal.

Penedès

Since the 1960s, winemaking in the Penedes region of **Catalan** has jumped to the forefront. This region is noted for two distinct types of wine: **Cava,** sparkling wine made in the traditional champagne method, and impressive white and reds that are vinified by using modern technology.

Cava wines are made from native grapes, including **Macabeo,** Parellada, and Xarel-lo, with some houses adding Chardonnay. These wines have excellent acidity, and the Blanc de Blancs are particularly fine. Legally, Cava wines must age 9 months in the bottle, although much is aged for 1 to 3 years. The two largest producers, **Codorniu** and **Freixenet,** are known internationally.

The notable still wines are a result of the efforts of the Torres and Jean León wineries. Torres was the first to introduce French varietals into this area, but more important was the use of modern vinification, such as temperature-controlled fermentation and aging in barriques.

Ribera del Duero

This important wine-producing DO in the Castilla-Leon region developed along the same lines as Rioja. In 1846, a new winery, Lecanda, imported Bordeaux technology. The name of this winery was later changed to Vega Sicilia, which today produces some of the world's most extraordinary red wine. The basis of this wine is the Tempranillo, which is blended with a small proportion of Cabernet Sauvignon. Its best wine is labeled Unico, which is aged a minimum of 10 years in oak and released after a minimum of 2 years in the bottle. A newcomer to wine making in this region is Fernandez Pesquera, who has received considerable accolades for his red wines.

Jerez-Xérès-Sherry

For a full discussion of this wine-producing region, see Chapter 5.

There are other important DO wine regions in Spain, such as Galicia and Rueda, both of which are producing fine white wines. There is little doubt that Spanish wines will continue to attract customers, and, if the past two decades are any indication, the results will be welcomed.

9

Beer

Beer

History of Beer

The origins of beer date back to before 6000 B.C., when it is presumed that some nomads accidentally discovered that wild barley, when soaked, fermented on contact with natural yeast. When consumed, this fermented beverage evoked feelings of relaxation and happiness. Clay tablets found in Mesopotamia, dating back to 6000 B.C., communicated that the practice of brewing beer was a well-established and regulated activity. Brewing was sometimes associated with priestly responsibilities. This beer, it is speculated, was probably cloudy, muddy brown, and, by today's standards, not palatable.

By 4000 B.C., the Babylonians were brewing over 16 varieties of beer, including the use of flavoring agents such as honey. In Egypt, around 3000 B.C., beer was made by partially soaking bread made from barley in water. When it came into contact with natural airborne yeast, the soaked bread fermented. Records indicate that hops, as well as other herbs and fruits, were used as flavoring by the Egyptians.

The Greeks and the Romans learned brewing from the Egyptians. Beer was a vital part of life and was consumed on many occasions. It was preferred over water due to the lack of potable water in most areas. The alcohol content eliminated pathogenic bacteria in the water used for brewing. Brewing was also established at this time among the barbarian tribes of Western and Northern Europe. The beer of this time did not resemble today's beer taste profile, largely due to the many herbs used for flavoring.

Brewing in Europe began to develop along two divergent paths. The loose grouping of tribes in England, the Celtic tribes, brewed a malted beverage without hops, which they called *ale*. The Germans, who shared a similar beer history with the English until the ninth century, commonly used hops. They discovered that the hops not only imparted desirable flavor characteristics, but also extended the life of the beer by acting as a natural preservative. The beer brewed during this time did not resemble today's beer taste profile due to the many herbs used for flavoring and the unavailability of pure yeast cultures. During this period, brewing permeated many sections of the culture. Monasteries, for example, refined brewing techniques. A brewmaster might supervise an adjoining brewery and bakery, garnering the title of master baker as well. Home brewing was done by every class of citizen. Queen Elizabeth I of England, for example, enjoyed a special brew prepared by her own brewmaster. The beer of this time was top fermented.

The nineteenth century marked the beginning of *lager* (the German word for "storage") beers. The ice-packed caves of the Bavarian Alps were used for cold fermentation. This cold fermentation allowed the use of a lager yeast, a bottom-fermenting yeast that requires cooler cellar temperatures. In the early nineteenth century, the founding fathers of the United States, Thomas Jefferson, Patrick Henry, James Madison, and Samuel Adams, passed legislation to promote the American brewing industry into an international market. During this period, the style of beer resembled the English traditional ales, porters, and stouts.

Traditional British-style top-fermented beers remained popular in the United States until 1840, at which time lager beers were introduced via the influx of German immigration. A Bavarian, John Wagner, is rumored to have brewed a lager in Philadelphia as early as 1840.

In 1842, the most popular lager-style beer was the Pilsner, sourced from Pilsen, Czechoslovakia. This beer was pale, clear, hopped, highly carbonated, and refreshing. Much of this beer's flavor distinction was attributable to the local water composition, which was very soft.

Around 1876, the art of brewing achieved a more scientific status, partly from the contribution of Louis Pasteur's pure yeast culture and fermentation process studies.

The brewing industry benefited from the Industrial Revolution during the late nineteenth century. Ice-making, refrigeration equipment, thermometers, and process control evolved at this time and encouraged the popularity of the colder-temperature lager beers in the United States.

There were 1269 U.S. breweries in 1860. This number diminished to just over 40 firms in 1970 due to the result of Prohibition, home refrigeration, and competition.

Twentieth-century advances, such as stainless steel and computer technology, have been incorporated in the brewing industry. Stainless steel vessels have begun to replace the copper or glass vessels. The Coors Golden Colorado brewhouse is an exception, with its all-copper brewhouse. It was produced by a German firm and retained because contact with copper is superior in heat transfer and beer-chemistry characteristics. Computer technology has infiltrated almost every brewery, from micro to major, and is used for process monitoring and automation. Beer packaging has evolved from wooden kegs to metal kegs, aluminum cans, glass bottles, and even plastic containers, all stemming from twentieth century technology.

In the late twentieth century, the beer industry comprises a wide spectrum of brewery sizes. The microbrewery has gained popularity and has offered consumers a wider choice of products. The larger brewers have been encouraged by this expansion to add a variety of beer types to their traditionally mild, subtly hopped product portfolios. Coors, for example, has seen increasing interest in its 10-year seasonal product offering, Winterfest, a dark German-style beer. The Coors portfolio of product offerings has expanded to include such beer types as a honey beer (George Killians' Wilde Honey) and a brown ale (George Killian's Brown Ale).

Primary Brewing Ingredients

Water

Quality beers are brewed with quality water. Beer is 90% to 95% water. Water's flavor and mineral content (hard-

ness, softness) impact the product and the process. For example, zinc and calcium are minerals critical to yeast during fermentation.

Historically, certain geographic locations have been renowned for distinctive beer styles. This distinction is partially attributable to the unique water composition of the area. In England, a "Burton" beer is a strong pale ale, the distinctive taste profile of which has evolved from the local hard (high mineral content, particularly calcium sulfate) water source. An U.S. example of product distinction influenced by water composition is Coors products. The Golden facility water is fairly soft (low in minerals), because the spring water has been naturally filtered through layers of sand and gravel. The Memphis and Shenandoah facility sites were selected primarily because of the water source composition, with these sources modeling the Rocky Mountain Spring water of Golden.

Malted Barley

Barley is the most significant solid ingredient used for brewing. It provides nutrients to the yeast and contributes to a beer's **body, flavor,** and **color.** Other cereal grains, such as wheat, oats, and rye, can be used as brewing ingredients. These grains, along with barley, are usually malted before use as a brewing ingredient. In the malting process, the grains are germinated to produce enzymatic systems within the grain. These enzymes convert starches to sugars, which will be fermented by the yeast. After germination, the malt is kilned, or dried. The temperature, time, and moisture level of kilning determines the flavor and color characteristics of the malt.

The majority of the malt used in beer is pale malt. Specialty malts (specially kilned), however, are used in small amounts in beer recipes to impart specific flavors and hues. Specialty malts include

- **Black malt:** Malted barley roasted at high temperatures for a black color and burned flavor that is often perceived as bitterness
- **Chocolate malt:** Malted barley roasted to a dark brown, which is sweeter (less bitter and burned) than the black malt and can impart chocolate flavor notes

- **Crystal** or **caramel malt:** Malted barley roasted to a lighter brown, which lends a caramel candy or toffee flavor and gold to reddish/brown hues

Coors grows and malts virtually all of its own barley requirements. Coors barley is a strain developed by the company to enhance qualities, such as disease resistance, that the company considers optimum for brewing. This barley is a two-row barley, which is plumper than a six-row, and is considered the highest quality of malting barley.

Hops

Hops are the cone-like flowers of the hop vine. The hop vine is a climbing plant, and there are many different varieties. They are generally cultivated in Germany, Czechoslovakia, New Zealand, Washington state, Oregon, and Idaho.

Hops have been used historically in beer for flavor and antimicrobial purposes. They impart flavor to the beer by adding **bitterness** and **aroma** from oils and resins in the hop cone or flower. Like spices, the hop variety, amount, addition time, and place will determine the flavor and aroma impact on the beer. Hop aroma and flavor descriptions vary from herbal, piney, and tobacco to citrus. Hops also act as an antiseptic that extends the life of the beer by inhibiting the growth of various beer-spoiling bacteria. Hops also aid in beer foam retention.

Yeast

Early brewers relied on wild yeasts, carried naturally in air, to ferment the malt sugars into alcohol and carbon dioxide. These wild yeasts, much like water, were distinctive by locality and produced beer inconsistent in flavor and body. Today, there are hundreds of pure brewing-yeast strains.

Yeast types, ale or lager, are identified by how they ferment beer. Ale yeasts rise to the **top** of the **fermentation** vessel, prefer temperatures of **59° F** to **75° F,** and generally provide a more fruity flavor profile. Beer types that generally use these top-fermenting ale yeasts include **ales, porters,** and **stouts.** Legally, in several U.S. states (e.g., Texas), a beer is classified as an ale based solely on a higher alcohol content instead of the type of yeast fermenting (top or bottom) that has been used. **Lager yeasts** are **bottom-fermenting** yeasts that prefer cooler temperatures (**42° F** to **48° F**) and ferment more slowly than ale yeasts. Bottom-fermenting yeasts generally produce a less fruity, cleaner beer with an occasional faint sulfur character that is described as "cooked corn." Examples of beer styles that generally use lager yeasts are **lagers, Pilsner,** and **Bock.**

Adjuncts

A beer adjunct is considered an additional source of starch or sugar added to the beer. Common adjuncts include corn (solid and syrup form), rice, or honey. Adjuncts were originally added to increase brewery yields with a less expensive starch source and to lighten beer's flavor profile.

Adjuncts also impart flavor to the beer. Corn and/or rice additions result in a smoother beer with a cleaner finish. Honey imparts a lingering sweet flavor that is characteristic of the flowers the bees visited during honey making.

The majority of modern domestic and international beer consumers prefer a lighter beer type, the recipe of which includes adjunct. Approximately 98% of the beer produced in the United States is of this type.

Brewing Processes

Malting

Malting is a natural process that occurs in four steps: **steeping, germination, kilning,** and **milling.**

1. In the **steeping** step, the barley is sprayed with water, aerated, and kept at cool temperatures to allow botanical growth.
2. In the growth or **germination** phase, the barley is maintained at 50° F and 100% humidity for ideal sprouting conditions. During the 5-day germination, the barley begins to form hundreds of internal enzyme systems.

3. The barley is roasted, or **kilned,** to arrest botanical growth, halt enzyme development, and develop malt flavors. Kilning temperatures are typically 90° F to 185° F and are maintained for 14 hours. For a darker, more bitter malt, the barley would be kilned longer and at higher temperatures. After kilning, the barley sprouts are removed and the malt is stored for several weeks to allow the flavor to mellow.

4. The malted barley is **milled** or ground to expose the interior starches to brewing water.

Brewing

Warm water is added to the malt to form a **mash** with the consistency of oatmeal. This mash is then heated and held at varying temperatures for varying lengths of time. If called for in the beer-style recipe, adjunct with water is then added to the malt mash to create a combined mash. At a critical temperature, called the saccharification or conversion temperature, the starches from the adjunct and malt are converted by the malt enzymes into fermentable and nonfermentable sugars. By adjusting the temperature and length of this saccharification hold, the brewer influences the body and alcohol content of the final product. The solid malt and adjunct particles are now filtered from the mash, and the result is a very sweet extract (see Figure 9–1).

The extract is transferred to a kettle, where the hops are added. The extract produced after the hop addition is called **wort** (a German term for "unfermented beer"), and this is boiled for 1 to 2 hours. This boil serves to **sterilize** the bacteria-vulnerable wort and to determine the amount of bitterness and aroma extracted from the hops. The wort is painstakingly kept aseptic or sterile throughout the remainder of the process.

Fermenting

The boiling wort is transferred from the kettle to a settling tank to allow unwanted proteins, or **trub,** to collect at the

Figure 9–1   Important steps in the beer-brewing process.

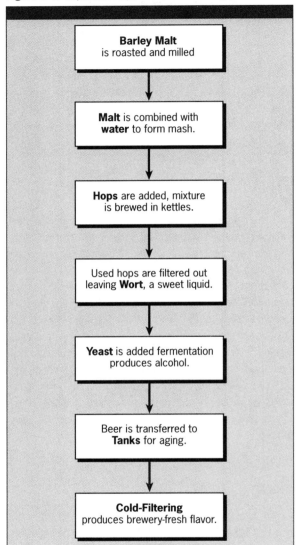

Barley Malt
is roasted and milled

↓

Malt is combined with **water** to form mash.

↓

Hops are added, mixture is brewed in kettles.

↓

Used hops are filtered out leaving **Wort**, a sweet liquid.

↓

Yeast is added fermentation produces alcohol.

↓

Beer is transferred to **Tanks** for aging.

↓

Cold-Filtering
produces brewery-fresh flavor.

bottom of the vessel. The hot wort is then decanted from this vessel and cooled to a temperature that is optimum for the yeast.

Air is injected into the wort in controlled amounts to promote initial yeast growth during the first 1 to 2 days of fermentation. Yeast, whether bottom (lager) or top (ale) fermenting, is added to the wort during the transfer from the settling tank to the fermenter. After the yeast addition, the wort is referred to as **fermenting,** or **green** beer. The fermenter is a temperature-controlled vessel in which the beer will remain for 3 to 10 days, depending on the desired beer style.

During this primary fermentation, the **balling,** or sugar content, of the beer decreases as the yeast metabolizes the fermentable sugars and produces alcohol and carbon dioxide. A majority of the beer's flavor components, such as esters (fruity aroma and flavor) and sulfur, are produced during this rapid-fermentation, sugar-reduction, and alcohol-production phase.

Lagering, Storage, or Aging

The beer is transferred from primary fermentation after the rate of sugar metabolism or fermentation is greatly reduced to secondary fermentation. The storage time varies by yeast type and brewing facility. A **top-fermented** beer is lagered or **aged** at a higher temperature for a shorter time than the lager or **bottom-fermented** beers. The aging time varies from 3 days to 3 months, depending on the brewer.

The intent of this secondary fermentation or aging is beer maturation. With the depletion of fermentable sugars, the yeast will begin to reduce the undesirable compounds that it produced during primary fermentation. Insufficient time or improper temperature control during aging can cause the final beer to impart sulfury, yeasty, or even buttery flavors.

Some brewers **krausen** the beer in aging to incite a more active secondary fermentation. Krausening is a process that adds a predetermined volume of unfermented wort and yeast to aging beer. This produces a more active secondary fermentation as a percentage of the aging beer undergoes primary or rapid fermentation.

Additional hops may be added to the beer after primary fermentation. This process is generally referred to as **dry hopping** and adds a distinctive hop flavor, aroma, and bitterness.

Beer Types

Bottom-Fermented Beer

- *Pilsner:* A pale gold beer with moderate hop flavor and refreshing taste. Most U.S. mainstream beers are made in the Pilsner style but are slightly lighter and less bitter when compared with the classic Pilsners of Czechoslovakia.
- *Lager:* A bright, light beer with high carbonation. This is the most common style of U.S. beer.

Domestic Beer Varieties

Pilsner

Lager

Light

(continued)

Domestic Beer Varieties (continued)

Red Lager

Micro Brewery
Specialty

- *Bock:* A dark, stronger-tasting beer. Bocks range in color and alcohol content but usually have a pronounced malty character.
- *Malt liquor:* A malt beverage brewed like beer but with a higher alcohol content.

Top-Fermented Beer

- *Ale:* A beer exhibiting a variety of characteristics, which might include descriptors such as pale, mild, brown, or bitter. Ale styles generally differ by amount of hops flavor, color, sweetness, dryness, and bitterness.
- *Porter:* A heavy, rich, dark beer with a chocolate or coffee flavor.
- *Stout:* A heavy black ale, similar to a porter but more full-bodied and creamier, with a roasted, burned flavor. Stouts can be sweet but usually are bitter (e.g., Guinness).

- *Saké:* Japanese rice beer. Often confused with wine, saké is high in alcohol (14% to16%) and can be served chilled (for best quality) or warm.

Storing Beer

Most beer bottles, kegs, or cans begin to cause flavor degradation within several months after packaging. Therefore, beer is best consumed as soon as possible after packaging. Bottle colors of brown and green lend some protection to beer by filtering out light. **Light,** especially fluorescent light, changes the beer chemistry by affecting natural hop constituents, which turns the beer "**skunky.**"

Ideally, packaged beer should be stored at **50° F** or cooler to maintain flavor integrity. Oxygen is also detrimental to the flavor of packaged beer. **Oxygen** combines with various components of the beer and causes notable deterioration in flavor and appearance. Oxidized beer is usually described as tasting like cardboard. Additives can reduce product oxidation, but the beer may lose purity and balance. **Pasteurization** to destroy bacteria can also lead to flavor oxidation.

Serving Beer

Pilsners and lagers are usually served at 44° F to 50° F; ales, at 50° F to 57° F; and porters and stouts, at 60° F to 65° F. A clear glass is the optimal serving choice for beer, to display color and clarity. The glass must be completely **cleaned** and properly **rinsed.** Any detergent residue will collapse the foam, decrease carbonation, and adversely impact flavor. "**Beer clean**" is the highest standard of cleanliness for serving glasses.

When serving bottle or canned beer, allow the glass to remain on a flat surface. Pour the beer so that the stream flows straight into the center of the glass. Do not tilt the glass or pour down its side (see Figure 9–2). When drawing from a tap, hold the glass at a 45-degree angle at about 1 inch below the tap and open the tap fully. As the glass

Figure 9–2 Pouring beer from a bottle or can

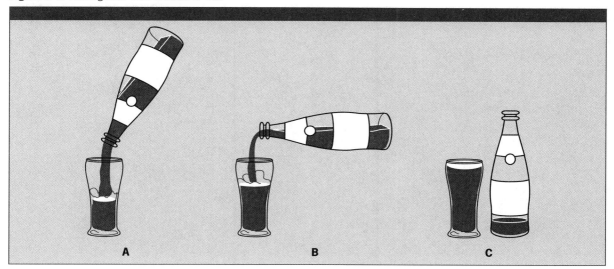

A   B   C

becomes half full, let the beer pour straight down the middle. Close the tap when the beer head has risen slightly above the rim (see Figure 9–3).

Draft Beer

Draft beer should remain cold (40° F to 50° F) because it has not been **pasteurized.** Draft **beer lines** must be **cleaned** on a frequent and regular basis to avoid bacterial contamination, which would impact negatively on the flavor of all beer served from them. Some states have specific laws governing how often draft beer lines are to be cleaned.

Carbon dioxide pressure must be monitored and controlled to maintain consistent carbonation and an even distribution rate. To accomplish this, a carbon dioxide regulator is usually connected to the tap system.

Microbreweries

Microbreweries, although often perceived as a new brewing-industry trend, are actually a renewal of the models of pre-Prohibition (and even more ancient) times, when a wide variety of beer styles were made by small breweries. Today, over 500 breweries exist in the United States, many of which are smaller enterprises serving a small restaurant or local area with customized or special beers. Most microbreweries do not have the equipment availability of the larger facilities, and many cannot use adjuncts. Many microbrews, however, tend to be all-malt beers that vary with additional ingredients such as fruits and spices.

Many microbrewers liberally add hops for flavor. These microbreweries usually do not have fresh hop freezer lockers, as does Coors, and therefore purchase processed hop pellets. Because of the complexity and cost, no microbreweries can afford to malt their own barley, as Coors does.

Beer and Food

Desirable Beer Attributes

- *Appearance:* Beer should be pleasing to the eye. It should be clear, carbonated, and attractive in color.

Figure 9–3 Drawing a beer from a tap

A few beer styles, however, are intended to be served cloudy.

- *Aroma:* The bouquet should be pleasant and appetizing. It should heighten the customer's desire to taste the beer.
- *Body:* The beer should be crisp and refreshing and reflect the style of the beer.
- *Taste:* Beer should be interesting and able to impart a variety of flavors. It should be complex yet balanced, with a beckoning flavor.
- *Finish:* Ideally, beer will possess an aftertaste, but it should not linger. It should be flavorful enough to be remembered, but not leave a lingering, hanging impression.

Complementing and Contrasting Beer and Food

Considering the variety of beers offered to today's consumer, the opportunity exists to match and enjoy beer in conjunction with food.

- *American Pilsners,* such as Coors and Coors Light, traditionally stimulate the palate. Specifically, they are a well paired accompaniment to light seafood dishes. These milder beers accent rather than overpower the seafood and allow full appreciation of both.
- *Pale ales* or *red lagers,* such as Killian's Red or Killian's Brown Ale, with their stronger flavor are an appropriate companion for beef. Both are strongly flavored and complement the other by creating balance.
- *Porters* traditionally accompany oysters in the half shell. The nutty, bitter porter contrasts the salty, flavorful oyster.
- *Rauchbier,* a Bavarian lager made from smoked malt, is a natural accompaniment for smoked Atlantic salmon.
- *Bière de Paris* is made from pure dark French malts. Its lively, spicy palate complements many French dishes (e.g., Filet de Sole Bonne Femme en bouchée).
- A dark Pilsner, *Coors Extra Gold,* matches nicely with spicy Mexican dishes due to its sweet nose, malty palate, and moderate hops.
- *Raspberry* and *cherry beers,* whether artificially or naturally flavored with fruit, pair favorably with desserts.
- *Dry stouts* are a contrasting and popular dessert accompaniment.

10

Spirits and Liqueurs

Spirits and Liqueurs

Distillation *was one of the first processes used to separate one liquid from another.*

Distillation

This method is simply the application of heat to a liquid, causing evaporation. Because different liquids evaporate at different temperatures, the mixture is heated only to a temperature at which one liquid will evaporate and the balance will remain in liquid state. This process takes place in special containers designed to trap the liquid as it evaporates so that it can condense back into a liquid state.

The early use of the term *distillation,* about 800 B.C., did not necessarily refer to spirits. At the time, distillation simply involved fermented liquid that, when allowed to evaporate, became stronger and more concentrated due to the loss of water. The term *distillation,* as used by the Romans, defined a filtering process. *Distillation* is derived from the Latin term *distillare,* meaning "to drip or trickle down."

The Romans used several different methods of filtration. One process, called *distillatio perfitrom,* involved passing wine through different kinds of materials to change the flavor. Another process of distillation was *distillatio per descensum,* by which the wine was placed in a perforated pot and allowed to drip into a lower pot containing additional flavoring elements.

In the first century A.D., the method of distillation changed to the type used today. This change was due to the type of container that trapped the condensation as the liquid was heated. This method began as an experiment but soon spread throughout Asia Minor, Asia, and Europe. Sometime later, this method was refined by the development of an apparatus that simplified the process.

Alembic was the name given to the apparatus developed by the Arabs. It was shaped like a hood with an extended tube. The alembic fits over a container of heated liquid, trapping the released vapors. The vapors condense and are led away from the heat via the tube to cool into liquid form. This distillation process was used by alchemists of the day, who sought a method to *transfigure* base metal into gold. Monasteries also showed an interest in distillation. They used the method to create medicines from herbs and roots.

With the use of distillation, the industries of the Eastern world were able to excel. Perfumes, colorings, and medicinal waters were derived from this method. *Kohl,* the original term given to what we know today as eye makeup, later became *Al Kohl* and referred to anything that produced a fine vapor during distillation. *Al Kohl,* or *alcohol,* soon became the term used to describe vapors produced from the distillation of fermented beverages. It was inevitable that someone would stumble onto the distillation of liquid to produce spirits.

It is believed that in the tenth century, the first alcohol was distilled in spirit form in Italy. Until then, no written formula for alcoholic spirits existed. In the centuries that followed, several nations referred to the product of distilled, fermented beverages in their own terms. The Arabs used the phrase *ruh al hamr,* or spirit of wine, while those schooled in Latin used *aqua vitae,* or water of life. Other terms, such as *eau de vie* (water of life) and *aqua ardens* (firewater) were coined.

Alchemists, delighted in the discovery of alcoholic spirits, called them the elixir of life. Throughout medieval times, it was hoped this discovery would produce a medicine to heal the entire body. Using the spirit as the base, roots, herbs, flowers, and fruits were added to create a medicinal concoction as well as to mask the taste. During the fourteenth century, Black Death overtook Europe. The spirit elixir was used for the first time on a large scale basis as a medicine. It also was distributed as a purifier of water for those who were not ill.

Gradually, the use of distillation passed from doctor, alchemist, and monastery to private use. Winemakers and brewers created private enterprises, using alcohol for other than medicinal purposes. Household distilleries emerged, and the method of distillation improved.

The still took on new shapes, which led to the design of the modern-day pot still. The still was no longer made of glass, as was the type used by the alchemist. It was transformed into a larger pot-shaped unit, made predominantly of copper which has the best heat transfer properties. The lower half was called the boiler, and the upper portion, the still head. The still head was shaped like an inverted funnel, its spout bent into a right angle that tapered off into a cooling coil.

The alcohol vapors produced by heating the fermented brew rose from the boiler to the still head. A pipe was connected to the head to lead the vapors away from the tube to be cooled. The pipe usually ran for some length, coiling through a tank of cold water beside the still, known as the condensation tank. By passing through the cold water, the vapors quickly condensed into spirit or liqueur.

Although the pot still helped to increase the amount of production, the distillation process itself was quite laborious. After each distillation, the still had to be cleaned and refilled. The distiller had to maintain a constant check on the still head and pipe. If the pipe became clogged, an explosion was possible. At the same time, the temperature had to be increased to 173° F, which is the temperature at which alcohol begins to boil and vaporize.

Despite these difficulties, production continued, and, with household stills, a new industry was born. The production of alcoholic beverages increased as the demand increased, especially for distilled spirits. This change moved distillers away from the production of sweet herbal concoctions toward new products, such as whiskey, gin, vodka, rum, and brandy.

In Western Europe, particularly in Ireland and Scotland, the product of the fermentation of grain was being distilled as early as the tenth century. The production of this distilled spirit led to the discovery of whiskey. The spirit produced by the Hibernians (Irish) was known as *usguebaugh,* whereas that produced by the Caledonians (Scots) was known as *ulsegebaugh,* or water of life. Eventually, both of these terms were shortened to *viskel,* then *whiskey.*

The distilling of whiskey was common in Scotland, where it was distilled in almost every home. The still thus became a common household tool. Ireland was not far behind in the vast production of whiskey. Inevitably, the distillation

Figure 10–1 The three basic categories of alcoholic beverages

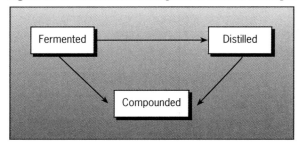

process and the use of the still were brought to the American colonies.

Initially, all whiskeys in the United States were made in the style of the Scots and the Irish, using barley malt as the predominant grain. The whiskey industry in the United States eventually started using corn rather than barley in distillation, because corn was more plentiful. Whiskey made with corn was a uniquely American invention. Corn whiskey became the popular spirit of the United States and was given a new name, bourbon.

All alcoholic beverages fall into one of three basic categories (see Figure 10–1):

- Fermented beverages made from products such as grains and fruits and have alcoholic strengths ranging from 3.2% to 14%.
- Distilled spirit beverages resulting from a pure distillation of fermented beverages.
- Compounded beverages made by combining either a fermented beverage or a spirit with flavoring substances.

Figure 10–2 summarizes the types and origins of alcoholic beverages.

Production Processes

There are five necessary steps in the production of distilled spirits, **mashing, fermenting, distilling, blend-**

Figure 10–2 Types and origins of alcoholic beverages

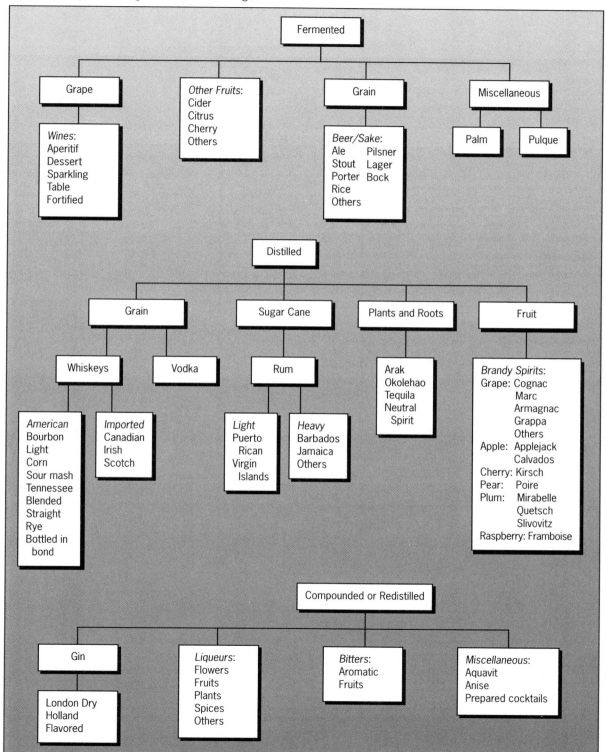

ing, and **aging** in oak barrels. For a flavored spirit, there is one more step, called **compounding**, in which no aging is done.

Mashing

Mashing is the process of turning grains to sugar. Whiskey may be produced from any type of grain, but corn, rye, wheat, and barley are used most often. The grains are first cleaned, then ground into meal. The meal is then cooked with water to release the starch. Dried barley malt is then added. The enzymes in the malt convert the grain starch to maltose or grain sugar.

Fermenting

The mash is put into a fermenter (large tank). Yeast is added, which consumes the sugar and produces alcohol. This process takes 2 to 4 days. The fermented mixture is called distiller's beer.

Distilling

Separating alcohol from water by applying heat causes the alcohol to evaporate; the vapors are trapped and condensed. The distiller's beer is heated in an enclosed tank to boil the alcohol but not the water. Remember, alcohol boils at 173° F, while water boils at 212° F. The steam from the boiled alcohol rises and is trapped. The vapors condense and become ethyl alcohol. United States law states that whiskey must be distilled at less than 190 proof (95% alcohol). It cannot be distilled at a higher proof because it would lose all the characteristics of the grain used and become a tasteless neutral spirit. Most whiskeys are distilled from 140 to 160 proof and some as low as 125 proof. Some of the impurities are removed through distillation; therefore, the colorless ethyl alcohol is still very harsh.

Blending and Aging

After distillation, the ethyl alcohol is diluted with deionized (demineralized) water and then aged. Aging takes place in charred oak barrels. The oak gives whiskey its **color,** the char **absorbs impurities,** and time alone **mellows the harshness.** The end product is smooth and textured with a rich bouquet. The character of whiskey depends on the length of time it is aged. Heavy-bodied whiskeys are aged for 8 or more years, whereas light-bodied whiskeys are aged for 4 years. If aged too long, whiskeys can absorb undesirable wood flavors. Whiskeys can be aged only in a barrel. Once bottled, the whiskey ages no further and remains unchanged until opened.

Compounding

Compounded beverages are made by combining either a fermented beverage or a spirit with flavoring substances. These beverages are derived from infusions, macerations, or percolations of products used. Distilling, or redistillation, is also a method of compounding. This process is used to flavor a fermented beverage or a natural spirit with flavoring substance. For example, gin is a spirit distilled with juniper berries.

American Whiskeys

Whiskeys vary in alcoholic strength from 110-proof American-bottled whiskey to 70-proof Canadian-bottled whiskeys. Most whiskeys sold in the United States are 80 to 86 proof, depending on the distiller and the brand.

The following designations are rigidly defined by law and are governed accordingly.

- Bourbon
- Corn
- Sour mash
- Tennessee

- Blended
- Straight
- Bottled in bond
- Rye

Bourbon

To be called bourbon, the whiskey must be made from at least 51% corn, be distilled at a proof not exceeding 160, and be aged in new charred, white oak barrels for at least 2 years. Examples are Jim Beam 80 proof, Early Times, and Old Grand Dad 86 proof.

Corn

Corn whiskey must be made from 80% corn mash and may be aged in used uncharred barrels. One example is Jim Beam Rye 86 proof.

Sour Mash

The difference between sour mash and other whiskeys is in the fermenting process. The yeast mash is soured with a lactic (milk sugar) culture (like sour dough bread) for a minimum of 6 hours. The fermented mash must contain at least 25% of the screened residue from the whiskey still, and the fermenting time must be at least 72 hours. Examples are Beam's Black Label 90 proof and Chester Graves 90 proof.

Tennessee

Tennessee whiskey is not bourbon, although the two are very similar. The difference lies in the extra steps taken after distillation. Tennessee whiskey is seeped very slowly through vats packed with charcoal, a process called leaching. Following the leaching process, the whiskey is placed in charred, white oak barrels to be aged. One example is Jack Daniels Black Label 90 proof.

Blended Whiskeys

Blended whiskeys are balanced and light bodied. A variety of straight whiskeys and grain-neutral spirits that complement each other are blended together to develop a composite flavor characteristic that will always be uniform. Blends must contain at least 20% straight whiskey on a proof-gallon basis and be bottled at not less than 80 proof. Seventy-five different straight whiskeys and grain neutral spirits go into premium blends. Examples are Seagram's 7 Crown 80 proof, Four Roses, and Corby's Reserve 80 proof.

Straight Whiskey

Straight whiskey is distilled at no more than 160 proof and aged at least 2 years in new charred oak barrels. Straight whiskey can be produced from corn, rye, barley, or wheat grains, using 100% of the selected grain. Examples are Wild Turkey Bourbon 86.8 proof and Old Charter (10 years old).

Bottled in Bond

Bottled in bond is a straight whiskey, usually bourbon or rye. The federal government requires that the whiskey be at least 4 years old, bottled at 100 proof, produced by only one distillery, and stored and bottled in a bonded warehouse under government supervision. Examples are Old Forester 100 proof, Beam's 100 proof (8 years old), and Old Grand Dad B/B 100 proof.

Rye

Rye must contain at least 51% rye grain, be distilled at no higher than 160 proof, and be aged in new charred oak barrels. One example is Jim Beam Rye 86 proof (7 years old).

Imported Whiskeys

Canadian Whisky

Canadian whisky is a whiskey blend and is light-bodied. It contains mostly Canadian corn, with a lesser amount of rye, wheat, and barley malt. For consumption in Canada, it is bottled at 70 proof. For export to the United States, it is bottled at 80 to 86.6 proof. Canadian whisky is usually 6 years old. If less than 4 years old, its age must be marked on the label. Examples are Seagram's VO 86.8 proof, Seagram's Crown Royal 80 proof, and Canadian Club 86.8 proof (6 years old).

Irish Whiskey

Irish whiskey contains no distilled spirit less than 3 years old. Irish whiskey is blended, deriving its individual personality from the native barley grain. It is made in pot stills and blended with pure, soft Irish water that has a very low mineral content. Irish whiskey is the only whiskey that is distilled three times. Only the choice "heart," or center part, of the distillate is retained each time, which yields spirits with a smooth and clean flavor. Irish whiskey is heavier and more full bodied than scotch and is usually 86 proof. Examples are John Jameson's 80 proof, Murphy's Irish 86 proof, and Dunphy's Irish (7 years old).

Scotch Whisky

Production of Scotch malt whisky begins with selection of the barley. After being cleaned, it is soaked in warm water for about 60 hours and then dried for 10 days or so, until it begins to sprout. The sprouted barley is called **malt.** Malt contains an enzyme, called diastase, which converts starches into sugars. The sprouted malt is then spread on screens over peat moss fires. The aroma of the smoke permeates the barley, which gives scotch its unique smoky flavor. After several weeks of drying, the malt is cleaned and ground into meal. The meal is then mashed, yeast is added, and fermentation takes place, The resulting liquid is called **mash beer.** The Scots use a distilling process different than that used in the United States: An old-fashioned pot still is used instead of a continuous still.

Most scotch whiskys are a blend of unmalted barley, malted barley, and other grains. However, some whiskys, such as Glenlivet, are made from a **single malt,** which means that the malt whisky is produced by a single distillery. Scotch whiskys are aged in used American oak barrels that are recycled from sherry producers. See Figure 10–3 for a flowchart of the distillery and production process for scotch. Examples of scotch are Cutty Sark (12 years old), Cutty Sark 86 proof, Chivas Regal Salute 80 proof (21 years old), Chivas Regal 86 proof (12 years old), and Glenlivet 86 proof (12 years old).

Gin

Gin is distilled from grain and receives its unique flavor and aroma from juniper berries and other herbs and spices, called **botanicals.** Gin can be made two ways: by being either redistilled or compounded. Most brands sold in the United States are distilled. Compounded gin is a mixture of neutral spirits and juniper berries. Distilled gin is redistilled completely and has the word *distilled* on the label. Gin requires no aging.

The terms, *dry gin, extra dry gin, London dry gin,* or *English dry gin,* all mean the same thing—lacking in sweetness. Dry gins are delicate, with the flavor of juniper and other botanicals more subdued. These gins blend perfectly with other flavors and are ideal for mixing.

Two factors differentiate English and American gins. The first is that English gin is distilled at a lower proof than American. The second factor is the water, which influences the character of the fermented mash and the spirits distilled from that mash.

Dutch or Genever gin is imported from Holland. It is highly flavored and rich in aromatic oils. It has a heavy taste and does not mix well with other ingredients. Dutch gins are full bodied, with a substantial juniper character.

Figure 10–3 Distillation and production process for scotch

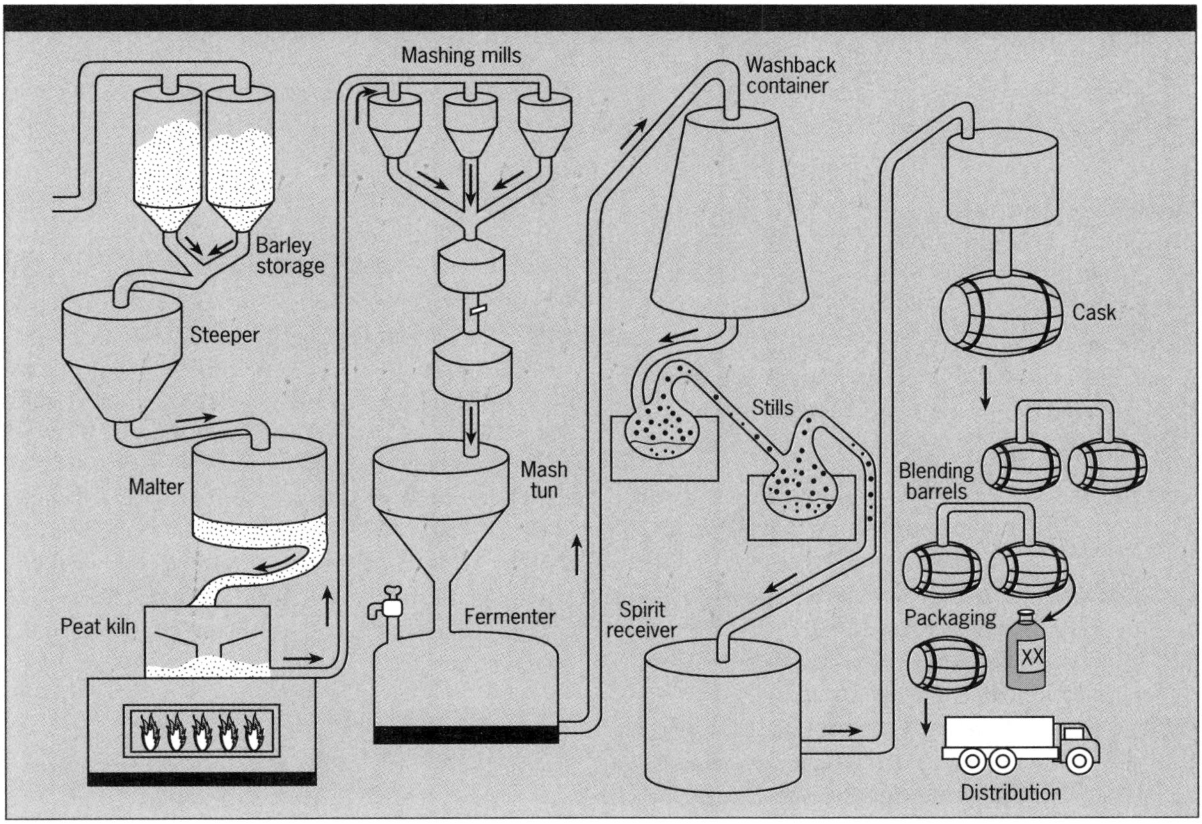

Vodka

Vodka was first distilled by the Smirnoff distilleries in Moscow in 1818. After the 1917 revolution, however, Smirnoff distilleries were disbanded. The formula for vodka was brought to America via Paris in 1930. For many years, Smirnoff was the first and only American-made vodka.

Vodka is made from potatoes and various grains, mostly corn, with some wheat added. It also may be made from white beets, as in Turkey (izmaya), or from molasses, as in Germany (closter). Vodka, like whiskey, is an alcoholic distillate from a fermented mash. Whiskey, however, is distilled at a lower proof to retain flavor. Vodka is distilled at a higher proof and then processed still further to remove all flavors. Vodka, unlike whiskey, is not aged.

United States distillers filter their vodka through activated charcoal to further remove all distinctive character, aroma, or taste so that the end product is odorless, colorless, and tasteless. Flavored varieties of vodka are popular mostly in Poland and Russia, where infusions and mixtures with herbs, grasses, leaves, spices, and seeds are used. Some are colored and, as vodka-based liqueurs, are sweetened and fruit flavored. They range from 70 proof and up.

The United States produces some fruit-flavored vodkas

as well. These are made from orange and lemon rinds and the pulp and skins of cherries.

Rum

Rum is an alcoholic beverage distilled from the fermented juice of sugar cane, sugar cane syrup, sugar cane molasses, or other sugar cane byproducts and is distilled at less than 190 proof. The proof is further reduced before bottling and it must be less than 80 proof).

Rum is produced wherever sugar cane grows, but most rums are produced in the Caribbean Islands. There are four main classifications of rum:

Light bodied	Very dry, with a light molasses taste. It is produced in Puerto Rico and the Virgin Islands.
Medium bodied	Gold, slightly mellower, and has a more pronounced taste than light-bodied rums. It is produced in Haiti, Barbados, Trinidad, and Guyana.
Full bodied	Much darker and sweeter. Has a pungent bouquet and a heavy molasses taste. Dark rums differ because of a slower fermentation and special maturation processes. It is produced in Jamaica, Martinique, and Demerara.
Light bodied (Batavia Arak)	A brandy-like rum of great pungency and used as any other rum. Arak is produced on the island of Java, Indonesia. Its fermentation process is different than that of other rums. The quality of Arak is obtained from the wild, uncultured yeast and specially cooked and dried Javanese rice that is placed in the fermenting tubs of molasses. The Arak is aged for 3 or 4 years in Java, then shipped to Holland, where it is aged for another 4 to 6 years, blended, and then bottled.

Rum also was produced in New England over 300 years ago from molasses imported from the West Indies. New England rum is now obsolete and was eliminated from the U.S. Standards of Identity in 1968. It was straight rum, distilled at less than 160 proof, with considerable body and pungency.

Brandy

The word *brandy* means "distilled wine" and has its roots in the Dutch *brandewijn,* meaning "burnt wine." Dutch traders distilled the highly acidic white wine from the Cognac region and found an appreciative market in Holland. Brandies are made by taking a wine base, from grapes or other fruits, and putting it through the distillation process. Although brandies are made in countries around the world, the best known are those of Cognac and Armagnac regions of France. Although all cognacs and armagnacs are brandies, not all brandies are cognacs or armagnacs. Only those brandies produced in the Cognac and Armagnac regions of France are entitled to carry the word *cognac* or *armagnac* on the label.

Cognac

Cognacs are the world's elite brandies, and they are rated as especially prestigious because of the grapes from which they are distilled, the chalky soil in which the grapes are grown, the humid climate, and the special distillation processes.

Three grape varietals are used predominantly: Ugni Blanc (Trebbiano) and declining amounts of Folle Blanche and Colombard. The highly acidic wine is fermented to only 7% to 8% alcohol. The double distillation reaches a 70% alcoholic spirit reflecting a ninefold increase in concentration of **congeners,** or flavor components.

Cognac is a brandy distilled from wine, made of grapes grown within the legal limits of the Charente and Charente-Maritime departments of France. The city of Cognac, on the Charente River, is the heart of the district. The entire Cognac region was delimited in 1909 and its seven subdivisions in 1936.

The quality of the cognac depends on soil. The soil at

its best is as chalky, as in Champagne. The quality ranking, based on the amount of chalk in the top soil. 35% chalk to 25% to 15%—is the progression from Grande Champagne to Petite Champagne to Borderies. Beyond the Borderies are the four bois, which have less and less chalk. The four bois are less delicate, with a distinct *goût de terroir,* or earthiness. The seven subdivisions, in order of quality, are

Grande Champagne
Petite Champagne
Borderie
Fins Bois
Bon Bois
Bois Ordinaires
Bois à Terroir

The **Grande Champagne** and **Petite Champagne** now account for about 30% of the total production of cognac. These names bear no relation to the sparkling wines of Champagne. *Champagne* in French means "open fields," a distinction made even clearer by the names of the five other districts, four of which refer to woodlands. Labels with the designation **Fine Champagne** mean that the cognac was made from 50% Grande Champagne and 50% Petite Champagne.

Cognac is distilled twice in pure copper pot stills soon after the wine has stopped fermenting. The wine is warmed in a tank and then boiled away by a steady coal fire. Two distillations are needed to get the fraction with exactly the right amount of alcohol. The first distillation produces a liquid of about 30% alcohol, called **brouillis.** This is redistilled to make the raw cognac, known as the **bonne chauffe,** which runs from the still white and clear at about 70% alcohol.

It takes 10 barrels of wine to make one barrel of cognac. The new cognac, which is colorless, is then aged in oak barrels. These barrels were traditionally made of Limousin oak, but the forest of Limousin can no longer supply all the needs of the cognac shippers.

Today, about half of the barrels in the cellars containing cognac are made of Tronçais oak. It is the interaction between oak and brandy, as well as the continual slow oxidation that takes place through the porous wood, that

gives cognac its superb and distinctive flavor. It is the barrel aging (during which the brandy also picks up color and tannin from the oak) that refines a harsh distillate into a pleasurable beverage. The longer the wood aging, the better the cognac. The cognac loses 3% to 5% of its alcoholic strength each year due to the porosity of the wood. The resulting loss is referred to as the Angel's Share.

Cognac, like all brandies, ages only as long as it remains in wood; it undergoes no further development once it is bottled. It is not the vintage that matters, as with wine, but the number of years spent in wood. Most good cognacs have spent 3 to 4 years in wood. Cognac takes on color from the aging process. It is then diluted to 40% alcohol with distilled water, and its sweetness and color are adjusted with sugar and caramels. Very special (VS) or three-star cognac means that it has been aged no less than 3 years. The Very Special Old Pale (VSOP) sold in London, beginning in Victorian times, cannot be less than 5 years of age. With older cognacs, such as Napoleons, Extras, and the XOs, there is a great variance in their ages.

Some of the best cognac houses include

Martell	Hine
Hennessy	Flapin
Remy Martin	Larsen
Courvoisier	Castillon
Otard-Dupuy	Delamain
Ricard Bisquit Dubouche	Denis-Mounie
Camus	Gaston de Lagrange
Salignac	Monnet
Prince de Polignac	

Armagnac

The world has only one other brandy that can be compared with cognac, and it, too, comes from western France. Armagnac shares only its refinement and its very high standards with cognac; the two brandies are poles apart in style and in the techniques used to make them.

Armagnac is an Appellation Controlée French grape brandy from Gascony. Its production, viticulture, distillation process, and aging are subject to detailed official inspection and strict controls.

Armagnac is a remote country region located in the heart of southwest France, between Toulouse on the east, Bordeaux and Bayonne on the west, the Pyrenees on the south, and the Garonne Valley on the north. It is divided into three sections: **Bas-Armagnac, Ténarèze,** and **Haut-Armagnac.** This is the production area entitled to appellation d'origine status. Bas-Armagnac is located in the plain of the north on the western side. It might be called the Grande Champagne of the region, except that it has sandy soil in place of chalk. Ténarèze is located in the plain of the north-central area of the region. Haut-Armagnac extends from flat plains in the northern part of the region, through the eastern part, and into the hilly area of the southern part.

Bas-Armagnac is the most westerly growing area, bordering on Les Landes. The land is sandy with little clay in the soil. Prune flavor and aroma are the dominant characteristics of these renowned brandies. Eauze (pronounced Ay-oze) is the capital, as well as the center of the Armagnac market.

Ténarèze, centrally located, has a predominantly argilo-calcaire soil (a clay and limestone mixture) and produces armagnacs with overtones of both prunes and violets that are considered on a par with those of Bas-Armagnac.

Haut-Armagnac is located in the eastern region, where the soil is mostly chalky with limestone outcroppings. Here, a large proportion of grapes is used for blending with the armagnac of the other regions; some is used for such regional specialties as prunes (and other fruit) in armagnac, as well as armagnac-based liqueurs and apéritifs. The capital of Haut-Armagnac is Auch, the largest city in the area, with a population of about 25,000.

The three principal grape varieties used in making armagnac are Ugni Blanc, Folle Blanche, and the Colombard. Other traditional varieties include the Jurançon, Clairette, Blanquette, Mozac, and Plante de Grèce.

Production Processes

Vinification

Only wines made from the aforementioned white grape varieties may be used to produce armagnac. They must be obtained through traditional wine-making methods without racking off, so that the wines still contain their lees. No oenologic product may be added. The ideal base wine should be high in fixed acidity and low in alcohol.

Distillation

Today, armagnac is produced mainly by the continuous method in a permanently installed copper still, called the alambic Armagnaçais. (The pot still, called alambic, a repasse, which is used to make cognac via the double distillation method, is currently being used in a limited way by several armagnac producers.)

When it first emerges from the still, armagnac is called *eau de feu* (firewater) and is colorless, with a powerful bouquet and flavor that mellows considerably after a few years in cask. Distillation is performed in the winter and must be completed before April 30 of the year following the harvest.

Aging

The alambic Armagnaçais' one-step technique gives armagnac a greater proportion of congeners or aromatic and flavoring elements than cognac. As soon as it comes out of the still, armagnac is stored in hand-made casks of the region's tannic-rich **Monlezun** oak. At this point, the cellar master takes over, carefully and constantly checking the aging process. The Monlezun oak helps develop the remarkable complexity of flavor and the sparkling, rich amber color for which armagnac is prized. When the dissolving of tannic matter and wood essences reaches its optimum rate, the brandy is transferred to either worked-out casks (i.e., no longer exuding tannin) or vats.

It is the cellar master's art of aging and blending that determines the essential quality of the firm's product, as well as its consistency. Once in a bottle, the brandy is stabilized and no longer ages.

Regulations and Label Language

On September 1 of the year following the harvest, armagnac receives the designation Zero (Compte 0); the following September 1, it receives the designation One (Compte 1); and so on. The word *armagnac* on the label categorizes all brandy from within the certified region. When armagnacs come exclusively from either Bas-Armagnac, Ténarèze, or Haut-Armagnac, their place of origin may be indicated on the label. Most, however, are a blend of two or three subregions.

Most armagnacs that are shipped to the United States are classified VSOP, VO, or Réserve. Any of these classifications indicates that the youngest brandy in the blend is at least Compte 4 (about 4½ years old). In the United States, a three-star armagnac indicates that the youngest brandy in this blend is Compte 2 (2½ years old). Extra, Napoleon, XO, Vieille Réserve, Hors d'Age, and similar label designations indicate that the youngest brandy is at least Compte 5 (5½ years old), although in these blends there will be greater amounts of older armagnacs. In general, all armagnacs contain much older brandies than regulations require.

Comparisons of the flavors of armagnac and cognac always classify armagnac as rustic, as having a sharper aroma, and as possessing a surprising smoothness. Armagnac also is drier than cognac. Sugar is not normally added, as it is to cognac.

Pomace Brandies

Pomace brandies are known as **Grappa** in Italy and **Marc** in France. Pomace brandies are distillates made from the pulp, skin, seeds and, stems (pomace) of grapes that are the remains of the pressing of grapes in winemaking (see Chapter 5). The pomace of other pressed fruit such as apples and pears is also used to make Eaux de Vies.

Consumers in the United States have been acquainted mostly with fiery and rather flavorless grappas but the 1990s have seen a proliferation of individual producers who make delicate brandies from single varieties such as Moscato, Bracchetto, and Nebbiolo. When oak-aged for one to two years, these brandies develop a more mellow quality. The best grappas, however, are not oak-aged but kept in glass. Grappas are also being distilled in the United States by producers such as Clear Creek in Oregon. Examples of Italian grappas are Esaffa Grappa di Barolo and Inga Grappa di Gavi Di Gavi. Marcs from the Burgundy and Champagne regions of France are particularly noteworthy.

How to Taste and Appreciate Brandy

Whatever its classified age, the following are recommendations on how brandies should be sipped and savored to appreciate their extraordinary aromas and flavors to the fullest.

Appreciation

Pour a little brandy into a clear, stemmed, glass brandy **snifter.** It should be about the size of an 8-ounce wine goblet, one that can be held comfortably in the palm of one's hand. The glass should not be more than one-third full. Hold the stem of the glass with thumb and forefinger. Examine the brandy's sparkling amber color. Gently swirl the brandy around, allowing the aroma to develop. Lift the glass to your nose and let the bouquet envelop the nostrils; then inhale, with short sniffs, the heady scents. Try to recognize the overtones of prunes, peaches, hazelnuts, and violets—what Gascons call the *goût de terroir,* the essence of the earth.

Tasting and Sipping

Next, taste, in slow sips, the smooth, deeply satisfying, grape flavor. Let the brandy sit on the tongue before rolling it about in the mouth for a moment or two. Chew it to experience the subtleties of the "velvet flame," an initial brief moment of "dancing fire" on the tongue, immediately followed by the sensation of velvety richness as the brandy is swallowed.

Rancio

Rancio is a somewhat imprecise term used to describe the richness felt on the palate, which develops in cognacs and armagnacs that have been aged in oak for 20 years or more. The deep, rich bouquets remind some tasters of a rankness, such as that found in Roquefort cheese.

Savoring

When the glass has been emptied, cup it in the hand or warm it between the palms and inhale deeply the aromas it still exudes. This is an old brandy custom called *fond du verre,* the bottom of the glass. It is said that a glass that has held a fine brandy will still retain the bouquet the next day.

Other Spirits

Tequila

Tequila has its own special flavor, which is almost tart. Tequila is obtained from the distillation of the fermented juice (sap) of the agava plant called pulque. This cactus-like plant takes between 10 and 12 years to mature. At harvest time, its long leaves or spikes are cut off, leaving only the bulbous central core, called the *piña* (pineapple). Each piña weighs between 80 and 175 pounds. Piñas are taken to the distillery, where they are cooked in pressure cookers for several hours. Then, they are cooled and shredded, and the juice is pressed out. The juice, along with fibrous pulp, is mixed with sugar, and the mash is fermented for about 4 days. To make tequila, the spirit must be redistilled to obtain the pure, colorless liquor. It is then aged in oak barrels for approximately 35 to 56 days. Gold tequila is left for 9 months or more in the 50-gallon oak barrels that give it its color. Premium tequila is aged for over 3 years.

Tequila can only come from the appellation of Tequila in the state of Jalisco or it is called mescal.

(Akvavit) Aquavit

Akvavit is made from a fermented mash of either barley malt and grain or potatoes and is flavored with caraway seeds. It is first distilled as a neutral spirit at 190 proof, reduced with water to 120 proof, and then redistilled with the flavorings. Caraway is the principal flavoring, but others, such as lemon and orange peel, cardamom, or anise,

are used. Akvavit is similar in production to gin, except that the main flavor is caraway rather than juniper berries. Akvavit generally is not aged and has an alcoholic strength of 86 to 90 proof. It is a popular beverage of Scandinavian countries where it is also spelled acquavit.

Bitters

Bitters consist of bitter and aromatic essences and flavors incorporated into an alcohol base. The flavors come from fruits, plants, seeds, flowers, leaves, bark, roots, and stems. Most bitters are proprietary brands. Their formulas are often closely guarded secrets and are handed down from generation to generation. These products are the result of infusion and distillation processes, and their one common characteristic is bitterness.

Bitters are classified by two categories: those used in a beverage and those used as a beverage. The best-known bitter is Angostura, which is made in Trinidad. This particular bitter is used as a spice in cocktails. Bitters such as Campari (from Italy) is believed to aid in digestion.

Proprietary Brands

Some proprietary brand names of the distilled spirits discussed in this chapter are provided in Figure 10–4.

Liqueurs and Cordials

A liqueur or cordial is a spirit, usually a brandy, whiskey, or grain alcohol, to which flavoring has been added. Various combinations of fruits, plants, flowers, herbs, and spices lend their flavors to the base spirit. To trace the popularity

Figure 10–4 Proprietary brand names of distilled spirits

American Whiskey
Seagram's 7
Bourbon
 Jim Beam (blended)
 Old Grand Dad (straight, bonded)
 Early Times (straight)
 Wild Turkey (straight)
Tennessee
 Jack Daniels (sour mash)

Imported Whiskey
Canadian
 Canadian Club
 Seagram's VO
 Seagram's Crown Royal
Irish
 John Jameson
 Bushmill
Scotch whiskey
 Cutty Sark
 J&B
 Dewars (White label)
 Johnnie Walker (Red label)
 Johnnie Walker (Black label) 12 years old
 Chivas Regal 12 years old
 Haig & Haig Pinch 12 years old
 Glenfiddich (straight malt) 10 years old
 Glenfiddich (straight malt) 12 years old

Gin
Beefeater
Boodles
Tanqueray
Bols Genever
Bombay
Bombay Sapphire

Vodka
Smirnoff
Fris
Absolut
Finlandia
Stolichnaya
Stolichnaya Cristall
Wyborowa (pronounced Vee-ba-rova)

Flavored Vodka
Absolut Citron
Absolut Peppar
Stolichnaya Pertsovstra
Stolichnaya Limonnaya

Rum
Virgin Island
 Barbancourt
 Lemon Hart
Jamaican
 Appleton—White
 Appleton—Gold
 Appleton—Dark
 Myers'—Platinum
 Myers'—Gold
 Myers'—Dark
Puerto Rico
 Bacardi—Silver
 Bacardi—Gold
 Bacardi—Amber
 Bacardi 151
 Bacardi—Black
 Captain Morgan—Spiced
Barbados
 Gosling Barbados
 Mount Gay Eclipse

Brandy (American)
Christian Brothers
Germain—Robin Fine

Cognac
Courvoisier, VS, VSOP, XO
Courvoisier Napoléon
Hennessy, VS, VSOP, XO
Martell, VS, VSOP, Cordon Bleu
Remy Martin, VS, VSOP, XO
Remy Martin Louis XIII

Armagnac
Cles des Ducs
St. Vivant
Marquis de Caussade
Demontal

Tequila
Jose Cuervo—Silver
Jose Cuervo—Gold
Sauza
Two Fingers

Apéritifs
Quinine apértif (bittersweet)
Campari
Cynar (fortified wine, 16 to 24% alcohol)
Lillet
Dubonnet, red and white

Other Types
Dry white wine (12 to 14% alcohol)
Dry sherry (fortified, 16 to 20% alcohol)
Champagne (12 to 14% alcohol)

of liqueurs, one can examine their fourteenth-century origins as elixirs brewed behind monastery walls and potions concocted by alchemists. While the students of alchemy searched for a fluid that could turn common metals into gold, the monks of several religious orders devoted themselves to producing liqueurs for medicinal purposes.

No discussion of the origins of contemporary liqueurs could proceed without mentioning two names that have bridged that span of centuries. Benedictine and Chartreuse exemplify the herbal blends that were developed by ancient religious orders.

Benedictine enjoys one of the most renowned reputations of all liqueurs. This famous French spirit, first made around 1510 by a member of the Benedictine order, is a complex mixture of herbs, plants, and spices incorporated into a cognac base. The present recipe for *Chartreuse* dates back to 1764, when the Carthusian monks of France expanded the original recipe to include 130 ingredients.

The intricate formulas for both the green and yellow variations of the liqueur remain in the hands of the Brothers to this day, entrusted to only five monks at a time.

Another of the first commercial liqueur distilleries—a company whose products continue to delight twentieth-century palates—was started by Lucas **Bols** in Amsterdam in 1575. Other early distillers still in operation are Rocher Frères, founded in 1705, and the house of Marie **Brizard,** which began producing liqueurs in 1755.

As the centuries passed, liqueurs kept pace with changes in popular taste, as suggested by the eighteenth-century alterations in the formula for making Chartreuse. The 1700s ushered in a shift away from what were often somewhat harsh, medicinal concoctions toward beverages more suitable for pleasurable drinking. As a result, there was greater experimentation with fruits and assorted sweetening agents.

Recipes grew increasingly elaborate, with one old English formula for a "cordial water" calling for 67 ingredients, including gold and crushed pearls. Liqueur producers also indulged their sense of humor in naming new drinks. Translated into English, some of the more popular liqueurs were titled Illicit Love, Old Woman's Milk, The Longer the Better, and Up with Your Shirt.

Today, the steps involved in the manufacture of liqueurs employ the same basic techniques used hundreds of years ago. The individual processes of **maceration, distillation,** and **percolation** can each produce a liqueur but are generally used in combination.

- **Maceration,** the simplest of these procedures, involves soaking in base alcohol the substances used for flavoring. After soaking the desired length of time, ranging from a few days to several months, the alcohol assumes the qualities of the substance. Fruits are used with this method, as well as ingredients such as coffee and vanilla beans.
- **Distillation** requires that the base spirits and flavoring substance be heated. The resulting vapor condenses in the still and forms a concentrated essence of the botanicals—usually plants, herbs, seeds, or dried fruit peels.

- **Percolation** is similar to the process of coffee making. The spirit or brandy is placed in a lower chamber, and the aromatics and flavoring agents are placed in the upper compartment. The spirit or brandy is continuously pumped over the compartment containing the aromatics and flavoring agents.

The final products of these processes, whether blended or allowed to remain pure, are cut with neutral spirits and water to produce a liquid generally ranging from 50 to 80 proof (25% to 40% alcohol). Sugar or honey is sometimes added to provide sweetness. The liquid is clear or just faintly tinted at this point, so color frequently is added.

Sharing the curative heritage of the herbal liqueurs are blends made from seeds such as caraway and anise, as well as mint and coffee. One of the oldest forms of liqueur, **anisette** has been enjoyed both for its aid to digestion and its pungent taste. Hippocrates was known to take the drink "anisum" from time to time. Although aniseed is the primary ingredient in anisette recipes, other seeds and plants or citrus peels also may be used to subtly augment the flavor.

Several contemporary liqueurs retain the romantic tales surrounding their origins. One of the more colorful histories accompanies **Drambuie,** a scotch whiskey–based liqueur. During the middle 1700s, the royal Scottish family of Stuart, the inventors of Drambuie, found themselves the victims of political turmoil and were deprived of their kingdom. In 1745, determined to reclaim the family birthright, Prince Charles Edward Stuart led an army of Highland clansmen in several successful battles against government troops. Although his forces pushed farther into England than had any previous Scottish army, defeat finally caught up with "Bonnie Prince Charlie" at Culloden in 1746. The prince fled to the island of Skye, off the Scottish coast, with a bounty of 30,000 British pounds on his head.

With fortune lost and the army disbanded, the prince had to rely on the goodwill of the island's inhabitants. Among those who aided him was John Mackinnon, forebear of the Mackinnon family that still produces Drambuie. In his gratitude for the kindness showed him, the prince gave Mackinnon the family recipe for a unique liqueur made of aged scotch whiskey, honey, and a secret essence of blended herbal oils, the exact formula for which is known today by only one Mackinnon in each generation. The name *Drambuie* is taken from the Gaelic *an dram buidheach,* for "the drink that satisfies."

The universal appeal of fruit is often enjoyed through a variety of liqueurs. Not long after the first shipments of exotic New World cargo appeared in Europe, the Dutch developed a liqueur that used bitter oranges from the West Indian island of **Curaçao,** and the product still carries the island name. Today, orange liqueurs are produced by many distilleries. One of the best-known and most successful is **Cointreau,** a product of France. The company that produces Cointreau has been owned by the family of Adolphe and Edouard Cointreau since 1849 and currently distributes its product in more than 200 countries. The base of Cointreau is a neutral spirit, which is processed with the peel of both the bitter oranges of the Caribbean and the sweet oranges harvested in Mediterranean regions.

Grand Marnier stands as the rival to Cointreau among orange liqueurs. Dating from 1827, the firm of Marnier-Lapostelle presently devotes about 80% of its production to this elegant liqueur. Cognac is used exclusively as the foundation of Grand Marnier, with which only the peels of bitter oranges are used. Unlike the clear Cointreau, Grand Marnier has a deep golden color.

Cherries are one of the most popular and available fruits the world over and probably could not help but turn up in liquid form. The house of **Peter Heering** has been producing a highly respected cherry liqueur since 1818. This Dutch firm uses an old recipe calling for the red cherries of South Denmark. Formally known as Cherry Heering, Peter Heering liqueur is consumed in many parts of the world.

Maraschino is a cherry liqueur with a markedly different character than that of Peter Heering liqueur. Special processing of the dark Marasca cherries of Yugoslavia, together with their pits, provides the cherry-almond flavor that distinguishes this liqueur. It was developed by Girolamo Luxardo in 1829 as a variation of a traditional, nonalcoholic beverage. The house of Luxardo has weathered considerable turmoil in its corner of Eastern Europe. After the original Yugoslavian distillery was destroyed in the Second World War, the current factory was built in Italy.

Closer to home, the famous U.S. product, **Southern Comfort,** benefits from a fruit readily accessible on its own soil. Originally produced in New Orleans, Southern Comfort subtly showcases the flavor of peaches, with undertones of oranges and herbs. These elements combine gracefully in a base of old bourbon whiskey.

The versatility of liqueurs is a key to their continued success. They are increasingly used as an ingredient in cocktails, offering almost limitless variety to the creative bartender. Gourmet cooking is another natural forum for liqueurs, particularly desserts. Because alcoholic content is dissipated with heating, only the concentrated flavor of the liqueur is imparted to the preparation.

Whether ancient herbal blends or exotic modern concoctions, liqueurs add a special touch to the eating and drinking experience. It is only necessary to look at their distinguished history and promising future to realize that liqueurs are one of the world's most enduring pleasures.

Production Methods

Liqueurs are made by mixing or redistilling neutral spirits with fruits, flowers, herbs, seeds, roots, plants, or juices to which sweetening has been added. Liqueurs and cordials differ from all other spirits because they must contain at least 2.5% sugar by weight. The sugar source may be cane, beet, maple, honey, or corn, or a combination of these. Liqueurs with a sugar content between 2.5% and 10% may be labeled *dry,* because they are not very sweet. Most liqueurs and cordials contain up to 35% sweetening agent.

There are two basic ways of extracting flavors when making liqueurs:

- Cold method, generally using fruit flavors
- Hot method, using plant products, seeds, peels, and flowers

Each method encompasses several processes, and each fruit or plant product is handled differently.

Cold Method

Infusion or Maceration
The cold method is used when the flavoring material is sensitive to heat. Cold extractions can take up to a year, because attempts to make the process go faster by using heat would destroy the flavor. If crushed fruits are steeped in water, the process is **infusion.** If fruits are steeped in alcohol, the process is **maceration.**

The water or brandy eventually absorbs almost all of the aroma, flavor, and color of the fruit or berry. In some cases, when the stones (seeds) of the fruit are present, some of the oil from the stones is also extracted, which accounts for the slight bitter almond undertone sometimes found in such liqueurs as apricot, peach, and cherry.

When ready, the liquid is drawn off and allowed to rest for several days in a storage tank (stainless steel) that will not impart any flavor, and then is filtered. The mass of remaining fruit still contains useful alcohol and some essential flavorings. To recover them, the mass is placed in a still, and the last drop of flavor is extracted by distillation. The distillate may then be added to the original maceration to give it more character. The finished maceration is then sweetened to the desired richness by adding sugar and/or other sweetening material in syrup form. The finished product is sometimes aged before bottling.

Percolation
Another cold method, percolation or brewing, is somewhat like making coffee. The flavoring agent, in the form of leaves or herbs, is placed in the upper part of the apparatus. Brandy or another spirit is placed in the lower part and is pumped up over the flavoring and allowed to percolate through it, extracting and carrying down the aroma and flavor. This process is repeated continuously for weeks or months until most of the flavor constituents have been obtained. The spirit is then distilled to obtain whatever flavor remains and then mixed with the original percolate. It is then filtered, sweetened with simple syrup, and often

bottled at once, although some plant liqueurs of this group are aged for a time.

Hot Method

Distillation
The hot extraction method is used mostly for seeds and flowers, such as anise, caraway, orange peel, mint, roses, and violets. These materials can withstand some heat and benefit from a quicker extraction of flavor than is provided by the slower cold methods.

The distillation method is normally performed in small- to medium-sized copper pot stills. The normal procedure is to steep the flavoring agent—plant, seed, root, or herb—in alcohol for several days, after which it is placed in the still with additional spirits and is distilled. A vacuum is created so that distillation can take place at a lower temperature, preserving more of the floral aroma. The resultant distillate, always colorless, is sweetened with simple syrup and colored with natural vegetable matter or approved food dyes.

Distinct Categories of Liqueurs

- **Fruit-flavored** liqueurs are the most popular. The label generally indicates which fruit was used to produce the liqueur; for example, the Midori label mentions melons, the Cocoribe label mentions coconuts, and the Peter Heering label indicates that the liqueur is cherry flavored.
- **Seed-based** liqueurs do not use a single seed; they use a variety of ingredients, with one seed flavor being predominate.
- **Herbs** will not stand out, except for mint or aniseed. Herb categories use a combination of herbs and sometimes seeds and flowers. (Chartreuse contains over 125 different ingredients.)
- **Peels** frequently provide the flavor. For example, the orange flavor of Curaçao comes from orange peels.
- **Crèmes** are indicative of the creamy texture and sweet taste of the liqueur. Crèmes take the name of the dominant ingredient. They are usually sweeter than other cordials and are fruit flavored.

Fruit Brandies

The fermented mash of fruits other than grapes is the source of a wide variety of unique brandies. There are three categories:

- Brandies made with apples and pears
- Brandies made with stone fruits, such as cherries, plums, and apricots
- Brandies made from berries, such as raspberries, strawberries, blackberries, and elderberries

Fruit brandies are produced when the fully ripened fruit is gathered and thoroughly mixed or mashed with wooden paddles in a wooden tub, where it is allowed to ferment—stones and all.

After 6 weeks, when fermentation is complete, the contents of the tub are placed in a pot still and distilled twice. A small amount of oil from the stones is distilled again with the spirit. The spirit is distilled to a fairly low proof (around 100 proof or less) so that the maximum fruit aroma and flavor are retained.

Some of the most popular fruit brandies are **Applejack** and **Calvados,** which are made from apples; **Apricot** brandy, made from apricots; **Kirsch** and **Kirschwasser,** made from cherries; **Prunelle** and **Slivovitz,** made from plums; **Framboise,** made from raspberries; and **Fraise,** made from strawberries.

How and When to Serve Liqueurs and Cordials

Liqueurs and cordials, being sweet and potent and containing certain beneficial essential oils, are natural digestives. They are popular as after-dinner drinks. During Prohibition, however, liqueurs were used widely as cocktail ingredients, because their rich sweetness helped to cover up the harsh bite of bootlegged spirits. A dash or two of a liqueur gave a cocktail added smoothness, texture, and palatability.

In France, certain liqueurs were used in the form of highballs. Crème de Cassis was mixed with French vermouth and soda or with wine to make **Kir. Frappés,** a popular way of serving liqueurs, are made by filling a small stem glass with shaved ice and pouring liqueur into it.

Proprietary and Generic Brands

Proprietary liqueurs are produced from closely guarded secret formulas and are marketed under **registered trademark** brands. Each is produced by only one house. No other house may produce a product exactly like it. **Generic** brands are those that are produced by many different companies all over the world. Because many producers use different flavoring formulas, there are variations in brands that use the same name. See Table 10–1 on page 286 for a list of proprietary and generic brands of liqueurs and cordials.

Table 10–1 Popular Brands of Liqueurs and Cordials

Alize*	From France; blend of passion fruit and cognac
Amaretto	Aromatic apricot-almond liqueur; distinctive flavor and bouquet; made from almonds and apricots steeped in aquavit, a fusion of alcohol; today, one of the great-selling cordial flavors
Amaretto di Saronno*	"The Italian liqueur of love"
Anisette	Sweet, mild, aromatic, with pleasant anise flavor reminiscent of licorice; white and red; flavor blend of aniseed (for which it is named) and aromatic herbs
B&B liqueur D.O.M.*	Delicate finesse of Benedictine D.O.M., with drier cognac
Benedictine D.O.M.*	Classic French herb liqueur
Boggs Cranberry Liqueur*	Tart, tangy taste of juice of native-grown cranberries; red
Campari*	Italian bittersweet spirits apéritif specialty; light ruby red; produced by infusion of aromatic and bitter herbs with orange peel
Chambord Liqueur Royale de France*	From France; rich aroma and taste of framboises (small black raspberries) and other fruits and herbs combined with honey
Chartreuse*	Classic herb liqueur with subtle flavor and aroma drawn from 130 wild mountain herbs distilled and blended in brandy; two varieties: green (110 proof, brisk, pungent, and reminiscent of exotic herbs) and yellow (80 proof; honey makes this the sweetest of the Chartreuse family)
Cherry Heering*	Danish cherry liqueur; flavor and aroma from the juice of fresh, ripe Danish cherries
Cherry Marnier*	French cherry-flavored liqueur; rich cherry taste with a flavor hint of the cherry pit
Cocoribe Liqueur*	Refreshing flavor of coconut and light Virgin Islands rum; white
Cointreau*	Classic French specialty orange liqueur; white; fragrant, mellow bouquet, with subtle hint of orange; produced by blending sweet and bitter Mediterranean and tropical orange peels
Cream liqueurs Baileys* (dominant brand) Carolans* Emmets* Leroux* Myers* O'Darby* Crème de Grand Marnier* Mozart Chocolate*	Dairy-fresh cream blended with spirits and natural flavorings; Irish whiskey most widely used spirit; brandy, cordials, rum, and vodka also used; flavor is rich, subtle, with mellow bite of spirit; shelf-stable; some brands use nondairy creams
Crème de Banana	Full flavor of fresh, ripe bananas; also called banana liqueur
Crème de Cacao (brown)	Rich, creamy, deep chocolate flavor drawn from cocoa and vanilla beans, with hint of spices added
Crème de Cacao (white)	Like brown crème de cacao, but not identical; with loss of color, chocolate flavor less intense
Crème de Cassis	Rich, fruity, with full flavor of black currants from Dijon, France
Crème de Framboise	Raspberry-flavored liqueur
Crème de Menthe (white)	Virtually identical to green crème de menthe; because the green coloring has not been added, can be used in more drink recipes

(continued)

*Proprietary brand.

Table 10–1 Popular Brands of Liqueurs and Cordials (continued)

Crème de Menthe (green)	Refreshing, tangy, natural mint flavor; cool, clean, pleasant to taste; made as spirit flavored with several types of mint and peppermint
Curaçao	Orange character, from the peel of bittersweet "green" oranges grown on the Dutch island of Curaçao in the West Indies; clear amber; like Triple Sec but slightly sweeter and more subtle orange flavor; lower proof
Drambuie*	Old scotch whiskey delicately honeyed and spiced; produced in Scotland by subtle blending of scotch with heather honey and gentle suggestion of herbs and spices
Dutch Delight*	Imported from Holland; cream dessert liqueur flavored with chocolate and vanilla
Frangelico*	Wild hazelnuts blended with berries and herbs
Fruit-flavored brandy	Flavor and aroma of selected ripe fruit identified by product name (blackberry, apricot, etc.); higher in proof and drier than companion liqueur (always 70 proof); always color of fruit
Fruit liqueurs	Flavor and aroma of fresh ripe fruit identified by product name (apricot, blackberry, etc.); lower proof and sweeter than companion fruit-flavored brandy; always color of fruit
Goldwasser	Flavor blend of herbs, seeds, roots, and citrus fruit peels; tiny flakes of gold leaf so light they cannot be felt on the tongue but shimmer in this clear liquid; also called gold liqueur
Grand Marnier*	From France; classic cognac-based orange liqueur; flavor and bouquet from peels of wild bitter oranges
Honey Blonde*	Honey-based imported liqueur from Denmark
Irish Mist*	From Ireland; flavor blend of four whiskeys, honeys, heather, clover, and essence of a dozen herbs; amber
Jägermeister*	From Germany; distinctive flavor blend of 56 roots, herbs, and fruits
Kahlua*	Coffee liqueur from Mexico; rich flavor and aroma of choicest coffees; dark brown
Kahlua Royale*	Mexican liqueur made from Kahlua, fine brandy, a hint of chocolate, and elegance of oranges
Kokomo*	Highly mixable tangerine-pineapple–flavored liqueur.
Kümmel	One of the oldest liqueurs; fairly dry, colorless, and usually 70 proof or over; essential flavor is caraway with a hint of cumin seed and anise
La Grande Passion*	French blend of armagnac with passion fruit
Lemonier*	Lemon-peel liqueur; imported from France
Licor 43*	Blend of vanilla and citrus flavors
Liquore Galliano*	Golden Italian liqueur; distinctive flavor of anise and vanilla; rich, sweet, palatable; natural flavorings of seeds, herbs, and spices
Liquore Strega*	From Italy; rich, fragrant, golden liqueur combining flavors of more than 70 herbs
Lochan Ora*	Imported from Scotland; distinctive scotch-based liqueur with subtle flavors drawn from ingredients from Curaçao and Ceylon
Malibu*	From Canada; flavor blend of white rum and coconut

(continued)

*Proprietary brand.

Table 10–1 Popular Brands of Liqueurs and Cordials (continued)

Mandarine Napoléon*	From Belgium; a tangerine liqueur; flavor and bouquet of ripe Andalusian tangerines and cognac
Metaxa*	Brandy-like Greek liqueur; grape base, slightly sweet, with a distinctive taste
Midori*	Imported from Japan; light, refreshing taste of fresh honeydew melon; green
Mohola*	From Japan; flavor of ripe mangos
Monte Teca*	Tequila-based liqueur imported from Mexico; rich, golden taste
Opal Nera*	Imported from Italy; color of black opal; anise and elderflower flavor with hint of lemon
Ouzo*	Sweet, white Greek liqueur; licorice-like anise flavor; slightly drier and stronger proof than anisette; when water or ice added, Ouzo turns milky white
Pear William	Delicate flavor of fresh Anjou pears from France's Loire Valley
Pernod*	From France; blend of select aniseed, special flavorings, and natural herbs in a spirit base
Peter Heering*	Danish cherry-flavored liqueur produced since 1818 from world-famous Danish cherries; formerly known as Cherry Heering
Petite Liqueur*	From France; cognac and sparkling wine with a hint of coffee; amber
Pimm's Cup*	Tall "sling" drinks imported from England (Pimm's Cup No. 1 is the gin sling)
Praline Liqueur*	Rich, mellow vanilla- and pecan-based flavor of the original New Orleans praline confection
Ricard*	Anise and herb liqueur from France
Rock and Rye	Whiskey-based liqueur that contains crystals of rock candy; flavored with fruits, sometimes containing pieces of fruit
Sabra*	From Jaffa, Israel; flavors of orange and fine chocolate are combined
Sambuca Romano*	Italian liqueur based on elderberry and anise flavors

Schnapps
  Apple Barrel*
  Aspen Glacial (peppermint)*
  Cool Mint*
  Cristal (anise)*
  DeKuyper Peachtree (peach)*
  Dr. McGillicuddy (menthomint)*
  Rumple Minze (peppermint)*
  Silver Schnapps (100-proof peppermint)*
  Steel (85-proof peppermint)*
	Light, refreshing, easy to enjoy, unlike traditional liqueurs, which are made predominantly for after-dinner sipping and are too sweet and syrupy for straight drinking; enjoyed with many mixers, especially peach with orange juice

Sloe Gin	Bouquet and tangy fruity flavor resembling wild cherries; red; made from the fresh fruit of the sloeberry
Southern Comfort*	High-proof American-made, peach-flavored liqueur with a bourbon whiskey base
Tia Maria*	Jamaican coffee liqueur with the flavor of fresh coffee; dark brown
Triple Sec	Crystal-clear orange flavor; like Curaçao but drier and higher in proof; flavor blend of peels of tangy, bittersweet "green" Curaçao and sweet oranges

(continued)

*Proprietary brand.

Table 10–1 Popular Brands of Liqueurs and Cordials (continued)

Truffles*	Liqueur du chocolate; delicate combination of spirits and imported chocolate flavors
Tuaca*	Golden Italian liqueur with hint of herbs and fruit peels in brandy base
Vandermint*	Imported from Holland; Dutch chocolate with touch of mint
Yukon Jack*	100-proof blend of Canadian whiskies
Wild Turkey Liqueur*	Bourbon base; herbs, spices, and other natural flavorings; amber

*Proprietary brand.

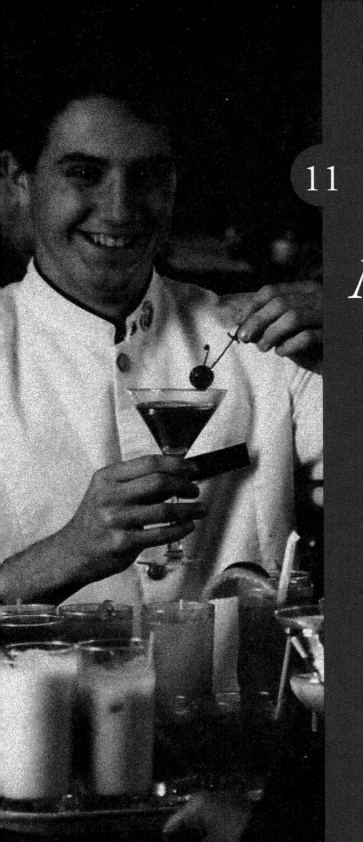

11

Mixology

Mixology

Mixology is the study of drink mixes. Those who study mixology—mixologists or bartenders—are required to master hundreds of beverage recipes. Most bartenders work in restaurants, bars, hotels, private clubs, and resorts and on cruise lines. This chapter focuses on the appropriate behavior and rules necessary to be a successful bartender, the current procedures to follow in setting up a typical bar, and a number of drink recipes.

What Makes a Good Bartender?

A good bartender should possess the following:

- **Good personal hygiene,** appearance, and knowledge of sanitary laws
- **Positive mental attitude,** including the ability to make guests feel welcome
- **Mixology expertise**
- **Organizational skills,** including accuracy and control of the environment
- **Knowledge of current events,** sports, or any topic suitable to the concept and clientele
- **Knowledge of the laws** regarding alcohol service and ability to recognize behavioral cues indicating level of intoxication

Rules for a Bartender

- Develop a good memory for the faces of your regular customers and their drink preferences. Greet them cordially.
- Handle complaints in a courteous manner. If the customer complains about a drink, either remedy it or mix another, while maintaining inventory control.
- After serving customers, step back or move away. Never give the appearance that you are listening to a conversation. Do not join in unless asked!
- Never hurry customers or be impatient if they are slow drinkers.
- Be cooperative and pleasant with fellow employees. Customers can sense and detect tension.
- Answer the telephone quietly. Never state that a particular person is present. Ask, "Who is calling?" first, tell the caller you will check to see if that person is available, then let the customer decide whether to answer the call.
- Keep ashtrays emptied and the bar dry and clean.
- Use a fresh cocktail napkin with each drink.
- Always use a fresh glass, unless otherwise requested by the customer.
- Use the appropriate glass and garnish.
- Pick glasses up by the stem or base only. Never pick up glasses by the rim or with fingers in the glass.
- Never fill a glass to more than one-fourth inch from rim.
- When in doubt, use a measure for drinks.
- When pouring more than one drink of the same kind, fill the glasses half full, then come back and keep filling until each glass is even. Never fill one glass at a time. Trying to even up already full glasses can be costly.
- Use cubed ice or large pieces of ice. Fine ice melts too rapidly and dilutes the drink too quickly.
- Follow standard recipes or house recipes, but take into account the customer's tastes and preferences. Following recipes too rigidly may drive customers away; being too lax will increase bar costs.
- Shake drinks rapidly in shaker. Too long a shake will dilute the drink. A 10-second shake will add a ½ to ¾ ounce additional volume of liquid to the drink.
- Always place the glass on the bar or rail so that the customer can see what you are doing. Then use the shaker or mixer glass.
- When finished with a bottle, put it back in its proper place. This saves time.
- Ring drinks on the guest check and lay it face down in front of the customer. Itemize by writing the order on the check.

Note: Never sit at the bar when on or off duty. It is unprofessional because it encourages familiarity with customers.

Bar-Opening Procedure

- Open the bar on time. All mise en place should be complete and the bar fully stocked and ready.
- Check the cash register by first clearing it. Count bank cash and record; then count and check bar guest checks.
- Place clean ashtrays (with books of matches) on the bar.
- Fill the three-compartment sink: (1) wash, (2) rinse, and (3) sanitize. Wash any glasses and leave them on the drain board (see Figure 11–1).
- Check bottled drinks; rotate and restock them according to established par stocks. Restock liquor issued for the day. Turn in empty bottles.
- Clean soda gun. Check soda cannister levels. Check carbon dioxide pressure.
- Check fruit garnish, fruit juices, cream, and other bar mixes. Wash containers, refill, and refrigerate.
- Prepare garnishes sufficient for one shift.
- Check all sundry supplies and bar implements.
- Wash and polish the bar counter; wash sinks and ice bins. Then wipe the neck of each bottle on the back bar. Line the bottles with labels and pourers facing the same direction.
- Visit the restroom for self-inspection.
- Keep the register key with you at all times.

Method for Washing Glasses by Hand

- Wash in first compartment with warm water at 110° F to 120° F, using washing compound, brush, and "elbow grease." *Remember:* Washing compound *does not* sanitize glasses.
- Rinse glasses in second compartment by immersion in clean, warm water. Change the rinse water frequently. Do not rinse glasses in dirty water.
- Sanitize glasses in third compartment by use of hot water or a chemical sanitizer. Rinse glasses in clean hot water at a temperature of at least 170° F for 30 seconds. In some states, a temperature of 180° F is required, or a chemical solution at a minimum of 75° F is recommended.
- Drain and air-dry glasses. Store them inverted, in a clean and dry place.

Using Chemicals

A sanitizing solution should contain one of the following:

- At least 50 parts per million (ppm) of available chlorine at a temperature of not less than 75° F
- At least 220 ppm of a quaternary ammonium compound
- At least 12.5 ppm of available iodine in a solution with a pH not less than 5.0 and a temperature not less than 75° F

A suitable field test kit should be available that will effectively measure the chemical concentration at any time.

Bar-Closing Procedure

- Wipe and thoroughly clean speed rack; wipe bottles and replace.
- Wash and dry empty glass shelves to receive clean glasses.
- Collect all used glassware and place on the counter above the sink area. Wash hands.
- Wash glassware one type at a time; Wash cream drink glasses last. Replace on shelf covered by air mats.
- Rinse and wash sinks, and dry them to prevent rust or scale.
- Wash and polish drainboard and other parts of the sink.
- Clean out ice bin and wipe dry.
- Sweep floor and remove garbage container.
- Wrap or cover all fruit garnish with lids or plastic wrap and refrigerate for the next day.
- Top all fruit juice containers, wash empties, and store.
- Fill in day's requisition for liquor, wine, and beer.
- Stock coolers for the next shift.

Figure 11–1 Standard bar unit and set-up

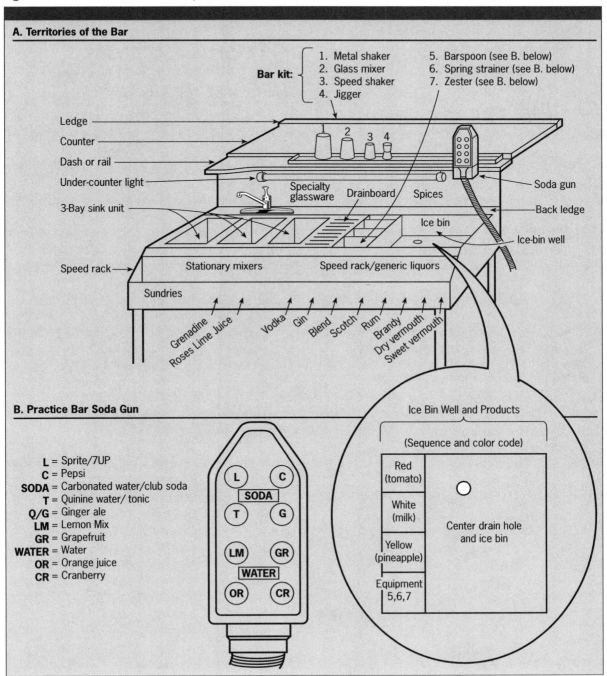

A. Territories of the Bar

Bar kit:
1. Metal shaker
2. Glass mixer
3. Speed shaker
4. Jigger
5. Barspoon (see B. below)
6. Spring strainer (see B. below)
7. Zester (see B. below)

Ledge
Counter
Dash or rail
Under-counter light
3-Bay sink unit
Speed rack
Sundries

Specialty glassware
Drainboard
Spices
Ice bin
Soda gun
Back ledge
Ice-bin well

Stationary mixers
Speed rack/generic liquors

Grenadine
Roses Lime Juice
Vodka
Gin
Blend
Scotch
Rum
Brandy
Dry vermouth
Sweet vermouth

B. Practice Bar Soda Gun

L = Sprite/7UP
C = Pepsi
SODA = Carbonated water/club soda
T = Quinine water/ tonic
Q/G = Ginger ale
LM = Lemon Mix
GR = Grapefruit
WATER = Water
OR = Orange juice
CR = Cranberry

L C
SODA
T G
LM GR
WATER
OR CR

Ice Bin Well and Products
(Sequence and color code)

Red (tomato)
White (milk)
Yellow (pineapple)
Equipment 5,6,7

Center drain hole and ice bin

- Count guest checks and check against issue register. Note checks that are not used.
- Close out cash register according to house policy.
- Check security and lock up.

Back Bar Setup

The back bar should be set up 1) to display bottles attractively to promote sales, and 2) functionally to assist the bartender. The setup should be standardized and arranged in the following order so the bartender can find the needed liquor in the most expeditious manner:

Row   Sequence

1   Proprietary-brand distilled spirits in sequence of products: Scotches, Canadians, imported whites, and Americans

2   Generic liqueurs and flavored brandies, arranged alphabetically, A–T

3   Rums and proprietary-brand liqueurs, arranged alphabetically, followed by seldom-used brands

First Row	Second Row	Third Row
Chivas Regal	Apricot-flavored	Bacardi Light Rum
Dewars	brandy	Mount Gay Gold Rum
Canadian Club	Crème de banana	Myers' Dark Rum
Seagram's VO	Blue Curaçao	Amaretto di Saronno
Seagram's 7	Dark crème de	Campari
Smirnoff	cacao	Cognac
Stolichnaya or	Light crème de	Cointreau
Absolut	cacao	Drambuie
Beefeater	White crème de	Frangelico
Tanqueray	menthe	Galliano*
Tequila	Green crème de	Kahlua
Old Grand Dad	menthe	Midori
Jack Daniels	Orange Curaçao	Peter Heering
	Peachtree	Southern Comfort
	schnapps	
	Peppermint	
	schnapps	
	Triple sec	

*Galliano bottle is to the left of the steps or shelf.

Cocktails and Mixed Drinks

History of the Cocktail

The cocktail is an American institution, and there are many versions of the name's origin. One version dates back to 1779 in a tavern located near Yorktown, New York, owned by Betsy Flanagan. Betsy's Tavern was a meeting place for the American and French officers of Washington's Army, who drank a concoction called a bracer. As the story goes, Betsy arranged for the patrons of her tavern to have a chicken feast. After the feast, they moved to the bar to continue the celebration with bracers. To their amusement, they found each bottle of bracer decorated with a cock's tail. A toast was requested, and one of the Frenchmen exclaimed: "Vive le cock tail."

It is worth noting that the development of hundreds of mixed drinks was in large measure a byproduct of Prohibition, because bootlegged liquors needed to be mixed with juices, cream, or sodas to become palatable.

Differences between Cocktails and Mixed Drinks

A **cocktail** is a fairly short drink made by mixing liquor and/or wine with fruit juices, eggs, and/or bitters, by either stirring or shaking the concoction in a bar glass (glass mixer). A **mixed drink** is liquor combined with a mixer, usually served in a tall glass over ice.

The object of a cocktail is the mixing of two or more ingredients to create a new flavor that is both pleasing and palatable. Unless requested by the customer, no single ingredient should overshadow the others. An unbalanced mixture produces an unsatisfying drink. Because cocktails are always mixed with ice, their strength varies with the length of time they remain in contact with the ice, which dilutes the liquor as it melts. Melting ice adds one half to three fourths ounce more liquid to a cocktail if it is shaken for 10 seconds and proportionately more if shaken longer.

Differences between cocktails and mixed drinks include

- Glassware
  1. Cocktails—**stem** glass
  2. Mixed drinks—**base** glass
- Procedure
  1. Cocktails—**stirred** or **shaken**
  2. Mixed drinks—**ice down–pour** or **speed shake**
- Presentation
  1. Cocktails—**up**
  2. Mixed drinks—tall, **with ice**

Procedures for Making Cocktails and Mixed Drinks

The following are definitions of the procedures used in mixing or building cocktails or mixed drinks:

For **cocktails served up:**

Stir: To gently agitate with ice; to chill and blend by stirring gently
Shake: To violently agitate with ice; to disperse or incorporate heavy ingredients

For **mixed drinks and cocktails requested on the rocks:**

Ice down–pour: To place ice in a service glass and then add liquor and mixer; serve as is
Speed shake: To agitate with ice; to disperse or incorporate heavier ingredients in a service glass with ice

Before each of these procedures is explained in greater detail, it is important to become familiar with relevant terminology and the types of alcohol that are used as bases of many cocktails and mixed drinks.

Terms Used at the Bar

- *Back:* Chaser, on the side
- *Float:* Last ingredient added to a drink after the usual procedure. Floats find their own space. *Do not incorporate.*
- *Free-pour:* The pouring of spirits or liqueurs from a bottle without the use of a measuring device, such as a jigger.
- *Hold/no garbage:* No garnish.
- *Jigger:* A legal measure of 1.5 ounces.
- *Light:* Short count on liquor; same amount of mixer.
- *On the rocks:* Served on ice, usually in RXS glass.
- *Shot of:* A measure of liquid, usually served straight up or neat; volume determined by the house.
- *Straight up or neat:* Served without ice; never comes into contact with ice.
- *Tall/long:* Drink is served in a 8- to 16-ounce highball or zombie glass; increase mixer, but not liquor.
- *Up:* Prepared with ice to chill; served without ice in a stem glass.

Eight Bases for Alcoholic Beverages

1. Vermouth — Cocktail category
2. Sours and Rose's lime juice — Cocktail category
3. Cream — Cocktail category
4. Polynesian or tropical — Mixed drinks category
5. Carbonated and juice-based highball — Mixed drinks category
6. Cordials — Two-liquor drinks
7. Wines and punches
8. Specialties — Frozen ice cream and spirited caffeines

Note: The base ingredient or mixer never changes. Liquor changes according to the name of the drink. The cocktails and mixed drinks presented on subsequent pages are only a sampling of a vast array of concoctions available in mixology.

The following tables illustrate procedures and glassware used for various types of drinks.

COCKTAILS

Category and Name of Drink	Procedure		Glass	
	Served Up	Served on the Rocks	Served Up	Served on the Rocks
Vermouth Base				
Martini	Stir	Ice down–pour	Cocktail	Rocks
Manhattan	Stir	Ice down–pour	Cocktail	Rocks
Rob Roy	Stir	Ice down–pour	Cocktail	Rocks
Negroni	Stir	Ice down–pour	Cocktail	Rocks
Gibson	Stir	Ice down–pour	Cocktail	Rocks
Short Sours				
All sours	Shake	Speed shake	Sour	Rocks
Bacardi Cocktail	Shake	Speed shake	Cocktail	Rocks
Between the Sheets	Shake	Speed shake	Cocktail	Rocks
Side Car	Shake	Speed shake	Cocktail	Rocks
Daiquiri	Shake	Speed shake	Cocktail	Rocks
Margarita	Shake	Speed shake	Champagne coupe	Rocks
Jack Rose Cocktail	Shake	Speed shake	Cocktail	Rocks
Kamakazi	Shake	Speed shake	Cocktail	Rocks
Gimlet	Shake	Speed shake	Cocktail	Rocks
Short Cream Base				
Brandy Alexander	Shake	Speed shake	Champagne coupe	Rocks
Grasshopper	Shake	Speed shake	Champagne coupe	Rocks
Golden Dream	Shake	Speed shake	Champagne coupe	Rocks
Pink Squirrel	Shake	Speed shake	Champagne coupe	Rocks

MIXED DRINKS (all on the rocks)

Category and Name of Drink	Procedure	Glass	Category and Name of Drink	Procedure	Glass
Long Cream Base			*Tropical-Polynesian*		
Orgasm	Speed shake	Highball	Mai Tai	Speed shake	Collins
Toasted Almond Bar	Speed shake	Highball	Planter's Punch	Speed shake	Collins
Girl Scout Cookie	Speed shake	Highball	Zombie	Speed shake	Sling/zombie
White Russian	Speed shake	Highball	Pina Colada	Speed shake	Sling/zombie
Long Sours			*Highball*		
(Tom) Collins	Speed shake	Collins	Soda Highball	Ice down–pour	Highball
Ward 8	Speed shake	Collins	Juice Highball*	Ice down–pour	Highball
Sloe Gin Fizz	Speed shake	Collins	*All Cordials*	Ice down–pour	Rocks
Singapore Sling	Speed shake	Sling/zombie			
Long Island Ice Tea	Speed shake	Sling/zombie			

*Exception to the rule for juice-based drinks: Speed shake juice-based highballs that have a **liqueur** with a juice mixer.

Vermouth Based Drinks

There is no standard recipe for Martinis on which all bartenders agree. Tastes change with time. The Martini has always been the most popular cocktail. It is a dry, sharp, and appetite-whetting drink. Through the years, the cocktail has become progressively drier. By the time it was referred to as a Martini, it had become a mixture of equal parts of gin and dry vermouth. Before the first World War, the standard recipe was two parts gin to one part dry vermouth. For 20 years after the repeal of Prohibition the standard recipe was four to one. Today's recipe has returned to two parts gin to one part dry vermouth.

The Manhattan was named after Manhattan, New York. As mentioned previously, to cut the harshness of bootlegged liquor, syrups and aromatic flavorings were used. The original Manhattan was made with bitters, sugar, and much more vermouth than is used today, in addition to whiskey or bourbon. The basic recipe for a Manhattan is sweet vermouth and whiskey. If dry vermouth is used, it becomes a Dry Manhattan. If both sweet and dry vermouth are used, it becomes a Perfect Manhattan.

A Rob Roy is a Scotch Manhattan. Scotch is used in place of whiskey or bourbon. The name *Rob Roy* comes from Scotland. One can make the same variations for a Rob Roy as for a regular Manhattan.

All vermouth-based cocktails are served up in a cocktail glass. The stir procedure is used, unless the customer requests the cocktail be on the rocks. Then the procedure is ice down–pour, and the drink is served in a rocks glass.

Mechanics of Stir and Ice Down–Pour Procedures

For the stir procedure:

- Chill a stemmed glass by filling it with ice. Set it aside (optional).
- Fill a mixing glass one-fourth full of ice.
- Pour base first; then add the liquor into the mixing glass.
- Hold the mixing glass with fingers closed at the base and stir. Hold the barspoon by its helix and roll it back and fourth between thumb and index finger for about 3 to 4 seconds. Gently remove the barspoon.
- Remove the ice from the chilled glass.

- Using a spring strainer over the mouth of the mixing glass, strain ingredients into the glass.
- Garnish.

The stir procedure is illustrated in Figure 11–2.

For the *ice down-pour* procedure:

- Fill a rocks glass with ice.
- Pour liquor first; then add the base. (Note the difference from the stir procedure.)
- Garnish.
- Add stirrer or sip-stix.

The following recipes utilize the stir or ice down–pour procedures in their preparation.

✓ **Martinis**

✓Martini
1½ ounces	Gin
¾ ounce	Dry vermouth
	Olive or zest

Dry Martini
2 ounces	Gin
½ ounce	Dry vermouth
	Olive or zest

∨ *Vodka Martini*
1½ ounces	Vodka
¾ ounce	Dry vermouth
	Olive or zest

Extra Dry Martini
2¼ ounces	Gin
¼ ounce	Dry vermouth
	Olive or zest

Smokey Martini or Silver Bullet
1½ ounces	Gin
¼ ounce	Dry vermouth
½ ounce	Scotch (float)
	Olive or zest

Gibson
1½ ounces	Gin or vodka
¾ ounce	Dry vermouth
	Cocktail onions

Figure 11–2 The stir procedure

1 Place a chilled cocktail glass on the rail, handling it by the stem.

2 With the scoop, fill the mixing glass ¼ full of cube ice.

3 Measure liquor and vermouth and add to the mixing glass.

4 Stir briskly in one direction 3 to 4 seconds.

5 Strain the liquid into the cocktail glass.

6 Add the garnish, using tongs, pick, or condiment fork. Serve on a cocktail napkin.

√ **Manhattans**

∨ *Manhattan*
1½ ounces Bourbon or blend
¾ ounce Sweet vermouth
Cherry

Southern Comfort or Deluxe Manhattan
1½ ounces Southern Comfort
¾ ounce Dry vermouth
Cherry or zest

✓*Perfect Manhattan*
1½ ounces Bourbon or blend
¾ ounce   Dry vermouth and sweet
                  vermouth combined
                  Zest or cherry

Dry Manhattan
1½ ounces Bourbon or blend
¾ ounce   Dry vermouth
                  Zest

- A Martini is garnished with either a cocktail olive or lemon zest.
- A Manhattan or a Rob Roy uses a Maraschino cherry. When using dry vermouth rather than a sweet, a lemon zest is used. When both sweet and dry are used, the garnish is optional—cherry or lemon zest.
- A Negroni is garnished with a lemon zest due to the addition of Campari (an Italian apéritif).
- A Gibson is garnished with a cocktail onion.

The following recipes also utilize the stir and ice down–pour procedures in their preparation.

Rob Roys

✓*Rob Roy*
1½ ounces Scotch
¾ ounce   Sweet
                  vermouth
                  Cherry

Dry Rob Roy
1½ ounces Scotch
¾ ounce   Dry vermouth
                  Zest

Perfect Rob Roy
1½ ounces Scotch
¾ ounce   Dry vermouth and sweet vermouth combined
                  Cherry or zest

Negronis

Negroni
1 ounce Gin
1 ounce Sweet vermouth
1 ounce Campari
               Zest

Negronis
¾ ounce Gin
¾ ounce Sweet vermouth
¾ ounce Campari
RXS glass, ice down–pour
Splash of club soda and zest
(1 dash bitters, optional)

Sours

Sours can be classified as **short** sours and **long** sours. **Short** sours are composed of liquor and/or liqueur with commercially prepared **lemon mix** or **lime juice. Long** sours contain the same ingredients, with the addition of a carbonated **soda** to cut the sour taste. Long sours are garnished with a cherry and an orange slice and are served in a tall glass.

All short sours are served in a cocktail or sour glass. The only short sours that are garnished are sour-type cocktails, such as whiskey sours or apricot sours. The garnish is a cherry. The shake procedure is used, unless the customer requests the cocktail on the rocks; then the procedure is a speed shake in a rocks glass.

Mechanics of Shake and Speed Shake Procedures
For the **shake** procedure:

- Fill a mixing glass one-third full of ice.
- Add liquor and/or liqueur(s).
- Add mixer and/or base ingredient(s).
- Place a metal cup or base over the top of the mixing glass (making sure the metal cup is sitting evenly, not at an angle).
- Give the top (bottom of metal shaker) a slight tap to create a vacuum.
- Pick the whole unit up off the bar and flip it over, so that the metal is facing down and the glass is to your shoulder.
- In a quick, even movement, move the unit back and forth in a rapid succession.
- After shaking, position the unit so that the metal shaker is still on the bottom. Hold the unit in your left hand, down low, near the base. Keep your hands away from frost-line area.
- Examine the metal cup for the frost line. Look at the top of the mixing glass for the side of the glass that is straight and not at an angle. The total unit should be to your right hand.
- With the left hand holding the unit for balance, hold your right hand at an angle and hit the side of metal shaker at the frost line to break the vacuum.

- Pull the mixing glass off and strain the liquid.
- Garnish as needed.

The shake procedure is illustrated in Figure 11–3.

Figure 11–3 The shake procedure

For the **speed shake** procedure:

- Fill a service glass with ice.
- Add liquor and/or liqueur(s).

1 Place a chilled sour glass on the rail, handling it by the stem.

2 Fill the mixing glass ⅓ full of cube ice.

3 Measure liquor, lemon juice, and sugar (or mix) and add to the mixing glass.

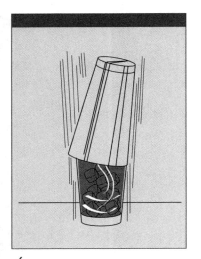

4 Tap the shaker over the glass, invert, and shake 3 to 4 seconds.

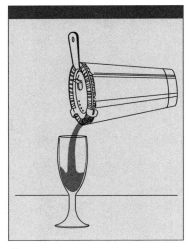

5 Remove the mixing glass and strain the drink from the shaker into the chilled glass.

6 Add the garnish, using tongs or a pick. Serve on a cocktail napkin.

7 Wash both shaker parts and invert them on the drainboard.

- Add the mixer and/or base ingredient(s).
- Place the speed shaker over the top of the glass.
- Lift the unit off the rail or dash and invert the glass into the speed shaker and shake. *Note:* When inverting the glass, do not allow the glass to shift, or an air pocket will form.
- Pull the glass from the unit and transfer the liquids back to the glass.
- Add the garnish.

The following recipes utilize the shake or speed shake procedures in their preparation.

Lemon Mix and Lime Juice-based Short Sours

✓Whiskey Sour

1½ ounces	Whiskey
2 ounces	Lemon mix
	Cherry
Glass:	Sour

Daiquiri

1½ ounces	Light rum
2 ounces	Lemon mix

✓ Bacardi Cocktail

1½ ounces	Barcardi light rum
2 ounces	Lemon mix
½ ounce	Grenadine

Margarita

Rim Champagne coupe with salt.
Set aside

1½ ounces	Tequila
1 ounce	Lemon mix
¾ ounce	Triple Sec

Blend or shake

Note: To rim or frost a glass, moisten the rim of the glass with a piece of citrus fruit; then dip the glass in a dish of salt or sugar.

Between the Sheets

B	½ ounce	Brandy
L	1½ ounces	Lemon mix
T	½ ounce	Triple Sec
Rye	½ ounce	Rum

Note: Using the "BLT on Rye" mnemonic is a handy way to remember the ingredients of this drink.

Jack Rose Cocktail

1½ ounces	Applejack
½ ounce	Grenadine
1½ ounces	Lemon mix
Rum	

Side Car

1 ounce	Brandy
½ ounce	Triple Sec
1½ ounces	Lemon mix

Kamakaze

1½ ounces	Gin or vodka
¼ ounce	Rose's lime juice
½ ounce	Triple Sec
	Lime wedge (optional)

✓Stone Sour

1½ ounces	Apricot brandy
1 ounce	Orange juice
1 ounce	Lemon mix
	Cherry
Glass:	Sour

Gimlet

1½ ounces	Gin or vodka
¾ ounce	Rose's lime juice
	Lime wedge (optional)

Long Sours

✓Tom Collins

1½ ounces	Gin
3 ounces	Lemon mix

Speed shake—Collins
Fill with club soda and 7UP

	Cherry and orange

Variations of Tom Collins

John Collins—made with whiskey
Joe Collins—made with Scotch
Ivan Collins—made with vodka

Singapore Sling

1½ ounces	Gin
4 ounces	Lemon mix

Speed shake—Sling/Zombie
Fill with club soda and 7UP
½ ounce float—Cherry-flavored brandy or liqueur
Cherry and orange

Variations of Singapore Sling

A fruit-flavored sling can be named from the flavoring (e.g., Strawberry Sling). The float would be strawberry‚ liqueur instead of cherry-flavored brandy or liqueur.

Sloe Gin Fizz

1½ ounces	Sloe Gin
4 ounces	Lemon mix

Speed shake—Collins
Fill with club soda
Cherry and orange

Ward 8

1½ ounces	Whiskey
4 ounces	Lemon mix
½ ounce	Grenadine

Speed shake—Collins
Cherry and orange

✓ *Long Island Ice Tea*

½ ounce	Vodka
½ ounce	Gin
½ ounce	Rum
½ ounce	Tequila
½ ounce	Triple Sec
1 ounce	Lemon mix

Speed shake—Sling/Zombie
½ ounce Coke—Float
Lemon wheel

Cream and Ice Cream Base

Cream drinks are usually very sweet, smooth, and pleasing to the palate. They are perfect after-dinner drinks, and many people order them instead of dessert. Cream drinks are ideal because they do not have a strong alcoholic taste.

There are two ways to prepare cream drinks: by **blending** or by using the **shake procedure**. A blender will thoroughly mix the ingredients and thereby give the drink a creamier and frothier texture than will the shake procedure.

All cream-based drinks may use ice cream instead of cream. Usually, vanilla ice cream is used, but any flavor that will mix well with the flavor of the liqueur may be used (e.g., coffee, strawberry, peach, or chocolate). Sherbets also may be used; if so, the name of the drink changes to a "freeze." The following is an example of a freeze:

Summer Rum Freeze

1½ ounces	Bacardi Rum
2 scoops	Lime sherbet
3 ounces	Pineapple juice
¾ ounce	Cream or milk

Place all ingredients in the blender. Blend until creamy. Pour into a tall goblet.
Garnish with pineapple spear or lime wheel.

Blend procedures:

- Place all ingredients in a blender. (Do not add ice unless crushed ice is available.)
- Blend until thick and creamy.
- Pour into a tall goblet or tall pilsner glass. Place on an underliner or napkin.
- Garnish with whipped cream, shaved chocolate, a cherry, or candied almonds.

The blend procedure can be used for any drink that is shaken, but it *should* be used when incorporating ice or solid food, such as strawberries in a Strawberry Daiquiri.

- Place the ingredients in the blender.
- Fill to one-fourth full or until the ice is covered by the ingredients.
- If a two-speed blender is used, blend 3 seconds on slow; then 7 to 10 seconds on high.
- Pour the ingredients, using a cocktail spoon to maintain an even flow.

Short cream drinks are served up in a Champagne coupe. The only cream-based drink that has a garnish is the Alexander, which requires a sprinkle of nutmeg to complete the drink. If blenders are not available, use the shake procedure. Long cream drinks are generally served in a highball glass, using the speed shake procedure, and they receive no garnish.

Note: White Russians are traditionally served in a rocks glass but occasionally are served in highball glasses, depending on house rules or customer preference. Traditionally, a White Russian was a layered drink, consisting of half-and-half cream set on top of the Black Russian. Today it is usually served tall using the speed shake procedure.

Cream-based Cocktails: *Short Creams*

✓*Brandy Alexander*

1 ounce	Brandy
1 ounce	Dark Cacao
1 ounce	Cream or milk
	Nutmeg

✓ *Grasshopper*

1 ounce	Light Cacao
1 ounce	Green Crème de Menthe
1 ounce	Cream or milk

Golden Dream

1 ounce	Galliano
½ ounce	Cointreau
½ ounce	Orange juice
½ ounce	Cream or milk

Pink Squirrel

1 ounce	Light Cacao
1 ounce	Crème de Nouyaux or Crème de Almond
1 ounce	Cream or milk

Cream-based Drinks: *Long-Creams*

✓*Orgasm*

1 ounce	Amaretto
½ ounce	Vodka
½ ounce	Kahlua
4 ounces	Milk

✓*White Russian*

1½ ounces	Vodka
½ ounce	Kahlua
4 ounces	Cream or milk

✓*Girl Scout Cookie*

1 ounce	Peppermint Schnapps
½ ounce	Dark Cacao
4 ounces	Milk

✓*Toasted Almond Bar*

¾ ounce	Amaretto
¾ ounce	Kahlua
4 ounces	Milk

Cordials and Highballs
Cordials: Two-Liquor Drinks

Two-liquor drinks grew in popularity in the 1970s. Their overall flavor is sweet and usually composed of a distilled spirit or brandy with an added liqueur. There should be more distilled spirit or brandy than liqueur in the drink. Too much liqueur will ruin the drink by making it too sweet.

All two-liquor drinks are served on the rocks, in a rocks glass, with the ice down–pour procedure. The exception to this rule is the Mud Slide, which needs the speed shake procedure.

Two-Liquor Drinks

✓*Black Russian*

1½ ounces	Vodka
¾ ounce	Kahlua

✓*Godfather*

1½ ounces	Scotch
¾ ounce	Amaretto

✓*Sicilian Kiss*

1½ ounces	Southern Comfort
¾ ounce	Amaretto

Mud Slide

¾ ounce	Vodka
¾ ounce	Kahlua
¾ ounce	Bailey's Irish Cream
Speed shake	

After 5

⅓ ounce	Kahlua
⅓ ounce	Bailey's Irish Cream
⅓ ounce	Peppermint schnapps

Layered in order

✓ *Stinger*

1½ ounces	Brandy
¾ ounce	White crème de menthe

Godmother

1½ ounces	Vodka
¾ ounce	Amaretto

✓ *Rusty Nail or Queen Anne*

1½ ounces	Scotch
¾	Drambuie

B 52

⅓ ounce	Kahlua
⅓ ounce	Bailey's Irish Cream
⅓ ounce	Grand Marnier

Layered in order

Highballs

As mentioned previously, a mixed drink contains a liquor and/or liqueurs combined with nonalcoholic mixers. One of the first mixed drinks was the **Gin and Tonic,** which originated in India during the late 1800s. British troops were required to take a daily dose of a medicine called quinine to guard against malaria. To offset the heavy bitterness of quinine, sugar and water were added. It was not too long before the troops started to add their favorite liquor, gin, to the medicine to make it even more palatable.

Another popular mixed drink is the highball, which became well known in the mid-1800s. **Highball** was a railroad term. Railroad workers would put a ball on a high pole to signal to fast, oncoming trains that the track was clear and there was no need to slow down. When the men had time enough to stop for a fast drink of whiskey and ginger ale, they referred to it as a highball.

The **Screwdriver,** another popular mixed drink, supposedly received its name from American oil workers in Iran who had the habit of mixing vodka with orange juice and stirring it with their screwdrivers.

The basic concept behind adding a mix to a liquor is to cut the alcoholic bite of the drink. Highballs are served in a highball glass, sometimes spelled **hi-ball.** For carbonated mixers, water, and juices, the procedure is ice down–pour; if a juice mixer is combined with a liqueur, the speed shake procedure is used.

Today's highball is made of many different combinations of liquors and flavored sodas. Water also is a base for a highball. Regardless of the combination, the **basic recipe** is as follows:

1½ ounces Liquor, or to customer preference
4 ounces Soda

- Pour liquor over ice cubes in a highball glass.
- Top with any flavored soda.
- No garnish is usually provided, except when serving a **Cuba Libre,** Gin and Tonic, or Vodka and Tonic, all of which have a lime wedge. Scotch drinks will usually have a lemon twist or zest for garnish. All other drinks are served without one.

Some of the most popular highballs are

Whiskey and ginger ale	Highball
White wine and club soda	Spritzer
Red wine and ginger ale	Wine Cooler
Dry gin and tonic water	Gin and Tonic
Vodka and tonic water	Vodka and Tonic
Scotch and club soda	Scotch and Soda
Seagram's 7 Crown and 7UP	7 and 7
Scotch and water	Scotch and Water Highball
Whiskey, ginger ale, and club soda	Presbyterian

Note: Drinks also may be ordered on the rocks with a splash of mix, according to the customer's preference.

An example of a classic mixed drink is the **Old Fashioned:**

1 package sugar
Stemless cherry
Orange slice

Dash of bitters
Splash of club soda
Muddle (crush using a muddler) these five ingredients to
release the oils and juice of the fruit. Add:
Ice
1½ ounces blended whiskey or bourbon
Float 1 ounce club soda

The following recipes utilize the ice down-pour procedure
in their preparation.

Highballs: Juice Base

✓*Comfortable Screw*
1½ ounces   Southern Comfort
4 ounces   Orange juice
Speed shake

✓*Bocce Ball*
1½ ounces   Amaretto di Saronno
4 ounces   Orange juice
Float club soda
Speed shake

/*Cape Codder*
1½ ounces   Vodka
4 ounces   Cranberry juice

Harvey Wallbanger
1½ ounces   Vodka
4 ounces   Orange juice
½ ounce   Galliano (float)

✓*Tequila Sunrise*
1½ ounces   Tequila
4 ounces   Orange juice
½ ounce   Granadine (float)

✓ *Madras*
1½ ounces   Vodka
2 ounces   Cranberry juice
2 ounces   Orange juice

Salty Dog
            Rim with salt
1½ ounces   Vodka
4 ounces   Grapefruit juice

Pearl Harbor
1 ounce   Midori
½ ounce   Vodka
4 ounces   Pineapple juice
Speed shake

✓*Basic Bloody Mary Mix*
1½ ounces   Liquor
4 ounces   Tomato juice
Dash   Salt and pepper
Dash   Lea & Perrins worcestershire sauce
Dash   Tabasco
Dash   ~~Lemon mix~~ Lime squeeze   .
1 teaspoon Horseradish (optional)
Dash   Celery salt (optional)
Speed shake—goblet
Garnish   Celery stalk or lime wedge

Variations of Bloody Mary
Bloody Mary is made with vodka.
Bloody Maria is made with tequila.
Virgin Mary is a nonalcoholic Bloody Mary.
Red Snapper is a Bloody Mary mix with gin, also called
a Bloody Jane.

✓ *Woo-Woo*
1½ ounces   Peachtree Schnapps
½ ounce   Vodka
            Cranberry juice to a ¼-inch rim
Speed shake

Alabama Slammer
½ ounce   Sloe Gin
½ ounce   Banana liqueur
            Orange juice to a ¼-inch rim
½ ounce   Southern Comfort (float)

✓ *Sex on the Beach*
½ ounce   Peachtree Schnapps
1 ounce   Vodka
2 ounces   Cranberry juice
2 ounces   Orange juice
Equal amounts to a ¼-inch rim
Speed shake

✓ *Sea Breeze*

1½ ounces	Vodka
2 ounces	Grapefruit juice
2 ounces	Cranberry juice

✓ *Tootsie Roll*

1½ ounces	Dark Cacao
4 ounces	Orange juice
Speed shake	

Scarlet O'Hara

1½ ounces	Southern Comfort
4 ounces	Cranberry juice
Speed shake	

Bloody Caesar

Rim goblet with salt and pepper	
1½ ounces	Vodka
4 ounces	Clamato juice
Speed shake	

✓ *Fuzzy Navel*

1½ ounces	Peachtree Schnapps
	Orange juice to a ¼-inch rim
Speed shake	

Watermelon

1 ounce	Southern Comfort
1 ounce	Crème de Nouyaux or Crème de Almond
	Pineapple juice to a ¼-inch rim

Polynesian-Tropical

Collins:	Mai Tai and Planter's Punch
Sling:	Pina Colada and Zombie

For all of these drinks, garnish with two of the following three items: cherry, orange, or pineapple chunk. Use the blender or speed shake procedure. (Note the use of mnemonics as an easy method for remembering ingredients.)

Mai Tai

S	½ ounce	Sugar or simple syrup
C	½ ounce	Orange Curaçao
R	1 ounce	Myers' Rum (dark)
R	1 ounce	Mt. Gay Rum (gold)
O	½ ounce	Amaretto
L	3 ounces	Lemon mix

Pina Colada

C	1 ounce	Coco Lopez
P	3 ounces	Pineapple juice
R	2 ounces	Golden rum (Mt. Gay)

Planter's Punch

G	½ ounce	Grenadine
L	1 ounce	Lemon mix
O	1 ounce	Orange juice
M	1½ ounces	Myers' Rum (dark)
S	½ ounce	Sugar or simple syrup

✓ *Zombie*

G	½ ounce	Grenadine
	1 ounce	~~White Light~~ rum (bar)
2R	1 ounce	Myers' Rum (dark)
L	2 ounces	Lemon mix
O	1½ ounces	Orange juice
C	1 ounce	~~Orange Curaçao~~
		triple sec

12

Federal and State Controls for Alcoholic Beverages

Federal and State Controls for Alcoholic Beverages

Liquor restrictions in the United States date back to colonial days and reflect the Puritan ethic that influenced that era. Regulations regarding liquor were directed initially at revenue collection but later the encouragement of sobriety.

History of Controls

The original controls were organized in 1733 by the governor of Georgia, who prohibited the importation of hard liquors into that colony. In order to raise revenue and act as a deterrent, a tax was levied on the selling of distilled liquors in 1790. This led to the Whiskey Rebellion, an uprising that was quashed by federal troops in Pennsylvania in 1794. In 1816, Indiana passed the first prohibitory law that banned the selling of liquor on Sundays. By the end of 1833, more than 5000 organized temperance groups totaled more than 1 million people. In 1838, Massachusetts limited the amount of liquor that one person could buy at one time. It was felt that drinking was a problem and should be controlled or stopped. In 1846, Maine passed the first prohibition law. On January 16, 1920, the National Prohibition Amendment (the eighteenth) became law. Prohibition cost the government about $1 billion per year, including losses in federal, state, county, and municipal revenues. Estimates are that Americans spent a total of $36 billion for bootlegged and smuggled liquor during Prohibition. On December 5, 1933, the Twenty-first Amendment was passed, repealing Prohibition, and the way was cleared for new controls. A system of federal regulation concerning trade practices and requiring permits was set up. In 1972, federal controls on alcohol became the responsibility of the newly named Bureau of Alcohol, Tobacco and Firearms (ATF).

The ATF enforces the codes and laws established by the legislative and executive branches of the federal government. For example, distilled spirits in the possession of a retail dealer must be in bottles or similar containers that bear internal revenue tax stamps. A portion of the strip stamp (green or red) must be kept affixed to each opened bottle. The penalty for unstamped liquors is a fine of not more than $10,000, imprisonment for not more than 5 years, or both.

The ATF exercises control over three broad areas:

- **Consumer protection:** Ensuring that each alcoholic beverage conforms to the Standards of Identity
- **Trade practices:** Preventing the sale of illegal spirits
- **Revenue collection:** The collection of revenues from distillers based on production of proof gallons

Retail dealers must obtain a federal tax stamp (FTS) to determine the type of alcoholic beverage they may sell. *Note:* It is also against federal law to utilize an empty liquor bottle for any reason or to "marry" (combine) the contents from two or more bottles of the same liquor.

ATF Definitions of Spirits

To understand the method by which the ATF levies taxes on alcoholic beverages, it is necessary to know some ATF definitions.

Alcohol: A volatile, colorless liquid obtained through the fermentation of a liquid containing sugar

Alcoholic beverage: Any potable liquid containing from 0.5% to 75.5% ethyl alcohol by volume.

Spirit: A potable alcoholic beverage obtained from the distillation of a liquid containing alcohol

Proof (American method): Once called "gunpowder proof." To test the strength of the liquor, old-time distillers poured it on gunpowder and struck a match. If the liquor blazed, it was too strong. Liquor at proper strength, mixed with the powder, would burn slowly with a blue flame. Mixing in 50% water produced a slow, steady flame. That strength was considered perfect and was called "100 proof." Today, the same scale is applied to the alcoholic content of a liquor on the following basis: Pure, 100% alcohol is 200 proof, and 1 degree of proof is equal to 0.5% alcohol. Divide the proof by 2 and you get the percentage of alcohol by volume. Proof is therefore a measure of alcohol strength. The proof number is always twice the percentage of alcohol. The remaining percentage comprises distilled water, coloring, and flavoring.

Proof Gallon Taxes (Domestic and Imported)

All alcoholic beverages produced in the United States, as well as all imported beverages, are subject to customs duties and internal revenue taxes. The tax rate is determined by the alcoholic content of the beverage. As mentioned in the preceding section, each degree of proof is equal to 0.5% alcohol; therefore, a spirit of 90 proof contains 45% alcohol, 1 gallon proof contains 75% alcohol, and 1 gallon at 150 proof equals 1.5 proof gallons. The trade term for a spirit of more than 100 proof is an *overproof spirit*.

A tax gallon is the gallonage on which duties and revenue taxes are paid. When the duties are determined, the tax gallons are equivalent to proof gallons at 100 proof or higher. If the spirits are less than 100 proof, the tax gallons are the actual wine gallons as measured quantitatively.

Customs Duties and Internal Revenue Taxes

Alcohol	Tax ($)
Wine per Gallon	
0%–14%	1.07
14%–21%	1.57
21%–24%	3.15
Sparkling	3.40
Carbonated	3.30
Beer per 31 gallons	18.00
Distilled spirits per gallon	13.50

Duties on imported alcoholic beverages are in addition to the federal and state excise taxes charged for alcoholic beverages. To determine the total tax on an imported beverage, add the federal tax, then the state tax, and finally the import duty. There also may be local sales taxes.

State Control

In addition to the federal government's control of the industry, individual states exercise a secondary control. Laws vary from state to state but cannot conflict with federal laws and must meet all federal regulations. State regulations may be stricter than federal regulations. Additionally, there may be local restrictions whereby counties disallow the purchase of liquor from another county and transporting it across county lines.

State control of the sale of alcoholic beverages is of three types:

- In **open-license states,** private businesses make both on-premise and off-premise sales of alcoholic beverages to all types of consumers. The operations vary in each state because of different taxes imposed on alcoholic beverages, and each state has different fees imposed on wholesalers and retailers. Furthermore, each state and/or municipality may have different hours for opening and closing and different provisions with respect to the number of licenses permitted.
- **Control or monopoly states** control the sale of **all** alcoholic beverages distributed in their territories.
- **Control or monopoly states** control only the sale of *distilled spirits* and certain kinds of *wines*. Beer and some wines are sold by private businesses.

Note: In open-license states, trade is conducted as in other competitive businesses. Open states collect revenues from excise and sales taxes. It is important to recognize, however, that control states are in the liquor business, and their function is also to make money. As a result, control states stock only those brands they believe will produce the most sales, thereby limiting consumer choice.

Dram Shop Laws

Aside from federal and state liquor laws, there is also a **dram shop law,** which originated in 1873. Dram shop is also known as **third-party liability.** In states that have dram shop, the innocent third party injured "in person, property, means of support or otherwise" by a drunken individual or minor can sue a restaurant, tavern, or liquor store owner and/or employees for having dispensed and sold the alcohol. Dram shop applies to the sale of beer, wine, hard cider, or distilled beverages.

In states where dram shop liability is not imposed through **Alcohol Beverage Control (ABC)** regulations, the courts apply **common law,** based on negligence and **third-party liability** case precedents. Courts normally favor the victim over the seller, server, or employer on the grounds that state ABC laws were violated or negligence was committed by dispensing liquor to an obviously inebriated patron or minor.

Dram shop lliability is the most critical issue affecting the nation's restaurants and bars since the repeal of Prohibition. Blood alcohol content, minimum drinking age, and first-offense penalties under dram shop or common law vary from state to state. The basic rationale behind dram shop and common laws is that it will help deter drunk driving, and thus decrease the number of alcohol-related accidents, which claim thousands of lives each year.*

Alcohol and the Body

Alcohol is a food product that is classified as an intoxicating drug that depresses the brain and central nervous system. Alcohol contains what are described as "empty calories." One ounce of pure alcohol (100%) has 210 calories; 1 ounce of whiskey (43% alcohol and 86 proof) has 75 calories; and a 12-ounce bottle of beer has between 120 and 210 calories. These empty calories contain no vitamins,

*See Appendix C for update.

minerals, or other essential substances. Alcohol also interferes with the body's ability to use other sources of energy.

Digestion

Alcohol requires no digestion. It is absorbed through the bloodstream and transported to all parts of the body in a very short period. A small amount is taken immediately into the bloodstream through the capillaries in the mouth. The remaining portion travels to the stomach, where 20% is absorbed through the stomach lining. The amount of food in the stomach is an important factor when drinking. Food mixes with the alcohol and slows down the absorption rate of the remaining 80% of alcohol as the stomach completes the digestion of the food.

The pylorus valve (the door between the stomach wall and small intestine) remains closed as long as there is food to be digested, but it is sensitive to the presence of alcohol. When a person drinks a heavy amount, for example, the large concentration of alcohol tends to get "stuck" in the stomach, because the pylorus valve, due to its alcohol sensitivity, remains in the closed position. When this pylorospasm happens, the alcohol trapped in the stomach may cause sufficient irritation and distress to cause a person to stop drinking (it is a self-protective mechanism that helps prevent overconsumption of alcohol). In the stomach, alcohol acts as an irritant. It causes the stomach lining to secrete excess amounts of hydrochloric acid, a digestive juice. A warm feeling is created in the stomach due to this irritation.

Absorption

Once in the small intestine, the remaining 80% of alcohol is absorbed into the bloodstream, the body's transportation system. Alcohol is soluble in water and is able to pass through cell walls.

The percentage of alcohol as well as the presence of carbonation are important factors in the **rate of absorption.** The higher the percentage of alcohol, the quicker it is absorbed into the bloodstream. Beer, however, contains some food substances that slow down its absorption rate. The rate of absorption into the bloodstream determines the level of intoxication. The faster the alcohol is absorbed, the more rapidly the blood alcohol level rises and the greater the impairment.

Absorption rate factors are

- Rate of consumption
- Height and weight
- Food in the stomach
- Amount of water in the body
- Medication (speeds up the effects of alcohol)

Intoxication

Alcohol affects the brain and central nervous system more rapidly than it affects other organs of the body. The blood alcohol content causes the effects of intoxication and/or impairment. To identify someone's particular level of intoxication, one must learn to recognize the following behavioral cues:

- Loss of **inhibitions:** Talkative, relaxed, overfriendly and exhibiting mood swings. People with lowered inhibitions fit into a happy-to-excited state of intoxication, depending on the extremity of their actions.
- Loss of **judgement:** Erratic behavior, foul language, anger, and impulsive acts. People who fit this description are most likely in the excited stage but are ap-

proaching the confused stage. Again, it depends on the extremity of their actions.

- Loss of **reaction:** Loss of train of thought, unfocused eyes, slurred speech and unsteady hands. People displaying these effects have reached the confused stage.
- Loss of **coordination:** Loss of balance, drowsiness, and lack of dexterity and/or coordination. People with these characteristics are in the fourth stage of intoxication, stupor.

Table 12-1 lists the five stages of intoxication with corresponding rates at which alcohol will accumulate in the blood stream, the common effects produced at each stage and the rate needed to metabolize the alcohol. The data are based on the effects of alcohol consumption by a 150–160-pound man. One drink represents 1 ounce of 100 proof distilled spirits, 3 ounces of sherry, 5 ounces of wine, or 12 ounces of beer.

Differing Effects of Intoxication on Men and Women

An average 120-pound woman becomes intoxicated faster than an average man of similar body weight due to a higher proportion of fat and correspondingly lower amounts of water in a woman's body. Alcohol is not fat-soluble. A woman and a man of the same body weight, both drinking the same amounts of alcohol, will have different blood alcohol levels.

Table 12-1 Five Stages of Intoxication

Stage	Drinks per Hour	BAC	Rate Needed to Metabolize
1: Happy	1	0.02	Less than 1 hour; talkative, relaxed, loss of inhibitions
2: Excited	2	0.05	Two hours; loud, boisterous, fewer inhibitions, loss of judgment
3: Confused	4	0.10	Four hours; loss of reactions, slurred speech, staggering, mood swings, double vision, some loss of coordination
4: Stupor	8	0.20	Eight hours; after 6 hours, still legally drunk; emotional, erratic behavior, unable to stand, loss of memory, barely conscious, approaching paralysis, loss of coordination
5: Coma	1 to 1¼ pints	0.40–0.50	No longer able to metabolize; in a coma and dangerously close to death; brain centers are anesthetized.
		0.60–0.70	Death occurs.

Source: Based on Health Communications Inc. Tips Progam.

The woman's will be higher, again due to less water in her body to dilute the alcohol. This difference in weight and body fat speeds the absorption rate in most women:

Drinks per Hour	BAC
1	0.03
2	0.07
3	0.14
1 pint	0.45; coma

Breakdown and Removal of Alcohol

The removal of alcohol from the body begins as soon as the alcohol is absorbed by the bloodstream. Ten percent of the alcohol is excreted through the breath, sweat, and urine. The rest has to be changed chemically: The alcohol has to metabolize and change into acetaldehyde. Acetaldehyde breaks down very rapidly to form acetic acid. The acetic acid then leaves the liver and is dispersed through-

out the body, where it is oxidized to carbon dioxide and water; 90 percent is metabolized and excreted by the liver.

The liver is the key organ in the breakdown process. The rate at which alcohol is metabolized by the liver may vary somewhat between individuals.

Deleterious Effects of Alcohol on Health

Although moderate drinking causes no direct harm, continued heavy drinking can result in permanent damage to the

- Digestive system
- Circulatory system
- Central nervous system
- Brain
- Liver
- Kidneys

Heavy drinking also can lead to malnutrition, ulcers, and gastritis.

A

Appendix A Wine Pronunciation Guide

Aloxe-Corton	ah lohs kor tohn		Banyul	Ban yul
Alsace	Ahl sahss		Barbera	bar BEH rah
Amontillado	ah mohn tee YAH doh		Bardolino	bar doh LEEN oh
Anjou	ahn zhoo		Barsac	bar sahk
Armagnac	ar mah nyahk		Beaujolais	boh zhoe lay
Asti Spumante	ahs tee spoo MAHN tee		Beaune	bone
Aurora	or RORE uh		Beaumes de Venise	Bome duh vuh nees
Baden	Bah din		Bergerac	Buhr zhe rahk

(continued)

Bernkastel	behrn kahs tel
Blanc de Blancs	blahn duh blahn
Bordeaux	bor doh
Cabernet Sauvignon	kah behr nay soh vee nyohn
Cahors	KAH or
Calvados	kahl vah dohs
Catawba	kuh TAW bah
Chablis	shah blee
Les Clos	lay kloh
Valmur	vahl moor
Chambertin, Le	luh shahm behr tan
Château	shah toh
Cheval Blanc	sheh vahl blahn
d'Yquem	dee kem
Grillet	gree yay
Haut-Brion	oht bree ohn
Latour	lah toor
Margaux	mahr goh
Mouton-Phillippe	moo tawn fee leep
Châteauneuf du Pape	shah toh nuf doo pop
Chenin Blanc	sheh neen blahn
Chevalier-Montrachet	shey vahl yay mohn rah shay
Chianti	kee AHN tee
Clos	Cloh
Corton-Clos du Roi	kor tohn kloh doo rwah
Corvo	kohr voh
Côte de Nuits	Koht de nwee
Côte Chalonnaise	Koht Sha lo nayse
Côte d'Or	Koht dor
Côte-Rôtie	Koht roh tee
Crianza	Kree ahn zah
Criolla	Kree oh ya
Cru	Crew
Cynar	CHEE nar
Dolcetto	Dohl chet toe
Dão	dow
Dubonnet	doo boh nay
Fino	FEE noh
Fleurie	fluh ree
Frascati	frahs KAH tee
Gevrey	zhev ray
Gewürztraminer	geh VURTZ tra meen er
Graves	grahv
Griotte	gree ut

Grumello	groo MEL oh
Haut-Médoc	Oht May dohk
Hessiche Bergstrasse	HES sih shuh BEHRG shtrah suh
Johannisberg Riesling	yoh hahn is behrk Rees ling
Jura	Jew rah
Juraçon	Jew rah sohn
Lacrima Christi	lah creem ah KREES tee
Lambrusco	lahm BROOS coh
Liebfraumilch	LEEB frow milkh
Lillet	lee lay
Mâcon	mah cohn
Maconnais	Ma koh nay
Madeira	mah DEER ah
Madiran	Ma DEE rahn
Malaga	MAH lah gah
Malmsey	MALM zee
Marsala	mahr SAH lah
Médoc	may dohk
Mercurey	mehr kyu ray
Meursault	Mer soh
Midi	Mee dee
Mittelrhein	MIT el rine
Montrachet, le	luh mohn rah shay
Moscato	mohs KAH toh
Mosel	MOH zel
Mosel-Saar-Ruwer	Mo zell sahr rooer
Moulin-a-Vent	moo lan ah vahn
Moulis	Moo lee
Muscadet	moos kah day
Musigny, Le	lay moo see nyee
Nebbiolo	neb bee oh loh
Nuit St. Georges	Nwee San Jor Jeh
Oloroso	oh loh ROH soh
Orvieto	ohr vee EHT oh
Pais	Pah eess
Pauillac	Poy yak
Pessac-Léognan	Pay sack Lay oh nahn
Pfalz	Fahltz
Pinot Blanc	pee noh blahn
Pinot Noir	pee noh nwahr

(continued)

Pomerol	Pah meh roll
Pommard	Poh marr
Pouilly-Fuissé	pwee yee fwee say
Pouilly Fumé	pwee yee foo may
Puligny-Montrachet	poo lee nyee mohn ray shay
Qualitätswein	Kval ih tates vine
Recioto	Reh chee oh toe
Rheingau	RINE gouw
Rheinhessen	RINE hes sen
Riesling	REES ling
Romanée, La	lah roh mah nay
Saint-Amour	san tah moor
Saint-Emilion	san tah meel yohn
Sancerre	san sehr
Saumur	Soh mur
Sauternes	soh tehrn
Savoie	Sa vwha
Sekt	sehkt
Sémillon	seh mee yohn
Soave	su ah veh
St. Estèphe	Sant es tef
Tavel	tah vel
Trimoulet	tree moo lay
Valpolicella	vahl poh lee CHEH lah
Verdelho	vehr DEL yo
Verdicchio	vehr DEE kee oh
Vernaccia	vehr NAH chah
Volnay	vuhl nay
Vosne Romanée	Vohn Roh mah nay
Vougeot	Voo zhoe
Vouvray	voo vreh
Württemberg	Vur tem behrg
Würzburger	vurtz behr gehr
Zinfandel	TZIN fan del

Appendix B Liquid Measurements

Distilled Spirits

1.75	liters	59.2 ounces
1.0	liters	33.8 ounces
750.0	milliliters	25.4 ounces
500.0	milliliters	16.9 ounces
200.0	milliliters	6.8 ounces
50.0	milliliters	1.7 ounces

Case packing requirements for 200 ml distilled spirits bottles may be changed from 60 bottles (as indicated) to 48 bottles per case under proposed rulemaking notice published by BATF.

Wines (All Types)*

3.0	liters	101.0 ounces
1.5	liters	50.7 ounces
1.0	liter	33.8 ounces
750.0	milliliters	25.4 ounces
375.0	milliliters	12.7 ounces
187.0	milliliters	6.3 ounces
100.0	milliliters	3.4 ounces

Jeroboam	102.4 ounces	4
Magnum	51.2 ounces	6
Quart	32.0 ounces	12
Fifth	25.6 ounces	12
Tenth	12.8 ounces	24
Split	6.4 ounces	48
Miniature	2.0 ounces	60

*Includes still wines, champagnes, and sparkling wines.

Table of Measurements

10 milliliters = 1 centiliter		0.338 ounce
500 milliliters = 50 centiliters = ½ liter		16.97 ounces = 0.52835 quart
1000 milliliters = 100 centiliters = 1 liter		33.8 ounces 0 = 1.0567 quart

1 ounce	2.9575 centiliter
16 ounces = 1 pint	0.4732 liter
32 ounces = 2 pints = 1 quart	0.9463 liter
64 ounces = 4 pints = 2 quarts = ½ gallon	1.8926 liters
128 ounces = 8 pints = 4 quarts = 1 gallon	3.7853 liters

Other Measurements

1 dash	=	⅙ tsp. or 1/32 oz.
1 tsp.	=	⅛ oz. to ⅙ oz.
1 tbsp.	=	3 tsp. or ⅜ oz. to ½ oz.
1 pony	=	1 oz.
1 jigger	=	1½ oz.
1 wine glass	=	4 oz.
1 tenth	=	⅘ pint or 12.8 oz. or 1/10 gal.
1 fifth	=	25.6 oz. or ⅕ gal.

70 proof (35% alcohol)	35 proof (35% alcohol)	38.8 under proof (or 61.2 proof) (35% alcohol)
80 proof (40% alcohol)	40 proof (40% alcohol)	30.0 under proof (or 70.0 proof) (40% alcohol)
86 proof (43% alcohol)	43 proof (43% alcohol)	24.8 under proof (or 75.2 proof) (43% alcohol)
100 proof (50% alcohol)	50 proof (50% alcohol)	12.5 under proof (or 87.5 proof) (50% alcohol)
150 proof (75% alcohol)	75 proof (75% alcohol)	31.3 over proof (or 131.3 proof) (75% alcohol)

Appendix C Corrections and Additions to Text

PAGE 8

"The food description should include the following:" is changed to:

Describing food to dining room guests should include the following:

- What are the main components
- How it is prepared
- How it is served
- The accompaniments
- The server's endorsement of the item (e.g., "It's a best seller.")
- A useful suggestion on a good beverage to accompany the dish.

Descriptions of certain courses may vary.

Soup Descriptions.

Soups are usually simmered. Use four (4) steps in describing soups:

1. Include the major ingredients in the soup
2. Mention the stock in which they were simmered
3. Include the texture of the soup (light, clear, creamy, thick, hearty etc.)
4. Mention the temperature especially if served chilled.

Examples:

- Diced chicken breast and mixed vegetables simmered in a light chicken stock, served piping hot.
- Fresh asparagus simmered in a creamy, seasoned vegetable stock and pureed.
- Fresh shucked clams and diced potatoes simmered in a creamy clam broth.

Salad Descriptions

Salads are generally tossed or arranged. If tossed, describe what major ingredients are tossed and what dressing accompanies them. If arranged, describe what major ingredients are served, the manner in which they are arranged and their accompanying dressing. If the salad contains cooked ingredients, be sure to state whether the ingredients are served chilled or warmed.

The following includes both kinds of salad descriptions:

- Fresh, tender spinach leaves, seasoned croutons and chopped, hard-boiled egg tossed in a warm bacon dressing.
- Grilled eggplant and roasted red bell peppers served chilled on a bed of wild field greens drizzled with a hazelnut vinaigrette.

Entrée Descriptions

Entrées should be described in three (3) steps. Be sure to maintain the sequence of the steps.

1. **The ingredients**
   This includes the specific <u>cut</u> of meat, fish, pasta, vegetable etc. and the pre-cooking preparation. For example, was the item marinated, breaded, encrusted, pounded out, boned, or stuffed? This should be included in the ingredient's description.

   Examples include:
   - A bone-in rib veal chop stuffed with spinach and feta cheese.
   - A lightly breaded filet fresh yellow-tail sole.
   - A dry-aged NY sirloin steak, encrusted with cracked black pepper.
   - A pita pocket stuffed with grilled fresh vegetables accompanied by humus.
   - A boneless breast of Long Island duckling marinated in a raspberry vinaigrette.

2. **The preparation**
   It is best not to use the actual word "cooked" in describing how it was prepared as it fails to articulate any definite method which imparts flavors or affects the texture of the item and fails to conjure up useful imagery for the guest.

   Examples would include:
   - Fried—this alludes to deep fat frying.
   - Baked—items cooked using a dry convected heat such as in an oven.

- Roasted—items cooked using a dry convected heat such as in an oven where the outside of the item is usually seared
- Broiled—the item is cooked on a gridlike surface with heat transmitted from above
- Grilled—the item is cooked on a gridlike surface with a heat source transmitted from below.
- Sautéed—the item has been cooked using a dry cooking method in a shallow pan using a minimum amount of fat or oil.
- Poached—the item has been simmered in water or a flavored liquid such as wine or stock.
- Simmered—the item is fully submerged by a cooking liquid and has been cooked slowly at a low temperature.
- Braised—the item has been seared in a pan that is then deglazed, and the item is then cooked slowly in the deglazed liquid in the oven. The other ingredients the item has been braised with should be included in the description.
- Steamed—the item has been cooked by applied steam from water or flavored liquids in a closed environment.
- Seared, charred, blackened, and barbecued are other notable cooking methods

If the item is left uncooked or the cooking method is obvious such as certain pastas, this part of the description would be omitted.

3. ***How the entrée is served***
   When discussing how an entrée is served, it usually refers to the accompaniments and a description of the sauce. There are only a few basic sauces to which the chef adds additional seasonings and or ingredients to create an endless combination of sauces. Most diners may not be familiar with the technical or culinary names of sauces. It is best, therefore, to describe the basic sauce with the chef's additions as illustrated by the following examples with the basic sauce highlighted:

   - A **white wine cream sauce** with Dijon mustard.

- A port wine **brown sauce** with chopped wild mushrooms.
- A spicy **tomato sauce** with capers and anchovies.
- A **white wine butter sauce** with fresh dill.
- A hollandaise sauce with fresh tarragon and tomato puree.

It is worth noting that foods that are braised, simmered and sometimes sautéed, are often not served with a separate sauce but with a sauce composed of the ingredients they were cooked with. On those occasions, simply describe those ingredients such as in the following examples:

- Osso Bucco—Tender baby veal shanks braised with white wine, onions, carrots, celery, garlic and tomatoes in a rich brown sauce.
- Sole Meuniére—Fresh fillet of sole sautéed with lemon and butter.

Combining the three steps
It is important to keep the food descriptions as brief as possible so as not to confuse or lose the guest's interest. The best descriptions of menu items are no longer than one sentence. Use the three steps in sequence as the following examples demonstrate:

- A fresh, boneless breast of chicken, sautéed and served with a light white wine brown sauce accented with a touch of Dijon mustard.
- A fresh fillet of Dover sole sautéed with lemon, butter and Muscadet white wine.
- A dry-aged NY sirloin steak, encrusted with black pepper, pan seared and served with a rich, peppery Cognac cream sauce.

Endorsing the product

(go back to the text where it begins: "Guests' attention must be focused on the selections that servers feel are particularly outstanding, by using appetizing adjectives...")

PAGE 22

Left column, "Hot Beverage Service"—fourth bullet ("Cream…"), add as last sentence:

"It should be noted that in some upscale establishments, the cream, half-and-half or milk is heated prior to service."

Right column, under "1. Proportion", after the 1st bullet, change as follows:

- The recommended formula is 20 ounces of fresh cold water to 1 ounce of freshly ground coffee.
- Always match the portion of coffee to the brewing capacity.
- The brew cycle must be completed before removing the decanter or pot.
- Do not combine old and new coffee

PAGE 23

Left column—under "4. Freshness", add as the first bullet:

- It is best to use the freshest coffee possible. Purchase roaster fresh, nitrogen flushed portioned packs.

Right column—under "5. Equipment", replace with the following:

- The cleaner the equipment, the better the taste of the coffee. Clean the grinder, dispenser, coffee maker, filter devices, spray heads, brewing containers thoroughly at the end of each shift.
- The selection of the equipment depends on the volume of fresh brewed coffee that will be consumed. For amounts less than 3 gallons of coffee per hour, a French press or a single pot brewer should be used. For 3 to 6 gallons per hour, an airpot brewing system should be used. Any amount over 6 gallons a modular system or an automatic urn system should be used.

- French presses are used at upscale establishments as they are both more costly to maintain and more labor intensive. French presses come in different sizes allowing flexibility if one is serving 10 ounces or 20 ounces at one time. The coffee grounds should be medium and the proportion is 1 to 1½ ounces of coffee to 20 ounces of boiling water.
- Pour the coffee into the French press pot and pour the boiling water directly into the pot over the grounds. Once the grounds have floated to the top, stir the coffee grounds 2 or 3 times rapidly around. Place the cover over the pot without plunging the press. Wait 3 minutes prior to plunging the press.
- Single pot brewers yield 60 ounces or 12 five-ounce servings. The brewers can be pour-through systems or are plumbed into a water source. Each pot requires 3 ounces of ground coffee. Coffee should not be held in the glass decanter or coffee pot for more than 15 minutes.
- An airpot brewer brews into an insulated serving decanter (airpot) that will maintain the temperature of the brewed coffee at 185 degrees F for an hour. Because it is insulted, direct heat is not applied to maintain this temperature and the coffee does not deteriorate as in a single pot brewer.
- Most airpots hold 75 ounces or 15 five-ounce servings. Use 3½ ounces of coffee and spread it evenly in the bottom of the filter-lined brew basket.
- An automatic urn is used in high volume foodservice operations. The average volume is 2.5 gallons of water to one pound of coffee, which brews 60 five-ounce cups of coffee. Use coarse ground coffee.
- If the urn is not equipped with an automatic mixing device, draw off the heavy coffee from the bottom of the urn and pour it back into the brew but not through the grounds, to ensure uniform mixing.
- Modular brewers are a combination of a brewing module (the water heating and volume control station) which is fixed in a permanent location and a mobile brewed coffee container of various capacities (5, 10 and 20 liters) with heating systems to keep coffee at 185 degrees F.

Paper filters
- Eliminate more soluble solids than other methods such as a French Press.
- Provide ease of sanitation—throw away the used filters
- Eliminate sediment and cloudiness in coffee
- Must be stored away from aromatic foods because filters can pick up odors and affect the taste of the coffee.

PAGE 24

Right column, last bullet —("When … result"), add as last sentence,

"Steamed milk should not reach any higher than 165°F."

Then add as last two bullets:

- Vent any leftover milk from the steaming arm by opening the steam valve again. Then turn off.
- Wipe the steaming arm with a damp cloth to remove excess milk.

PAGE 69

Right column, under Tureen Service there is a step missing. After the first bullet ("Preset the … on underliners"), add as a second bullet:

- Place the underlined soup plate, bowl or cup in front of the guest from the right side using the right hand.

PAGE 118

Left column, insert the following bullet after 1773

- At the Paris Exposition Universelle of 1855, Edouard Loysel de la Santais invented a prototype of the espresso machine.

Right column, after the first paragraph on Robusta, insert the following:

Varietal and Specialty Coffees

Of the entire coffee bean production, only 10% represents gourmet or specialty quality. A varietal coffee is a coffee comprised entirely from one type of coffee bean from a single growing region. Antigua Guatemalan, Jamaican Blue Mountain, Hawaiian Kona, Costa Rican Tarrazu, Kenyan AA, Ethiopian Yrgachev, or Sumatran Gayo Mountain are all examples of varietals. A blend is a mixture of two or more types of beans that complement each other. There are no definite rules about blending. Blending defines the coffee roaster's image for the public.

Certified Organic Coffee

The market for organically grown and processed products has expanded considerably in the last few years. There is a difference between products that claim to be "organic" and those that are "certified organic". "Organic" is only a manufacturer's claim while "certified organic" products such as coffee have been verified through inspection and evaluation by an independent third party inspector.

To become organically certified, the processor must keep detailed records of the materials and methods used in processing the product. The product must also be made with at least 95% certified organic ingredients. This means the coffee farmer must follow strict agricultural practices that prohibit the use of synthetic fertilizers or pesticides. The farmer must also practice shade-tree canopy preservation surrounding the coffee plantation to provide habitat for migratory birds. This allows the coffee to be designated as "bird friendly." Certified organic coffee must be kept separate from all other coffees throughout its production and processing.

The Coffee Plant

(Continue with the original 2nd paragraph that was under "Robusta"—"The coffee plant matures … sweet cherries")

PAGE 119

Right column, under "Coffee Classifications" add as a continuation of the 1st sentence ("...altitude of growth")

by the International Coffee Organization (ICO). The ICO has lost its standing in the past decade and the following classifications are not so readily accepted or conformed to.

PAGE 121

Left column, add as bullets before "Cappuccino":

- *Ristretto* (Restricted) is made using ½ a shot of espresso, served in a demitasse cup with sugar on the side and "water back."
- *Doppio* (Double) is a double shot of espresso served in a demitasse with sugar on the side.
- *Macchiato* (Marked) is a single shot of espresso, marked with a "shot" of hot milk, served in a demitasse with sugar on the side.
- *Lungo* (Long) is a long single shot of espresso served in a demitasse with sugar on the side.
- *Caffe Breve* is made using a single shot of espresso and 4 oz of steamed/foamed half-and-half, served in a 6 ounce cup with sugar on the side.
- *Corretto* (Corrected) is a single shot of espresso with a 1 ounce shot of liqueur served in a demitasse.

(Change "Cappuccino")

- *Cappuccino* is made by combining a single shot of espresso with 4½ ounces of thick foam of steamed milk, served in a 6 to 8 ounce cup or glass with sugar on the side.

Left column, under "Decaffeinated Coffee", add as the first sentence:

The U.S. Food and Drug Administration (FDA) guidelines state that decaffeinated coffee must have 97% of caffeine removed from the green bean prior to roasting.

Change "water method" to:

- *Conventional water method.* The green beans are treated with steam and water to open their cellular structure and then flushed with a decaffeinating agent such as methylene chloride or ethyl acetate to draw out the caffeine. The beans are then treated with steam and water to evaporate all remaining traces of the decaffeinating agent. It is completely safe as there is no traceable amounts of the agent left.

Eliminate the bullet "Methylene chloride."

Right column, under "Tasting Terms", add as first two paragraphs:

Cupping is the traditional procedure in the coffee industry to evaluate the quality of samples of green coffee beans. The cupping process is designed to enable the buyer to assess **aroma, acidity, taste** and **body.** A cupping is not so very different to a wine or beer tasting."

Aromas are very important as they relate to our ability to smell and "taste" the flavor of the coffee. Aromatic characteristics include floral, spicy, fruity, woody, winey, nutty, sweet, musty, earthy.

(Leave "Acidity" as is, insert "Taste" before "Body" and eliminate "Flavor")

Taste is affected by sweetness, sourness, bitterness and saltiness, but it is also the overall impression felt by the tongue. Characteristic tastes include sweet, sour, bitter, mellow, bland, fresh, sharp.

Add to "Body" at end of paragraph:

Characteristics of body include buttery, watery, heavy, thick, light, and thin.

PAGE 133

Left column, insert the following paragraph after paragraph about "Semillon"

Viognier. Viognier originated in the Rhone region of France and though close to obscurity until recently found its best expression in Condrieu and Chateau Grillet in northern Rhone. It has many characteristics of Chardonnay in that it is somewhat full bodied, has good acidity and is malleable to the winemaker's art. However, when Viognier comes in little to no contact with oak, it has a distinctive floral and peachlike aromas. This variety is being planted in increasing amounts in California.

PAGE 163

Left column, insert after the 6th bullet ("Tasters ... wine tastings"), the following bullets:

- Professional tastings are conducted while seated with usually 6 to 15 wines poured in equal amounts of no more than 1½ to 2 ounces.
- The purpose of professional tasting is to be able to better differentiate between the wines by comparing one to the others.
- It is best for the taster to sniff through all the wines before actually sipping any of them as wine on the palate will linger and interfere with the taster's ability to evaluate the next one.

Delete bullet "Two ounce portions of wine should be served."

PAGE 229

Right column, 1st paragraph—insert after the sentence "There are 17 Grand Cru vineyards ... Comite Interprofessionel du Vin de Champagne.":

The rating system is known as the *echelle des crus* in which points are assigned to all vineyards which subsequently affects the prices fixed for the grapes from those vineyards.

PAGE 274

Right column, heading "Gin" and the text on gin should be on page 280 under "Other Spirits".

PAGE 313

Left column, add to the "Dram Shop Laws" text at the end:

It is worth noting that it is also against the law to serve four classifications of patrons:

- Anyone who is legally intoxicated or would become intoxicated by serving him/her an alcoholic beverage
- Anyone who is a known alcoholic
- Anyone who has a propensity towards alcoholism
- Anyone who is legally under age.

(After the text on Dram Shop Laws, there should be a text on Identification)

Identification

All states mandate that only those 21 years and older are legally able to purchase alcoholic beverages whether at on-premise or off-premise establishments. It is imperative that the server be aware of his/her own liability if they serve an underage patron. There are criminal, administrative and civil sanctions that can be applied against a server, manager or owner of an establishment that fails to take reasonable steps to enforce this law. As an added precaution, a server should check the identification of any patron who looks 25 years old or younger.

Given today's technology, it is not very difficult to forge identifications. Establishments should rely on publications that are updated yearly on identifications from across the U.S. as a means for increasing reliability of the identification. Identifications should be carefully inspected. The following identifications are legally acceptable:

- A state issued picture driver's license
- A state issued picture identification card

- A military identification with picture
- A U.S. passport

There is no requirement for an establishment's employees to accept any identification issued outside the state it is located in. Some states, such as Rhode Island, require alcoholic licensees to have a "Minor's Book" located at the bar which requires a questionably legal patron to sign it. A good guide to follow is, if a server has any doubts about the legal age of a patron, politely refuse the patron any alcoholic beverage.

Glossary

À la carte   Foods prepared to order; every item priced separately.

À la Russe   Foods prepared in a Russian way.

ATF   Also known as BATF, for Bureau of Alcohol, Tobacco and Firearms.

AVA   American Viticultural Area, a legally defined and designated wine growing area of the United States.

Abboccato   Semi-sweet, for wine.

Abfüllung   Bottling or bottler.

Accompaniments   Items that accompany a course; a food item mandated by the chef.

Acetaldehyde   Component giving sherry its distinctive bouquet. Not desirable in other wines.

Acetic   Vinegary.

Acetobacter   Bacteria present in wine which feed off oxygen and convert wine to vinegar.

Acid   Important element in wines, which includes tartaric, citric, malic and lactic acids.

Acidity   Refreshing tartness due to the presence of fruit acids.

Aging   The complex process that allows slow oxidation to take place in wood barrels, transforming the wine or spirit into a more complex beverage.

Agrafe   A metal clip that holds a champagne cork in place during the second fermentation.

Aguardiente   A distilled spirit.

Albariza   A chalky soil found in the Jerez-Xérès-Sherry region of Spain.

Alcohol   The compound, generally ethyl alcohol or ethanol, that acts as both a preservative and an intoxicating agent.

Al fresco   Outside dining (i.e., on sidewalks, patios, lawns, and poolsides).

Amontillado   A dry type of sherry with nutty flavors, in the style of Montilla from Jerez, Spain.

Ampelography   The study of identifying grape varieties.

Amphora   An ancient two-handled ceramic container used by ancient Greeks and Romans for the storage of wine.

Angel's share   The amount of alcohol in cognac or armagnac that evaporates during aging.

Anthocyanin   The pigmentation contained in the skins of grapes, especially black grapes, that gives wine its color.

Añada   Wine made from the harvest of a particular year in Spain.

Apéritif   A wine or wine-based beverage to stimulate the appetite.

Appellation d'Origine Contrôlée   System of wine laws enacted in 1935 in France.

Appetizer   A food dish usually served as the first course of a meal.

Arches   *See* Legs.

Aroma   The smell or fragrance emanating from a grape used in making wine.

Aromatic (or Aromatized) Wine   An apéritif wine that has been infused with botanicals, such as vermouth.

Assemblage   The blending of different wines in the making of Champagne.

Asti   A sweet sparkling wine made in the area surrounding the Piedmont town of Asti in Italy.

Astringent   An adjective to describe wines that lead to a sensory response to tannins which caused the mouth to feel dried out and puckered.

Atmosphere   A unit of pressure equal to 15 pounds per square inch.

Attack   The first impression that the wine makes on the palate.

Auslese   A Qmp wine made from hand-selected late-harvest grapes.

Autolysis   The breakdown of lees or dead yeast cells, which become reincorporated into the wine giving it a "tasty" bouquet.

B&B   Bread and butter.

Bacchus   The Roman god of wine.

Back bar   The display area behind the bar, which has two or three shelves of liquors and liqueurs, cabinets, shelving, and possibly beer coolers.

Banquet   A dining function in which all guests are served at one time and all facets of the meal are prearranged (i.e., the menu, the number of guests, price, and so on.)

Banquette   A type of seating arrangement in which guests are seated facing the dining room with their backs against a wall or partition.

Bar back   A bartender's helper or apprentice bartender.

Barrique   An oak barrel holding 225 liters.

Basket press   A wine-shaped press shaped like a tub in which grapes are placed and pressure is applied by means of a large screw, which presses the grapes and allows the juice to run out through slotted sides.

Battonage   The stirring of lees to impart its flavors into wine.

Beerenauslese   A Qmp classification of German wines made from overripe, oversized, individually picked grapes.

Bentonite   A montmorillonite clay used as a fining agent for wine.

Bereich   A designated district delimiting a wine-producing area.

Bitter   One of four sensations identified by the taste buds.

Blanc de noirs   White sparkling wine or champagne made entirely from white grapes, usually Chardonnay, with more fruit flavor than a Blanc de blancs.

Blanc de blancs   Champagne or sparkling wines made entirely from white grapes, usually Chardonnay.

Blazer   An oval, rectangular, or round pan used primarily for tableside cooking.

Bloom   White waxen coating on grapes to which wild yeasts become attached.

Blush wine   A white wine made from black grapes whose must was left in brief contact to produce a blush-colored wine.

Boal   *See* Bual.

Bocksbeutel A flask-shaped bottle used in Franken, Germany, Portugal, and Chile.

Bodega A wine cellar or warehouse, but also a term used to designate a producer or shipper.

Body The tactile impression of fullness left by a wine on the palate.

Bonne-chauffe The second distillation of Cognac.

Botrytis cinerea A special mold, also called "noble rot," which allows grapes to dehydrate and become very sweet and aromatic.

Botti A large wooden cask.

Bottle shock Unbalanced condition that wine suffers immediately after bottling.

Bottom-fermented Lager-style beers that ferment at cooler temperatures for longer periods of time than ales.

Bouquet The smells that develop as a result of the fermentation and aging processes.

Bowl The part of the glass that holds the wine.

Breathe To allow a wine to come into contact with air to dissipate the tannins and shed any off-odors.

Brigade French for "team."

Bristol cream Sherry that was traditionally made in Bristol, England, blending oloroso with sweet Pedro Ximénez wine.

Brix A measurement of sugar by weight in a solution; sometimes referred to as *balling*.

Brouillis The "heart" of Cognac distillation.

Brut Very dry; no perceptible sugar in sparkling wines or champagne.

Bual Semi-sweet Madeira wine named after its grape variety.

Buffet A display of ready-to-eat dishes presented on a table or sideboard.

Buffetier A server whose primary responsibilities include setting up, breaking down, maintaining, and serving the buffet.

Bung hole The round opening originally located at the top of a barrel.

Bung A cork or wooden plug that fits into the opening at the top of a barrel, for a tight seal.

Busser A server whose primary responsibilities are those of clearing, pouring water, changing ashtrays, and resetting tables.

Cage Wire mesh wrapped around a sparkling wine cork; also wire hood.

Call liquor Brand-named distilled spirits, which have proprietary labels.

Capitolare Classification of fine Italian wines that are not DOC because the primary grape is nontraditional, (e.g., Cabernet Sauvignon).

Capsule An aluminum, plastic, and (much less often) lead covering to give a more aesthetic appearance to a bottle.

Carafe A glass bottle with a wide mouth used to decant wine or in which to leave a house wine.

Carbonation Injection method in which carbon dioxide is forced into wine to make it sparkling. Used for the lowest quality and least expensive sparkling wine.

Carbonic maceration A vinification process whereby the yeast is forced to ferment from the inside of the grape under carbon dioxide pressure. Normally used in Beaujolais and in the making of fruity and fresh-tasting red wine.

Carte du jour Menu of the day.

Cask A wood barrel used for aging wines.

Casserole dish An oven-proof dish used in the baking and service of various dishes.

Cava Sparkling wine made by the classic or Champagne method.

Cave   A wine cellar.

Cépage   Grape variety.

Chai   A cellar or above-ground facility for storing and aging wines.

Chamat   Bulk fermentation of sparkling wine.

Chambré   A decanting process to help bring wine to room temperature at 64° F.

Champagne   Sparkling wine from the Champagne region of France made from the méthode Champenoise.

Chapeau   A thick "cap" consisting of skins, stems, pips, and so on, that rise to the surface during red-wine fermentation.

Chaptalization   Augmenting of the sugar levels of must by adding beet sugar.

Charente   The valley in the heart of the Cognac region.

Château   French for "estate".

Check register   A managerial tool used to record the check number issued to specific servers. Used as a control to prevent employee theft.

Chef de service   Dining room manager.

Chef de rang   Station captain.

Chiaretto   A light-colored Italian red wine.

Chiller/cooler   A wine bucket that holds the temperature of the wine but does not lower it.

Church key   A slang term for a beer bottle opener.

Clairet   Rosé wine made from bleeding maceration tanks of red wines.

Claret   An English term to describe light red wines.

Clarete   A Spanish term to describe light red wines.

Classico   The central zone of an Italian DOC wine region.

Clos   Generally, an area enclosed by a wall. A French term used particularly in Burgundy as equivalent to a château.

Cold stabilization   A process for clarifying wines by bringing the temperatures of the wine to 25° F to 30° F and precipitating tartrates and other solubles.

Colheita   A Portuguese name to denote a port of a particular vintage.

Commis de rang   Front waiter.

Commis de suite   Back waiter.

Commune   Town or village.

Condiments   Seasonings or additional ingredients for a food or beverage, which may be requested by guests (e.g., salt, pepper, and Worcestershire sauce).

Congeners   Flavor components that provide spirits with their aromas and flavors.

Cooper   A professional craftsperson who makes wooden barrels.

Copita   A tulip-shaped stemmed glass that holds 4 ounces and is used for serving sherry.

Cordial   A term for an after-dinner beverage, usually referring to a liqueur.

Corkage fee   A fee charged by an establishment for opening and serving a wine that a customer has brought.

Corked   A wine that smells moldy and cork-like from the mold *Trichloroanisole* (TCA).

Côte   French for "hillside" or "slope."

Cover   A single place setting at a guest table.

Crash kit   All necessary paperwork, including dupe pads and a reconciliation sheet, in the event a computerized point-of-sale system ceases to function.

Cream sherry   *See* Bristol cream.

Crémant   A sparkling wine made only from Chardonnay. Less sugar is added to the liqueur de tirage, reducing the level of alcohol and carbon dioxide during the second fermentation. This results in a wine with half the amount of atmospheres of pressure.

Cru French for "growth" and "a vineyard"; refers primarily to the classification in the system.

Cruet A small glass bottle for holding vinegar or oil in tableservice.

Crumbing The removal of food particles left on the guest's table by using a folded napkin and small plate or a crumber.

Cuvée A blend of wine that is selected for a single bottling.

Cuvier Fermenting room.

Damask A pattern in the weave of linen.

Dash One-sixth teaspoon.

Débarrassage The process of clearing a guest's table of plates, flatware, and so on.

Decant To pour wine from its bottle into a decanter to separate it from sediment or to accelerate its exposure to oxygen.

Dégorgement The process or removing all sediments in Champagne by freezing the lees in the neck of the bottle and allowing it to be forced out by its own pressure prior to refilling and placing a permanent cork in the bottle.

Demi-tasse A half-sized cup used for serving espresso.

Demisec Semi-dry or off-dry.

Denominacao de Origem Portuguese system of wine laws.

Denominacíon de Origen Spanish system of wine laws.

Denominazione di Origine Controllata (DOC) Italian system of wine laws.

Dessert wine A still wine that naturally contains over 14% alcohol and is normally sweet.

Deuce A party of two or table for two.

Dioise method Similar to the transfer method in the making of sparkling wine but with a single fermentation.

Dionysus The Greek god of wine.

Discs The gradation of color around the outer rim of the surface of wine in a glass.

Dolce Italian for "sweet."

Domaine French for "estate."

Dosage A syrup made of wine and sugar that is added to Champagne or sparkling wines after dégorgement, which determines the sweetness level of the wine.

Doser A container holding ground espresso, which dispenses exact portions.

Doux Sweetest level of champagne.

Draft (or Draught) beer Unpasteurized beer, which may be bottled or canned.

Dupe (or Dupe pad) Hand-written order with one or two duplicates for kitchen use.

Edelfäule German for *Botrytis cinerea* or "noble rot."

Edelzwicker Alsatian blend of noble grape varieties.

Égrappage The process of destalking the grapes before pressing.

Eiswein The German term for wine that is made from pressed frozen grapes, resulting in an intensely flavored and sweet wine.

Enology *See Oenolgy.*

Enophile *See Oenophile.*

Entrée The main food item served during a meal.

Erzeugerabfüllung German for "estate bottled."

Estate bottled A legally defined term requiring 100% of a wine to be grown, crushed, produced, and bottled at a single estate; equivalent to Mise en Bouteilles au Château.

Esters   Organic components that offer the fruit aromas in wine.

Estufa   The heating chamber used in the process of making Madeiras.

Ethyl alcohol   The principal form of alcohol in all alcoholic beverages.

Extra-dry   A term reflecting a higher degree of sugar in sparkling wines, even though they are not perceptibly sweet.

Family-style service   Sizable portions of food served on a platter or in a tureen, presented to a table of patrons, who will help themselves.

Fattoria   Italian for "farm."

Fermentation   The process whereby yeasts convert natural sugars into alcohol and carbon dioxide.

Fiasco   (pl. Fiaschi) The traditional straw-wrapped bottle used for inexpensive Chianti.

Filtering   The procedure used to clarify wine prior to bottling.

Finger bowl   A small bowl filled with warm water and usually a slice of lemon. It is used by the guest to cleanse the fingers when eating foods that require use of the fingers. The bowl should be accompanied by a napkin.

Fining   The process of clarifying wine by adding an agent such as bentonite, egg whites, casein, or albumen, which will coagulate suspended particles in wine.

Fino   A pale, very dry, and elegant style of sherry from Spain.

Fire   Expression used to inform the kitchen staff that a course should be ready to serve in a short period of time.

Flatware   A category that includes all fork, knives, and spoons used in the dining room.

Flight   A row of glasses in a table setting.

Float   The last ingredient poured onto a drink, which is not incorporated by a specific procedure.

Flor   The development of yeast that forms a coating on top of some sherries and Jura wines.

Flute   An elongated stemmed glass used in the service of sparkling wines.

Forecasting   Predicting the future business activities and needs of an establishment.

Foxy   An adjective describing the wild grapey aromas stemming from native *Vitis labrusca* grapes.

Frappé   A European-style beverage that consists of a liqueur poured onto crushed or shaved ice.

Free-pour   The pouring of spirits and liqueurs from a bottle without using a measuring glass such as a jigger.

Frizzante   Effervescent but not as bubbly as a sparkling wine.

Front of the house   The public areas of an establishment where the server meets the guests, such as the dining room, lobby, guest room, and meeting room.

Garnish   A fruit or vegetable added to a plate or platter to enhance eye appeal.

Garrafeira   A Portuguese term denoting a wine that has been especially aged.

Gebiet   A German wine-producing area.

Generic wine   Wines labeled in the United States after place names of Europe to describe a facsimile style, such as Chablis.

Governo (al' uso)   A process used in the production of Chianti, in which sweet concentrated must is added to fermented wine, causing a second fermentation that results in a higher alcoholic content.

Grand Cru   Great growth; a legal classification.

Grappa   An Italian distillate made from the pomace of grapes.

Grosslage   A collection of individual vineyard sites in Germany.

Group   The part of an espresso machine into which the portafilter is placed.

Guéridon   A wheeled cart from which food is served in the dining room.

Guest of honor   A guest for whom an event or meal is being celebrated.

Halbtrocken   Semi-dry wine from Germany.

Heads   A term used in the distillation process to describe the elements that vaporize first.

Hearts   The essence of the distillation process, which provides the basis of a distilled spirit.

Hectare   A land measurement of 2.47 acres.

Hectoliter   A measurement equal to 26.4 gallons.

Highlighting   The practice whereby a particular item is emphasized so as to leave a lasting impression.

Hops   A vine that develops flowers in small cones. Used as a "bittering" agent for beer.

Hors d'oeuvre   French for "outside the main item." Usually a palate teaser or small, portional food item.

Hospices de Beaune   A charity hospital located in Beaune, Burgundy, which hosts an important yearly wine auction.

House brand   Brands of spirits that are generic and generally of lower quality and price.

Hybrid grapes   Dozens of American grape varieties, with *Vitis vinifera* varieties such as Vidal Blanc.

Hydrometer   A gauge used to measure specific gravity and potential alcohol concentration.

Imbottigliato   Italian for "bottled."

Import duty   A tax levied on all imported distilled products.

Infusion   Cold process for compounding spirits to make them liqueurs. Flavors are extracted from botanicals by steeping them in water.

Intermezzo   A brief pause or course, such as a sorbet to cleanse the palate between two courses.

Isinglass   *See* bentonite.

Jack   A tray stand.

Jeroboam   A large bottle of wine that is equivalent to four 750-milliliter bottles of wine.

Jigger   A legal definition for a 1½-ounce pour of a spirit.

Jug wine   A description for an American vin ordinaire, usually bottled by the liter or in a larger container.

Kabinett   The distinct and lowest category of German QmP wines.

Keg   A container holding 15.5 gallons of beer.

Kir   A popular apéritif made by adding Crème de Cassis to white wine.

Knife rest   An object on which the blade of a knife is placed at a place setting to prevent it from damaging a fine tablecloth.

Krausening   A secondary fermentation process whereby actively fermenting beer is added to a lager to enact carbonation and alcohol.

Lagar   Large stone or concrete tanks in which black grapes are crushed in traditional port vinification.

Lager   A bottom-fermented beer that is stored or lagered for considerable time.

Leaching   A process for filtering spirits, such as whiskey or vodka poured through finely ground charcoal.

Lees   Dead yeast cells and other solids that remain in the wine after fermentation.

Legs   The streaks formed on the inside of a glass bowl after a wine has been swirled; also known as tears.

Limousin   An oak forest in central France that is famous for the oak that is harvested to make barrels for aging wines and cognacs.

Linalool   A chemical compound found in wines, which offers a very floral aroma, especially in Riesling, Gewürztraminer, and Muscat varieties.

Line   The side of a buffet table.

Liquoroso   A sweet fortified wine.

Liter   A metric unit of liquid measurement equal to 33.814 ounces.

Logbook   A record book used for tracking information such as dates, weather, guest counts, and sales.

Maceration   The extraction of aroma, color, flavor, and tannins from the skins of grapes, usually during fermentation in vinification. Also the extraction of aromas, flavors, and colors by steeping a botanical fruit.

Maderized   A wine that is somewhat oxidized and has a baked odor and taste. Usually describes a wine that is overaged or stored improperly.

Magnum   A bottle that can hold 51 ounces of wine.

Maître d'   French for "master of"; refers to a manager of a dining room.

Malmsey   British derivation of the grape variety Malvasia; used to describe sweet Madeira wines.

Malolactic fermentation   A secondary fermentation of wine in which malic acid is converted into lactic acid.

Malt   Sprouted barley used in making beer or spirits, especially scotch.

Manzanilla   A light refreshing sherry from San Lucar de Barrameda.

Marc   *See* Pomace and Grappa.

Meniscus   The outer rim of wine in a glass, which can be perceived as clear.

Mercerization   The process by which natural linens are chemically treated to prevent great shrinkage and fast deterioration.

Merrowing   The hemming of polyester cloth by a rolled stitch.

Meso climate   Unique climate of a subsection of a vineyard region.

Méthode Champenoise   Wine that undergoes a second fermentation in the bottle through the addition of more sugar and yeast. The wine is clarified by riddling and dégorgement prior to a dosage being added.

Millésime   Harvest.

Mis(e) en Bouteilles au Château   Estate bottled.

Moelleux   French for "soft and luscious."

Momie   A weave in linen, usually blended natural and synthetic fibers, that provides a richer texture.

Monopole   A wine blended by a négociant and given a brand name.

Mousseux   A sparkling wine other than champagne from France.

Muddler   A wooden instrument used for crushing fruit in an old-fashioned manner.

Must   Unfermented grape juice prior to fermentation.

Mutage   The adding of a spirit to fermenting wine to stop the fermentation process, resulting in a sweet wine.

NV   Nonvintage.

Natural   Designation for bone-dry sparkling wine. Same as Brut Sauvage.

Neat   *See* Straight up.

Négociant   An individual or company that purchases, produces, or blends wine and ships it.

Nevers   Famous forest supplying oak for cooperage.

Nose   The combination of aromas and bouquets, which the taster can discern in three separate attempts.

Nouveau   The French term for a new wine. The Italian term is *novello*. Used in describing red wines that should be drunk within 6 months of vinification.

Oeil de perdrix   French for "eye of the partridge"; used to describe a pale blush color.

Oenology   The study of wine and wine making.

Oenophile   One who enjoys the study and the consumption of wine.

Oidium   A powdery mildew that attacks grapes.

Olfaction   The sense of smell.

Oloroso   A dark sherry produced without flor. It is usually made sweet.

On the rocks   When a beverage, usually a mixed drink, is served on ice.

Order   Foods selected by patrons and recorded by a server, who relays the request to the kitchen by voice, in writing, or by computer.

Organoleptic characteristics   Those elements of food or beverage that are perceived by the senses.

Oxidation   The changes in wine caused by exposure to oxygen.

P.X.   Initials used for Pedro Ximérez; a sweet varietal wine also used in the making of cream sherry when blended with oloroso.

Palo Cortado   A type of sherry that is very rare, because it begins as a Fino until the flor dies.

Par stock   Established minimum and maximum amounts of a product in inventory.

Passito   An Italian sweet wine made from grapes that have been shriveled in the sun.

Pasteurization   The heating of a substance, such as milk, to 140° F for 20 to 25 minutes to kill microorganisms and prevent or slow fermentation.

Percolation   A cold method of extracting the aromas and flavors from botanicals, fruits, and spices in compounding spirits.

Pergola   A system for trellising grapevines so that the grapes hang from overhead.

Pétillant   Slightly effervescent, spritzy.

Phenols   *See* Tannin.

Phylloxera vastatrix   A root louse that devastated the vineyards of Europe, Australia, and California in the 1880s. This species continues to be a problem in California.

Pith   The white bitter layer of citrus fruit that lies between the skin and pulp.

Planchon, Jules-Emile   French scientist and agronomist in the nineteenth century who arrived at the solution of grafting American rootstock onto *Vitis vinifera*.

Pleat   A fold in the tablecloth draping or skirting that presents a more aesthetic appearance.

Pomace   The residual skins, pips, and stems of grapes after pressing.

Pony glass   A small stemmed shot glass holding 1.5 ounces, used in the service of cordials.

Portafilter   The small basket holding the correct amount of espresso coffee in the espresso machine.

Potage spoon   A spoon used for a cream or thickened soup.

Press   A machine that applies pressure on grapes to extract juice.

Prestige Cuvée   Super-premium champagne.

Prix fixé   A menu offering several courses at one set price.

Prohibition   The prohibition of all alcoholic beverages in the United States, due to the Eighteenth Amendment, which was enacted in January of 1920, until its repeal by the Twenty-first Amendment in December of 1933.

Proof   A measurement of the strength of alcohol (2 degrees proof are equal to 1% alcohol).

Proprietary   The brand name that a specific winery, brewery, or distillery gives to one of its products, which no other may use.

Pruning   The process of removing excess vines to stimulate growth and vigor during the subsequent growing season.

Punt   The indentation in the bottom of a wine bottle.

Pupîtres   The French term for an A-frame rack used in the riddling process of the Champagne methods.

Qualitätswein bestimmter Anbaugebiete   (QbA) Germany's quality wines of designated areas of origin.

Qualitätswein mit Prädikat   (QmP) German wines of distinction; the highest quality level of wines from Germany.

Quinta   A wine estate in Portugal.

Racking   The siphoning or pumping of wine from one container to another, to clarify it by leaving the sediment behind.

Rancio   The rich nutty flavor found in cognacs and armagnacs that have been aged for 20 years in wood.

Réchaud   A heating unit designed to be used on a guéridon for tableside cooking.

Recioto   A wine made from passito grapes, such as Amarone.

Récolte   Harvest.

Remuage   The French term for riddling.

Reservation   An arrangement established between a guest and an establishment for dining on a specific date and at a specific time.

Reserve   Has no legal standing in the United States, but is a marketing tool to promote the best quality wine that a winemaker can produce.

Residual sugar   The amount of sugar left in wine after fermentation has stopped.

Riddling   The process of turning and shaking champagne bottles to collect all the sediment in the neck of the bottle.

Robe   The hue or depth of color of wine.

Ruby port   A port that is aged in wood for 3 to 4 years and then bottled; fairly tannin and sweet.

Saccharomyces cerevisiae   The most common strain of yeasts used in wine making.

Saigner   French for "to bleed"; used to describe the process of releasing some must during maceration to concentrate the remaining must.

Schloss   German for "château" or "estate."

Sec   French for "dry."

Section   A number of tables assigned to a server or service team.

Sélection de Grains Nobles   Classification of Alsatian wines made from grapes that are affected by *Botrytis* and are individually picked.

Sercial   (Port) The direct varietal of Madeira wines.

Serging   The hemming process for linen.

Service plate   A plate used to replace a showplate and used as an underliner for all courses preceding the entrée. When any course is served on a plate of the same size, the service plate should be removed.

Service set   A large fork and spoon held in a specific way and used to transfer food items from one service container to another.

Service station   A small work area or supply closet in the dining room, usually containing items used frequently during service.

Service towel   A clean, pressed, cloth napkin used by a service person during service for holding hot plates and wiping small spills.

Serviette   A plate covered with a neatly folded napkin, or merely a napkin used to carry items such as flatware to a guest's table.

Shot   A measure of liquid, usually straight up. Also defines the length of steam that passes through the portafilter in an espresso machine.

Showplate   A decorative plate used to make the tabletop more attractive.

Side duty/work   Defined duties for each service person to perform prior to and after service.

Silencer   A pad or cloth (rubber or felt), placed between the table and the tablecloth to reduce noise.

Solera system   A system to blend each vintage with the prior one so that a blend remains consistently the same.

Sommelier   A wine steward.

Spätlese   German Qmp wines made from grapes harvested a minimum of 1 week after the regular harvest.

Speed rack   A stainless steel rack located on bar sinks that contains bottles of spirits and mixes that meet the greatest customer demands.

Spittoon   A container used for spitting wine or other beverage during tasting.

Splash   A very small amount of an ingredient added to a drink.

Spritzer   A tall beverage made of wine and carbonated mixer.

Spumante   Italian for "sparkling."

Station   A group of tables assigned to a server or team of servers.

Straight up   A bar term indicating that the spirit has not come in contact with ice.

Stuck fermentation   A fermentation that has stopped naturally before all the sugar has been converted to alcohol.

Sulphurization   The adding of sulphur to inhibit bacterial growth and oxidation.

Sur lie   The aging of wine on the lees after fermentation.

Sur pointe   The neck-down position of champagne bottles in storage after riddling but prior to dégorgement.

Süssreserve   The unfermented must that is filtered and added back into German wine to add flavor and sweetness.

Suzette pan   A circular pan; the most frequently used pan for tableside cooking.

Table d'Hôte   From the table of the host. In the modern context, a menu in which the price of a complete meal changes according to the entrée selected.

Table wine   A still wine containing 14% alcohol or less.

Tails   The elements in wine or mash that are the last to vaporize.

Tall   A mixed drink that is diluted and served in a taller glass.

Tannin   A phenolic compound that is extracted from the skins, pips, and stems of grapes during maceration. Tannins may cause wine to be astringent when young but also act as a preservative and give wine structure or body.

Tartrates   The salts of tartaric acid that can precipitate and form crystals in wine.

Tastevin   A shallow silver cup used for examining wine in Burgundy. Also, when placed on a chain, the cup is used as the symbol of the sommelier.

Tawny port   Port wine that is aged 10, 20, 30, or 40 years in wood, resulting in an amber-brown color, with sandalwood spiciness and traces of dark fruit, such as dates.

Tea bottle   A pear-shaped glass bottle used for steeping tea.

Tea cozy   A knitted or padded cover for a teapot, used to insulate it and prevent the tea from losing its heat as quickly.

Tears   *See* Legs.

Terroir   The French term that defines the concept of place, including soil, terrain, climate, and water retention.

Tête de Cuvée   The French term for a producer's best bottling of champagne, generally made from free run-off juice from the press.

Tips   The origin of the word is an acronym: **t**o **i**nsure **p**rompt **s**ervice. It is a payment for service and is calculated as a percentage (usually 15% to 20%) of the bill. Tips are assigned according to the establishment, but most often the server keeps the tips he or she has been left.

Tirage   The liqueur de tirage is the mixture of wine, yeast culture, and sugar that is added to Champagne wines to cause the second fermentation.

Toast   The process of applying fire to wood/oak barrels in the cooperage process. The greater the application, the more pronounced the oak flavor in wine.

Top shelf   A category of distilled or compounded spirits that are proprietary premium brands.

Topping off   The addition of wine to compensate for evaporation in the barrel during the aging process.

Training/trellising   Methods of harnessing the growth of vines to optimize their vigor and productivity.

Transfer method   A method for producing sparkling wine, in which the wine is transferred from the bottle after the second fermentation, filtered in bulk with the dosage added, and rebottled under pressure.

Tray stand   A collapsible two-legged stand that is hinged and has straps on its upper arms to give more stability. Used by servers to hold trays of food carried in to the dining room.

Triage   The sorting and selection of good-quality grapes after harvesting but before crushing or pressing.

Trocken   German for "dry."

Trockenbeerenauslese   The category of German QmP wine that has the highest amount of sugar at the time of harvest. The grapes are late-harvested and picked when shrivelled once they are affected by *Botrytis*. These are very expensive wines.

Turn sheet   A management tool that is used to distribute guest's parties evenly throughout the stations of the dining room to ensure smooth service.

Ullage   The space in a barrel between the wine and the barrel that is caused by evaporation. It is also referred to as the space between the wine and a cork, which is significant when appraising older bottles.

Umami   Viewed in the Far East as a fifth taste component that can be perceived by taste buds in the mouth. An example of a umami glutamate compound is MSG (monosodium glutamate).

Underliners   Any plate placed under a service item containing food or beverage.

Upselling   A technique used by servers in an attempt to have guests try a higher-quality or higher-priced item (e.g., Absolut instead of house vodka).

Varietal   A wine made predominantly or exclusively from a particular grape variety, such as Chardonnay.

Vendange   French for "vintage" or "harvest."

Vendange tardive   The term for late harvest wine from Alsace.

Véraison   The point at which grapes turn from green to their true colors in early June.

Verdelho   An off-dry Madeira wine.

Vin Santo   Italian for "holy wine"; an amber dessert wine classically from the Tuscany region.

Vintage   The harvesting of grapes; also the designation of a wine label for the year the grapes are harvested.

Vitis labrusca   An American species of grapevine.

Vitis vinifera   The European grapevine species considered to be the premium for making wines.

Waste plate   A plate placed before guests for the discarding of bones or shells.

Weingut   German for "wine estate."

Wine thief   A tube made of glass or other material that is used to extract wine samples from barrels to check their condition.

Wire hood   *See* Cage.

Worm   The twisted screw that is inserted into the cork.

Wort   The liquid resulting from the grinding and mashing of malted barley and other grains, which is boiled with hops.

Bibliography

American Diabetes Association and the American Dietetic Association, *Exchange Lists for Meal Planning*, American Diabetes Association, Diabetes Information Service Center, Alexandria, VA, 1986.

American Spice Trade Association, *Food Service Seasoning Guide*, Food Service Department, American Spice Trade Association, New York, 1969.

Boxer, Arabella; Charlotte Parry-Crooke; Lewis Esson; and Jocasta Innes, *The Encyclopedia of Herbs and Flavorings*, Cresent Books, New York, 1984.

Brody, Jane, *Jane Brody's Nutrition Book*, W. W. Norton, New York, 1981.

Cichy, Ronald F., *Sanitation Management*, Educational Institute of the American Hotel and Motel Association, East Lansing, MI, 1984.

Crawford, Holly W., and Milton C. McDowell, *Math Workbook for Foodservice Lodging*, 3rd ed., Van Nostrand Reinhold, New York, 1988.

Dalsass, Diana, *Miss Mary's Down-Home Cooking*, New American Library, New York, 1984.

Dittmer, Paul R., and Gerald G. Griffin, *Principles of Food, Beverage and Labor Cost Control for Hotels and Restaurants*, 3rd ed., Van Nostrand Reinhold, New York, 1984.

Dondi, Beda A., and Mary Frey Ray, *Professional Cooking and Baking*, Bennett & McKnight, Encino, CA, 1981.

Dowell, Philip, and Adrian Bailey, *Cook's Ingredients*, Dorling Kindersley, London, 1980.

Dykstra, John J., *Infection Control for Lodging and Food Service Establishment*, John Wiley & Sons, New York, 1990.

Escoffier, A., *The Escoffier Cook Book*, Crown Publishers, New York, 1969.

Eugen, Paul, *Classical Cooking the Modern Way*, Van Nostrand Reinhold, CBI, New York, 1979.

Farrell, Kenneth T., *Spices, Condiments, and Seasonings*, AVI Publishing, Westport, CT, 1985.

Food and Drug Administration, Division of Federal State Relations, State Training and Information Branch, "Hazard Analysis and Critical Control Points," Draft, May 1991.

Fuller, John; John B. Knight; and Charles A. Salter, *The Professional Chef's Guide to Kitchen Management*, Van Nostrand Reinhold, New York, 1985.

Gisslen, Wayne, *Professional Cooking*, 2nd ed., John Wiley & Sons, New York, 1989.

Gunst, Kathy, *Condiments*, G. P. Putnam's Sons, New York, 1984.

Haines, Robert G., *Math Principles for Food Service Occupations*, 2nd ed., Delmar Publishers, Albany, NY, 1988.

Hamilton, Eva May; Frances Sizer; and Eleanor Whitnew, *Nutrition Concepts and Controversies*, 5th ed., West Publishing, St. Paul, MN, 1991.

Heath, Henry B., *Source Book of Flavors*, AVI Publishing, Westport, CT, 1981.

Herbst, Sharon Tyler, *Food Lover's Companion*, Barron's Educational Series, New York, 1990.

Lendal H., *Standards, Principles and Techniques in Quantity Food Production*, 3rd ed., CBI, Boston, MA, 1966.

McVety, Paul J., and Bradley J. Ware, *Fundamentals of Menu Planning*, Van Nostrand Reinhold, New York, 1989.

Peterson, James, *Sauces: Classical and Contemporary Sauce Making*, Van Nostrand Reinhold, New York, 1991.

Montagné, Prosper, *Larousse Gastronomique*, Edited by Charlotte Turgeon, Crown Publishers, New York, 1977.

National Restaurant Association, *Current Issues Report*, Nutrition Awareness and the Foodservice Industry, National Restaurant Association, Washington, DC, 1990.

Pauli, Eugene, *Classical Cooking the Modern Way*, Edited by Marjorie S. Arkwright, R.D., Van Nostrand Reinhold, New York, 1979.

Peddersen, Raymond B., *Foodservice and Hotel Purchasing*, CBI, Boston, MA, 1981.

Saulnier, L., *Le Repertoire de la Cuisine*, Distributed in the United States by Christian Classics, Westminster, MD.

Stobart, Tom, *Herbs, Spices and Flavorings*, Overlook Press, Woodstock, NY, 1982.

The Culinary Institute of America, *The New Professional Chef*, 5th ed., Edited by Linda Glick Conway, Van Nostrand Reinhold, New York, 1991.

The Surgeon General's Report on Nutrition and Health, Public Health Service Publication No. 88-50211, Public Health Service, U.S. Department of Health and Human Services, Washington, DC, 1988.

U.S. Department of Health and Human Services, *Dietary Guidelines for Americans*, USDA Home and Garden Bulletin No. 232, U.S. Department of Health and Human Services, Washington, DC, 1990.

Wason, Betty, *Cooks, Gluttons and Gourmets, a History of Cookery*, Doubleday, Garden City, NY, 1962.

Books on Beer, Wine and Liquor

Anderson, Burton, *The Wine Atlas of Italy and Travelers' Guide to the Vineyards*, Simon and Schuster, New York, 1990.

Ashley, Maureen, *Encyclopedia of Italian Wines*, Simon and Schuster, New York, 1991.

Bespaloff, Alexis, *Complete Guide To Wine*, Penguin Books, New York, 1994.

Broadbent, Michael, *The New Great Vintage Wine Book*, Alfred A. Knopf, New York, 1991.

Coates MW, Clive, *Grands Vins*, University Of California Press, Berkley, Los Angeles, CA, 1995.

Dallas, Phillip, *Italian Wines*, Faber and Faber, London, 1983.

Erickson, Jack, *Star Spangled Beer*, Running Press, Philadelphia, PA, 1988.

Faith, Nicholas, *The Story Of Champagne, Facts On File*, New York, 1989.

Finch, Christopher, *Beer*, Abeville Press Inc., New York, NY, 1989.

Grossman, Harold J., *Grossman's Guide To Wines Beers And Spirits*, Charles Scribner's Son, New York, 1983.

Halliday, James, *Wine Atlas of Australia and New Zealand*, The Wine Appreciation Guild, San Francisco, CA, 1991.

Halliday, James, *Wine Atlas of California*, Penguin Books, England, 1993.

Hanson, Anthony, *Burgundy*, Faber and Faber, London, 1994.

Hazan, Victor, *Italian Wine*, Alfred A. Knopf, New York, 1982.

Jackson, Michael, *The Beer Hunter*, Discovery Communications Inc., Compact Disc, 1995.

Jackson, Michael, *The World Guide to Beer*, Running Press, Philadelphia, PA, 1982.

Jefford, Andrew, *Port*, Exeter Books, New York, 1988.

Johnson, Hugh, *The Atlas of German Wines and Traveler's Guide to the Vineyards*, Simon and Schuster, New York, 1986.

Johnson, Hugh, *Hugh Johnson's Modern Encyclopedia Of Wine*, Simon and Schuster, NY, 1994.

Johnson, Hugh, *Vintage, The Story Of Wine*, Simon and Schuster, New York, 1989.

Johnson, Hugh and Halliday, James, *The Vintner's Art*, Simon and Schuster, NY, 1992.

Johnson, Hugh, *World Atlas of Wine*, Simon and Schuster, NY.

Katsigris, Costas and Porter, Mary, *The Bar and Beverage Book*, John Wiley & Sons, Inc., New York, NY, 1990.

Laube, James, *California's Great Cabernets*, Wine Spectators Press, California, 1989.

Laube, James, *California's Great Chardonnays*, Wine Spectators Press, California, 1990.

Lichine, Alexis, *Guide To The Wines and Vineyards of France*, Alfred A. Knopf, New York, 1989.

Lipinski, Robert A. and Kathleen A., *The Complete Beverage Dictionary*, Van Nostrand Reinhold, New York, NY, 1992.

Lipinski, Robert A. and Kathleen A., *Professional Guide To Alcoholic Beverages*, Van Nostrand Reinhold, New York, NY, 1989.

New World Guide to Beer, Running Press, Philadelphia, PA, 1988.

Parker, Robert M. Jr., *Burgandy*, Simon and Schuster, New York, 1990.

Parker, Robert M. Jr., *Parker's Wine Buyer's Guide*, Simon and Schuster, New York, 1993.

Pieroth, Kuno F., *The Great German Wine Book*, Sterling Publishing Co., Inc., New York, 1983.

Platter, John, *South African Wine Guide*, Mitchell Beazley, London, 1994.

Read, Jan, *The Simon and Schuster Pocket Guide to Spanish Wines*, Simon and Schuster, New York, 1983.

Read, Jan, *The Wines of Portugal*, Faber and Faber, London, 1987.

Rosengarten, David and Wesson, Joshua, *Red Wine with Fish*, Simon and Schuster, New York, 1989.

Spurrier, Steven, *A Du Vin Complete Wine Course*, G.P. Putnam's sons, New York, 1983.

Stevenson, Tom, *Champagne*, Sotheby's Publications, London, 1986.

Torres, Miguel A., *Wines and Vineyards of Spain*, Editorial Blume, Milanesat, 1982.

Index

bags, 124
flavored, scented or spiced, 123–124
growing, 122
herbal, 123–124
historical aspects, 122
processing leaves of, 122–123
Tea cozy, 26
Tea service, 25–26
Temperature
for grape growing, 136
wine, 21–22
for wine storage, 162
Tempranillo, 135
Ténarèze, 278
Tennessee whiskey, 273
Tequila, 280, 281
Terms, glossary of, 325–337
Terroir, 137
Third-party liability, 315
Tignanello, 247
Timeliness, of server, 6
Tips, history of, 117
Toaster, 97
Tossed salad, tableside, 40
Touraine, 227
Transfer method, for sparkling wine, 147
Trays, 83–84
Tray stands, 84
Trentino-Alto Adige, 249
Triage, 140
Trout, boning of, 73
Tureen service, 69

Ugni Blanc-Trebbiano, 133
Ullage, 144
Umbria, 249–250
Umqua Valley, Oregon, 187
United States
wine labeling requirements, 157–158
wine-making history, 130–131
wine production
in California, 175–185
in Eastern States, 189, 191
in New York, 188, 190–191
in Pacific Northwest, 185–188
Upselling, 4

Valle d'Aosta, 248
Valpolicella, 248

Varietals, wine, 155, 157, 159
VDN (Vin Doux Naturel), 151
Veal
Veal Piccata, 49
Veal Scallops in Wine Sauce, 48
Vendange Tardive, 231
Veneto Region, Italy, 247–248
Verdelho, 150
Vermouth, 151
Vermouth-based cocktails, 299–301
Vernaccia di San Gimgnano, 246
Vienna roast coffee, 120
Vin Doux Naturel (VDN), 151
Vino Nobile di Montepulciano, 246
Vin Santo, 246
Vintage, wine, 137, 138–140, 156–157
Vintage port, 148
Viticultural practices, 137, 159
Vitis vinifera, 127
Vitis vinifera, 131, 132, 175, 185, 188
Vodka, 275–276, 281
Volnay, 220
Vosne-Romanée, 218
Vougeot, 218
Vouvray, 227

Wagon service, 68
Waiter. *See* Server
Walla Walla, Washington, 188
Washington, wine production in, 187–188
Water
for beer brewing, 260
for making tea, 25
Water service, 17–18
Whiskeys
American, 272–273, 281
imported, 274, 281
White wine
Bordeaux, 208
fermentation, 142
pressing, 141
White wines, opening procedures, 19
Willamette Valley, Oregon, 187
Wind, grape growing and, 136
Wine. *See also specific varieties of*
aromatized or apértif, 151–152, 281
cold-stabilization of, 132
consumption, average, 205
for cooking, 46
defined, 127

fortified, 147–151
grapes for. *See* Grapes
history of, 127–131
making, practices for, 159
aromatized or apértifs, 151
carbonic maceration, 144–145
dessert wine, 145
fortified wine, 147–151
sparkling wine, 145–147
special, 144–145
of table wine, 140–144
measurements, 323
pairing with food, 168–171
production, 127. *See also under specific countries*
pronunciation guide, 319–321
proprietary brands, 281
purchasing, 155–156
label decoding for, 156–157
labeling requirements for, 157–162
quality level, 156
service, 18–22
storage, 162
tasting, 162–163
savor and, 167
sight and, 163
sipping, 164, 166, 167
smell and, 164, 165
spitting/swallowing, 167
swirling and, 163–164
terminology for, 167–168
temperature, 21–22
varieties of, 132–135
Wine Sauce, Veal Scallops in, 48
Wine service basket, 20
Wine steward, 39
Wood port, 148
Württemberg, 239

Yakima Valley, Washington, 188
Yarra Valley, Australia, 194, 196
Yeast, for beer brewing, 261
Yield management, for grape growing, 137–138
York Mountain, California, 182

Zabaglione, 56
Zester, 59
Zinfandel, 135